Praise for *Lincoln's Forgotten Friend, Leon.*

"Eckley brings renewed and deserved attention to Swett, who practiced law with Lincoln, played a key role in Lincoln's 1860 nomination and 1864 campaign, and who, after Lincoln's death, wrote about his intimate knowledge of Lincoln's career."
—HENRY S. COHN, *The Federal Lawyer*

"Swett's life and fate deserved to be rescued for scholars and lay readers, both for his association with Lincoln, which yielded interesting comments on the president's character, and for his own path up from ragged circumstances. Robert S. Eckley, always a 'Lincoln man,' merits our gratitude for this fine study."
—DAN MONROE, *Journal of the Illinois State Historical Society*

"*Lincoln's Forgotten Friend, Leonard Swett* is a scholarly and thoughtful biography of Leonard Swett (1825–1889), an attorney who became a loyal friend of Abraham Lincoln long before Lincoln was elected President. . . . An excellent contribution to public and college library biography shelves, highly recommended."
—JAMES A. COX, *Midwest Book Review*

"The story of Abraham Lincoln cannot be told adequately without including those Maine men who were close by his side. Among them was Leonard Swett, born and raised in Turner; he eventually became one of Lincoln's closest advisors. . . . Now Swett's story has been told in *Lincoln's Forgotten Friend, Leonard Swett.*"
—*Bangor Daily News*

"Leonard Swett, who met Abraham Lincoln as a young circuit-riding lawyer in Central Illinois, is referred to as the president's 'forgotten friend.' He might have remained largely 'forgotten' if not for a book by former Illinois Wesleyan University President Robert S. Eckley and the efforts of Eckley's children to help their father finish the book as he slowly succumbed to amyotrophic lateral sclerosis, more commonly known as Lou Gehrig's disease."
—*Bloomington Pantagraph*

"With the publication of this well-documented and well-written book, another of those 'original Lincoln men' is rescued from obscurity. Swett was Lincoln's confidant in the elections of 1860 and 1864. His loyalty to Lincoln may have stymied his own ambitions to be governor or congressman. During his successful post-war legal career in Chicago, he wrote or spoke valuable reminiscences of Lincoln, many of which are published here."
—MARK A. PLUMMER, author of *Lincoln's Rail-Splitter: Governor Richard J. Oglesby*

"Eckley's title says it truly: Leonard Swett has long been Lincoln's 'forgotten friend.' But no more. This needed book reveals the important friendship—political and personal—that developed between the men during Lincoln's midlife (late 1840s on). And, just as important, Swett comes alive for the reader as a fascinating character in his own right."
—ROBERT BRAY, author of *Reading with Lincoln*

Lincoln's
Forgotten Friend,
Leonard Swett

Lincoln's Forgotten Friend, Leonard Swett

Robert S. Eckley

Southern Illinois University Press
Carbondale

Southern Illinois University Press
www.siupress.com

24 23 22 21   4 3 2 1

Cover and frontispiece: photograph of Leonard Swett courtesy of George
Buss, Freeport, Illinois; Leonard Swett's autograph courtesy of the Abraham
Lincoln Presidential Library; *cover*: "Standing Lincoln" bronze statue, by
Augustus Saint-Gaudens, photograph courtesy of Andrew Horne, from Wi-
kimedia Commons and licensed under Creative Commons Attribution Share Alike.

ISBN 978-0-8093-3839-9 (paperback)

The Library of Congress has cataloged the hardcover edition as follows:
Eckley, Robert S.
Lincoln's forgotten friend, Leonard Swett / Robert S. Eckley.
   pages cm
Includes bibliographical references and index.
ISBN 978-0-8093-3205-2 (cloth : alk. paper)—ISBN 0-8093-3205-1
(cloth : alk. paper)—ISBN 978-0-8093-3206-9 (ebook)—
ISBN 0-8093-3206-X (ebook)
1. Swett, Leonard, 1825–1889. 2. Lincoln, Abraham, 1809–1865—Friends
and associates. 3. Lawyers—Illinois—Biography. 4. Bloomington
(Ill.)—Biography. I. Title.
E457.2.E24 2012
977.3'03092—dc23
[B]   2012012090

Printed on recycled paper ♻

To my wife, Nell, and our children,
Jane Lennon, Robert George, Paul Eckley, and Rebecca Melchert

Gallery follows page 106

Preface

While serving on the board and as president of the Abraham Lincoln Association, I noticed a lack of literature on certain of Lincoln's friends and acquaintances. In particular, I could find little about one contemporary and colleague named Leonard Swett, to whom Bloomington historians had alerted me earlier. Swett belonged to a small coterie of Lincoln associates who had a close relationship with and extended exposure to the widely admired yet enigmatic man. The Lincoln circle of friends provides historians with an avenue for better understanding of our greatest president. Although many of these figures wrote memoirs or have been the subjects of book-length studies, little has been written about Leonard Swett. Among the few writings that do exist are several articles by the historian Harry Pratt; Willard King's biography of David Davis, which contains numerous references to Swett in his collateral roles; and an extensive article on his life written by his son, Leonard Herbert Swett, and published by the McLean County Historical Society.

The dearth of material on this friend of Lincoln's prompted me to conduct research and write several articles on Swett. In reading Swett's writings and speeches, I was struck by his eloquence and unique ways of putting things, and this in addition to my desire to fill the gap in the existing literature led me to write a full-length biography.

Swett knew many, if not all, of the personalities in Lincoln's political universe. Although he never held a position of importance in the Lincoln administration, which is likely the main reason why he has been overlooked by historians, he had considerable influence as a friend to Lincoln, often making suggestions and recommendations. He freely roamed the halls of the White House and was entertained by the president, despite not having any kind of title or position. For example, as described in chapter 7, about a month before coming out with the Preliminary Emancipation Proclamation, Lincoln invited Swett into his cabinet room, where, in a private meeting, he read Swett several letters on the pros and cons of emancipation. That Lincoln did so, no matter how one-sided the discussion, demonstrates the confidence he held in Swett. By asking his friend to serve as a sounding board as he articulated and tested his arguments in this crucial judgment, Lincoln displayed considerable trust in and reliance on Swett. This kind of behind-the-scenes influence—and the fact that Lincoln took his advice so often, and for so long—makes him an important character in his own right.

While doing the research for this book, I found that scant information exists on Swett's personal life, including his marriage to his first wife, Laura, and family life with their only child, a son named Leonard Herbert. Swett and Laura were married for thirty-two years, but he spent much of this time traveling for his legal career and involvement in politics. A mere six letters survive from Laura, some written to her husband and others to his friends and colleagues. A larger number of letters are in the archives from Swett to his wife, however, and I paid special attention to what information I was able to glean from all of these personal missives, as well as their tone. From reading their existing correspondence, I concluded that despite the great amount of time the couple spent apart, they enjoyed a loving marriage. Although few of Laura's letters survive, those that do show that she was an intelligent woman who shared her husband's interests in literature, politics, and the law, and in fact, she initially accompanied him on his travels until she suffered from a tragic malady. She kept his friend and law partner William Orme informed of activities at home while he was in the service during the Civil War, and she boldly wrote to David Davis on Fanny McCullough's and her husband's behalf after the judge had gone to Washington to serve on the U.S. Supreme Court.

Despite the gaps in personal information, Swett's colorful life and eloquent writing, for which he was renowned in his day, make for an interesting story. Because of the lack of details on his marriage and home life, the book focuses on his legal cases and political ambitions, characterizing Swett chiefly through his work and his relationship with Lincoln, touching on his personal life where information is available, and clarifying his place among the important personages of his day about whom more has been written.

History has an unpredictable way of focusing its beam, and we do not know exactly why Leonard Swett slipped through the cracks of history into the murky bin of obscurity and neglect. It is time to shine the light on Lincoln's friend from Bloomington whom, up until now, history has overlooked.

Lincoln's
Forgotten Friend,
Leonard Swett

Introduction

On a spring day in 1857 in central Illinois, a young lawyer named Leonard Swett rose to defend a man accused of a notorious murder. There was no question the defendant had committed the homicide. He had shot the victim four times in cold blood in front of numerous witnesses and was apprehended on the spot. Swett knew the odds were stacked against him. The case would have been a tough one for even the most seasoned attorney. But a man's life was at stake, and the young attorney's defense was his only hope for survival.

Swett was just thirty-two years old at the time. He had made his way to the Illinois prairie a few years earlier, near death when he arrived in Bloomington, having barely survived the rigors of war and prolonged illness. On the other side of the aisle, the tall prosecuting attorney made the case for conviction in a plainspoken manner. He was no ordinary lawyer. Widely considered the leading attorney on the Eighth Judicial Circuit, he was older and more experienced. His name was Abraham Lincoln.

This historic case in which Leonard Swett squared off against Abraham Lincoln would have profound implications for future trials. In what appeared to be a clear-cut case for conviction, the young lawyer emerged victorious, proving his mettle in this challenge as an advocate. When asked to defend a murderer in a subsequent case, Lincoln wisely sent Swett as his replacement.

Outside the courtroom, the two men forged an enduring friendship. During their spring and fall tours on the Eighth Circuit, which initially took them to Springfield, Bloomington, Urbana, Danville, and ten other county-seat towns in central Illinois, they traveled together on horseback or by horse and buggy. On these long, arduous journeys across the prairie, they spent weeks together in primitive inns and taverns, often sharing crowded rooms and meager meals. So began their long and close association, which continued until Lincoln's assassination.

Several of Swett's contemporaries, as well as later historians, testified to Swett's close relationship with Lincoln. In correspondence, Henry Clay Whitney said that Swett and David Davis "were more intimate" with Lincoln than were his other friends. When Josiah Holland approached David Davis, in his capacity as administrator of Lincoln's estate, for biographical information on the president shortly after his assassination, he responded that "[William] Herndon and Swett were [Lincoln's] intimate personal and political friends" and could provide "more detailed information concerning the past fifteen years of his life than perhaps any other parties." Newspaper publisher and Lincoln biographer Alexander K. McClure wrote that Swett "doubtless did counsel [Lincoln] with more freedom than any other man." More recently, historian and biographer Doris Kearns Goodwin mentioned Swett as one of Lincoln's "unusually loyal circle of friends" along with David Davis, Norman Judd, and Stephen T. Logan—four men essential to his 1860 nomination.[1]

Swett's long friendship with Lincoln allowed him to observe firsthand the man who would be president—the master politician with his sharp mind and deliberate pace, mood changes and melancholy straits, and inherent goodwill. Throughout Swett's life, he made substantial contributions to Lincoln biography and understanding of the man through a considerable volume of writing pertaining to Lincoln and his friends and colleagues, the Civil War, and other related topics. Roughly thirty different collections or pieces of writing by Swett survive in letters, speeches, newspaper and periodical articles, and book sketches. He wrote ten of these contemporaneously with events from 1854 to 1864. The writing in these segments is expressively eloquent and polished overall, suggesting that he planned to incorporate them into a biography of Lincoln during his later years. Swett also penned an important essay on Lincoln's character in early 1866, but it was not until a decade later, in 1876, that he began his extensive lectures and reminiscent writing on Lincoln.

Among his writings on Lincoln's friends and associates, Swett wrote memorials to the Dickey family, describing their Civil War losses, and to

David Davis, as well as a segment on Davis's 1862 appointment to the U.S. Supreme Court. He penned a segment on Lincoln's unexpected reaction to the cashiering of General Fitz-John Porter for his failures in the second battle of Bull Run, still recalling vividly twenty-one years later Lincoln's uncharacteristic outburst. He wrote brief descriptions of the heavy losses General Ulysses S. Grant incurred as he pounded south in the early summer of 1864, as well as an excerpt on the same subject in a letter to his law partner and friend, General William Orme. Swett also authored a *North American Review* article titled "Conspiracies of the Rebellion," and he wrote the dedication speech for the "Standing Lincoln" statue by Augustus Saint-Gaudens in Chicago's Lincoln Park.[2]

Swett's relationships with others who wrote about Lincoln and Swett's contributions to their writings demonstrate his prominence in the realm of Lincoln biography. He was part of a select group of aspiring memoir writers with close contacts to Lincoln, and these colleagues shared and debated their experiences with Lincoln from differing vantage points over an extended period. The chief writers and target sources of the best literature from Lincoln's friends were William Herndon, Ward Hill Lamon, Henry Clay Whitney, Alexander McClure, John Nicolay and John Hay, Jesse Fell, Orville Browning, and Isaac Arnold. Swett's relationships with these individuals and their comments about him in their writings are illuminating.

After Jesse Weik rescued William Herndon's massive concept of Lincoln's biography, together they produced a work of lasting value. Herndon and Weik used two long passages authored by Swett in their biography of Lincoln, including verbatim Swett's essay on Lincoln's characteristics, which he had first written in 1866 and revised slightly in 1887, and his description of Davis's appointment to the U.S. Supreme Court, penned in 1887.[3] Weik interviewed Swett in 1889 after publication of the biography and then, more than two decades later, included Swett's reactions in the preface to his 1922 work, *The Real Lincoln: A Portrait*, along with details on Swett's meeting Davis and Lincoln in Danville in 1854. However, Weik grossly distorted the latter story. Herndon held a high regard for Swett's knowledge of Lincoln and, in 1889–90, in an effort to improve subsequent editions of the Herndon-Weik biography, wrote eight letters to Swett's second wife, Maria, seeking additional information on the Lincoln-Swett relationship.[4]

Ward Hill Lamon's biography caused much controversy in its day. Davis and Swett objected to offensive information on Lincoln that Lamon sought to publish and succeeded in having some of the material redacted. Lamon stopped his project temporarily but reengaged in the work later. In an exchange of letters on their writing projects about Lincoln in the mid-1880s, Swett and Lamon explained their works, sought help, and offered criticism.[5]

Henry Clay Whitney was one of the most prolific sources for Herndon, with sixteen interviews, statements, and letters, some lengthy. Whitney had practiced law primarily on the Eighth Circuit until Lincoln appointed him to the position of army paymaster in 1861. After the war, he moved to Chicago, where he occasionally saw Swett. In his writings, he referred to Swett frequently and obviously thought very favorably of him. Whitney did not like Davis much but thought "Lincoln did right to appoint him but awfully wrong to not give Swett anything." Whitney's major contribution to Lincoln biography was his 1892 *Life on the Circuit with Lincoln.* His familiarity with the participants made for an important book, despite its discursiveness and occasional inaccuracies.[6]

Newspaper publisher Alexander K. McClure had a less important but still significant relationship with Swett from 1860 on. McClure introduced an excerpt of Swett's letter to Herndon on Lincoln's characteristics in his 1892 memoir *Abraham Lincoln and Men of War-Times*, writing, "Leonard Swett is well known to have been one whose counsels were among the most welcome to Lincoln, and who doubtless did counsel him with more frequency than any other man." In a meeting a day or two before the 1864 nomination for vice president, he claimed that Swett "earnestly and even passionately protested against the overthrow of [Hannibal] Hamlin," but that after Lincoln explained his position, "he wisely declared [Joseph] Holt to be his candidate, as a foil to protect Lincoln."[7]

John Nicolay and John Hay, who had been Lincoln's private secretaries, interviewed Swett while working on their ten-volume biography, *Abraham Lincoln: A History.* Both knew Swett well from his frequent visits to the White House, but neither had a close relationship with him. In the summer of 1878, Nicolay asked Swett about Lincoln's drafting of the Emancipation Proclamation, taking detailed notes on the conversation. These notes suggested that Lincoln had been at work on the document in mid-August 1862. At least five subsequent statements by Swett on the subject were consistent with Nicolay's notes.[8]

Several others who knew Swett also wrote or aided in the writing of reminiscences about Lincoln. Jesse Fell of Bloomington, who had been involved in the political campaigns of Lincoln and Swett, was another of Herndon's informants and played a role in influencing Lamon's book. Orville Browning, who associated with Swett socially and in a number of legal endeavors, left behind a diary and many letters mentioning Lincoln. Isaac Arnold, who spent at least three years as Swett's law partner, wrote two books on Lincoln.[9]

Swett was blessed not only with extensive contemporaneous exposure to Lincoln but also with the ability to write and tell a good story. Many of his stories have been factually corroborated, and he made no attempt to enhance his own significance to Lincoln in his speeches or writing. Although some of the other historians had serious shortcomings, their perspectives helped shape and sharpen Swett's collective writings during his years in Chicago.

Contrary to the impression of many scholars, however, Swett's extensive writings have never been collected and assembled. Some were never published; many are found only in archives and obscure nineteenth-century publications, largely inaccessible to contemporary readers. Although historians have picked over the bones of these writings, contemporary Lincoln literature refers to only a few of Swett's written works in brief bits and short quotations and barely touches on his highly successful legal career except to comment on his fame in criminal defense, which was not the larger part of his work. Nevertheless, Swett's work should not be viewed as a peripheral or ephemeral part of Lincoln biography. When assembled, his contributions add essential content to the body of knowledge of the whole of Lincoln's life.

Likely the main reason why historians have overlooked Swett is his failure to achieve any kind of important position, either by election or through appointment by Lincoln. Although Swett was respected as a great lawyer and an eloquent writer and speaker, he never achieved success in politics. Despite his political aspirations and four attempts at a political career, only one met with success, and he served just a single term in the state legislature. In 1856, he sought the nomination for a seat in Congress, but he lost out to an abolitionist Republican. Lincoln did not challenge the nomination but was angry and wrote, "It turned me blind."[10] In 1858, Swett won a seat in the Illinois House of Representatives in support of Lincoln, the only political position he ever held. In 1860, he sought unsuccessfully the Republican nomination for governor of Illinois. Swett was among three Republican candidates, and Lincoln decided not to take sides. Swett missed the convention because he was at work on a murder trial; had he been there, it is possible he might have won the nomination. Finally, he ran for a House seat in 1862 against John Todd Stuart, which was a fairly close race, with Swett losing by 5.6 percent. He tried time and again to get an appointment from Lincoln, but here too he was not successful.

Perhaps the biggest question surrounding Swett is why Lincoln never gave him an important or permanent appointment, despite their close association and obvious mutual respect. Although Lincoln gave Swett three temporary appointments and offered him a position as commissioner in a settlement negotiation in Peru, which Swett turned down to take what he thought would be a more lucrative assignment in California instead, he never got the kind of appointment he hoped for. Friends, even his closest ones, asked him for an explanation. Subsequently, historians and others have sought the answer to this question, often positing flaws in his character, behavior, or other shortcomings without much evidence to support their contentions. Or they have suggested that perhaps Lincoln knew Swett well enough *not* to appoint him to a responsible position, without examining all the available information for answers.

What may have been the most important reason that Lincoln did not appoint Swett to a more important and permanent office was that after he became president, Lincoln quickly learned that he had Swett's loyalty and company *without position or compensation.* Swett gave his loyalty to Lincoln free of charge. Lincoln and Swett obviously enjoyed one another's company, or they would not have spent as much time together as they did. Their long association on the circuit had established mutual trust and a pattern of frank exchange of ideas, and Swett freely spoke his mind, at times disagreeing with Lincoln. He had no inclination to shade his expression of opinions to curry favor. Lincoln appreciated Swett's ability to discuss diverse and wide-ranging subjects, to sound out various individuals, and to provide him with appraisals and evaluations of a complex of political situations. They discussed many key decisions, including emancipation, the second vice presidential nomination, and the peace crisis of 1864. If Swett had been appointed to almost any post of major responsibility, these chats would have turned in a different direction and he no longer would have been free to give Lincoln his frank opinions. Lincoln would have lost Swett's ready availability for trustworthy consultation.

Another factor may have been Lincoln's determination to build a coalition of Republicans of various stripes as well as War Democrats, which he strove to do throughout his years as president. He was steadfast in his decision not to appoint men from Illinois throughout his fourteen cabinet appointments, despite the important political support the Illinoisans gave him. Lincoln also failed to give appointments to several others, besides Swett, who were close to him. Neither William Herndon, Lincoln's former law partner, nor Orville Browning, who coveted a Supreme Court position, received an appointment. Similarly, James Conkling, a loyal Springfield friend of Lincoln's who had assisted in both presidential elections, requested a European appointment but did not receive one.

Lincoln also may have felt that plenty of time remained for appointing Swett, who was thirty-five years old in 1860. Despite their long friendship, Lincoln was Swett's mentor and sixteen years older, and he may still have viewed Swett as his young protégé. He chose Caleb Smith over Schuyler Colfax, who was about Swett's age, as secretary of the interior, partly because he felt that as Colfax was a much younger man, he could better afford to wait.[11]

Finally, some have suggested that Swett's excessive drinking on occasion may have been a factor in the appointment question. Lincoln held definite thoughts on drinking, but he was guarded in expressing his views. He raised the question of Herndon's drinking in their final interview in Springfield, and in an early letter to Richard Oglesby regarding the election of Richard Yates, a Whig candidate for Congress in 1854, he asked whether Yates was a drinker, carefully avoiding the implication that the answer was critical or determinative.[12] Lincoln obviously would have known of Swett's occasional excesses while both were on the circuit, and he possibly had been aware of Davis's effort to encourage Swett and Lamon to curb their use of alcohol in the form of their abstinence pledge that Davis penned in 1864. Although Lincoln readily appointed Lamon, who appeared to exceed Swett in his drinking habits, the two men functioned at different levels. That Swett's drinking by itself was a factor is doubtful, but there is insufficient evidence to know how it may have influenced Lincoln.

Swett himself addressed the appointment question with what may be the best answer. When pressed by Herndon about it a little more than two years before Swett's death, he replied, "An unknown number of people have almost every week since [Davis's appointment], speaking perhaps extravagantly, asked me in a quasi-confidential manner, 'How was it that you and Lincoln were so intimate and he never gave you anything?' I have generally said, 'It seems to me that is my question, and so long as I don't complain I do not see why you should. I may be pardoned also for saying that I have not considered every man not holding an office out of place in life.'"[13]

Lincoln's assassination became a pivotal point in Swett's life. One could argue that Swett's adult life might be divided into two distinct parts: the period while Lincoln was alive and that after Lincoln's death. In his early career, Swett had adjusted to a life on the road while working on the Eighth Judicial Circuit, and he continued this peripatetic lifestyle after his marriage to Laura and the birth of their son. His travel increased still further with his work in the Illinois General Assembly and his efforts on various campaigns for himself and others. Once Lincoln was nominated for president, Swett took longer trips out of state to aid his friend and fulfill his requests. His commitment to work on behalf of Union regiments also took him away. Perhaps the challenges of involvement with politics and the war simply seemed more compelling than the settled life of family and a legal practice.

During this period, Swett took Laura and their son with him when he could, possibly in part as a temporary solution to the problem of his long absences. Early in their marriage, however, an illness had left Laura with physical disabilities that limited her capacity to live away from home in unpredictable situations, so Swett's family accompanied him infrequently, only as Laura's health allowed. They traveled with him to St. Louis in late 1861, when he worked on the Commission for War Claims, and to California for four-plus months in 1863, when Lincoln sent Swett to serve as emissary for the U.S. government in a mine claim issue. Swett's whole family also went to Gettysburg with the presidential party in November 1863. The following year, Laura spent the summer with her husband in Washington, visiting wounded soldiers in the hospitals.[14]

Throughout this period of Swett's life, he also continually experienced money troubles. Although his income as a lawyer was probably adequate, he always suffered from some degree of financial ineptitude and never accumulated much wealth, instead accumulating considerable debt. He was more of a spender than a saver, not having learned to closely monitor his personal finances. His pursuit of three offices as well as his efforts on behalf of Lincoln in four campaigns took him away from his legal work for months at a time. In addition, he largely paid for his own expenses associated with campaigning, as organized political funding and campaign contributions are relatively recent phenomena. During all of this, Swett focused on the excitement and stimulation of the issues of democracy and put off the mundane business of trying to reduce his debts. He anticipated an appointment after Lincoln took office and hoped it would be lucrative enough to erase much of his accumulated obligations, but this never materialized. He tried his hand at investing but was not successful here either, because he assumed too much risk and was impatient for quick results. Some of his friends also credited him with being overly generous.

But Swett's life completely changed after Lincoln died in 1865. Immediately thereafter, the now-forty-year-old Swett moved to Chicago, where he finally put down roots with his family. Once Swett determined to stand on his own two feet without relying on Lincoln or Davis and gave up on politics to focus on his legal career, he soon built a thriving practice that enabled him to finally repay the debts that had plagued him for much of his life.

Swett met and perhaps exceeded his goal of a legal practice in Chicago. The highly successful law firm he built there demonstrated that he had more talent and potential than his political efforts of 1856–62 or his lack of appointments from Lincoln revealed. Swett was extremely good at picking up a case and working it to its conclusion. He worked with uncanny bursts of speed and intensity. Although he did not have Lincoln's gift of strategic thinking, he had a superb formal education, a deep understanding of history, a natural instinct for the courtroom, and a flair for public speaking. His friend David Davis, who achieved success in a political career, lacked Swett's speaking ability. Lincoln and Davis moved on to greater political heights, but Swett eventually found his bearings in the courtroom and in his Chicago law practice and was a highly gifted lawyer.

Greater appreciation is due to Leonard Swett for the invaluable contributions he made to Abraham Lincoln's career, as well as for the extensive body of writings he left behind that further illuminate Lincoln and his world. He aided Lincoln in both of his presidential nominations and at times influenced him while in office, but more than anything else, he was Lincoln's friend, from their traveling days together on the Eighth Circuit to the warm welcomes he received on his many visits to the White House during the Lincoln presidency. The quality of their friendship and what it meant to history cannot be adequately measured. Friendship may be the least measurable of human possessions and contributions, especially after it is gone. At its very heart, it is an intangible thing. This is the story of Lincoln's forgotten friend.

He had come to Bloomington to die.

—George Washington Minier, writing about Leonard Swett
on his arrival in Bloomington, Illinois, in July 1848

1. A Wandering Youth

Leonard Swett's roots go deep into the fabric of America. His ancestors came to America on the *Mayflower* and, as with Lincoln's forebears, were among the earliest settlers of the Massachusetts Bay Colony. His great-grandfather, Dr. Stephen Swett (1734–1807), settled in Gorham, Maine, and served in the Revolutionary War as a surgeon to a Massachusetts regiment. Leonard's father, John Swett Jr. (1789–1859), served in the War of 1812, and then cleared a farm out of the wilderness in the foothills of the White Mountains. He chose a piece of land three miles from the small village of Turner, Maine, near the Androscoggin River and sixty miles north of Portland.

John and his wife, Remember Berry (1794–1883), had six children: four daughters and two sons. Born on August 11, 1825, Leonard was their fourth child, the second son. Leonard's older brother and an older sister both eventually married into the Ricker family. Danville Swett married Ann Ricker, and his sister Sarah married Albion Ricker. John and Remember's farm remains in the Ricker family today. Leonard's two younger sisters, Rose and Mary Ellen, married two brothers in Maine, Justus and Joseph Briggs. Although Leonard wound up venturing far from the farm, his ties to Maine remained strong throughout his life. Leonard was closest to his sister Rose, with whom he kept up a regular correspondence after he moved away from home.

John Swett cultivated a productive apple orchard on his Maine farm. To support his family during the off season, he sold local products such as lumber, scythes, and wooden bowls. At the time, the village of Turner consisted not only of farms that grew apples and corn but also of sawmills and gristmills.

Leonard's mother, Remember, enjoyed music and started a family orchestra in which he played the flute. She also encouraged her children to sing and enrolled them in the local choir. Leonard apparently assimilated this instruction, because later his contemporaries often referred to his melodious speaking voice, and he became an ardent lover of opera. All of the Swett children attended school in Turner, walking or riding horses back and forth, often in the snow. Eager for their children to be educated, John and Remember arranged for them to board in town in severe weather.[1]

At age twelve, Leonard began three years of Latin and Greek lessons with the Baptist minister in Turner. Then for the next two years, he attended North Yarmouth Academy, on the coast north of Portland forty miles from his home. Established in 1814, the academy was progressive for its time. When Leonard began attending in 1840, more than half its students were girls.

The common law of primogeniture has historically provided that the eldest son inherit the entire family estate, to the exclusion of other siblings. Although the law had been abolished in the New England colonies before the Revolutionary War, John and Remember Swett decided that their oldest son, Danville, should inherit the farm. Perhaps to compensate for this distribution, they decided to send Leonard to college so that he could train for a profession. They chose Waterville College (today Colby College), in part because of its Baptist connection. Founded in 1813, Waterville was on the west bank of the Kennebec River fifty miles from the Swett home.

When Swett began as a freshman in 1842 at age seventeen, Waterville had five faculty members and some sixty students. The majority of these students came from Maine, and only one was from outside New England. Before admission, the school expected students to have a thorough acquaintance with English, Latin, and Greek; the Gospels; geography; and mathematics through quadratic equations. A significant portion of Waterville's students were preparing for careers in teaching, the ministry, law, or medicine. With a student-faculty ratio of eleven to one, the academic program was rigorous. Waterville placed a heavy emphasis on the classics, both Latin and Greek, including grammar and writing, history, and literature.[2] Leonard Swett's classical references in his writings and speeches over the next forty years likely reflected his academic studies here. In addition, he studied chemistry, physics, biology, rhetoric, French, political economy, philosophy, modern history, the U.S. Constitution, and Christianity. Waterville fostered its students' public speaking and writing skills with weekly declamation exercises and biweekly themes for the three upper classes. Swett also attended weekly religious services and was free to make his own choice of denomination.

The small class of 1845, the year ahead of Swett's, included several students who went on to illustrious careers. One of the seven graduates that year, Theophilus Capen Abbott, became president of the University of Michigan for twenty-two years, from 1863 to 1885. A classmate of Swett's, Josiah Hayden Drummond, who was his closest friend and junior-year roommate, became an attorney in Portland, a member of both houses of the Maine legislature, and Speaker of the Maine House of Representatives. Swett maintained a friendship with Drummond throughout his life, and they interacted as Lincoln supporters in 1860 and as delegates to the nominating convention for Lincoln in 1864. Later they joined in legal work for a life insurance company.[3]

But Leonard Swett would not graduate with his class. For some reason that he never explained in his writings, he did not finish college but dropped out in 1845 after his third year. College attrition was high at Waterville, as at other colleges during that time. Swett's class of eleven sophomores became nine juniors, and only five went on to graduate. His decision not to finish his college education may have been due to family financial concerns, as his younger sisters also needed to be educated. Or it may have been that a college degree was not necessary for a career in law and Swett was eager to get started. History is replete with young men and women who left their college educations unfinished to pursue careers, and reading law as an apprentice was an established way to prepare for admission to the bar in nineteenth-century America. Although wages often were not part of the bargain, it still was not always easy to find an able attorney or firm with which to affiliate. However, Swett found a promising connection with George Foster Shepley.

Shepley had obtained his law degree in the traditional manner, graduating from Dartmouth and Harvard Law School. He was also the son of the chief justice of the Maine Supreme Court, Ether Shepley. In 1844, George Foster Shepley and Joseph Howard, an older and established attorney in Portland, formed the law firm of Howard & Shepley. The following year, Swett began reading law with the firm, where he remained for nearly two years. In 1847, Swett decided to move on, but he did not sever his ties completely with Shepley. As with many of Swett's other friends, their lives intersected in other venues as their careers evolved. Swett encountered Shepley again in 1862 when he took his former employer, now the military governor of Louisiana, to visit Lincoln at the Executive Mansion.[4]

During the winter term of 1847, Swett taught at what apparently was a public elementary school in Gray, Maine, between Portland and Auburn. He lost some of his youthful innocence as he struggled to establish discipline among his sixty students, both boys and girls. Swett wrote to his sister Rose that this was one of the most difficult schools in the region. He had to flog four or five of the larger girls, he said, and broke a two-foot-long ruler on the large boys. "I have heretofore always been an advocate of moral suasion," he wrote, "[but] this . . . whipping experiment . . . has made me a convert to compulsive measures."[5]

By December 1847, however, Swett left this teaching job, as well as his home state of Maine, to seek his fortune on a journey that was to change the course of his life and eventually lead him to Illinois. Now twenty-two years old, and lacking in resources, he felt that New England offered few opportunities in law and teaching and decided to venture elsewhere. He went first to Pennsylvania, stopping in both Philadelphia and Pottsville. These visits were initial steps in an improvisational plan to go south, working his way along as a book agent for a northern firm.[6] He chose New Orleans, the nation's third-largest city at the time, as his next destination. Rather than travel across the Allegheny Mountains to the Ohio River and then down the Mississippi River in midwinter, he decided on an all-water route around Florida.[7] This two-week sea voyage was the first of many trips he made throughout his life, and it sparked his lifelong enthusiasm for travel and adventure.

On January 6, 1848, Swett embarked on the *Robert Burton*, a sailing vessel manned by a captain and several sailors, "ten weather beaten tars . . . boys of the old school," who showed up on the morning of departure "handsomely drunk." Swett stood on the quarterdeck to give the hills of the North a long farewell gaze, and then turned to watch the ship roll with a heavy groundswell out into the open sea. With the plunging and cresting of the prow, bouts of seasickness overtook him. In time, however, he acclimated to the ship and the sea, and he soon began to enjoy the warm currents of the Gulf Stream.[8]

The ship proceeded along the dangerous shoals of the Bahamas, difficult to navigate because of the currents. Then the weather changed and a squall overtook them. "A cloud suddenly appeared on the water with long ragged portions of vapor pointing from it in a manner to give it what seamen call a windy appearance." The captain paced the deck but made no concessions to the storm, "seemingly indifferent to the danger and utterly regardless of consequences." The sailors stopped their work, and everyone watched the progress of the gale, but the captain bore the same calm demeanor. "The only change which the closest scrutiny could detect," Swett wrote to his sister, "was that the puffs from his cigar were more frequent." Much to Swett's relief, the captain stopped and watched the clouds for a few moments, then finally said to his mate, "This will be too much for us." With the captain's order to reeve the topsails, the sailors flew into a frenzy of activity. "The ship yielded to the heavy weight which pressed her and leaning nearly to her beam ends dashed through the water like a race horse." For several hours, the crew struggled to save themselves and their ship as the waves rose ever higher, threatening to swallow the vessel. Finally they passed from danger's jaws, leaving the gale behind them to navigate quieter seas.[9]

Upon his arrival in New Orleans, Swett found his New England sensibilities under siege and denounced the morals of the city. "Habits and amusements are countenanced which are wicked and deplorable," he wrote to his sister Rose. "The people here think the wrong consists not in committing the offense but in the bad manner of doing it. If done quietly and orderly the wrong is never thought of."[10] He described the inhabitants of New Orleans as "a confused and heterogenious [sic] mass composed of all classes, grades and nations." The Creoles comprised "all the native born citizens of the City," he said, and included "the worthless and profligate and as if in offset, . . . the 'bon ton' or 'elite' of the town." Swett described the migratory class as having "every variety of feature. There is the Englishman who steps with stately tread from the deck of his well laden ship, the shrewd and enterprising Yankee, the blustering backwoods man, the Mexican with his lasso, the Wild Comanche, and the keen eyed gambler watching for his prey."[11]

On the levee at midday, Swett saw a hundred ships and vessels and all types of people "mixed and mingled in most delightful confusion." He portrayed the merchants as energetic and influential makers of commerce who sought the city for its winter climate but retired north for summers and autumns. He observed the boatmen "as forming a distinct feature among the people of Orleans. They live an aquatic life upon the river, but [are] easily distinguished from the crowd as they swagger."[12] To Swett, New Orleans had the feel of a foreign city, with its exotic blend of peoples and prominent use of the French language. Two decades earlier, Abraham Lincoln had walked these same levees among a similar mixed crowd.

Despite all this, Swett found many pleasant aspects to the city, although he disliked the weather. The streets were surprisingly orderly and safe. Regardless of his Yankee views and contrasting values, he forecast continued growth and prosperity for New Orleans. The city amazed him, with its position on the curve of the river, the huge number of ships in the harbor, the snakes and alligators filling its outlying marshes, its licensed gambling, and its moral code diametrically opposed to that of his puritanical background. Swett also may have encountered romantic disappointment here. In a letter several years later, he referred to "the remembrance of a lady now living in New Orleans where I had the misfortune to fall in love." He gave her name to a horse, Nell, a cream-colored mare that became his favorite.[13]

Swett spent several weeks in New Orleans, then headed north up the Mississippi River in the early spring of 1848. He wrote home about the "gardens of plantations along the banks . . . beautiful beyond description," saying that "the trees bordering the banks have put on their green covering and the open fields are verdant with growing grass. A southern spring is a spring indeed." At Natchez, Mississippi, he saw the town rising on a bluff nearly perpendicular to the river and observed the citizen planters enjoying the cool of the evening on the balconies and piazzas. He wrote to his sister later, after having made the entire trip up and down the river twice, that his favorite part of the Mississippi was above Cairo, Illinois, where forest trees stood as tall and graceful figures, diversifying the landscape.[14]

At Cairo, Swett's ship turned up the Ohio River, heading eastward to Madison, Indiana. Here, eight weeks after landing in New Orleans, his resources ran dry. Despite his plans, his book sales had been negligible, and he was unable to land a job. Disappointed and confused by his inability to find employment, Swett enlisted on March 16 as a replacement in the Fifth Indiana Volunteers of the U.S. Army. He joined an "awkward squad," a group of stubborn recruits that was mustered into the army a month later to fight in the Mexican-American War under U.S. general Winfield Scott.[15]

According to his many retellings of the story, an event that occurred during his training traumatized him and taught him a lesson for life. The drill sergeant bullied the new recruits and yelled foul language at them in a manner common to the nineteenth-century army but foreign to the ears of this New England college boy. After a time, apparently provoked beyond restraint, Swett sprang from the ranks and charged the sergeant with his bayonet. Swett was quickly restrained and locked up in the guardhouse. Facing the possibility of a court-martial and perhaps even execution for insubordination, he contemplated death by hanging and blanched at what his family would think.[16]

The tense proceeding afforded him an opportunity to use the legal skills he had acquired during his last two years in Portland. He "told the story of his life, how through self-denial his parents tried to prepare him for an honorable and useful life, how he had enlisted, expecting to do his duty but that he had forgotten himself in the excitement caused by abuse which he seemed in no way to deserve." After hearing him plead his case, the commanding officer pardoned him with a severe reprimand. Swett thus won his first real case and saved his own skin. Considering how the threat of a hanging "concentrates the mind," he resolved to control his anger in the future.[17]

With the rest of his squad, Swett retraced his voyage downriver to New Orleans and across the Gulf of Mexico to Vera Cruz, which was and still is the largest port in Mexico. There he took his place in the regiment guarding General Winfield Scott's supply line through Jalapa to Mexico City, with the supplies carried by wagon train along the same route taken by Hernán Cortés in 1519. Looking west from the beach, Swett admired the "beautiful snow-capped Orizaba" (Citlaltépetl), the highest peak in Mexico, with its amazing cone rising 18,696 feet, resembling Fujiyama near Tokyo.[18]

Swett did not guard wagon trains for long. In the moist, warm climate, he came down with a debilitating fever and symptoms of malaria. He was transported back to Vera Cruz to a makeshift hospital in the Roman Catholic cathedral, where he suffered for much of May 1848. He heard a doctor near his bed say that he would probably die within a few hours, and as contemplating the possibility of execution had earlier, the physician's words energized him and soon he rallied. When asked if he could walk to the bark *Robert Morris* with the first group of convalescing soldiers returning to the United States, he replied, "I think I can walk that far towards home, but do not think I could walk that distance in the opposite direction." He reached the ship but was so weak he had to be hoisted aboard in a rope sling.[19]

Swett came close to death yet again on the passage to New Orleans. The vessel had rations for only four days for 125 sickly soldiers, and the drinking water had been stowed aboard six months earlier. The ship was becalmed for four days during the Gulf crossing, and the voyage lengthened to thirteen days. Because of the heat and inadequate provisioning, nearly a third of the soldiers died and their bodies were thrown overboard. After the ship was towed to New Orleans from the mouth of the Mississippi and anchored off Andrew Jackson's historic 1815 battlefield, the commanding officer went ashore on a multiple-day drinking spree. Meanwhile, more soldiers died. When the officer returned, the survivors were brought ashore to the nearby barracks. A Regular Army captain came aboard and, after learning of the gross negligence, spoke contemptuously to the commanding officer. Swett commented later, "His swearing seemed to me religious devotion."[20]

Swett now learned that the Mexican War had ended more than a month before his enlistment. News had traveled slowly from Mexico City after the Treaty of Guadalupe Hidalgo ending the war was signed on February 2, 1848. From New Orleans, the army immediately transferred Swett back to Jefferson Barracks in St. Louis, where he was mustered out on July 8, 1848. Although he had served as an orderly sergeant for a time in the company, his discharge papers ranked him as a private and described him as being afflicted with amebic dysentery.

He started for home by steamboat up the Illinois River, but his fever returned. People advised him to get away from the river, so he disembarked at Peoria, Illinois, and from there set forth on foot, walking eastward toward home.[21] His most likely route would have been along a dirt road southeast to Tremont, the county seat of Tazewell County, then due east through the town of Mackinaw. Between Tremont and Mackinaw, he would have crossed the Mackinaw River, a small stream that he could have forded easily if he did not encounter a bridge. By the time he stumbled into the town of Bloomington, Illinois, a couple days later, he must have realized that in his poor health, he would not be able to make the long trek back to Maine.

Bloomington was established along the northern border of the settlement of its namesake Blooming Grove, so called for its numerous flowers and trees, and soon after, in 1837, became the McLean County seat. By then its population was some seven hundred. Over the next decade, the town grew quickly, and when Leonard Swett arrived, Bloomington could claim about three thousand residents.

Swett's arrival in this burgeoning town did not go unnoticed. George Washington Minier, a schoolmaster and later a minister, recalled, "As I was seated near the little hotel at Bloomington I saw a tall, gaunt, emaciated young man come up the street just able to walk. I was attracted to him and spoke to him. He told me he was a discharged soldier, he lived in a distant state, that his people did not know his whereabouts and that he had come to Bloomington to die, and when he breathed his last he wished me to write his parents of his fate. I encouraged him and told him that God still had work for him to do."[22]

At the time, Swett carried a mere 123 pounds on his six-foot, two-inch frame. Minier took the ailing young man under his wing and gave him food and shelter. The kind schoolmaster had recently opened the first high school in Bloomington that was exclusively for young women and recognized Swett's potential. By September 1848, Swett began reading law and assisting at the school. He wrote to his sister that his health was good and that he weighed 155 pounds, "nearly as much as I ever weighed."[23]

That year, Swett also met the lawyer David Davis. While sitting outside a corner store in downtown Bloomington, Swett caught sight of a man of great height and girth. His first thought was that the man's "immense tread was the tread of Hercules."[24] That same year, Davis was elected judge of the Eighth Judicial Circuit in Illinois, and in him Swett later came to recognize other parallels to that hero of extraordinary strength.

Davis was thirty-three years old at the time and had practiced law in Illinois for thirteen years. A native of Maryland, he had attended Kenyon College in Ohio, an institution established by Episcopal bishop Philander Chase, uncle of Salmon P. Chase, who was later a member of Lincoln's cabinet. In his last year at Kenyon, Davis met Edwin M. Stanton, another man who later served on Lincoln's cabinet. After studying law in Massachusetts, Davis left for the Midwest and opened a law office in Pekin, Illinois. In the fall of 1835, he lobbied for a railroad connection for clients at the Illinois state legislature and met Jesse Fell, whose Bloomington law practice he bought soon after. Around this time, Davis also made the acquaintance of John Todd Stuart, Whig leader of the legislature, and Stuart's law partner, Abraham Lincoln, then a freshman legislator. These lawyers became better acquainted over the next thirteen years, prior to Davis's election in 1848 as judge of the Eighth Circuit.[25]

The warm reception that Swett received from Minier, Davis, and others in central Illinois proved to be both lifesaving and life-shaping. By mid-January 1849, Swett was practicing law. "Have just about business enough to support me," he wrote to Rose. The following week, he started teaching school in Waynesville, about twenty miles south of Bloomington. Apparently he had not totally lost his wanderlust, despite his travails aboard ship and in military service, as he wrote to his sister about the gold rush: "The California fever is raging severely. All are more or less infected and probably about fifteen or twenty will go from this town among whom perhaps I shall be numbered."[26] For the time being, however, Swett devoted himself to teaching and preparing for the bar exam, which he passed in June 1849 at age twenty-four. The exam was oral, and no records survive.[27] In early fall of that year, Swett moved to Clinton, Illinois, nineteen miles south of Bloomington, where he established his law practice. There he remained for the next four years.

Swett's bruising journey up and down the big river and into Bloomington ended the first phase of his practical education. That he had not only survived but also rebounded to become a lawyer with his own practice was a tribute to his Yankee ingenuity and strength of character, as well as to frontier hospitality and good fortune.

As friendly, as perhaps men ever lived.
—*Leonard Swett*, Chicago Tribune, *February 21, 1876*

2. The Road to Mount Pulaski

Clinton, on the central plains of Illinois, was a frontier prairie town founded in 1835 after Jesse Fell, a lawyer and land speculator from Bloomington, and James Allen, a representative in the Illinois state legislature, stopped to rest their horses on the open prairie halfway between the cities of Bloomington and Decatur. Fell and Allen found this place ideal for a settlement, as there was nothing nearby, and named the town in honor of DeWitt Clinton, an early American politician and U.S. senator from New York. When Swett moved there in 1849, it was a small town of a few hundred inhabitants, built around a central square.

The plains surrounding Clinton and other frontier towns in central Illinois still resembled Louis Jolliet's 1674 description: "There are prairies three, six, ten, and twenty leagues in length, and three in width, surrounded by forests of the same extent; beyond these, the prairies begin again, so that there is as much of one sort of land as of the other. Sometimes we saw the grass very short, and, at other times, five or six feet high; hemp, which grows naturally there, reaches a height of eight feet."[1] Prairie grasses included bunchgrass, big bluestem, and in the wet spots, slough grass. The forests consisted mostly of oak and hickory trees, along with white pines, walnuts, cottonwoods, tupelos, sassafras, and gums. Native fruit trees and shrubs also grew in abundance, including cherries, crab apples, mulberries, plums, persimmons, and raspberries. The woods once held much wildlife, but civilization soon pushed out the larger animals, leaving only foxes, occasional wolves, deer, quail, and pheasants.

Beneath the prairie grass lay fertile soils that turned black when dampened by rain. The settlers cleared swaths of this land for farms, and towns grew out of the early settlements. Milk and eggs were staples for prairie town residents, and their meals often consisted of stews or hashes, such as salt pork cooked with green peas, string beans, beets, onions, cabbage, and pumpkin. On special occasions, they might dine on beef or chicken.[2]

Stagecoach lines soon connected the prairie settlements with other towns and cities. Elected officials, important citizens, and people traveling from the east rode the stagecoaches, drawn by teams of four or six horses. The coaches also carried mail, which was distributed and delivered on a regular basis. The town residents usually rode in their own buggies and wagons.

Most prairie towns, like Clinton, had a few taverns (hotels), rooming houses, mercantile stores, churches, and log cabin homes. In Clinton, the settlers built a plain brick courthouse without a cupola or a bell in 1849, the same year Swett moved to town. They dedicated it with a celebratory dinner and dance. Earthen streets and plank sidewalks surrounded the structure. After Swett had taken up residence there, he began advertising his availability as a lawyer in the *Weekly Pantagraph*, the Bloomington newspaper. As Clinton grew rapidly, so did Swett's legal practice, and he took cases from surrounding counties as well. Traveling back and forth on horseback to appear in court or meet with clients, he slowly adjusted to the extreme weather and primitive conditions in mid-nineteenth-century central Illinois.[3]

In one letter to his sister, written in February 1850, Swett described his return trip from a trial in a neighboring village. The road home lay across an open prairie, and for about nine miles there was not a tree or shrub to shield him from the wind. Mounted on his spirited mare, he arrived in town in less than an hour but, he wrote, "old Boreas had done his work . . . both cheeks, my nose and an ear was frozen." Little more than a year later, he recounted the details of a trip on horseback to Marion, Illinois. With each step, his horse's hooves sank into the mud, sometimes six to twelve inches. Fortunately, the temperate Indian summer days in the fall offset these experiences. Then Swett engaged in deer hunting, which he called "chasing deer," the only sport he enjoyed.[4]

Shortly after his move to Clinton, Swett also accompanied Judge Davis on the Eighth Judicial Circuit. In central Illinois, towns were small and far apart, and no one county could provide lawyers and a judge with full-time work adjudicating suits and claims. For this reason, circuits were formed through which to handle legal cases. Each circuit was a district comprising several counties, and the court, a judge, and several lawyers traveled from county to county on the circuit. The lawyers were assigned to one side or the other, to prosecute or defend, and they gathered evidence, met with clients and witnesses, and then tried their cases before the judge with juries selected from the local population.

In the fall of 1849, Davis was making his second tour of the Eighth Circuit, which then consisted of fourteen counties across central Illinois, from Springfield and Pekin on the west to Danville on the east. Although it had existed in the area for only ten years, by 1849 the Eighth Circuit was already more than just a geographic designation of judicial centers. It was a group of individuals who shared common interests in the law, politics, judicial spectacle, storytelling, cards, drinking, music, church services, billiards, and other avenues of socializing and camaraderie. The geography of the region established certain conditions, opportunities, and obstacles for the residents as well as members of the bar.

The settlements in the Eighth Circuit skirted the timberline. Dim trails led from one county seat to the next, each with a few hundred to several thousand residents, a log or wooden courthouse, and a log jail. Before railroads through the area were completed in the mid-1850s, the judge and lawyers traveled on horseback or in carriages, crossing streams and muddy sloughs, often without bridges. Swett recalled how "the quail whistled to his mate as we passed along, how the grouse with his peculiar whirr arose from his hiding place in the grasses, how the wolf fled and the red deer was startled from the grassy dell."[5]

Mount Pulaski was a small town, home to several hundred citizens, on the Eighth Circuit between Clinton and Springfield. It had the feel of a country outpost, with just a few buildings and streets. It was in this tiny town that Swett had his first encounter with the man whose destiny changed his own.

While Swett and Judge Davis sat in the town's only hotel, another man arrived on horseback. When he entered the hotel, Swett noticed him immediately, a tall man with a circular blue cloak thrown over his shoulders. The man passed through the room and went out another door without speaking.

His curiosity piqued by the stranger's appearance, Swett turned to the judge. "Who is that?" he asked.

"Why don't you know him?" Davis replied. "That is Lincoln."

A few minutes later, the tall man returned. Swett stood up and shook his hand, making the acquaintance of Abraham Lincoln for the first time. The exact date is uncertain, but several historians believe it was October 8, 1849. At that time, Swett was twenty-four years old, Davis was thirty-four, and Lincoln was forty. Swett recounted this version of his initial encounter with Lincoln at least three times.[6]

Lincoln made a formidable impression on young Swett, who in turn soon gained the attention and friendship of the older man. Lincoln had toured the Eighth Circuit since its inception in 1839 and had seen its expansion from eight to fifteen counties. After a disappointing two-year term in the U.S. Thirtieth Congress, he rejoined the circuit and fully rededicated himself to the practice of law, leading the circuit along with Davis.[7]

After Swett and Lincoln met, observers noted several striking similarities and subtle differences in their appearances. Lincoln took full advantage of his commanding height. Swett was almost two inches shorter than Lincoln but still a tall man, well above average in height for his time. Both were described as angular, gaunt, and lanky, with black hair and swarthy complexions. Lincoln's gray eyes were often a source of comment, whereas Swett's eyes were black with noticeable intensity. Although Lincoln was called homely, Swett was an extremely attractive young man with a commanding presence. Each man discovered and used his own unique advantages bestowed by heredity.

The courts on the Eighth Circuit commenced around the first of September and closed by Christmas, starting again in February and running until June. Depending on the county's size and number of residents, the court would last three to five days. Early in the morning on the first court day, the guards brought in the first defendant from the log jail. In civil cases, the litigants arrived on horseback with their witnesses. Until the morning the court opened, the judge and the lawyers may not have heard of the parties or the case. As Swett said, "The consideration and trial of each case began and ended with itself; we were continually roused to devise a new policy, new tactics, fresh expedience with each new retainer."[8]

Life on the circuit provided an ideal training ground for a bright and ambitious young lawyer like Swett. He recalled that each county was different in its population and class of business, so each court brought new parties and witnesses to be represented, "new and different juries to entertain, cajole and convince; new and distinct conditions of chaos" from which to evoke order. The circuit afforded Swett opportunities to develop his listening skills, practice his candor, and hone his eloquence and persuasiveness. Because "life on the circuit was in the nature of a school of events," he learned to "deal off-hand and on the spur of the moment, with emergencies."[9]

Swett initially represented litigants in cases common to a new country and a rural environment, such as disputes over border lines and deeds, damages caused by wandering cattle, and brawls that broke out during country festivities. All of these tested his advocacy skills, but he possessed an unusual knack for criminal cases, which were the subject of great community interest. Another Clinton attorney, Clifton Moore, later wrote his impression of Swett during this period, whom he first met in 1849: "He was a scholarly man, read Latin and Greek fluently besides being a fine belles-lettres scholar, and was from the start looked upon as much more than an ordinary law student. His fine address, dignified manner, as well as his power of reasoning and persuasion, and above all his capacity to cross-examine a witness, and extort the truth, gave him at once a position and practice much more remunerative than that of many older members of the bar."[10]

The arrival of the judge and lawyers for the semiannual court marked the most important time of year for the isolated residents of central Illinois in the 1850s. Shopping was delayed until court week. County statesmen offered their wit and humor. "The local belles came in to see and be seen, and the court house from early morn till dewy eve—and the tavern from dewy eve till early morn—were replete with bustle, business, energy, hilarity, novelty, sarcasm, excitement, and eloquence." Moore observed that everyone "attended court whether they had business or not, and usually there was one case at each term, in each county, that everybody wanted to hear, and which gave Mr. Lincoln and Mr. Swett a fine opportunity to display their forensic ability. And then after court would adjourn in the evening the crowds that would gather around them to hear their stories were almost suffocating."[11]

The Eighth Circuit proved to be fertile ground for lawyers and yielded a staggering blend of gifted competitors. The editor of the Danville newspaper wrote in May 1856, "The bar of Illinois has among its members men of as much intellect, as much genius, as much prestige as any State in the West." Swett described the "splendid galaxy of talent" and said of attorney Stephen T. Logan of Springfield, Lincoln's second law partner and one of the circuit's oldest members, that he was "keen and incisive as a Damascus blade, and who it is conceded, for quickness and strength, was the best trial lawyer the state ever produced." David B. Campbell, the state's prosecuting attorney, frequently traveled with Davis, Lincoln, and Swett and played the violin in the evenings. The young attorney Shelby Cullom, also from Springfield, went on from the circuit to become Speaker of the Illinois House of Representatives, a congressman, governor, and a U.S. senator for thirty years. Samuel C. Parks and Harvey Hogg also practiced on the circuit; Parks was appointed by Lincoln to the Supreme Court of the Idaho territory, and Hogg became an early antislavery advocate and Republican supporter of Lincoln who was elected to the state legislature in 1860. Lawrence Weldon was elected to the legislature in 1860 and appointed by Lincoln as the federal district attorney in southern Illinois in 1861. Daniel W. Voorhees came from Indiana to practice in the eastern counties of the Eighth Circuit with a "torrent of eloquence." Voorhees served as a War Democrat in Congress during the Civil War and later was elected three times to the U.S. Senate.[12]

Ward Hill Lamon came from Berkeley County, Virginia, to Illinois in 1847 at age nineteen. Soon after being admitted to the Illinois bar, he became Lincoln's only law partner outside Springfield. Their partnership lasted about five years, and they tried many cases together before Lamon became the state's attorney for the Eighth Circuit in 1856. While his nomination for this position was pending, a Danville newspaper editor warned that "when reckless dissipation is combined with other objections, we, as public journalists, boldly object to Ward H. Lamon, and beg the delegates to pause before they recommend him for our Prosecuting Attorney." The editor was Phillippa W. B. Carothers, wife of the publisher of the *Danville Independent*. Later she rescinded some of this criticism, perhaps having learned that her husband had engaged Lamon as counsel for his coal-mining business. A large man with a dramatic and flamboyant personality, Lamon amused Lincoln on the circuit with his minstrel vocalizing, later criticized for its off-color racial humor. Lamon became a loyal supporter and dedicated follower of Lincoln, as well as a lifelong friend of Swett.[13]

After Swett became a regular on the Eighth Circuit, he joined Davis, Lincoln, and Lamon in traversing the entire circuit, which few others did. This small band journeyed together along the road, covering some four hundred miles over three months twice a year. Swett, Lincoln, and Lamon rode the trails on horseback. Davis, who weighed about three hundred pounds and was considered the monarch of the circuit, drove a carriage pulled by two horses. The four men slept at the same small hotels, ate their meals together, and "lived as intimately and, in a manner, as friendly, as perhaps men ever lived."[14]

Swett recalled the scant provisions of the times—beds too short, coffee burned or bad, and food indifferent—but he also remembered that Lincoln never complained. Davis described the Mount Pulaski House in 1851 as "perhaps the hardest place you ever saw . . . everything dirty, and the eating horrible." The woman who waited on tables "looked as we suppose the witch of Endor looked," referring to the sorceress visited by Saul in the Old Testament.[15] However, the warm welcomes at each county seat, the freedom of the long days spent in the open air, the trivial adventures interspersed with the trials of the various cases, and the companionship more than compensated for the irritations and discomfort of circuit riding. The evenings were filled with merriment, stories and fiddle playing, jokes and reminiscences, as well as plans for the upcoming schedule. Another form of entertainment was wrestling matches among Swett, Lincoln, and Lamon.[16]

Swett and Lincoln also squared off in the courtroom in a divorce case on the Eighth Circuit in 1852. In *Thorpe v. Thorpe*, Lincoln and another attorney represented the wife, Eliza, who was suing her husband, Moses, for lack of support. Swett was part of a team of four lawyers defending the husband. The Thorpes had each been married before and had children from their former unions. The suit extended over several sessions in different locations and attracted a great deal of local attention for its colorful allegations. Moses Thorpe asserted that Eliza called him "a cursed old son of a bitch; an old hell houne [*sic*], an old Devil & such kindred expressions" and that "she did not intend to live with him long . . . and [intended to] make a pile of money out of him." Eliza introduced a letter from a younger woman stating that Moses had misrepresented himself as a widower to commit adultery. Defense witnesses countered that Eliza drank and stayed out all night with other men. Witnesses for Eliza, including her former doctor from Indiana, attested to her good character and sobriety. Eliza abandoned her suit at this point, and the action was "stricken from the docket . . . for want of prosecution." Swett's specific role in the defense of this case is unknown, but his participation on the team is a significant indication of his progress as a lawyer.[17]

Another example of Swett's widening practice was a case in 1853, when he again went up against Lincoln. This time, Swett was employed as the prosecutor for Vermilion County, on the eastern edge of the circuit, with its county seat in Danville. In this capacity, Swett obtained a manslaughter conviction against Walter Bosley, who had been charged with murder and was defended by Lincoln.[18]

Gradually, Swett's presence on the Eighth Circuit became more regular. By 1854, Swett and Lincoln were working on many cases together, sometimes on the same side but often on opposing sides. By the beginning of the spring session that year, Swett's success on the circuit was the envy of most lawyers. Since he started on the circuit, he had represented a large number of defendants in criminal cases, but none of them had been convicted of any charge except one for stealing rum. During the spring session of 1854, he defended every criminal indicted, about twenty in number—three for shooting, one for stabbing, one for horse stealing, one for counterfeiting, and the remainder for lesser misdemeanors—and ended up with only one felony and four misdemeanor convictions. He successfully defended a doctor in a malpractice case for five thousand dollars, which became the favorite case of the circuit session. As a token of gratitude, the doctor threw a party at his home that included Swett and announced that he was inviting only professional men, a group of fourteen doctors, eleven lawyers, and seven preachers.[19]

Swett grew in political stature as well, following in the footsteps of Lincoln. Lincoln served as a Whig presidential elector in Illinois in 1840, 1844, and again in 1852. In 1852, Swett also was named an elector for the Whig Party candidate, General Winfield Scott, who had been his top commander in the Mexican-American War. Swett stumped for Scott in the Third Congressional District and gave a rousing three-hour speech at the Springfield courthouse, across the street east of what is now the Old State Capitol, on October 29, 1852. The *Illinois State Journal* reported that Swett "was fully posted upon the topics of the day, and secured the attention of the densely crowded room. . . . His speech was replete with political information, keen irony and passages of surpassing eloquence. The meeting adjourned with three cheers for Scott, three cheers for Graham [Whig candidate for vice president], three cheers for Dick Yates [candidate for Congress], and three cheers for Swett!"[20]

As Swett made the rounds on the circuit, he also was seeking a wife. He had been confiding in his sister about his search since he left home, telling her that he was corresponding with an old sweetheart in Lewiston, Maine, and pronouncing her a "girl of merit" who wrote glorious letters full of poetry. He dropped his contact with her around the time of his departure for New Orleans, however. When he arrived in Clinton, he rented a room from a man from New Hampshire, Charles Brown, and his wife, Martha. In October 1850, he wrote to his sister about an offer made to him by Brown: free use of the house they occupied, with his share of the furniture, for two years, "on one condition but that a dreadful hard one to wit: to get married."[21]

The Browns introduced Swett to Martha's sister, Laura R. Quigg, a well-educated woman and devout Presbyterian. Laura was from a close family with five children in southern New Hampshire, probably the second of four daughters. Her father, Abel Quigg, was a merchant, and the family emphasized education and appears to have enjoyed modest wealth.[22] At the time Swett met Laura, she was living in Massachusetts. Eventually the entire family migrated to Illinois, and Swett became closely affiliated with them.

Laura was three and a half years younger than Swett. Only a few of her letters exist and no known picture of her survives, but a pass through military lines issued in 1861 described her as five feet, eight inches tall, with blue eyes and brown hair. Laura's intelligence appealed to Leonard Swett. He and Laura shared an artistic appreciation of literature and creative expression, and both were interested in politics and the law. Their courtship apparently lasted beyond the time frame of Brown's offer, as Swett lamented to his sister in April 1854 that he "expected a letter from [Laura] this morning and didn't get it. These women are funny institutions any how."[23]

Three months later, on July 20, 1854, the *Pantagraph* reported without elaboration that Laura and Leonard had married in Bradford, Massachusetts. The couple returned promptly to Illinois and settled in Bloomington. In the early years of their marriage, Laura sometimes joined Swett as he traveled. According to Henry Clay Whitney, an attorney friend on the circuit, "Occasionally the accomplished wife of Leonard Swett would accompany him on the circuit; and in such cases those two, Lincoln and myself, would go together in a two-seated vehicle; and we would have to talk sense on such a trip."[24] With her interest in politics and the law, along with an impressive background in literature, Laura might have been a more important figure on the Eighth Circuit had she not contracted a debilitating disease a short time later.

After moving back to Bloomington, Swett formed a law partnership with Amzi McWilliams that lasted little more than a year. McWilliams had arrived in Bloomington in 1848, the same year as Swett, and they tried several cases together before forming their partnership. The association ended when McWilliams started the 1855–56 term as prosecuting attorney for the Eighth Circuit. Subsequently, McWilliams ran for prosecutor in the new Eighteenth Circuit, which included Springfield, but it is unknown whether he was successful. Later, he moved to St. Louis, where he died in 1862. Davis described McWilliams as "a low vulgar Man" but commented that Lincoln was attracted to him, possibly because of his "sharp-witty" mind.[25]

Swett next entered into what turned out to be a more lasting partnership with William Ward Orme, who was seven years younger than Swett. A native of Washington, D.C., Orme had attended Mount St. Mary's College in Maryland before moving to Bloomington in 1850. He was accepted into the bar in 1852 and soon became deputy McLean County clerk to William McCullough, whose oldest daughter, Nannie, he married in 1853. After the partnership with McWilliams ended, Swett purchased the assets of the McWilliams & Swett firm for $445 and McWilliams's library for $358. He established the firm of Swett & Orme on January 8, 1855. Laura Swett's younger brother, David A. Quigg, had just graduated from Dartmouth and moved to Bloomington to read law with Swett & Orme.[26]

Although the quality of life was slowly improving, life on the prairie frontier in the mid-nineteenth century could still be perilous. A year after Laura Swett arrived in Bloomington, cholera struck the town and twenty people perished. William Orme sent his wife to Washington, D.C., to protect her from the disease. Laura, who remained in Bloomington, managed to avoid contracting cholera, but the following winter she suffered from an unspecified polio-like illness that affected her locomotion. Her disability waxed and waned for the rest of her life. Swett wrote to his sister in early 1860, "My wife is much better in her general health than a year or two ago." He displayed a mature acceptance of the inevitable, writing to Lincoln a year later, "She is not yet and never will be a strong healthy woman but as long as she supplies this deficiency by excess of goodness I do not feel like complaining."[27]

During these early years of Swett's law practice, he continued the peripatetic lifestyle he had embarked on when he left his home in Maine. Even after marrying and establishing a law firm, Swett never stayed home for long and continued to ride the circuit, following his interests in travel and politics. Because of Laura's poor health, she was no longer able to join him and remained behind alone at home. Although Swett was absent for much of their relationship, his love and respect for her were apparent in the profusion of letters he sent her as he traveled. William Orme tended to the firm's office duties while Swett was away. This division of labor capitalized on the talents of both men, as Swett showed limited aptitude for the business side of the practice. He adapted easily to the rigors of life on the road and seemed to yearn for any possible adventures around the next corner. And indeed, the road provided Swett with opportunities he could not have had in one place. The road to Mount Pulaski led to the road to Washington.

The great triumvirate consisted of Davis, Lincoln, and Swett . . .
—*Henry Clay Whitney*, Life on the Circuit with Lincoln, *1940*

3. The Great Triumvirate of the Eighth Judicial Circuit

Four years into his law practice and the itinerant life on the circuit, Swett, now age twenty-eight, scrutinized its leadership, Davis and Lincoln, who as mentors gave shape to his thoughts and actions. Davis's frank manner of expressing himself cloaked a wholehearted sincerity and earnest respect for his friends and associates, as well as for those who sought justice in his court. And despite Lincoln's apparent lack of sophistication, his careful deliberations revealed his obvious wisdom. Swett's characterization of Lincoln as "wise as a serpent" was later refined to describe a man of "great directness and extreme simplicity."[1] Swett happily joined in their legal activities and found harmony with their Whig politics.

The adventures and exploits of what Henry Clay Whitney referred to as the "great triumvirate" of the Eighth Circuit—Lincoln, Davis, and Swett—make a fascinating tale.[2] As they traveled together on the circuit from Clinton to Urbana on October 22, 1853, Swett, who had become curious about how Lincoln had reached his respected position given his humble background, asked Lincoln about his life before they met: "I have heard a great many curious incidents of your early life, and I would be obliged if you would begin at your earliest recollection and tell me the story of it continuously."

In a rare instance, Lincoln talked about himself. "I can remember our life in Kentucky," he responded, "the cabin, the stinted living, the sale of our possessions, and the journey with my father and mother to Southern Indiana." He was about seven years old at the time. Two years after moving to Indiana, his mother died. "It was pretty pinching times," he said, "at first in Indiana, getting the cabin built, and the clearing for the crops; but presently we got reasonably comfortable, and my father married again." Lincoln had few recollections of his mother, but Swett said that "he spoke most kindly of her and of his step-mother."

Lincoln also told Swett "of earning his first half dollar. Standing upon the shore of a river [the Ohio] a steamboat was passing along in the middle of the stream. Some one on board the boat called to him to come with a small boat. He went, took off a passenger and was paid the half dollar. Afterwards, playing upon a flatboat which was fastened so as to reach out into the stream, he dropped his half dollar from the farthest end of the boat." Lincoln said, "I can see the quivering and shining of that half dollar yet, as in the quick current it went down the stream and sunk from my sight forever."

The story of Lincoln's want of formal education is well known, and he told it to Swett in detail. "My father had suffered greatly for the want of an education, and he determined at an early day that I should be well educated. And what do you think he said his ideas of good education were? We had an old dog-eared arithmetic [book] in our house, and father determined that somehow, or somehow else, I should cipher clear through that book." Lincoln began to attend a school in a log house in the neighborhood, but after six weeks he withdrew to go to work on behalf of his father, Thomas Lincoln, who had become responsible for a note he had endorsed for a considerable sum. The elder Lincoln explained to his son that he wanted to hire the boy out and receive the fruits of his labors.

As a strong, athletic, and good-natured boy, Lincoln stood "ready to out-run, out-jump and out-wrestle or out-lift anybody in the neighborhood." He managed to get hold of what few books existed in the vicinity—"the Bible, Shakespeare, Bunyan's *Pilgrim's Progress*, Weems' *Life of Washington* and *Life of Marion*"—and devoured them. He "read through every book he ever heard of in that country" within a fifty-mile radius.

When Swett discovered that both he and Lincoln had made trips up and down the Mississippi River, he was most interested in Lincoln's story of his first flatboat trip down the river. Somewhat familiar with the landscape and the hardships of the river, he could readily envision the descriptions that Lincoln shared.

Flatboats were crude, rectangular craft usually made of planks. They had flat bottoms and were navigated with long oars. They were, practically speaking, miniature barges. A flatboat sometimes had a small enclosure where the boatmen could sleep or take cover from inclement weather. These boats were not good on the open sea but were designed for inland waterways, especially rivers. With no sail or engines, they depended on the currents to carry them to their destination and were typically one-way craft, because they were of no use on a return trip against the current. At the end of the voyage and after the delivery of the produce or goods a boat carried, it was dismantled and the wood was reused or burned as fuel.

The boatmen did not need great expertise to simply follow the current of the river. Yet these trips were dangerous, sometimes life-threatening, and away from the home port, anything could happen. The simple craft could be damaged easily, requiring that crews be adept at repairs to reenter rapid currents and deep water. A successful trip required a strong back, perseverance against conditions in the wild, and the mental fortitude to make good decisions and avert danger where possible.

According to Swett, Lincoln made his first trip to New Orleans in 1828 at age nineteen, with a neighbor boy named Allen Gentry. Gentry's father, James, owned a little store and dispatched the boys with some cargo. Departing from Rockport, Indiana, they headed down the Ohio River to where it flowed into the Mississippi, and then took that great river south to New Orleans. With the many bends and twists in the river, the trip took several weeks as they made about ten miles' progress each day. Steamboats could keep going day and night, but flatboats had to tie up at night for safety. Lincoln and Gentry carried with them what they had procured from the Indiana countryside, including apples and corn. For the remainder of their needs, they stopped along the riverbank, tied up, dropped a crude anchor to keep the vessel from drifting off in the currents, and went ashore to trade with the local inhabitants.

In Lincoln's era, sugarcane grew in the river delta, and the portion of the lower Mississippi River that ran through the cane fields was called the Sugar Coast. One night along the Sugar Coast, the boys stopped near Natchez to do some trading and tied up their flatboat for the night. During the night, Lincoln heard a noise on board and climbed out of the hatchway to take a look around. Several intruders had slipped aboard the boat, intent on pilfering its contents, but were surprised to find that it had occupants. In the dark of night, Lincoln could not make out any details of their appearance and described them later only as seven black men. One of the thieves attacked Lincoln as he emerged from the hatchway, aiming a blow at his head with a heavy stick. But the blow glanced off the frame around the opening before it struck him, so he did not receive its full impact. Despite their injuries in the scuffle, Lincoln and Allen managed to drive the attackers from the boat. The thieves vanished into the night, and Lincoln and Gentry immediately cut the cable, weighed anchor, and headed downriver in the darkness.

Lincoln avoided a serious head injury in the attack but sustained enough of a wound to leave a scar on his temple, which he displayed to Swett when he told him the story. Swett recounted this harrowing adventure to others some thirty-two years after Lincoln related it to him and is the only source to give Natchez as the locale. In reference to the race of the men who attacked Lincoln, Swett wrote in 1885, "A negro came very near smashing the head of the future emancipator of his race." At the end of the trip, Lincoln and Gentry returned home via steamboat.

When Lincoln was twenty-one, his family migrated from Indiana to Illinois. Arriving in the spring, they "built a cabin for the coming winter and broke land for a crop the next year." Lincoln spent a year in Macon County and departed the following March. "His step-mother tied up all his earthly possessions in a bundle, and Lincoln . . . started off with his father's and mother's blessing" to find his way in the world. In his 1885 essay, Swett painted a verbal portrait of Lincoln leaving home with his possessions tied around a stick thrown over his shoulder to go out and seek his fortune: "See him as he goes on foot through the grasses of the prairie—a tall, lithe, young man, a stick and a pack upon his back, starting out on an unknown journey."

Lincoln conceived the idea of building a flatboat with his cousin, John Hanks, and his stepbrother, John Johnston, and taking produce down the Mississippi. After contracting with Denton Offutt in Springfield, Illinois, to take his produce to New Orleans, they set about building the boat on the river just north of town. When they finished four weeks later, they started down the Sangamon River but got hung up on the dam at New Salem, Illinois. Lincoln managed to solve the arduous problem, which required him to balance the load forward, impressing Offutt and a number of bystanders. This story has often been told in much detail, but Swett reported only that "the dam was successfully passed at high water by some device." Eighteen years later, Lincoln confronted a somewhat similar situation. He then applied for and received the only patent ever obtained by a president.

After being the center of attention briefly in New Salem, Lincoln and the others proceeded downriver to St. Louis, where they dropped off John Hanks. The rest of the men continued south to New Orleans, Lincoln's second visit to the area. Once back in Illinois following this trip, he lost little time in returning to the place of his public feat as flatboat captain, New Salem.

The stories Lincoln told Swett of his early years included many familiar topics: Lincoln as a rail splitter; his pleasure at being elected captain of his local militia unit in the Black Hawk War; his part ownership in a New Salem store, which saddled him with a joint eleven-hundred-dollar loan he called "the national debt"; learning the skills of a Sangamon County surveyor; and serving four terms in the state legislature. Swett could not forget Lincoln's serious demeanor when he said, "That debt was the greatest obstacle I have ever met in life; I had no way of speculating, and could not earn money except by labor, and to earn by labor eleven hundred dollars, besides my living, seemed the work of a lifetime. There was, however, but one way. I went to the creditors and told them that if they would let me alone, I would give them all I could earn, over my living, as fast as I could earn it." His work as a surveyor helped, and the income from being a legislator was a giant step. "At that time," Lincoln said, "members of the legislature got four dollars a day, and four dollars a day was more than I had ever earned in my life." Even so, he still carried part of that debt into his life as an attorney after his marriage.

From his memory of these conversations with Lincoln about his early life, Swett emphasized the contrast with other writers' descriptions of Lincoln's childhood and youth. "Mr. Lincoln told . . . the story of a happy childhood . . . nothing sad . . . nothing of want, and no allusions of want, in any part of it." He told his stories "with mirth and glee, and illustrated by pointed anecdote, often interrupted by his jocund laugh which echoed over the prairie . . . such boys are *not* suffering, but are rather like Whittier's 'Barefoot boy with cheeks of tan.'"

In the legislative canvass of 1834, John Todd Stuart recommended to Lincoln that he study law and lent him books to get started. Lincoln became one of the "long nine," referring to legislators over six feet tall. He told Swett that at the close of his term, he was persuaded to move to Springfield and study law. "William Butler, still remembered as State Treasurer . . . , loaned him money and board," said Swett, "and he immediately commenced studying and practicing law. He rose in his profession with great rapidity and soon became distinguished as a leader in it." Lincoln became a leader of the Whig Party in the state, canvassing in 1836, 1840, and 1842. He championed Henry Clay in 1844 and was elected to Congress in 1846. In 1848, he made a canvass for President Taylor, and he returned to the circuit the following year to practice law. Soon after, he met Leonard Swett for the first time in Mount Pulaski.[3]

Swett also used his days on the Eighth Circuit to observe and note those qualities of both Lincoln and Davis that contributed to their professional success. In Judge Davis he saw an openness and hospitality that he resolved to emulate. Swett recalled that when a stranger visited the court, Davis immediately noticed and provided for him. His kindness to young lawyers often dismayed the older members of the bar, many of whom were inclined to take advantage of the junior lawyers' inexperience.

One incident involved Henry Clay Whitney as a young lawyer in Danville. After Whitney submitted a written pleading to Judge Davis, Usher T. Linder, the opposing counsel, demurred to the plea on the grounds that it was inadequate, and Davis sustained the demurrer. Whitney amended the plea but still failed to get it right. Again Linder demurred and Davis sustained the demurrer, but this time the judge provided the young lawyer with more detailed instructions on the form of the proposed amendment. After another round, Davis said to Whitney, "Give me that plea." According to Swett, Davis read the language over, "amended it to suit himself," and gave it back to Whitney so that Linder lost his demurrer. Linder visited the judge that night in his room and found Davis alone and writing. "Come in, Linder," said the judge. "Oh no," said Linder, "I see you are writing pleas in some of your numerous cases. I will not disturb you."[4]

Swett also learned from Davis to use common sense in seeking justice. He saw that Davis knew and understood the rules of law but used these rules as guides rather than mandates for his decisions. Swett described Davis as a natural judge, taking to justice by instinct, as a hound takes to a scent. Davis used the rules so far as they could guide him, but when they were inapplicable, he threw them out. Swett recalled one occasion when Davis held court together in Springfield with the federal district judge on the bench, Judge Samuel H. Treat, his predecessor on the Eighth Circuit and an old friend. A shrewd lawyer, "one of the keenest land sharks this State ever produced," brought an eviction action to take possession of a large farm for almost nothing. Davis listened to the claim and the applicable law at the trial. He crossed his legs, swung around in his rotary chair, looked back at the lawyer trying the case, and said, "You can talk to Treat. You can talk to Treat. Before this court you can not steal a man's farm in that way."[5]

Davis also used his ingenuity and instinct to arrive at a decision in an estate case with two groups of claimants. A German man had married in his homeland but abandoned his wife and family, coming to Indiana, where he married again and raised another family. By the time of his death, he had accumulated an estate worth $1 million. His heirs in Germany and Indiana both made claims for the entire estate. This time Davis was riding the circuit while serving as a U.S. Supreme Court justice. He heard this case with another federal judge, Walter Q. Gresham. At the conclusion of the proofs at trial, Judge Davis consulted with the other judge in chambers and said, "It is a pity about this case. There is property enough for both. The situation is not the fault of either party, but of the man who is dead. Let us make them divide it." The other judge replied, "That is right. You are good at that. Suppose you engineer the matter."

The two judges went back into court and sent for the lawyers on both sides. Davis expressed grave doubts about the merits of the case, at least as much as he thought the attorneys would bear, and suggested they consult and negotiate with each other to see if an agreement could be reached. After some time, the lawyers came back into court with a decree, entered by consent, declaring both families to be heirs and dividing the money equally between them. Swett commented that Davis "knew just enough law to be a great judge, and not enough to spoil him. The poorest lawyers I have ever known are men who know the most law." He was implying that those excessively devoted to procedure and detailed precedents are tempted to neglect the essence of the case before them.[6]

In another case in 1852 at Champaign, a lawyer filed a petition for a young girl's stepfather and guardian, seeking permission to sell an improved farm that the minor child owned. After hearing the application, Davis ordered the land sold and the proceeds paid to the court's clerk, a man known for honesty and fidelity. In the next year, the clerk reported that he had received the money from the sale. Davis ordered the clerk to travel to Cincinnati and invest the money in land warrants then available for about a dollar per acre. When the clerk arrived back in court in Danville with the warrants, Davis "adjourned court and went to the land office in person" to enter the

THE GREAT TRIUMVIRATE   39

warrants in the child's name. When she came of age, the warrants were worth fifty thousand dollars. By example, Davis taught Swett both fidelity to a trust and ingenuity in creating solutions.[7]

In observing Lincoln as a trial lawyer, Swett found him to be the peer of any man. He noted that Lincoln's strength was based on his ability to identify the material point on which the case turned. Swett watched Lincoln gain standing before the court and jury by adroitly giving away all immaterial issues so that he might successfully win the one point on which the case hinged. Swett described Lincoln's technique at trial, saying that when most lawyers would object, Lincoln would say that he reckoned it would be fair to let one fact or another into evidence to be considered by the judge or jury. When Lincoln's adversary could not quite prove what Lincoln knew to be true, Lincoln would say that he reckoned it would be fair to admit the truth of such a fact. If Lincoln did object and the court overruled his objection, Lincoln would say that he reckoned he must be wrong.[8]

If Lincoln used this approach well into the case without his adversary realizing what he was doing, the opponent would find that he had secured "the Greeks too late and wake up to find himself beat." By giving away six points, Lincoln would carry the case on the seventh. Swett said that Lincoln was as "wise as a serpent in the trial of a cause" but had "too many scars from his blows" for him "to certify that Lincoln was harmless as a dove."[9]

Swett undoubtedly honed his skills of persuasion by following Lincoln's example of using logic to analyze a case and then presenting his case in a clear and lucid fashion. Swett developed acuity in logic, the faculty of keen analysis, and great pathos. He used his imagination to adorn and illustrate his point and acquired the rare ability of "causing his hearers to see as he saw, to think as he thought, and to feel as he felt."[10] Swett learned from Lincoln to present his adversary's strengths more forcibly than the opponent could, and then answer each negative point fairly and fully.[11] To allow an adversary to make a point without a counterpoint or fail to address a weakness in the other side's case meant a loss of credibility with the judge or jury and the possible loss of a case.

But Swett and Lincoln differed in a number of ways. Swett brought to the courtroom his schooling in classical literature, history, and mythology, while Lincoln's mind was filled with the knowledge of the times in which he lived. Lincoln used the language of everyday conversation rather than that found in books. By listening to Lincoln as he used commonplace and conversational words to describe facts and issues, Swett developed his skills of oration and mastered the art of communicating with people of all levels on the juries. He comprehended the value of speaking in plain words to the jury members and carefully chose examples from literature to sprinkle into his arguments when appropriate. With practice on the circuit, he developed into an eloquent speaker known for his scholarly presentations.

Swett believed that the public misunderstood Lincoln's character in considering him to be a frank, guileless, and unsophisticated man. Swett felt that this was not true at all. "Beneath Lincoln's smooth surface of candor and apparent declaration of all his thoughts and feelings, he exercised the most exalted tact and wisest discrimination." Further, "any man who took Lincoln for a simple minded man would very soon wake [up] with his back in a ditch." Swett also became known as a man of exquisite tact, influenced in the cultivation of this trait by Lincoln. He never spoke disparagingly of others and had only good words for other lawyers.[12]

Another trait Swett took note of was Lincoln's inquisitive nature. Traveling on the circuit, Lincoln would take his seat next to the driver, and by the journey's end, he would know all that the driver knew. If they stopped at the blacksmith's shop, Lincoln would stay with the blacksmith over his forge to learn how to make nails. While walking along a sidewalk in a country town, if Lincoln saw an agricultural implement new to him, he would stop to learn how it worked and figure out why it worked better than its predecessor tool. "Life was to him a school, and he was always studying and mastering every subject that came before him. He knew how to dig out any question from its very roots, and when his own children began to go to school, he studied with them, and acquired in mature life the elements of an education."[13]

Swett saw Lincoln on the circuit, with a "'geometry,' or an 'astronomy,' or some book of that kind, working out propositions in moments of leisure." One day, he saw Lincoln sitting on the sidewalk near Barnett's Tavern in Clinton at a session of the circuit, studying his geometry. When he understood the point of a proposition, he got excited and wanted to share it with someone. He went up to a man nearby who was caring for some horses and explained the proposition to him until the man said, perhaps in self-defense, that he understood it.[14]

The men had time for many pleasures while on the circuit, and both Swett and Lamon consumed alcohol excessively on occasion. Their excesses on the road have been confirmed in the reminiscence literature of life on the

Eighth Circuit. Mrs. P. W. B. Carothers, editor of the *Danville Independent*, wrote in May 1856, "The bar of Illinois has among its members men of as much intellect, as much genius, as much *prestige* as any State in the West. It has great legal talent, but it has also the most *drunken* lawyers of any bar on the face of the earth." Lincoln was not a drinker, and both he and Davis were strongly opposed to drunkenness. Lincoln was guarded in expressing his view on the matter, leaving this largely unspoken. Davis was more outspoken on the issue, however, and "deplored Swett's and Lamon's excessive drinking and their occasional irresponsibility."[15]

Swett wrote, in his description of Lincoln's early years, that "he told me, not more than a year before he was elected President that he had never tasted liquor in his life."

"What!" Swett exclaimed. "Do you mean to say you never tasted it?"

"Yes, I never tasted it," Lincoln said.

Swett explained that Lincoln had opposed selling whiskey when he was a partner with William Berry in operating a store in New Salem. "A difference . . . soon arose between him and the old proprietor, the present partner of Lincoln, in reference to the introduction of whiskey into the establishment. The partner insisted that, on the principle that honey catches flies, a barrel of whiskey in the store would invite custom, and their sales would increase, while Lincoln, who never liked liquor, opposed this innovation. The result was that a bargain was made by which Lincoln should retire from his partnership in the store. He was to step out as he stepped in." However, it turned out that not only had Lincoln's partner "been his own best customer at that whiskey barrel," but he had also "failed to pay the debts," and "there were eleven hundred dollars for which Lincoln was jointly liable." Lincoln struggled with this heavy debt for much of his life. This whole incident only served to strengthen his aversion to alcohol.[16]

When Swett started on the circuit in the fall of 1849, the Eighth Circuit had consisted of fourteen counties in central Illinois. As populations grew and development continued, the circuit was reconfigured, and the six southern counties were taken away in early 1853. Four years later, the three western counties were sheared off, leaving only the five counties from Bloomington to Danville. In the mid-1850s, travel throughout the Eighth Circuit shifted from horseback and buggy to rail. The Illinois Central and the Chicago and Alton lines opened up, along with the east-west railroads serving the area. Also, the impediments posed by having to cross minor rivers draining the prairies—the two Vermilions, the Sangamon, and the Mackinaw—were greatly reduced by the addition of bridges.

While Swett, Lincoln, and Davis habitually toured the entire circuit, other attorneys participating in the spring and fall swings around the circuit came and went. Their number dwindled in the late 1850s, as the towns' growth enabled lawyers to find enough work in their own counties of domicile or in an adjacent county or two. During these years, Swett and Lincoln still thrived in the itinerant lifestyle, continuing a pattern that Swett followed for much of his life. Away from home for weeks or months at a time, they lived in small hotels or boardinghouses and ate wherever meals were available. This way of life allowed them to make and maintain many acquaintances and friendships, but it was not a life of thrift, at least not on Swett's part. As he moved farther away from his New England puritanical background, he apparently forgot the lessons of caution learned at home and lost any tendency toward parsimony.

During their years on the Eighth Circuit, Lincoln and Swett appeared together in more than ninety cases of record. Sometimes they appeared as co-counsel on the same side, but just as often they appeared on opposing sides, as was the case in the murder trial of Isaac Wyant. Swett appeared with Lincoln in more cases before the bar than did any other attorney except for Lincoln's partner, William Herndon. This gave Swett the opportunity to study Lincoln's practices, especially the way he zeroed in on the essential argument of a case. There is evidence that they consulted informally in numerous other cases where formal records do not survive. More than twenty of the recorded cases involved claims of trespass against the railroads, usually the Illinois Central Railroad, which retained Lincoln as defense counsel. The two men also associated in assumpsit or breach-of-contract cases and larceny and forgery claims.[17]

Representing the defendant, Swett beat Lincoln in a slander case tried in DeWitt County in May 1854. After that case, Lincoln always wanted Swett on his side in jury trials. This may mark the beginning of Swett's demonstration of his ability to concentrate on details to find the essence of each argument. Swett assisted Lincoln informally in *Peter Spink v. Charles Chiniquy* in defense of Father Charles Paschal Telesphore Chiniquy, who was accused of slander. The May 1856 trial in Champaign County lasted three days. Although plaintiff Peter Spink had been found innocent of charges of perjury, he claimed that Father Chiniquy had publicly slandered him to his parishioners in L'Erable, a village settled by French Canadians in northeastern Illinois in the 1850s. The case attracted great attention, and many people attended the trial, including a nephew of George Washington, Spotswood Augustine Washington. At the end of three days, the case was still ongoing, so it was carried over until the fall term of the court.[18]

By this time, Lincoln had determined the contest unworthy of its cost and effort, and he sought an end to the argument. Following his practice of avoiding excessive litigation, Lincoln persuaded the parties to sign the following agreement, written in his own hand, and then submitted it to the court with an order for dismissal: "This day came the parties and the defendant [Chiniquy] denies that he has ever charged, or believed the plaintiff [Spink] to be guilty of Perjury; that whatever he has said from which such a charge could be inferred, he said on the information of others, protesting his own disbelief in the charge; and that he now disclaims any belief in the truth of said charge against said plaintiff. It is therefore, by agreement of the parties, ordered that the suit be dismissed, each party paying his own cost—the defendant to pay his part of the cost heretofore ordered to be paid by said plaintiff."[19]

The disputatious Father Chiniquy separated from the Roman Catholic Church four years later in a quarrel with the bishop. Some three decades after this trial, Chiniquy claimed to have visited Lincoln three times while president. In a lengthy book, Chiniquy stated that they discussed Jesuit assassination plots against Lincoln, but a later inquiry found the visits dubious. Chiniquy made spurious anti-Catholic accusations and other charges that were repeated over the next four-score years.[20]

In October 1855, two events occurred that pitted Swett against Lincoln in the courtroom: a deadly fire and a premeditated killing. The case following the fire went on to a hung jury and a later settlement, but it produced the infamous "chicken bone story" shared by lawyers for decades. The Wyant murder case had far-reaching implications and is an illustration of an early application of the insanity defense.

In the first case, a fire broke out in the block south of the old McLean County Courthouse in Bloomington on the night of October 16, 1855. One man died and another, Samuel G. Fleming, sustained two broken thighs when the chimney of the Morgan House collapsed on him. Three doctors, including Thomas P. Rogers and Eli K. Crothers, splinted Fleming's legs. Three weeks later, they removed the splints to check his progress. Although his left leg had mended well, they found that the right leg was crooked. The doctors suggested that they reset his leg, and Fleming and his family agreed to this intervention. They gave him chloroform and started the manipulation, but Fleming screamed for them to stop, as the pain was too great for him to bear. Dr. Crothers explained that if the leg did not heal properly, it might not be able to sustain his weight. Fleming and his family members continued to object, however, so the doctors discontinued the procedure. After his right leg healed but remained crooked, Fleming sued the doctors for malpractice.

Swett and Lincoln faced off in *Fleming v. Rogers & Crothers.* The *Fleming* case emerged as a celebrated one because of the legal talent employed and the challenge posed to the evolving medical profession in Bloomington, and it involved extensive medical testimony. Each side retained three pairs of attorneys, making a total of twelve attorneys on the case. Asahel Gridley and John Wickizer were the most established pair on the plaintiff's side. Gridley was a prominent attorney, banker, and property owner in Bloomington, who resigned his legal practice soon after this case. Lincoln later appointed Wickizer to the U.S. Quartermaster Corps during the Civil War, and he continued in government service for much of his life. Swett and Orme also appeared for the plaintiff. William Hanna and John M. Scott, both friends of Swett and Lincoln, were an additional pair for the plaintiff. Scott later became a long-term member of the Illinois Supreme Court. Hanna, a Lincoln political supporter, was struck by lightning in his bed and killed in 1870; his wife, amazingly, escaped unscathed. When Swett appeared on the plaintiff's team, Lincoln and John Todd Stuart, Lincoln's former partner, were quickly retained for the defense, possibly an example of Swett's burgeoning reputation. David Brier from Indiana and Jesse Birch constituted the second pair for the defense, and L. L. Strain, who died before the trial started, and Andrew W. Rogers rounded out the defense team.

During the plaintiff's case, his attorneys called fifteen doctors and twenty-one other witnesses. The defense presented the twelve remaining doctors practicing in Bloomington in support of its case. Every doctor in town testified on one side or the other. After being carefully coached by Dr. Crothers on age-related changes in bone structure that impact healing, Lincoln demonstrated his argument for the jury by using brittle chicken bones. He "seized on the bones as the best means of making things clear to the jury" and argued that a crooked leg was better than no leg, if an amputation had been required.

The jury deliberated for eighteen hours without reaching a verdict. The court ordered a change of venue and set a new trial for April 1857 in Logan County. Before the trial started, however, the parties reached an agreement to dismiss the case, with the doctors paying the costs of defense. Despite this anticlimactic conclusion, the case lived on in perpetuity as the "chicken bone case" because of Lincoln's novel approach to explaining the evidence.[21]

The second case, the March 1857 trial of Isaac Wyant in Bloomington for cold-blooded murder carried out in front of several witnesses, became one of the most notorious cases on the Eighth Circuit. It pitted Swett for the defense against Lincoln, handpicked by the state's attorney to lead the prosecution. Swett used his observations and knowledge of Lincoln to his advantage. Although he was going up against "a man without peer," he was, after his years on the circuit as part of the great triumvirate, well acquainted with Lincoln and the practice of law. He was thirty-two years of age. Lincoln, at age forty-eight, was just four years shy of the presidency. Lincoln was equally familiar with Leonard Swett, his younger friend, as they had shared meals and stories, buggy rides and travels across the prairie, and cases in the Eighth Circuit. He had adequate witnesses to the public murder of Anson Rusk at the hands of Isaac Wyant. And he had much more experience than Swett.

The summer before the murder, a dispute had arisen between the Rusk and Wyant families over a piece of land. One family preempted the land, and the other attempted to impeach the claim. The matter evolved into an extended family feud. Wyant, thirty-four and reportedly a bully, beat up one of the Rusk relatives. One day, the two families ran into each other on a road north of Clinton, Illinois. Anson Rusk shot Isaac Wyant in the arm and threatened to kill him and the rest of his family. Wyant's nephew later claimed that the Rusks fired a number of shots at the family.

The next day, after administering chloroform, a doctor amputated Wyant's arm below the elbow to prevent the spread of infection. He testified that the amputation had occurred sixteen hours after the shooting. From that time on, as members of the Wyant family testified, Isaac Wyant became obsessed with the idea that Rusk would find him and kill him, and he acted peculiarly in other respects.

On October 12, 1855, Wyant followed Anson Rusk into the county clerk's office in the Clinton courthouse and shot Anson Rusk four times in cold blood in front of several bystanders. He carried two revolvers with him to make sure he got the job done. Later investigation revealed that his adversary carried two pistols in his pockets. The sheriff immediately apprehended Wyant and put him in a jail cell.

Ward Hill Lamon, the prosecuting attorney, quickly retained Lincoln to head the prosecution. Assisting Lincoln were Clifton Moore, Davis's partner in land investment activity, and Harvey Hogg, a Bloomington attorney. Isaac Wyant asked the jailer whom he recommended as an attorney. The jailer suggested Leonard Swett, and the Wyant family soon retained the law offices of Swett and Orme. Orme assisted with the defense, but Swett spent many hours over the next year developing the defense and fashioning an explanation for the murder.[22]

While the trial was ongoing, he took his meals with Ann Gideon Parker and her husband, who ran a hotel in Clinton. Ann knew Swett from his early days in Clinton, when he had boarded at the hotel. She recalled that he was incredibly nervous in preparing for the trial, often getting up from the table to pace the floor, and told her he had read the Bible through twice to find every help that scripture might provide him in his defense.

"Swett, why do you work this way to save a murderer?" she asked him. "For you know he killed the man."

"This man looks to me to save him, he has given me all he has to do so, and I must serve him," he replied. His answer revealed "the secret of a great career," she said: "faithfulness to an obligation."[23]

Swett was a creative thinker who did not mind taking risks, and he made the innovative decision to explore insanity as a possibly significant defense that could influence the jury. Although lawyers often use the insanity defense today, it was still experimental in the 1850s. Unbeknownst to the prosecution, Swett made a study of the human mind and mental illness. He mastered the anatomy of the brain and other relevant medical evidence, meeting with physicians and other authorities at an insane asylum in Illinois. He also traveled to New York and Massachusetts seeking information while on an extended visit with his family in Maine.[24]

Despite a change of venue moving the case from Clinton to Bloomington, public interest moved right along with it, and the courtroom was packed from the beginning to the end of the trial. Lincoln gave his opening statement on Tuesday, March 31, 1857, and called six witnesses, including those who had seen the shooting plus two doctors. He closed the case for the prosecution that evening.

The next day, Swett opened with a lengthy statement and called several of Wyant's family members to testify about the man's aberrant behavior and the family's history of insanity. Then he called several witnesses to testify about the earlier shooting by Rusk. The families disagreed as to whether Wyant had been carrying a knife the day the families met on the road and the first shooting occurred. Swett called one of the doctors involved in the amputation, and an Indiana minister long acquainted with Wyant described him as a "fearless and undaunted man" but said he was vastly changed after the loss of his arm. Swett put five additional doctors on the stand, including three practitioners in the field of insanity. The doctors offered the opinion that Isaac Wyant was insane, explaining the impact of the fears on his mind, suggesting that the dosage of chloroform given for the amputation had induced insanity, and citing a repetitive nervous tic, a picking of the head, as an indication of madness. The doctors supplied strong evidence that Wyant was in constant fear of his life after the shooting. At one point, Wyant had become so paranoid he thought his sister was going to kill him. The strongest testimony came from the doctor heading the Illinois State Hospital for the Insane. He was well respected and had previously headed a hospital in New Hampshire for eight years. Finally, the evidence showed that both Rusk and Wyant were armed on the day of the murder, as each carried two pistols. Swett called a total of eighteen witnesses before resting his case.

Lincoln recovered quickly from the unexpected barrage of defense witnesses. On rebuttal, he called twelve new witnesses, including several local physicians, and recalled two others, one of the doctors involved in the arm amputation and one with knowledge about other fights that had involved Wyant. On cross-examination of a local medical doctor, Swett asked some preliminary questions about the anatomy of the brain without revealing the extent of his studies. According to Herbert Swett in his biography of his father, when the physician tried to showcase his own knowledge, Swett quietly lifted a copy of *Gray's Anatomy* from under his pile of law books and handed the book to the doctor on the witness stand, remarking, "I see that Dr. Gray states quite the contrary. Perhaps you had better correct Dr. Gray in this matter."[25]

The rebuttal by the prosecution ended on Thursday evening. Hogg spent three hours summarizing for the prosecution on Friday morning, and Orme argued for the defense for a similar interval before yielding to Swett. On Saturday morning, Swett finished his closing argument, and Lincoln did his best for five hours in the afternoon. The local paper in Bloomington, the *Pantagraph*, observed that the closing arguments of "the senior counsel . . . were models of forensic eloquence." Swett's skillful defense made a life-changing impression on at least one individual who attended the trial. A seventeen-year-old named Joseph Fifer, who later served as the governor of Illinois, said he first resolved to become a lawyer on hearing Swett's plea in Wyant's defense.[26]

The jury received brief and clear instructions for finding a verdict of guilty or not guilty, and then adjourned for supper. They retired to their rooms for approximately five and a half hours and then, after a short deliberation, returned to the courtroom early Sunday morning, April 4, 1857, with a verdict. Their decision called for acquittal on condition that the defendant be committed to the state institution for the insane. Isaac Wyant was found not guilty of murder by reason of insanity. Swett thus was one of the early attorneys to use the insanity defense successfully in the West.[27]

A conversation about a year later provides some insight into Abraham Lincoln's compassionate nature. He discussed the Wyant case in early 1858 with the attorney general of Indiana, Joseph Ewing McDonald (1819–91), whom he knew and who attended the Danville court on occasion. McDonald, later a Democratic congressman and a U.S. senator, told Lincoln that he "had been Wyant's counsel frequently and had defended him from almost every charge in the calendar of crimes; and that he was a weak brother and could be led into almost everything." As Lincoln had no prior knowledge of these cases, he asked McDonald many questions. The following morning, Lincoln reported that "his sleep had been disturbed by the fear that he had been too bitter and unrelenting in his prosecution . . . that [he thought] he was 'possuming' insanity." He said with remorse, "Now I fear I have been too severe . . . the poor fellow may be insane after all."[28]

As a result of the Wyant verdict, Leonard Swett's name became associated with the insanity defense, and he became well known as a successful and flamboyant criminal defense attorney. The first derivative of the Wyant case occurred shortly after its conclusion, when Lincoln received an appeal for help from the father of Robert C. Sloo Jr., in Shawneetown, a Gallatin County town in the Ohio River bottomlands. The elder Sloo was a clerk of the circuit court and was running for reelection. His opponent for office had published several anonymous articles in the local paper describing him as "violently abusive . . . casting injurious imputations upon his family." Sloo's son criticized the unknown writer for making these inferences about his family. Once unveiled, the author of the articles, John E. Hall, threatened the son, and the younger Sloo, who already had shown signs of mental instability, took a revolver to the courthouse and killed his father's opponent.

After the young man's father reached out to Lincoln for help, the older lawyer paid Swett the ultimate compliment and nod of respect. "I want you to go in my place," Lincoln said.

"I am unknown to the parties and they would not be satisfied with the change," Swett replied.

"Mr. Swett, if I can get you to go, it is not fair to that young man and his family that I should go," Lincoln said earnestly.[29]

Accordingly, Swett took the referral and represented the defendant. The prosecution was ably led by William J. Allen (1829–1900), the U.S. district attorney from Marion, and John A. Logan (1826–86), later a popular Union general and three-term U.S. senator. Logan was known as "a fire-eater."[30] Swett associated with Thomas G. C. Davis of St. Louis and Alton, Illinois, plus a Kentucky lawyer and two additional local attorneys.

Swett enlisted as expert witnesses three doctors from the Wyant trial. The trial took place in a converted railroad depot in Shawneetown. The depot overflowed every day with spectators to the point of suffocation, and the crowd spilled outdoors as far as the proceedings could be heard. In the days of the Eighth Circuit, people eagerly anticipated and attended the trials. They listened for hours to the testimonies and arguments to make up their own minds and follow the pursuit of justice. Swett's argument lasted four hours and concluded at dusk. A former member of the bar in Clinton, Lawrence Weldon, later a U.S. Court of Claims judge in Washington, said of Swett, "In fluency of language, copiousness of thought, and aptness of illustration, he never surpassed this effort. The trial had commenced with all the doubts against the defendant, but even before the argument began, the certainty of acquittal was plain." After a deliberation that appeared to be a formality, the jury promptly brought in a verdict of not guilty by reason of insanity.[31]

By this point, Swett and Lincoln were the sole lawyers who continued to tour the entire Eighth Circuit with Judge Davis. Swett wrote to his college roommate in 1860, "For perhaps five years, Lincoln and myself have been the only ones who have habitually passed over the whole circuit." Henry Clay Whitney, who participated in the Eighth Circuit during its last seven years of renown, 1854–60, clearly identified its apex in this definitive remark: "When I first knew the eighth circuit, the great triumvirate consisted of Davis, Lincoln, and Swett: and their social consequence was in the order named."[32]

The first work of our forefathers . . . was to
proclaim the territories . . . forever free.
—*Leonard Swett, introducing Lincoln in*
Bloomington, September 4, 1858

4. Politics Overtakes the Law

While Swett was serving on the Eighth Circuit, the events of the day drew him, along with the other two members of the great triumvirate, into politics. During this time, the practice of law on the circuit often took a backseat to the political activities and dialogue of these unpaid servants in a growing democracy.

In May 1854, Senator Stephen A. Douglas introduced the Kansas-Nebraska Act in Congress, and it quickly passed and became law. Besides creating the territories of Kansas and Nebraska, the act repealed the Missouri Compromise of 1820, which had excluded slavery from the rest of the new territories acquired in the Louisiana Purchase, and gave the settlers the right to make their own decision about whether to allow slavery in their territory. This unexpected action rattled opposing political forces, and Lincoln and many others renewed their efforts to contain the extension of slavery. Lincoln attacked the Kansas-Nebraska Act on a number of occasions in Bloomington and elsewhere, but he did not give his full arguments until he responded to a speech by Douglas with a three-hour speech of his own, delivered in the State House of Representatives Hall in Springfield on October 4.

Stirred by the slavery issue and the repeal of the Missouri Compromise, Lincoln decided to run for Senate, and Swett became one of his most valuable supporters. Although the Senate seat occupied by Douglas was not in contest in early 1855, that of Lincoln's old Democratic adversary, James Shields, was. At that time, a vote among state legislators determined the winner, and with the newly elected legislature being composed over-whelmingly of new members and disparate parties, Lincoln hoped to gather enough support among them to gain the seat. Judge Davis, Lincoln's former law partner Stephen T. Logan, Ward Hill Lamon, and others provided assistance. In December 1854, Swett wrote to Lincoln offering his support, saying, "Use me in any way." Lincoln promptly dispatched him to northern Illinois to assess possible supporters.

Swett made at least two trips in ten days, during which he wrote four letters to Lincoln. While he was away, he mentioned that there was illness at his home, but he did not make clear its exact nature. Apparently Swett did not feel compelled to stay home to tend to his family, instead visiting Wilmington, Joliet, Ottawa, LaSalle, and other locations in northern Illinois on Lincoln's behalf. Swett wrote to Lincoln that "the Tribune controls things" in Chicago and "is secretly in favor of" a local judge, although "[State Senator Norman] Judd was leaning for you," and "[Governor Joel] Matteson is secretly working for himself and hopes to be a compromise candidate." He wrote that his informant there "thinks it important for you to send some decent man" to Chicago "and endeavor to enlist them."[1]

Swett also spent an afternoon with T. Lyle Dickey, judge of the adjoining judicial circuit in Ottawa, along with the judge's son-in-law, W. H. L. Wallace, and another local politician. Swett knew Dickey as an attorney and occasional judge on the Eighth Circuit. Dickey agreed to go to Kendall County to try to influence the new members of the legislature there to support Lincoln. The judge persuaded the Democratic leader of LaSalle County to work on that county's two members to go for Lincoln "in preference to any other Whig and go for a Whig rather than have the election layover." Swett summarized his efforts in this way: "I think from all I learned that in that region you need not fear any other Whig." Other discussions involved members of the legislatures in Kankakee and Kendall Counties. All in all, it was a good week of "politicking."[2]

A heavy snowstorm delayed the voting by nearly two weeks. When the combined houses of the state legislature finally convened in early February, the first ballot gave Lincoln forty-five votes, but he needed fifty-one to win. The incumbent, Shields, received forty-one, and Lyman Trumbull, an Anti-Nebraska Democrat (as those who opposed the Kansas-Nebraska Act were called), garnered only five. A smattering went to a few others, including one vote for Governor Matteson. The next six ballots did not shift much, but by the eighth ballot, the Douglas Democrats revealed their hand, suddenly throwing their support to Matteson. On the ninth ballot, Lincoln had lost all but fifteen of his supporters. Matteson now had forty-seven votes. Trumbull, who had started with only five Anti-Nebraska Democrats, stood at thirty-five votes. On the tenth ballot, Lincoln persuaded all of his supporters to switch to Trumbull to prevent Matteson from being elected. Trumbull won the seat and ended up serving in the Senate for the next eighteen years. Lincoln felt his defeat sorely, although he later gained support from Anti-Nebraska Democrats for his action and said he had experienced more pleasure from Matteson's defeat than pain from his own loss. Davis and Swett never warmed to Trumbull's righteous persona, even when he later joined the Republican ranks.[3]

The Republican Party was in the process of formation during this period, combining many of those opposed to the extension of slavery from among northern Whigs, Free Soilers, Know-Nothings of the American Party, and dissident Democrats in the various states. The party was first established in Wisconsin and Michigan in 1854. In Illinois, the statewide Anti-Nebraska Party collected these factions for two years and held its convention in Bloomington on May 29, 1856, which resulted in the creation of the state's Republican Party. To avoid being labeled an abolitionist, Lincoln had chosen not to join the earliest Republican group in Illinois. But now he was ready to join and gave his famous "lost speech" as the last speaker at the convention.

Swett, who had already become a Republican, attended this convention as well and considered his own political future. The *Pantagraph* of Bloomington endorsed him for the Republican nomination in the Third Congressional District, a twelve-county region stretching across the northeastern part of the state, from Bureau to Will County on the north and from McLean and DeWitt to Vermilion County on the south. A full-scale editorial endorsement followed in the *Pantagraph* on June 11, clearly identifying "Slavery extension" as the major issue and saying of Swett, "For vividness of imagination—for bold and impassioned eloquence, united in logical compactness of argument—though not a stranger to forensic and parliamentary eloquence of a high order—we have seldom heard his equal, and never his superior."[4]

The Republican National Convention met in Philadelphia on June 17–19, 1856. Although Lincoln and most of the Illinois delegation favored U.S. Supreme Court justice John McLean of Ohio for the Republican presidential candidate, John C. Fremont, the "Pathfinder of the West," won easily on the first ballot, with 359 votes to McLean's 196. John M. Palmer, an Anti-Nebraska Democrat who had opposed Lincoln for Senate in 1854 and had led the Bloomington Anti-Nebraska Convention in May, now as a delegate favored Lincoln for the Republican vice presidential candidate, as did most of the Illinois delegation. They succeeded in getting him nominated, but the favorite, former senator William L. Dayton of New Jersey, also won on the first ballot, with 253 votes to Lincoln's 110.

These were heady days for the thirty-year-old Swett. Later that summer, he returned home to Maine for a visit. While there, he joined Charles Russell Train, a Massachusetts delegate to the Philadelphia convention, in speaking at a political rally for Fremont in Concord, Massachusetts.[5] Swett's own political career now was beginning to take shape.

Shortly after Swett visited his family in Maine, his older brother, Danville, who was to inherit the family farm, instead followed Leonard back to Illinois, migrating to McLean County with his family. The Maine farm then passed to their eldest sister and her husband, Sarah and Albion Ricker. Leonard reported in a letter to Rose that they had "bought a farm of 240 acres which Danville is to have for his home."[6] Leonard's part in the financing of this farm, about eight miles from Bloomington, involved his cosigning for a large debt for his older brother, assuming his debt and discharging his brother's obligation after realizing that his brother had no ability to pay.

Swett also quickly resumed his political activities on his return to Illinois, and on July 2, when the Ottawa nominating convention met to name the Republican congressional candidate for the Third Illinois District, he faced off against the incumbent, Jesse O. Norton, and Owen Lovejoy, a Congregational minister from Princeton, Illinois. Lovejoy was an abolitionist and brother of the martyred Elijah Lovejoy, who had been killed nearly two decades earlier for publishing abolitionist materials. Lincoln disappointed Swett by not supporting him against Lovejoy. Lincoln had decided, for political reasons related to his own candidacy, not to take one side or the other in this race. On the first ballot, the count was twenty-four votes for Lovejoy, nineteen for Swett, and nine for Norton. The second ballot showed no change. After a twenty-minute recess, Swett and Norton both withdrew in favor of a more conservative candidate, who then lost to Lovejoy.

Lincoln arrived in Princeton two days later to participate in Fourth of July festivities and wrote to Judge Davis, "Seeing the people there—their great enthusiasm for Lovejoy—considering the activity they will carry into the contest with him—and their great disappointment, if he should now be torn from them, I really think it best to let the matter stand." When he learned the result of the convention, Lincoln said, "It turned me blind." Two days later, he used the same phrase in a letter to Henry Clay Whitney.[7] Many Whigs in the southern counties of the district did not support the Lovejoy nomination, and Lincoln encountered political difficulties maintaining their allegiance to the Republican Party. Davis came around, but Dickey threatened to bolt. A dissident group nominated Dickey for the seat sought by Lovejoy, but ultimately Dickey withdrew from the race a couple months before the election.[8]

Lincoln's speaking schedule intensified as the campaign progressed in the late summer and fall of 1856, and Leonard Swett was not far behind him on the campaign trail. Swett spoke on August 30 at a large Fremont Club meeting in Major's Hall in Bloomington. Having recently returned from a trip to the Northeast, he reported on the enthusiasm in New York and New England for "Fremont and Freedom," as had become the Republican campaign slogan. James Buchanan had won the Democratic presidential candidacy, and on September 16 at Major's Hall, Lincoln "tore the day-time speeches of the Bucks [Buchanan supporters] at their great meeting into ribbons." Two days later, Swett stood again at the same podium, "cutting up Judge Douglas" and other speakers. He spoke in Pana, about a hundred miles south, four days later with McLean County judge John M. Scott of Bloomington and several others. At the Springfield State Republican Convention on September 25, Swett was among a group of nine candidates for lieutenant governor and received eight votes. John Wood of Adams County (Quincy) won, with sixty-three votes.[9]

The following month saw the candidates and their supporters at podiums across the state. On October 9, 1856, a huge Republican meeting for McLean County and towns beyond attracted ten thousand people to Bloomington. The event featured a parade and an afternoon and evening of speeches. The speakers included Owen Lovejoy and, at the outer edge of the crowd and out of earshot of Lovejoy, Swett and former U.S. congressman from Illinois Richard Yates. Trumbull and Lincoln gave simultaneous speeches in Peoria. On October 13, Swett spoke at Clinton, along with Lincoln, Judge John Scott, Judge Dickey, Clinton lawyer Lawrence Weldon, and Springfield lawyer John Rosette, a former Democrat. Over the next few days, Swett also participated in events in West Urbana (now Champaign), Atlanta, and Decatur with Trumbull, Lincoln, Yates, Herndon, and others. The same program of speakers held forth at a gathering of fifteen thousand to twenty thousand in Jacksonville on November 1.[10]

Fremont won in Bloomington but lost in Springfield and Quincy. Lovejoy carried McLean, Champaign, and Vermilion Counties in the election but lost in DeWitt. Ward Hill Lamon, Swett's friend and colleague on the Eighth Circuit, won nearly 54 percent of the vote to become prosecuting attorney of that circuit.

Around this time, Swett worked with several others to establish a public teachers college in North Bloomington, and in May 1857, Illinois State Normal University, the first public university in Illinois, became the twenty-second teachers college in America. In Swett's Fourth of July oration in Bloomington that year, he traced the origin of normal schools in America and emphasized the need for teachers. He concluded by pointing out the importance of education in a democracy: "Monarchies maintain peace by standing armies, but republics could only depend upon the intelligence among the people to save them from internal discord."[11]

Earlier that year, on March 6, 1857, the U.S. Supreme Court's decision in the *Dred Scott* case that the African American slave was not a citizen had intensified political tensions. The extension of slavery into the new territories had gained legal status following the Kansas-Nebraska Act, and Illinois entered the arena of the controversy as Lincoln repeatedly challenged Douglas. Around the time of the decision, Swett, Lincoln, and Davis were embroiled in the *Wyant* and "chicken bone" cases on the circuit, which for a time absorbed most of their energy. Within three months, however, Lincoln spoke to the Illinois House of Representatives in Springfield in response to a speech two weeks earlier by Senator Stephen A. Douglas. Lincoln talked about the situation in Kansas since the Kansas-Nebraska Act and then launched into a lengthy attack on the *Dred Scott* decision, as well as Douglas and Chief Justice Roger B. Taney, who had delivered the majority opinion in the case, for diverging from the intent of the founding fathers in 1776 and the meaning of the Declaration of Independence.[12]

The following year, on June 16, 1858, Lincoln opened his canvass for the Senate against Douglas at the Republican State Convention with an address known as his House Divided Speech. Lincoln formed his political positions slowly, after thinking them through carefully. When he felt secure in his path, he resisted any modification or change to the principles and arguments established in his mind. So it was with his "house divided" concept, which, according to Swett, was "apparently made for the campaign." The "house divided" idea originated from a Bible verse, Matthew 12:25, and Lincoln probably first saw it used in relation to slavery in America in a sermon by Theodore Parker that he read earlier that spring as he planned his campaign against Douglas.[13]

The significance of the "house divided" concept lies in its biblical anteced- ent, its complexity and overt reference to a possible breakup of the country, and its uniqueness to Lincoln. No other major argument in the Lincoln- Douglas Senate campaign elicited more challenges or questions. Swett later described how, during the campaign, a group of Lincoln's friends, including Swett, "insisted it was a great mistake," to which Lincoln responded, "You may think that Speech was a mistake, but I never have believed it was, and you will see the day when you will consider it was the wisest thing I ever said."[14] Regardless of his friends' opinions, this opening speech appears to have made a defining contribution to the Lincoln presidential nomination and candidacy two years later.

In the late summer of 1858, Swett was suffering from a recurring un- named illness and headed for Mackinac Island, Michigan, to recuperate. He embarked on an extended trip on the Great Lakes, meeting family members in Chicago and Milwaukee en route, and did not attend the Lincoln-Douglas speeches or debates during this time. Although Laura was now six months pregnant, he left her at home to fend for herself. Once Swett arrived on Mackinac Island, he made the acquaintance of James O. Putnam from Buffalo, New York, and established a friendship that he later used to support Lincoln's nomination for the presidency.[15]

Swett returned in time to introduce Lincoln at a large rally on September 4, 1858, in Bloomington between the third and fourth debates. The choice of the thirty-three-year-old Swett was most likely easy and uncontested. Davis was not much good at giving speeches and regarded Swett as having oratorical skills second only to those of Lincoln. The *Pantagraph* described the event as a Republican mass meeting and magnificent demonstration and called Swett's reception speech "eloquent and beautiful."

The newspaper also transcribed Swett's speech, in which he expressed his views on slavery. Swett anchored his opposition to the extension of slavery to the acts of the founding fathers, pointing out that "the present form of slavery" existed at the time of independence, "forced upon the forefathers" by the power of the mother country. He explained that "the first work of our forefathers . . . was to proclaim the territories . . . forever free, to restrict as soon as practicable the further importation of slaves, and place the institution where the public mind would rest in the belief that it was in the course of ultimate extinction." Instead, he observed, the forefathers' policy was now "claimed to be a violation of the very constitution they made and gave us." Swett argued that "the whole policy to make this country the great heritage of free men is subverted, and in its stead prevail other maxims which, in their tendency, nationalize and perpetuate the crowning evil of our land."[16]

Swett then charged Lincoln with representing the citizenry by repudiating Douglas's heresies: "The eyes of the nation are upon you. You are expected to deal heavy blows—to parry unscrupulous and artful thrusts, to unmask every sophistry, and drag to light the naked deformity of the dangerous policy you are combating." Swett offered "not only the affectionate welcome of the people, but their entire approval . . . on every field you have met your wary adversary." He exhorted Lincoln to "go on as you have nobly begun; be cheered by the approval, the sympathy and unshaken confidence of the thousands assembled here to greet you."[17]

Following Swett's introduction, Lincoln spoke. His remarks took the form of a reply to a speech Douglas had given in Bloomington in July. Lincoln based his resistance to the extension of slavery on the acts of the founding fathers and repeated the first two paragraphs of his House Divided Speech. "A dozen times had the slavery question been declared to be *settled* forever," he said. "Will war follow from adopting the policy which was originally adopted by the Government, and from which war never *did* follow—from which no trouble came?" Lincoln also made a plea for "at least a fair and impartial hearing" from the old-line Whigs in attendance.[18] He was referring to his former law partner, John Todd Stuart, for whom he had canvassed twenty years earlier, as well as to Judge T. Lyle Dickey and others who feared that the Republicans would support abolition. Despite this plea, however, Dickey defected to support Douglas.

Swett, Lincoln, Dickey, and Davis had been old-line Henry Clay Whigs together, but Dickey had been raised in Kentucky and, although he freed his own slaves, feared abolition, likely afraid of the disruption it would cause. Shortly after the Lincoln speech, Swett arrived at his Bloomington office early one morning to find Dickey waiting for him. The judge had taken the night train down from Ottawa and arrived at about daylight. Dickey asked Swett to send for Davis. When Davis arrived, Dickey told his friends that he had decided to join the Democratic Party. The three men spent the day together, telling stories of their days on the circuit. "Politics, in fact, was the only subject absolutely avoided," said Swett, "for all the ground there had in many an interview been trampled over before." Late that afternoon, Davis and Swett accompanied Dickey to the train, where they shook his hand and said good-bye. "He did not stop," Swett said, "until he ran into the very heart of the democratic party."[19]

Lincoln was bitterly disappointed when Dickey supported Douglas against him in this Senate race, along with other old-line Whigs such as Horace Greeley, editor of the *New York Tribune*, and Republican senator William Seward of New York. In addition to defecting, Dickey solicited an opinion from Senator John J. Crittenden of Kentucky, generally regarded as wearing the mantle of Henry Clay. In response, Crittenden sent a letter in August supporting Douglas. Dickey released this letter for publication a week before the election, searing Lincoln, who had thought this action was possibly decisive.

As Swett aided Lincoln in his 1858 senatorial campaign, he found that it differed from the one in 1854. Now the railroads were more fully developed; the Republican Party was better established, if still prone to factions; and the legislature was less subject to turnover. And this time, Lincoln was more ensconced as the Republican candidate, so his demands on his supporting friends such as Swett were also different. Lincoln needed to inform voters in order to bring their influence to bear on their legislators, and he used county and legislative district voting records from 1856 to determine which districts they "must struggle for" and those in which there was "no use in trying." Through this analysis, he targeted the central Illinois districts most likely to produce results in his favor.[20] Influencing legislators through their constituents proved a tricky business, however.

At about the time of the rally in Bloomington, Swett felt pressured to enter the race to represent McLean County in the state legislature in order to support Lincoln's candidacy there. It is clear that he did not want to run in this race, as he told the county convention held in Lexington on September 6, 1858, "[I have] engagements in the courts of McLean, Logan, DeWitt, Champaign and Vermillion [*sic*] counties, which will require nearly all my time between now and election day, and I sincerely hope the Convention will not insist upon my nomination." Davis also mentioned in a postscript to a letter to Lincoln that Swett "does not want to run." With his busy law practice, Swett had little time for campaigning. Furthermore, he likely considered that the campaign would be a financial strain, as he was still in debt from helping his brother purchase a farm. And although he would be reimbursed as a state representative, his time spent serving in government would not replace the forgone earnings from his legal practice.[21]

After nominating other county office candidates, the convention returned to the selection of the candidate for the state House of Representatives and, by acclamation, chose the man who had introduced Lincoln two days earlier. Swett "made a few feeling and appropriate remarks . . . of the kindness and partiality with which he had been treated by the people of McLean county" and accepted the nomination in order to support Lincoln: "The vote of McLean County must be given for [Lincoln] . . . and the hope that I can be instrumental in elevating him to the place now occupied by Stephen A. Douglas is one of the reasons which have induced me to accept the nomination."[22]

Swett's September 6 nomination gave him less than two months to plan and execute his canvass of McLean County. His Democratic opponent, John Gregory, a large landowner from the Gridley area in the northern edge of the county, about fifteen miles north of Bloomington, was a well-respected livestock producer. A group of old-line Whigs in the county, of which Gregory was one, had asked him to run. Gregory accepted the nomination on September 20, by which time Swett already had spoken in Lexington and arranged appearances through October 2 at the Republican Club of Bloomington, Leroy, Old Town, Saybrook, Pleasant Hill, Towanda, Carlock, Concord (now Danvers), Dale, and Heyworth. Swett returned to his practice for about two weeks before falling ill with an unspecified malady serious enough to confine him to bed. On the evening of October 21, he spoke in Atlanta in Logan County, where Douglas had appeared that afternoon. He responded to Douglas again at a Republican gathering the following day at the dedication of the new Phoenix Hall in Bloomington, across from the courthouse.[23]

In the meantime, the Democrats had difficulty with local organization, as reflected by a split between President James Buchanan and Senator Douglas at the national level. The Democrats asked a local Douglas supporter,

Dr. E. R. Roe, to participate in joint sessions with Swett, but Roe told the *Pantagraph* that he was not a Democrat. The Democrats were willing to adopt him, however, as long as he supported Douglas. Swett was to have a series of joint meetings with the Democratic Third Congressional District candidate, George W. Armstrong, on October 25–29 in Concord, Lytleville, Lexington, Towanda, and LeRoy, with the proviso that substitutions could occur on either side. Although Swett missed the first two meetings, neither Armstrong nor another Democrat showed up for any of them.[24]

Swett's speeches, as revealed by the *Pantagraph*, bear enough similarity in structure and content to Lincoln's to suggest that Swett was a close student of his mentor. However, he had a knack for a clever story of his own here and there to establish a distinction. Swett usually followed the same format in his speeches as Lincoln, using the same guideposts of American history, beginning with the prohibition of slavery in the Northwest Territory by the Congress of the Confederation, and then concentrating most heavily on the Compromise of 1850 and the changing positions of Douglas, who had earlier supported the Missouri Compromise but then yielded to the slavery cause with the Kansas-Nebraska Act. Swett also devoted a little more time in his speeches to state and local positions and interests.

The final tally of votes in McLean County showed a 57 to 43 percent victory for Swett, who thus won his first and only political office. Although he lost heavily in areas populated by more southern migrants with Jacksonian Democratic leanings, he ran a strong race in the Bloomington-Normal area, even carrying his opponent's home of Gridley Township.[25] In McLean County, at least, the old-line Whigs had proved to be distracting rather than decisive. Lincoln won his race by a similar vote margin in the state, but then lost in the gerrymandered legislative apportionment in early 1859 by 54 to 46 percent—a bitter result for a developing democracy.

Nine days after the 1858 election, on November 11, Leonard and Laura's only child, a son they named Leonard Herbert, was born. Laura remained frail after the debilitating illness she had suffered three years earlier, but young Bertie arrived in good health. Letters written by Swett and Laura throughout Bertie's childhood expressed anxieties about their son's health, even exceeding those often associated with late-nineteenth-century life and mores. They tended to magnify his health problems, perhaps because he was their only child in an age of high juvenile mortality, making any threat of illness seem all the more dire. Additionally, with Laura's physical limitations, her remaining home alone with their son while her husband traveled made every childhood illness a major event. From the letters, Bertie appears to have been a typical boy who caused no unusual problems, yet there is abundant evidence of overindulgence, as he occupied a great deal of his parents' time and attention.

While Swett took to the road in the fashion of many professional men of his day, the hardship of parenting in the pioneer West fell heavily on Laura. Therefore, it is not surprising that she was becoming increasingly unhappy about his long absences from home. Her friend Fanny McCullough, the daughter of the county clerk and the younger sister of Orme's wife, occasionally stayed with her on cold nights, with the two sleeping together to keep warm as was typical in the nineteenth century. Although Laura's infirmity limited her mobility, she joined the Second Presbyterian Church soon after her arrival in Bloomington. Notwithstanding her disabilities and extended periods without her husband, Laura was a strong and intelligent woman able to surmount her difficulties and raise her son, sustained largely by her strong religious faith, family, and friends.

Laura also was unhappy about not having a home they could call their own, which had been her expectation based on her family background. The Swetts did occupy and own a house for a period in Bloomington, although the records are incomplete, but for much of Leonard's time on the circuit, they boarded in hotels or had similar living arrangements. This may have been satisfactory to Leonard, but it did not suit Laura.[26]

In addition, Swett's debts and inability to manage money contributed to their marital problems. His extravagance must have started early, as he assured his sister Rose in a January 12, 1849, letter that he had "not been very extravagant. . . . Since I have learned how difficult it is to earn money, I think I have learned to be prudent."[27] But Swett never really acquired habits of thrift. He also did not seem to have much of a mind for business. When he established his law firm with Orme in early 1855, his partner managed the business side of their practice in recognition of Swett's desire to be on the circuit.[28] Unfortunately, Swett had assumed a large debt for his brother's purchase of a farm in central Illinois, and this generosity resulted in a long period of indebtedness that lasted well over a decade.[29] During the late 1850s, Swett's indebtedness was compounded by poor health in his family, primarily his wife's, but both he and his son also apparently suffered from various maladies. Whether he took time off from work to care for Laura is unknown, but it is likely that he incurred expenses associated with medical care and treatment, possibly therapy, and probably household help.

As both Swett and Lincoln had households to support, they were back in court within days after the 1858 election. When the new year began, both men were in Springfield, Swett to attend the legislative session on January 5, 1859, to begin his two-year term. Any hope of Lincoln's defeating Douglas died as the conclusion of the November election played out with the vote of the state legislators. Swett and Lincoln joined the political arena on March 1 in Chicago, where the Republicans were victorious in a municipal election. Both men spoke at Republican headquarters, along with Alonzo W. Mack, an attorney, banker, and state senator from Kankakee. Swett's speech on that occasion does not survive, but Lincoln argued for Republican unity around the central theme of opposing the extension of slavery.[30] Shortly after, they returned to the circuit.[31]

In April, Swett, Lincoln, and Henry Clay Whitney defended store owner Thomas Patterson in Champaign County court on a charge of manslaughter for killing Samuel Dehaven. Patterson claimed that the drunken Dehaven had threatened to strike him with a spade during an argument, whereupon Patterson threw a two-pound scale weight at Dehaven, striking him behind the ear. Dehaven died the following day. According to Whitney and Judge Davis, Swett took the laboring oar in defending Patterson, because Lincoln thought the man was guilty and did not contribute to the defense.[32] The jury found Patterson guilty, and Davis sentenced him to three years in the penitentiary. A year later, Swett and Davis obtained a pardon from the governor, which Lincoln also endorsed.[33]

Swett and Lincoln associated in at least nine significant cases during 1859, including three in which Lincoln sat in as judge in Davis's absence. Although Swett was now serving in the legislature and Lincoln's political activities increased during the second half of the year, both men maintained full court calendars throughout much of 1859. At some point during the summer, Laura's health grew worse. She "became so feeble as to be carried wherever she went," and Swett took her and his infant son, who was also sick and "holding onto life by a slight tenure," to Minnesota in hopes of recovery. Burdened as he was with an ill family, he must have longed to get back on the road again.[34] In mid-October, after his return to the circuit, Swett, Lincoln, and Lawrence Weldon celebrated the Republican victories in Pennsylvania, Ohio, Indiana, and Minnesota with talks in the DeWitt County courthouse.

Sometime in 1859, Swett decided to run for governor of Illinois, and the *Clinton Central Transcript* backed his candidacy as early as August. Although he had been reluctant to run for state legislature, Swett felt that the position of governor would be attractive for the political recognition it offered, as well as opening the door for future opportunities such as the patronage accompanying the office and the possibility of election later to the U.S. Senate. However, his bid for governor encountered numerous hurdles from the start. He lacked the financial resources and time to devote to the race. Additionally, he was not well known beyond the narrowing Eighth Circuit, and to succeed, he needed Lincoln's clear and express support.

But Lincoln was not in a position to provide an endorsement for Swett. At that juncture in the emerging 1860 campaigns, Lincoln was mediating a bitter feud between two Chicago Republican leaders, Norman Judd, a member of the National Republican Committee also running for governor, and "Long" John Wentworth, the publisher of a leading Chicago paper who was running for a second term as mayor, having served in that office in 1857–58. Judd was in a three-way contest for the gubernatorial nomination with Swett and Richard Yates, a former Whig congressman from Jacksonville—all friends of Lincoln. Judd, a former Anti-Nebraska Democrat, had played a key role in defeating Lincoln's bid for the Anti-Nebraska nomination for the Senate in 1855 by supporting Trumbull. Now many Republicans criticized him for his former action, and Lincoln decided to intervene both for the sake of the party and to gain Judd's support for his own campaign. Accordingly, Lincoln wrote a letter for publication in Illinois newspapers on December 14, 1859, to three "prominent businessmen and Republicans of Chicago," testifying to Judd's loyalty to the Illinois party since its organization in 1856 and denying "any unfairness to me at the time of Senator Trumbull's election." Twice Lincoln stated his neutral position: "It is not my intention to take part in any of the rivalries for the Gubernatorial nomination" and "I . . . am, very anxious to take no part between the many friends, all good and true, who are mentioned as candidates for a Republican Gubernatorial nomination."[35]

This was the second time Lincoln deemed that he could not support his advocate, Swett, for political reasons relevant to his own candidacy. Although Lincoln probably explained his position and intentions directly to Swett, it hurt Swett to have his mentor choose this course, not only in his prospects for the nomination but likely personally as well.

Things were also coming together for Lincoln's presidential nomination. On December 21, 1859, the *Central Illinois Gazette* of West Urbana ran an editorial supporting both Lincoln for president and Swett for governor. Such comments were appearing more frequently for Lincoln but less often for Swett. One old friend and colleague who did give his support to Swett was Judge Davis, who wrote to a Beardstown lawyer and political friend in early 1860 that "Mr. Swett of this place is in my opinion the very man to make the race [for governor]. He is an able man & efficient speaker. I really do not know (Mr. Lincoln alone excepted) a more efficient man as a lawmaker in the State. He is a self possessed [man] with no arrogance of manner or speech but with a consciousness that he is able to debate with any man."[36]

Despite their candidacies, Swett and Lincoln were still taking on legal cases, and on January 17, 1860, Swett appeared in the Illinois Supreme Court for Richard T. Gill on an appeal of a default judgment taken against him and two associates for five hundred dollars in Logan County. Lincoln represented the lender, Samuel Hoblit, an old client of Lincoln's from his first law partnership, with John Todd Stuart. Apparently Lincoln's firm had filed the subpoena against Gill in the wrong county, and Justice John Dean Caton wrote a cryptic decision in favor of Swett's client, stating that Gill "was bound to obey the summons, or if that was impossible, he was bound to do nothing."[37]

In the last week of January 1860, Swett and his colleague Ward Hill Lamon were among a private caucus of Republican leaders and Lincoln friends who met in the office of Secretary of State Ebenezer Peck in what is now the Old State Capitol. At this meeting, the group sought Lincoln's concurrence in announcing his candidacy for president. Lincoln "asked until the next morning to answer us . . . the next day he authorized us to consider him and work for him if we pleased as a Candidate for the Presidency."[38]

Around this time, during the heat of the nominating race, Swett's sister Rose apparently asked him if he would ever return to Maine. Swett replied in a letter dated March 18, 1860, "I shall live and die here. Its people are my people and I feel as though no other place would be home to me."[39]

The spring saw Swett on the campaign trail from Chicago to southern Illinois, picking up support in the process. The *Pantagraph* reprinted favorable comments from the *Olney Times* and the *Belleville Advocate* during the third week of April, showing Swett's success in gaining adherents in these areas. The *Olney Times* stated, "We believe the Republicans in this section of the state, will give him their undivided support; his political record is without a blemish, and his character as a statesman has been established by the record, and his services in the Republican ranks exemplified." The *Belleville Advocate* wrote, "Mr. Swett . . . appears to be drawing to himself a majority of the suffrages of the party, if the expressions of opinion by Republican presses in all parts of the State are to be taken as evidence . . . his former party relations, as well as his personal character, contribute to make him in general opinion, the most available candidate." After Swett spoke in Jasper County, just north of Richland County, where Olney is located, the Olney editor commented, "We scarcely ever listened to a more forcible and argumentative speech than made on this occasion. His hearers were highly pleased, and even the most ultra Democrats acknowledged the force of his deductions. The speaker won imperishable honors for his eloquent and well timed remarks."[40]

Swett's campaign suffered from one of his political alliances, however. After Lincoln's defeat in 1855, although Lincoln had moved quickly to maintain relationships with Democrats Lyman Trumbull and Norman Judd, Swett and Davis, who were Whigs, remained cool to both and became more closely associated with "Long" John Wentworth. Now, while Swett and Judd were contending for the Republican nomination for governor, Judd exposed Swett's friendly connection with Wentworth, writing to Ozias Hatch in Springfield that "S[wett] trades [makes allies] with everybody that offers."[41] When Davis and another of Swett's friends, fellow attorney Harvey Hogg, learned this from Hatch, both defended their friend, writing back that Swett denied the charges of making political combinations.[42] But Swett's candidacy had been damaged. Even a Yates supporter urged the use of Swett's connection with Wentworth to "keep the fire warm between the Judd and Swett men so neither of them is hostile to you in the event of a failure to nominate their men your chances will be good."[43]

In the final days of his campaign, a promise Swett made to Lamon to prosecute a manslaughter case distracted him. *People v. Alexander Kilpatrick*, a four-day trial in Danville, required the attention of the three principal players—Swett, Davis, and Lamon—and kept them from where they should have been on May 8, 1860: at the Republican State Convention in Decatur, eighty miles to the west. Whitney claimed that Swett's absence discouraged his supporters. The *Chicago Tribune* reported of the opening day of the convention: "Wentworth made a speech last night attacking Judd and puffing Swett calling him the Henry Clay of the West. He damaged the latter more than the former."

An informal poll that day of the majority of delegates showed that Judd had two votes fewer than the number required for nomination. Going into the convention, each candidate had appeared strong in the counties where he was best known. Judd led primarily in the northern counties; Swett's strengths were in the central and eastern counties, including most of those the Eighth Circuit had encompassed; and Yates held sway in the south-central portion of the state.[44]

The next day, Swett gained further support, as Thomas J. Turner of Freeport, in Stephenson County on the northern boundary of Illinois, placed Swett's name in nomination for governor. Turner had served as a Democrat in the U.S. Congress during the same term as Lincoln and had been a representative and the Speaker of the Illinois House in 1854–56 as an Anti-Nebraska Democrat. He had introduced Lincoln at the Freeport debate two years earlier. The origins of Turner's support of Swett remain unknown, but John W. Shaffer, Lincoln's chairman in the Freeport debate, was a friend of Swett's. Turner knew Lincoln well as a fellow attorney, and as a knowledgeable politician he may have sensed that Lincoln would have backed Swett had he been free to do so. Whatever his motivation, he carried the entire Stephenson County delegation of nine for Swett on the informal ballot, making it the only county giving him its entire support among the top two northern tiers of counties.[45]

From this point on, however, things began to deteriorate for Swett. The *Tribune* reported, "Swett's friends may go to Yates and nominate him on the 4th or 5th ballot." Judd and Yates both gained votes on the first formal ballot, while Swett's support began to erode. On the second ballot, the same thing happened, and on the third, Judd's support began to slip. Realizing that he had no chance of winning, Swett asked his supporters to vote for Yates on the fourth ballot to keep Judd from carrying off the prize. Following his direction, those who had voted for Swett now threw their support behind Yates, who tallied 363 votes to Judd's 237 on the last ballot. Both Judd and Swett reacted positively to unite the party behind the newly chosen candidate.[46] Immediately after Yates's nomination, Turner moved to nominate Francis A. Hoffmann, one of the founders of the Republican Party and a Lincoln supporter, for candidate as lieutenant governor by acclamation. With a cheer, it was done.

The next day belonged to Lincoln. Even a century and a half later, many think it providential that Lincoln was nominated and elected to the presidency, considering his lack of experience compared with the other candidates. But Lincoln knew how to help providence along. His December 1859 letter of assistance for Judd to Chicago Republicans had a small price attached. On February 9, 1860, he wrote to Judd, reminding him of the letter and suggesting that it "would hurt some for me to not get the Illinois delegation . . . can you not help me a little in this matter, in your end of the vineyard?" Within a week, the *Press* and *Tribune* finally came out in strong support of Lincoln, and Judd, who had influential ties to the papers, asked Lincoln what he thought of their position, clearly implying his responsibility for it. Lincoln crafted an even more delicate letter to Senator Trumbull, who reportedly favored Justice McLean, saying, "The taste is in my mouth a little," and adding this special admonition: "A word now for your own special benefit. You better write no letters which can possibly be distorted into opposition, or quasi opposition to me. There are men on the constant watch for such things out of which to prejudice my peculiar friends against you."[47]

At the Republican State Convention in Decatur on May 10, 1860, John M. Palmer, one of the five Anti-Nebraska Democrats who had denied Lincoln's election as senator in 1855, now made the crucial resolution tying the Illinois delegates to Lincoln: "That Abraham Lincoln is the choice of the Republican party of Illinois for the Presidency and the delegates from this State are instructed to use all honorable means to secure his nomination by the Chicago Convention, and to vote as a unit for him."[48] Lincoln had obtained the support of the entire Illinois delegation. Now Swett faced the challenge of helping his friend get enough votes to win the party's nomination at the national convention the following week.

A thousand steam whistles, ten acres of hotel gongs, a tribe of
Comanches . . . might have mingled in the scene unnoticed.
—Swett to his college roommate, describing the response
to Lincoln's nomination on May 18, 1860

5. From the Wigwam to Washington

As soon as Lincoln won the nomination for president at the state convention in Decatur, Swett and Davis went to work ensuring that he
would win the party's nomination at the Republican National Convention
scheduled for May 16–18, 1860, in Chicago. Davis believed that if he could
go to the national convention as a delegate, he would be able to do more
to get Lincoln nominated than anyone else could, so he set his sights on
becoming the delegate-at-large for the state of Illinois. The Illinois convention agreed. Unlike his friend Swett, Davis was not a great public speaker,
but he had superb organizational and management skills, which he now
put to use on Lincoln's behalf.[1]

While Swett remained in Bloomington for a couple more days, Davis
went to Chicago the Saturday before the convention started. On his arrival,
he found that no one had yet set up a headquarters for Lincoln, so he
promptly arranged for rooms at the Tremont House, a stone hotel at the
corner of Lake and Dearborn Streets.[2] Davis arranged with the proprietor
of the Tremont House to pay for "the evacuation of certain rooms by
private families, and soon marked the suites as the Illinois Headquarters."[3]
Davis chose this hotel for its location just five blocks east of the Wigwam,
where the convention would be held. The Wigwam was a temporary two-
story wooden structure built to house the convention. Constructed in
little more than a month with financing by Chicago businessmen, it was
large enough to hold the 466 delegates from various states plus about ten
thousand spectators.

"Without anybody electing him to the position," Swett wrote, Davis "at once . . . became the leader of all the Illinois men."[4] When Swett arrived two days later, on Monday, May 14, Davis told him, "If you will put yourself at my disposal day and night, I believe Lincoln can be nominated." Davis's enthusiasm was contagious, and for the first time, Swett felt hopeful that they could achieve this objective.[5]

Lincoln did not appear at the national convention, which was typical of a candidate seriously seeking the nomination in that era. According to Swett, Lincoln had told him at the state convention that "he was almost too much of a candidate to go" to the national convention, but "not quite enough to stay at home." The unifying resolution for Lincoln at the end of the Decatur convention had been a master stroke, and given the divisive elements of his temporarily united Illinois delegation, it was likely a wise decision not to appear at the national convention.[6]

The maneuvers and manipulations at the state convention had left some with hurt feelings, and Davis knew he needed to hold together the fractious factions. Although all twenty-two members of the Illinois delegation were allied in voting for Lincoln, Swett later wrote to his former college roommate, Josiah Drummond, that "there were eight who would gladly have gone for [Senator William] Seward" of New York, because the northern Illinois counties at that time were overwhelmingly Republican. Seward had entered the convention as the strongest candidate, with support from eastern states as well as party members in northern Illinois. Swett thought that these delegates "intended in good faith to go for Lincoln" but said they "talked despondingly" and expected to vote for Seward in the end. They could count on the delegates from the central and southern parts of the state to support Lincoln, whether he won or lost. The contingent also included some delegates who wanted "to turn up on the winning side" without doing any work. "These men were dead weights," Swett said. A group of colleagues from the Eighth Circuit, along with some state officers and "a half dozen men from various portions of the State, were the only tireless, sleepless, unswerving and ever vigilant friends" of Lincoln working for him at the convention.[7]

Davis maintained harmony among the Illinois delegates by keeping them busy talking to delegates from other states about Lincoln's candidacy and positions. Seated behind a big table at the headquarters in the Tremont House, Davis organized committees to visit the various delegations.[8]

Following Davis's lead, Swett marshaled support for Lincoln, but he always insisted it was a group effort and never took the credit for himself. Davis also used more than a dozen other lieutenants in this process.[9]

Davis's strategy was to secure enough votes on the first ballot to make Lincoln a serious contender, knowing that Seward had the largest initial following. To do this, he and the Illinois contingent needed to convince the leaders and delegates from other states of Lincoln's political availability, the soundness of his principles, and the lack of serious opposition to him. Lincoln was a new name on the national level, and Davis hoped to lay the groundwork for him as the second choice once the lesser candidates and "favorite sons" showed their shortcomings. The plan was to get a hundred votes for Lincoln on the first ballot, with the expectation that certain increases would follow afterward. To influence any doubters, Davis and Swett wanted to show that support for Lincoln was growing.

Davis first approached the delegates from Indiana, whom Swett said were almost "equally divided between [Missouri attorney Edward] Bates and [Supreme Court justice John] McLean." After three days of talk, the Indiana delegates united behind Lincoln, bringing him an additional twenty-six votes. Indiana remained united with the Illinois delegates for Lincoln throughout the convention.[10]

Swett organized a group of Lincoln supporters from Maine to visit the delegates for that state, and Samuel C. Parks did the same for Vermont. Davis assigned similar envoys to the other states' delegates and had every man "come back and report to him." Working this way, Davis knew the situation with every delegation. Swett and Illinois lawyer Orville Browning also gave talks supporting Lincoln's candidacy before various state delegations.[11] To make a show of the support for Lincoln, Davis also enlisted Richard Oglesby, a man with "stout lungs," to "fill the building's public spaces with a strong-voiced brigade of shouters" at the appropriate time.[12]

By the time Seward's supporters appeared at the convention, Lincoln's main opponent had almost enough delegates to win the nomination. Bates held second place, and if he did not do well on the first ballot, he intended to throw his delegates behind another candidate who opposed Seward. The Pennsylvania delegation wanted Senator Simon Cameron, and New Jersey wanted former senator William L. Dayton. The Davis-Swett team gained points by getting both of these states to unite with Illinois and Indiana in opposing Seward. Next, they worked to secure more votes for Lincoln on the second ballot, getting Delaware and Vermont to agree to vote for Lincoln if their candidate lost on the first ballot and securing the promise of some additional votes on the second ballot from New Hampshire. In Swett's words, "It all worked to a charm."[13]

In the middle of the night before the nomination, Swett and Davis had a crucial meeting with two leading delegates from Pennsylvania about whether the state would support Lincoln. The Pennsylvania delegates agreed in the wee hours of the morning to give forty-eight of their votes to Lincoln on the second ballot if he appeared to be gaining strength. Swett described how they prevailed over Seward's supporters in winning over the Pennsylvania delegates: "Everybody who knows politicians knows that what they worship is the god of success. The friends of Mr. Lincoln knew this, and saw their chance in securing, upon the failure of Mr. Seward to carry the Convention, a great demonstration of strength as between Mr. Lincoln and the other candidates. This chance lay in Pennsylvania. . . . [T]he Seward men were laboring with the delegates from that State, and so were the friends of Mr. Lincoln. . . . Our arguments prevailed, and [they] agreed to come to us upon the second ballot, . . . [a] blow in the centre which disorganized the forces of the great opponent and revealed the coming man."[14]

On Friday morning, May 18, the day of the nomination, some twelve thousand people, including friends of all parties, gathered at the Wigwam. Most of these people were from central Illinois and Indiana, a boon to the Illinois delegation. The business and commerce of downtown Chicago came to a halt as spectators lined the streets. To keep those who spilled outside the Wigwam informed about the goings-on, "a line of men formed on the roof starting near a skylight close to the speaker's stand, and one man reported to the next," until a man "with stentorian lungs in front of the building . . . then announced the proceedings to the masses gathered in the streets."[15]

Seward was the first to be nominated, resulting in a deafening shout. "I confess," Swett wrote, this "appalled us a little." Next came nominations for Bates, McLean, Cameron, and Chase, which met with moderate applause. Then it was Lincoln's turn. Swett wrote, "Our people tested their lungs" and were a little louder than the other groups. The Seward supporters screamed even louder when a Michigan delegate seconded his nomination. Then Caleb B. Smith of Indiana seconded Lincoln's nomination, and five thousand people leaped out of their seats, making the previous applause sound in comparison like soft vespers. Swett wrote, "No language can describe it. A thousand steam whistles, ten acres of hotel gongs, a tribe of Comanches, headed by a choice vanguard from pandemonium, might have mingled in the scene unnoticed."[16]

After the first ballot, Lincoln was solidly in second place, with more than twice as many votes as any of the other three serious contenders behind Seward—Cameron, Chase, or Bates, in that order.[17] "Our increase after the first ballot was a little more than we calculated," said Swett. The second ballot brought Lincoln within three and a half votes of Seward, while each of the other candidates received fewer votes. On the third ballot, "the ground swell was irresistible and bore our man through, and the shout from the Wigwam and the shout from the street, as the man from the top shouted 'Old Abe, hallelujah!' and the cannon with its mimic thunder, told the city and surroundings we had won."[18]

Swett and Davis's lieutenants—the "boys" as Swett called them—had pounded the pavement and worked the backrooms and hallways, sleeping just two hours a night. Davis was overjoyed that he and Swett had achieved their goal in helping Lincoln win the party's nomination. "At the Chicago Convention," wrote Swett, "when Lincoln's nomination became a fixed fact, when delegations were changing their votes and everything was in the confusion of coming to Lincoln, when everybody was shouting and in the hurrah of Bedlam, Judge Davis threw his great arms around a friend and cried like a child."[19] Swett wrote to Drummond that Davis was the kingmaker for Lincoln and that were it not for Davis, Lincoln never would have been president. Of Lincoln, he wrote, "He is a pure-minded, honest man, whose ability is second to no one in the nation," pointing out that "he has raised himself from the captaincy of a flatboat on the Mississippi, to the captaincy of a great party in this nation." Showing his great faith in and esteem for Lincoln, he added, "When he shall be elected he will restore the government to its pristine purity."[20]

Allegations that Swett and Davis made obligations or promises to obtain votes for Lincoln divided participants at the convention and later historians as well.[21] However, Swett also wrote to his roommate, "No pledges have been made, no mortgages executed, but Lincoln enters the field a free man. He will continue so until the day of the election."[22] Nothing in his subsequent dozen letters to Lincoln regarding cabinet formation contradicts this belief.

After the convention adjourned, a man identified in sources only as Mr. Humphreys came to visit Swett. Humphreys, formerly of Bloomington, had moved to New York and become associated with that state's delegation. He told Swett that Seward's campaign manager, Thurlow Weed, was feeling bad about Seward's loss and suggested that some members of Lincoln's team should call on him. Swett asked him for an introduction, but Humphreys said he did not feel he knew Weed well enough. Swett informed Davis of the situation, and the two hurried to the Richmond Hotel to meet Thurlow Weed for the first time.[23]

Swett recalled that Weed did not complain about Seward's loss or speak in anger. With strong disappointment, he said, "I hoped to make my friend, Mr. Seward, President, and I thought I could serve my country in so doing." Swett later wrote of Weed, "He was a larger man intellectually than I anticipated, and of finer fiber. There was in him an element of gentleness and a large humanity which won me, and I was pleased no less than surprised." Despite an age difference of twenty-eight years, Swett and Weed found common interests and communicated well. Weed was headed on to Iowa, and Swett suggested that he return through Illinois on his way back east so that he could meet Lincoln. Swett and Davis arranged for Weed to telegraph them in Bloomington with the dates he could be in Springfield, and they would then take him to see Lincoln.[24]

As they had arranged, Swett later accompanied Weed to Springfield, where he introduced Weed to Lincoln on May 24, 1860. This was typical of the unheralded role Swett often played in aiding Lincoln. Lincoln remembered that he and Weed had met in Albany, New York, in 1848, when Lincoln was on a speaking trip to New England. Lincoln and Weed got along well together and discussed the prospects of the campaign and the condition of the country. Lincoln paid close attention as Weed formulated his objective of promoting party unity.

Shortly after Lincoln's nomination, Swett spoke at Phoenix Hall in Bloomington, where delegates had packed the house to ratify the Republican National Convention's action. Swett gave an exposition of the Republican platform, "the modus operandi" of the convention, and as the *Pantagraph* described it, "a few of those masterly appeals of which he is so capable."[25]

After the convention, Swett received several letters raising questions. In addition to writing his own replies to the letters, he also forwarded these letters to Lincoln and in some cases asked Lincoln to review the responses before sending them out.[26] In one letter, a man named John W. Shaffer from Freeport, Illinois, wanted assurance that those who had supported Seward or

Cameron at the convention would receive fair treatment relative to Lincoln supporters. Lincoln suggested that Swett add a postscript telling Shaffer to "come down and see me." James O. Putnam, whom Swett had met on his trip to Mackinac Island in 1858, was now a Republican elector-at-large and wrote to Swett about Lincoln, "I think him one of the most remarkable speakers of English, living? [*sic*] In all that constitutes logical eloquence, straight-forwardness, clearness of statement, sincerity that commands your admiration and assent, and a compact stren[g]th of argument, he is infinitely superior to Douglas, I think." Swett forwarded the letter to Lincoln, who saved these kind words. Former Pennsylvania congressman Joseph Casey, who had been the leader of Cameron's supporters at the convention, also wrote to Swett about competition Cameron was facing from gubernatorial candidate Andrew Gregg Curtin's faction for political appointments in Pennsylvania. This worried Lincoln, especially because of the pressure on him to give a cabinet position to Cameron, as he did not want the party splitting into factions.[27]

In the months between Lincoln's nomination at the convention and his election as president, Swett closely observed his friend's political strategies and tactics. He found them to be "peculiar" and wholly different from those of other politicians.[28] Swett later explained that Lincoln calculated the law of forces and ultimate results, as the world to him functioned by cause and effect. Lincoln believed that certain great causes tended toward specific results and felt that those results could not be changed, hastened, impeded, or altered by personal interference or political manipulation. The great cause of his time was the agitation of slavery, and the ultimate result would be its overthrow. Lincoln's personal political tactics consisted quite simply of getting into the right place and staying there until time and events caught up with him. He did not believe that political combinations or personal efforts could influence the direction of his campaign. He believed that if elected, he could not have been defeated, and conversely, if defeated, he could not have been elected.[29]

Initially, Swett and others failed to understand Lincoln's theory and course of action. Lincoln said and did things they did not understand in the context of current events. Swett reflected on the "house divided" concept Lincoln had used at the beginning of his senatorial campaign against Douglas in 1858. Swett and others had thought the sentiment of the "house divided against itself" seemed wholly unfortunate and inappropriate. But later he realized that Lincoln viewed the concept as an abstract truth to stand on, waiting for events to catch up and find him in the right place. Swett wrote that Lincoln saw the elementary truth in this concept and found it necessary to the growth of the Republican Party.[30]

As a result of his beliefs, Lincoln wanted nothing done in the way of political management once he was a candidate for president. After the Chicago convention, there was great dissatisfaction in the East over Lincoln's nomination, and Swett thought that a great deal of effort would be necessary to unify the party and bring harmony, but Lincoln seemed to disagree. In keeping with his political philosophy, Lincoln felt that external forces would lead the party to unify without individual effort. If unification occurred, it would be because of the strength of the cause. If the cause was not strong enough to bring about unification, individual effort would not be an adequate substitute. After his nomination, Lincoln sat in an office provided in the State Capitol in Springfield, which Swett described as Lincoln's "Mecca," and received all guests, listened intently, told stories, and watched as the great forces gradually produced order out of chaos and brought him to final triumph.[31]

Between the nomination in May and Election Day in November 1860, Swett participated in the canvass for Lincoln. He spoke at Republican rallies in early June in the towns of Lincoln, Springfield, and Decatur and throughout the summer and early fall in other areas in central Illinois. He met with Lincoln on several occasions, corresponded with him, and conveyed exchanges through colleagues. Lincoln wrote to Swett on July 16 asking to see him concerning a trip for Swett or Davis or both to the East to respond to requests for speaking engagements and political reconciliation.[32] After Swett and Davis made a pass through central Illinois in late July with Trumbull, Lovejoy, Oglesby, and others, Davis left for the East in early August.

Meanwhile, Swett swung through the Ninth Congressional District in southern Illinois during the first half of August, traveling farther south into seven more counties. He traversed Illinois cities from Centralia and Salem to Fairfield, Carmi, Grayville, Mount Carmel, Albion, and Olney, speaking once or twice a day in the sweltering heat to crowds of eight hundred to six thousand. The *Chicago Tribune* followed his endeavors with interest, and a reporter cheered his appearance in Centralia by writing, "We are waking up in Egypt. . . . Mr. Swett held the people, as if by magic, for three hours, in one of his most eloquent efforts. The multitude assembled in Yankee Stinson's big show tent, which was not sufficient to hold the crowds, hundreds being compelled to stand outside in the broiling sun. Great enthusiasm prevailed, and shouts after shouts for 'Old Abe' rent the air." Swett wrote to Lincoln about the great optimism in this district: "The general remark of every one, wherever I have been, is that our vote in the 9th will be increased about ten fold."[33]

By late summer, Lincoln had heard about concerns over election prospects in Pennsylvania and Indiana.[34] He dispatched Swett to Indiana to speak in Terre Haute and Vincennes on October 1 and 2. Swett knew people from these areas because of his Eighth Circuit work in Danville. Perhaps his meetings with four old friends, all Indiana leaders from circuit visits, made as much of an impact as his speeches. He met with Richard W. Thompson, who had served in the Thirtieth Congress with Lincoln and was now a Constitutional Union Party member supporting Lincoln. Thompson had received or been the subject of several careful letters drafted by Lincoln earlier.[35] Swett also saw Daniel W. Voorhees, a Democratic U.S. district attorney running for a seat in Congress; John P. Usher, a former Whig and Republican supporter of Lincoln; and Thomas H. Nelson, a founding member of the Republican Party.[36] Swett wrote to Davis from Terre Haute to report on his discussions and said the men were confident of Lincoln's victory. Davis wrote to Lincoln a few days later, "Swett has returned and says that at Terre Haute and Vincennes, the meetings were magnificent."[37]

Elections for state officers occurred on October 9 in Pennsylvania, Ohio, and Indiana and served as indicators that the crucial lower northern states were leaning heavily Republican. Although the outcome seemed assured, important states still in contention included Illinois (where both leading candidates resided), New York, New Jersey, and California, for a total of 57 electoral votes out of 303. Electioneering continued. Swett and Yates spoke at a large mass meeting in Urbana less than two weeks before the election. After an appearance of the governor of Ohio on October 15 in Springfield, Davis smelled victory and wrote to his wife, Sarah, in his own candid style, "Politicians are gathering round Lincoln. The cormorants for office will be numerous & greedy."[38]

On the last day of October, Swett gave one more major address in Bloomington's Phoenix Hall. The *Pantagraph* reported, "The meeting . . . was a magnificent success in every respect. The Hall was completely full. . . . The presence of the speaker, Hon. L. Swett, was greeted with unanimous shouts of applause. He spoke something more than an hour and a half in such a manner as to secure the most flattering attention, and eliciting applause from time to time. As a whole, the speech was one of the most opportune of the season—fair, manly, and conclusive on every point. Noble as was the speech in all its bearings and characteristics, it rises higher still in all respectable estimation by contrast with the miserable slang and subterfuge that have been so often heard from other sources in this campaign. . . . With three cheers for Lincoln and the whole Republican ticket, three cheers for Mr. Swett, and continuous rounds of applause, the vast audience retired."[39]

On Election Day, November 6, 1860, Davis voted and then went down to Springfield to receive the returns with Lincoln. Swett stayed behind in Bloomington and wired Lincoln that evening about the local voting: Bloomington "and 5 towns heard from [in McLean County] majority five hundred fifty two 552 gain one hundred & seventy one 171." Here it appears that Swett was comparing the gain in the number of votes by which Lincoln won in McLean County over Fremont's majority in the county in the 1856 presidential race. Lincoln won in eighteen Union states. Douglas finished second in the popular vote but won electoral votes only in Missouri and New Jersey, although the latter's electoral votes were split, with Lincoln winning four and Douglas only three. In Missouri, the Douglas majority over John Bell, the Constitutional Union Party candidate, was less than five hundred votes. John C. Breckinridge won in eleven of the other slaveholding states, and Bell in three. Of the states Breckinridge won, Delaware and Maryland did not secede, and of those won by Bell, Kentucky did not. In an ominous signal, Lincoln received no votes in ten slaveholding states and less than five thousand in four others.[40]

From his distant perch in Bloomington, Swett took great delight in the final outcome. Lincoln's win sent electricity throughout the party, and merriment and celebration ensued among Lincoln supporters.

Now that he was president, Lincoln set about the task of appointing his cabinet. Although he invited and patiently listened to others' advice, Lincoln clearly made his own decisions based on the principle that his choices should serve his overriding objective of uniting the strongest possible political coalition under his party leadership. He used this primary criterion for all the cabinet appointments he made during his presidency. Competence of cabinet members also was essential for success.

Both Davis and Swett played roles in the cabinet selection process to serve Lincoln's central purpose. Lincoln used the two men in the designation of cabinet candidates from Indiana and Pennsylvania because of the role these states' delegates had played in creating the groundswell of support for Lincoln's nomination. They soon experienced the reality of Davis's comments about the numerous "cormorants for office."[41]

No candidate required more time and caused more perplexity than the choice of Senator Simon Cameron from Pennsylvania. Cameron's backers subjected Swett and Davis to unrelenting pressure. Their leverage hinged on their involvement in the last-minute conversion of the Pennsylvania delegation to support Lincoln on the second ballot. Cameron's manager, Joseph Casey, visited Lincoln in Springfield on November 8, two days after the election, to speak on Cameron's behalf. Casey wrote to Swett twice over the next two weeks, stating in his second letter, "From some things that occurred when I was at Springfield my mind has since been in doubt as to whether Mr. Lincoln has been made *fully acquainted* with the conversations and understandings, had between you & Judge Davis on the one side, & myself, on the other, at the Tremont House, the night before the nomination."[42]

Another Cameron lieutenant, John Sanderson, also sent a letter, which Swett passed on to Lincoln. "I am annoyed that these applications of Cameron's friends are made so prominently through Judge Davis & myself," Swett commented to Lincoln. "Yet on the whole, from what occurred at Chicago I think they have a right to do it." Swett denied that he or Davis had agreed to advocate for Cameron but confirmed that their negotiations with Cameron's men had induced the Pennsylvania delegates to vote for Lincoln on the second ballot. If Lincoln did not give Cameron a cabinet position, Swett said, it would create great dissatisfaction.[43]

Late in November, Swett wrote to his old college roommate Josiah Drummond seeking suggestions for additional cabinet members. Drummond responded with a five-page letter that Swett passed on to Lincoln, along with another letter from John Sanderson in support of Cameron. Drummond discussed about twenty possible candidates for the cabinet but recommended against John Bell and Edward Bates. He advised, "Take no fossils, take *live* men. This victory is unanimously a victory of the young, bold, vigorous men. Let the policy of the party be carried out by such men." Four of the men Drummond recommended became members; a fifth rejected Lincoln's offer.[44]

Swett became an elector-at-large for the state of Illinois, and as such, he joined ten other electors to cast their votes at noon on December 6, 1860, in the Senate Chamber of the Illinois State Capitol. The electors selected Swett to serve as their messenger to carry their ballots to Washington. That evening, James Conkling, a member of the Republican state central committee and an elector for the Springfield district, hosted a dinner for the electors, which Swett attended along with the Lincolns.

Lincoln and Swett did not miss the opportunity to talk about cabinet appointments, and Lincoln mentioned the idea of Swett going on a political scouting expedition in Washington. They also discussed the advisability of seeking ideas from Thurlow Weed. Swett wanted to facilitate a connection with Weed and had already written to him about the possibility of his making another trip to Illinois. Lincoln suggested that Swett and Davis issue Weed another invitation, and on the evening of December 18, Weed arrived in Bloomington, where he spent part of the next day conferring with Swett and Davis. The three men traveled to Springfield on December 20 and met with Lincoln for the entire day. Lincoln greeted them graciously and showed them into the parlor of his home. Swett was keenly aware of the crucial nature of this rendezvous—the future was at stake. Weed and Lincoln sat opposite each other, both seeming to Swett to be anxious yet cautious. He found both men remarkable in appearance and stature, as "both had rough, strongly-marked features, and both had risen by their own exertions from humble relations to the control of a nation whose destinies they were shaping."[45]

Initially they discussed the appropriate posture of the new administration relative to the different states and political parties. In his autobiography penned twenty years after the meeting with Lincoln, Weed described his views: "I believed then, as I know now, that but for the conservative sentiment awakened in the Republican party the North would have been fatally divided. I believed then, as I know now, that by insisting that the war was prosecuted to maintain the government and preserve the Union, the Democratic masses, with some of their leaders, would remain loyal; while, on the other hand, if the whole Republican party proclaimed it a war for the abolition of slavery, a united South would prove too strong for a divided North."[46]

Then Lincoln moved on to the subject of cabinet making. He told Weed he had already chosen William Seward for secretary of state, but "the rest of the cabinet . . . was an open question although some names had been fixed upon, unless serious objections should arise, and others were being favorably considered." The conversation turned to Cameron's possible selection as a cabinet member. Swett felt this was the only subject on which Weed did not speak with entire freedom. "He spoke kindly of Gen. Cameron, said that Pennsylvania was entitled to a place in the cabinet, and undoubtedly that State would be for him. He thought, however, it would be wiser to give him some place other than the Treasuryship. He thought Mr. Chase the proper man for that place, and both agreeing, this seemed to pass as fixed."[47]

Lincoln suggested Edward Bates and Caleb B. Smith. Weed approved of both of these men but strongly opposed Montgomery Blair and Gideon Welles. Weed wanted former Whigs wherever possible. Lincoln explained that he had given his vice president–elect, Hannibal Hamlin, the privilege of naming the secretary of the navy, and Welles was Hamlin's choice. However, he remained open to hearing Weed's opinion as to whether Welles was unfit for the position, although it was unlikely that he would have overridden Hamlin's choice. As for Blair, Weed "insisted if Mr. Lincoln took him into the Cabinet he would regret it," as "Blair blood was troublesome." Weed advanced the name of Henry Winter Davis and hoped for more support from Judge David Davis, Henry's first cousin, than he received. Then Weed brought up John Gilmer from North Carolina. Lincoln responded favorably and asked Weed to visit Gilmer in Washington and, if he had no doubt of Gilmer's fidelity, present him with a letter from Lincoln inviting him to be a cabinet member.[48]

After the discussion of Gilmer, Weed challenged Lincoln regarding a cabinet potentially made up of four former Democrats and three "Whig background Republicans." Lincoln's reply was memorable. "You seem to forget that I expect to be there: and counting me as one, you see how nicely the cabinet would be balanced and ballasted."[49]

Swett observed that Lincoln and Weed "took to each other," and their relationship became more agreeable and friendly as time went on. Weed did not try to secure anything for himself or anyone else in these meetings, which impressed Swett. Later, as tough questions arose, Lincoln sent for Weed to consult with him and ask him for suggestions on how to handle various issues. On many occasions, Lincoln had Swett deliver his messages to Weed. Although Swett noted that "Weed was a man always wanting political positions for the army of friends who depended on him," Weed set

aside the wishes of people who were looking to him for political appointments or favors in order to focus on what was in the best interests of the
country. He cheerfully did what he was asked without demanding or reaping
political rewards.[50] Swett's respect for Weed continued to grow over time.

At the end of their meeting on December 20, this quartet of Republican
Union preservationists learned that South Carolina had that day become
the first state to secede from the United States. Excerpts from Lincoln's
letters to leaders and members of Congress in the weeks after the November
6 election paint a portrait of the unraveling of the Union.

On November 29, 1860, Lincoln drafted remarks for Senator Trumbull
to make as part of a speech in Springfield, stating that "the States will be
left in as complete control of their own affairs respectively, and at as perfect
liberty to choose, and employ, their own means of protecting property,
and preserving peace and order within their respective limits, as they have
ever been under any administration." On December 13, Lincoln instructed
Illinois congressman Elihu Washburne to "prevent, as far as possible, any
of our friends from demoralizing themselves, and our cause, by entertain-
ing propositions for compromise of any sort, on *slavery extension.*" Two
days later, he asked Congressman John Gilmer of North Carolina, "Is it
desired that I shall shift the ground upon which I have been elected? I can
not do it. . . . On the territorial question, I am inflexible." On December
17, Lincoln wrote to Weed, "I believe you can pretend to find but little,
if any thing, in my speeches, about secession; but my opinion is that no
state can, in any way lawfully, get out of the Union, without the consent
of the others." The following day, Lincoln stated in a letter to *New York
Times* editor Henry Raymond, "Mr. Lincoln is not pledged to the ultimate
extinctinction [*sic*] of slavery; does not hold the black man to be the equal
of the white, unqualifiedly as Mr. S[eward] states it." On December 22,
he wrote to Congressman Alexander Stephens of Georgia, soon to be the
vice president of the Confederacy, "I fully appreciate the present peril the
country is in, and the weight of responsibility on me. . . . Do the people of
the South really entertain fears that a Republican administration would,
directly, or *indirectly,* interfere with their slaves, or with them, about their
slaves? If they do, I wish to assure you, as once a friend, and still, I hope,
not an enemy, that there is no cause for such fears."[51]

In the meantime, on December 18, in an attempt to stave off secession,
pro-Union senator John Crittenden of Kentucky proposed a compromise

that called for a series of amendments to the Constitution. The Senate Committee of Thirteen considering the compromise deadlocked on December 22. Senator Seward, the Republican leader of the committee, was not present, and he chose not to break the deadlock once he arrived with Lincoln's instructions "that the constitution should never be altered to authorize Congress to abolish or interfere with slavery in the states, that the Fugitive slave law should be amended by granting a jury trial to the fugitive . . . [and] that Congress should recommend that the states revise legislation concerning persons recently resident in the state and repeal all in conflict with the constitution."[52]

The Southern states now sought to regain what they had lost at the election in November by threats of secession. Lincoln apparently did not yet understand the seriousness of their intent, as evidenced even as late as February 15, when he said in his speech in Pittsburgh, "There is no crisis."[53] At the same time, the leaders of the slaveholding states misread the strength of the likely resistance of the yet-to-be-formed Lincoln administration. Emboldened by the acquisitions of the Mexican War, the Compromise of 1850, and the Kansas-Nebraska Act, the slavery powers now demanded more concessions, and the Republicans attempted to make accommodations. Lincoln thought he could hold the line and looked for help and guidance to Senators William Seward and Lyman Trumbull, Congressmen Elihu Washburne and William Kellogg, and many others. He had a government to form before taking office on March 4, and the contending factions of his party did not make the task any easier, especially with the political union itself in jeopardy.

Into this maelstrom, Lincoln sent the thirty-five-year-old Leonard Swett on his first visit to Washington. Cabinet discussions had intensified, with the secession crisis becoming paramount. Lincoln wanted Swett in the capital to listen, get information, and report back to him. Additionally, as a devoted ally, Swett understood Lincoln's positions and could describe and interpret the president-elect's moderate Republican policies to others in government. Swett also needed to be in Washington to fulfill his duties as an elector.

No detailed journal or chronicle of Swett's Washington trip exists, but his letters and those of others provide a reasonable record. While on the trip, Swett wrote a dozen letters and several telegrams to Lincoln. He also wrote four pertinent letters to Laura, as well as other correspondence to

Judge Davis, Seward, Weed, Cameron, Henry Winter Davis, Washburne, and Lamon.

Leaving from Bloomington the day after Christmas 1860, Swett briefly met Laura in Chicago, where she may have been visiting relatives, and then departed the same evening for the twenty-four-hour trip to Pittsburgh. Once again Laura would have to fend for herself while her husband's duties took him away from home for an extended period. From Pittsburgh, Swett left immediately for Harrisburg, where Cameron's manager, Joseph Casey, met him at four the next morning. He caught a few hours of sleep and met Cameron for dinner. During their meeting, Swett extended an invitation on behalf of Lincoln for Cameron to meet the president-elect in Springfield, and Cameron and Casey gave Swett foreboding news that the "cotton states" were talking about secession. He wrote the same day to Laura, "A long and deadly war seems a terrible thing, but I surely believe it is upon us." At three in the morning of the twenty-ninth, he boarded a train to Washington, arriving seven hours later. Cameron left Harrisburg about the same time for Springfield and saw Lincoln on December 30. The following day, Lincoln wrote Cameron of his intention to appoint him either secretary of the treasury or secretary of war.[54]

Sometime over the next couple days, Swett wrote a misdated letter to Lincoln expressing his shock on encountering the crosscurrents in Washington and advising the president-elect to come to Washington immediately. For some unknown reason, however, Swett did not send this letter, and it is likely that Lincoln never saw it.[55] But the words reflect Swett's amazement at the realities of the crisis. Swett had contacted General Winfield Scott, the army chief, who forwarded him on to Colonel Charles P. Stone, inspector general of the army. Stone was responsible for coordinating information on possible attacks on Lincoln.[56] Swett wrote to Lincoln in the unsent letter that Scott was busy gathering troops, despite the difficulty of the task in the climate of treason. Scott was doing all he could, he said, and would bring in troops from New York and West Point if necessary. Swett believed the South was gaining strength "because their policy is well conceived by a few men & then carried out by all. Jeff Davis & a few others meet privately & dictate action to Congress & the whole South. They have plan trim [sic] & method." In contrast, the Buchanan administration supported the Union but wavered feebly. Republicans in Congress were not united on a single opinion. "Our party here is like a stream with a thousand currents

& counter currents," Swett wrote. Some of the Republicans were fearful and saw the situation as dangerous, whereas others predicted that the South soon would be starving. Swett implored Lincoln to come to Washington. "We are like sheep without a shepherd & 'dumb before the shearer,'" he wrote. Because Swett neglected to mail this letter, however, Lincoln never read any of these important words.[57]

Swett expressed similar sentiments in a letter to Laura, telling her, "I find myself in the very midst of treason and conspiracy, which has been rife here for months & which may soon end in open war."[58] Swett clearly felt overwhelmed by the confluence of opinions in the capital, and he reacted to the bellicose Washington scene with shock and dismay. President Buchanan's responses to the situation were equivocal. His December 1860 message to Congress, for example, had included the statements that "the people of the North have no more right to interfere" and that "secession was unconstitutional." Swett became even more concerned on learning that only Maryland's governor, Thomas Hicks, stood between that state's adherence to the Union and secession. It doubtless alarmed him still further when an uncle of his law partner, William Orme, a Washington resident and a devout Union man, informed Swett that "union men here admit their interests are with the South & they intend to go with her."[59]

Swett interviewed Seward twice before December 31, the date of his next letter to Lincoln. During this interval, Seward led the peace negotiations in Washington for the new administration. Sometimes he followed Lincoln's instructions, but other times he followed his own inclinations. Swett transmitted Seward's impressions about the condition of the country to Lincoln, writing that Seward thought the Southern men had President Buchanan under their power, and if they could persuade Maryland and Virginia to join them, they hoped to prevent Lincoln's inauguration on March 4 by taking possession of the telegraph wires and the railroad from Baltimore to Washington. Seward felt, however, that this plan was so dark and frightening to the South that the scheme would break down before March 4. Swett agreed but worried that "from the rapid change of events . . . no human being can tell what the future has in store."[60]

Regarding the cabinet selections, Seward advised that Lincoln dispatch a rapid selection of the "ablest" men from the North to Washington without delay to oppose the danger. He disagreed with Lincoln's idea of selecting faction leaders in hopes of unifying the party. Swett described Seward's reasoning as "all very well for fair weather times ought he thinks now, to succumb to this cause." According to Swett, Seward believed that "a complete union of all patriotic men will be made in the fiery crucible . . . in which we will be tried. It is strength and character and ability he wants." Swett solicited Seward's choices for cabinet members and found that he favored Charles Francis Adams and Welles, and liked John Fremont for secretary of war, but opposed Cameron and Bates. He recommended Caleb Smith of Indiana, with the balance of appointments from the South.[61]

As the year concluded, Swett discovered that Senator Trumbull and others were pushing to include former Illinois senator Norman Judd in the cabinet. On January 1, 1861, Swett wrote a forceful letter to Davis insisting that the judge see Lincoln immediately to try to stop that possibility. The selection of Judd could make trouble for Lincoln, as Cameron and Seward opposed it. Swett had advised Lincoln that the cabinet needed to be assembled without delay, and he agreed with Seward on its makeup: "Lincoln's whole theory of uniting the elements of our party by coupling in a Cabinet rival chiefs is a very bad one. . . . It is strength unanimity of sentiment & action he wants." Davis went to Springfield on January 7 after receiving messages from Lincoln asking him to come. The Judd movement ended two days later, much to Judd's disappointment.[62]

Swett also wrote to Laura on January 1, wishing her and his son a happy New Year and declaring, "Union stock is improving." He launched into a discussion of the potential trouble on March 4 and how it rested on the action or inaction of one man, Governor Hicks of Maryland. A majority of Maryland state legislators favored secession and were pressing Hicks to convene a session of the legislature. Swett explained to Laura that if Hicks allowed the legislature to meet, a vote for the state to join the rebellion was almost a certainty. The South could then take control of the railroad to Washington and prevent Lincoln's arrival for his inauguration. Hicks had resisted the pressure up until this point, but Swett feared he might succumb. Leaders in Washington had arranged for Swett to meet with Hicks the following day. In his letter, Swett affirmed to Laura that he would start for home after a week in Washington, but as it turned out, two more weeks elapsed before he departed.[63]

The following day, Swett met with Governor Hicks as well as Maryland congressman Henry Winter Davis, whom Lincoln was still considering for a position on the cabinet. No record of this meeting has turned up, but

Congressman Davis wrote to his cousin, Judge David Davis, three days later, "I was glad to make the acquaintance of your friend Mr. Swett. I trust his mission will place Mr. Lincoln in the possession of the real state of our country which the northern people are *slowly* waking up to." The letter also gives a summary of the discussion with Swett and the subject of cabinet choices. Davis again tried to remove himself from consideration for the cabinet, proposing instead one of two North Carolinians, John Gilmer or former U.S. senator George E. Badger.[64] He also emphasized the importance of retaining the loyalty of some of the slaveholding states by recommending that a cabinet member be selected from North Carolina, Tennessee, or Kentucky.

On January 4, Swett wrote to Lincoln again, this time seeming more reflective and less overwhelmed by the secession crisis. Cameron returned to Pennsylvania from his visit with Lincoln, and he or his supporters announced his cabinet appointment. Swett reported that no one in Washington knew that Lincoln had asked Seward to be secretary of state. Nevertheless, both Cameron and Seward actively showed leadership in Washington's unfolding drama. Cameron visited General Scott and urged him to get authority from the president for security for the inauguration. Scott ordered enough light artillery to ensure peace and quiet and told Cameron that Buchanan was acting "nobly" now.[65]

The next day, Swett wrote to Lincoln warning that the Massachusetts men had called on him to discuss appointments and that there was tension among the Republican factions in the North over possible future announcements. He lobbied Lincoln against making any more appointments for the time being, advising that as things had evolved, Seward and Cameron had taken responsibility and were doing all they could, even though Lincoln had not yet announced Seward's appointment. Swett suggested letting the two Washington insiders continue to go it alone in order to "keep everything profoundly still." That evening, however, Cameron received a telegram from Lincoln withdrawing his appointment, and Lincoln sent a cryptic letter of rescission at the same time.[66]

Swett not only served as Lincoln's eyes and ears on the ground but also interpreted the events in Washington and offered counsel along with his reports. And Lincoln, so familiar with his old colleague from the Eighth Circuit who had occasionally bested him in the courtroom, knew how to listen to his loyal friend. In his letter of January 5, Swett also discussed the cabinet choices various faction spokesmen or groups advocated and provided his analysis. The appointment of a man from New England had been the subject of many discussions, with most of the Massachusetts men favoring Adams, although no one had found fault with Welles. "Of course if you appoint Wells [*sic*] Adams friends will howl & vice versa," Swett commented. "There is not a Congressman here who don't think you ought to consult <u>him</u> & take him or <u>his</u> friend in the cabinet." In Swett's opinion, Welles was the best choice for the New England appointment. Swett also wrote Lincoln his take on another man whose name had been raised, U.S. representative Schuyler Colfax from Indiana, whose appointment would have disappointed New Englanders: "Everybody thinks Colfax is a clever fellow but a gun of too small bore."[67]

Swett then described for Lincoln the diverse opinions on the men from the South under consideration. Seward's group supported the North Carolinian John Gilmer, but Swett had heard Gilmer was "timid . . . changeable [with] no opinion of his own." He compared another candidate, U.S. representative Emerson Etheridge from Tennessee, to attorney and banker Asahel Gridley, a man they both knew well from Bloomington, saying that Etheridge was "talented, but a rattling man," and cast his own vote for Henry Winter Davis, whom he said "has more ability than any of them." Swett also described the reaction to the announcement of Seward's appointment: it was "like Cameron's . . . warmly advocated & opposed."[68]

Regarding security for the inauguration, General Scott now had "complete control," Swett wrote. "He has today reinforced fort-Washington 12 miles below. I think the danger has passed." He clarified this a day or two later, apparently concerned that Lincoln might have misconstrued his statement that "the danger has passed." He was not referring to secession, he said, but meant "that sufficient military strength was being concentrated here to ensure [the safety of] your inauguration." On the "general question of secession," Swett added vaguely, "so far as I can see, the South are making steady progress."[69]

The next challenge for Swett involved mediating Lincoln's withdrawal of his intention to appoint Cameron. This reversal had occurred after Lincoln met with one of Cameron's adversaries from Pennsylvania, Alexander K. McClure, a journalist and the state Republican chairman. The Pennsylvania governor-elect, Andrew Gregg Curtin, also expressed opposition to Cameron. When Cameron returned to Washington from Harrisburg, he called on Swett on January 8, and they had a long conversation, which Swett informed Lincoln about in a letter the same day. Cameron showed Swett Lincoln's letter rescinding his appointment and complained that Lincoln had impugned his character in the withdrawal. Had Lincoln simply written that he had changed his mind for reasons of state, Cameron would not have taken offense, but instead, he felt assailed. After a lengthy discussion in which Swett assured him of Lincoln's good intentions, Cameron agreed to announce that he would not take a cabinet position. Swett telegraphed Lincoln, "The man I invited to see you will not accept [the appointment] don't act until you get my letter." In his letter, Swett also said that Cameron would remain loyal to Lincoln but hoped for a full explanation of his thoughts and actions at some future time. He transmitted Cameron's request that Lincoln not give an appointment to Dayton of New Jersey, whom he considered one of his enemies. Swett pointed out that this seemed to be Cameron's main concern. He advised Lincoln not to appoint anyone from either Pennsylvania or New Jersey, or otherwise it would lead to antagonism. Swett said that Cameron had acted "nobly & manly about the whole affair." He then commented on the secession crisis: "Things look fearfully here. If Virginia goes, Maryland is very doubtful."[70]

Following Swett's letter and a visit by John Sanderson, a state senator and close friend of Cameron's, Lincoln wrote a letter of apology and explanation to Cameron on January 13, which said in part, "I wrote that letter under great anxiety, and perhaps I was not as guarded in it's [sic] terms as I should have been; but I beg you to be assured, I intended no offence." He sent a substitute rescission letter for Cameron to use, asking him to destroy the original, which Cameron apparently did. Lincoln indicated that he had learned from Swett's letter, as well as one from Sanderson, that Cameron's "feelings were wounded."[71] This situation illustrates Lincoln's methods at work: taking the counsel of trusted friends, listening to constituents, making a sound decision, getting what he wanted, and being careful about the tracks he left in the political sands.

More good advice from Swett followed in his next two letters. Before Lincoln's first letter to Cameron arrived, offensive reports about the Pennsylvania senator appeared in the press. Ever the vigilant watchdog, Swett wrote to Lincoln again on January 14, requesting that he send another letter to Cameron, unaware that Lincoln had already done so. The next day, Swett cautioned Lincoln against appointing a cabinet member from Maryland until "it is certain it will not secede and the danger is past." He warned of the need for the full allegiance of all candidates, implying that an announcement by Lincoln about any appointment at this time could cause trouble.[72]

On January 17, his last day in Washington, Swett met with a group arranged by Seward consisting of the "Virginia Unionists" and, in Swett's words, "some extreme Southern Senators, to see if something could not be indicated which might do to restore peace."[73] It is likely the group included staunch supporters of both preservation of the Union and secession. No solutions emerged from this meeting, however. Things remained unresolved as Swett readied for his departure the next day.

During his time in Washington, Swett had sometimes found himself in vulnerable positions among the outspoken factions within the Republican Party seeking favors or positions. Twice in January, Elihu Washburne, the Republican congressman from Galena, Illinois, wrote strongly negative letters to Lincoln about Swett's activities. He complained that Swett was acting as the agent of the Weed-Seward dynasty, to the detriment of the Republicans, and condemned Swett's activities regarding Cameron's appointment, which Washburne strongly opposed.[74] These letters revealed more about Washburne and the Radical Republican faction, however, than they did about Swett. At various times, either the Radical Republicans or the Peace Democrats, later called Copperheads, posed major problems for Lincoln. With the first Republican president having been elected and the nation disintegrating, the various factions within the party—former moderate or old-line Whigs, abolitionists and former Democrats, plus an assortment of former Free Soilers and Know-Nothings—all were struggling for recognition and leadership.

While Swett was engaged in negotiations in Washington, more disturbing events had been unfolding. Three more states seceded between January 9 and 11, and several more were soon to follow.[75] On January 10, Confederates fired on the steamer *Star of the West* as it entered Charleston Harbor on its way to resupply the U.S. Army at Fort Sumter. Its captain turned the ship around. Major Robert Anderson, in command at Fort Sumter, lacked clear orders and therefore took no action. The restraint with which both sides handled this shocking episode deferred an outbreak of hostilities for the time being.[76]

Swett finally left Washington on January 18, 1861, with William Kellogg, a congressman from Canton, Illinois, with whom he intended to make the trip home. But when they arrived in Harrisburg, Swett broke down, exhausted and suffering from chills. He wrote to Laura that night, telling her about his sickness and ending his letter on a personal note that indicated he missed her and was longing for home: "I am very anxious about home. I hope you are well. My trip has not been a pleasant one, but full of work and anxiety." The next day he wrote to Lincoln, saying that he would be there shortly and cautioning him not to make any decisions until he arrived. "I think I have important considerations to present to you," he said. "[Do not] definitely determine when you will go to Washington until I see you."[77]

Swett remained in Harrisburg for three nights and then moved on to Pittsburgh. But his fever worsened, and he succumbed to a urinary tract infection. Without antibiotics, doctors could prescribe only rest and specific dietary regimens. He stayed at the Monongahela House in Pittsburgh for more than a month, struggling to recover from an assortment of maladies that included a persistent fever and possibly hepatitis. During this time, he wrote Laura almost daily and hired an African American assistant to help him recuperate. On January 24, he sent Lincoln words of caution about his travel arrangements for his inaugural trip to Washington. General Scott advised that Lincoln should send a messenger rather than a letter concerning the route he would take. Scott also said he intended to secure Baltimore to ensure Lincoln's safety en route to his inauguration. Swett told Lincoln that he would travel to Springfield as soon as he was able.[78]

While Swett recuperated gradually in Pittsburgh, Lincoln stopped there for the night of February 14–15 on his way to Washington and stayed at the hotel where his friend was lodged. This gave them an opportunity to confer. Lincoln and Swett likely discussed security precautions, cabinet formation, and Swett's appointment preferences. Before departing Pittsburgh, Lincoln gave the longest talk of his journey on the morning of the fifteenth from a front balcony of the hotel in the rain. Many people mentioned that there was more than a superficial resemblance between the two men, and when Swett walked into the reception that morning, "there was a tremendous outburst of enthusiasm," explained in a very short time by the appearance of the real Mr. Lincoln.[79]

Swett finally was feeling well enough to make the trip home to Bloomington a week and a half later, arriving on February 25. The day he returned, he wrote to his friend Ward Hill Lamon, inquiring about the "mysterious transit through Maryland" on the inaugural trip. Because of the threat to Lincoln, he had made the journey for his inauguration traveling incognito from Pennsylvania to Washington through Baltimore without stopping, and Lamon had accompanied Lincoln as a bodyguard. Swett also offered Lamon some observations on Washington, D.C.: "It is the worst place in the world, to judge correctly of anything. A ship might as well learn its bearings in the Norway Maelstrom, as for you people to undertake to judge anything correctly upon your arrival there. You are the subject of every artful and selfish appliance. . . . You have to decide all of moment in a few days, before you can discover the secret springs of the action presented to you. . . . There is but one safe rule and that is to stand by and adopt the judgment you formed before you arrived there. The atmosphere of Washington and the Country are as unlike as the atmosphere of Greenland and the tropics." Swett asked Lamon to share this advice with Lincoln, concerned about his "bewilderment of that City of rumors," and concluded, "I do ache to have him do well [as president]." Laura Swett, who had suffered her husband's absence and worried about his illnesses while he was on the road, glanced over his shoulder as he wrote to Lamon. Then she added a line asking Lamon not to forget his many friends back home and jokingly requesting that he use his influence to get her an office.[80]

I write . . . because I am so impressed with the
injustice of now overlooking Judge Davis.

—Swett to Lincoln, January 25, 1862

6. And the War Came

Leonard Swett's long absence from home had undoubtedly strained his relations with his wife and son. In addition, he still had lingering effects from his illness and had not yet fully recovered. Compounding all this were the pressing debts Swett had accrued over the last few years. Besides the debt he had assumed in helping his brother, the entire two-month trip to Washington had been largely at Swett's own expense, as were his earlier travels during the presidential convention, the campaign, and other journeys for political reconnoitering. Swett had yet to realize that the reward for political activity, even if well intentioned and responsible, could be meager or nonexistent. Devoted to the man he had helped get elected president, he had given freely of his time and scarce resources. Now he felt that he needed to make a large sum of money in a short period to take care of his family and remain under conditions conducive to good health. He would have to give up the hard ways of the road and the adventures associated with it. In this frame of mind, he wrote to Lincoln, as agreed when they saw each other in Pittsburgh, about his wishes for a post in the new administration.

Rather than simply asking for a suitable position within Lincoln's grasp, or at least some activity in which he could remain visible and available until a better position could be identified, Swett poured out his troubles to Lincoln in an ambiguous letter penned on Inauguration Day, March 4, 1861, appealing for personal sympathy. He chronicled the debts he had incurred over the years in the service of politics, both in running for office and in campaigning for Lincoln, as well as his accumulated expenses for medical care, detailing the maladies of his wife and child, both of whom were also in ill health. He then asked the president to use his sense of justice and fairness to determine the appropriate position for him.

With all that Lincoln was facing as he took office, he needed problem solvers on the scene, not someone else's problems to solve. Incredibly, Swett failed to recognize this in his self-absorption of the moment, although he was aware of Lincoln's work ethic and the demands facing him in office in Washington. Swett even went so far as to request a highly compensated assignment overseas in a favorable climate. If such a situation were not available, he said, he should stay hard at work at home to discharge his debts. Swett must have had an inkling of the inappropriate tenor of his requests, because he asked Lincoln to return the letter to him after reading it. He also sent similar but briefer letters to Davis, Cameron, Seward, Orme, Lamon, and Weed.[1]

Thurlow Weed sent Swett a discouraging reply to his appeal. Weed lamented Swett's illness and absence when appointments were under consideration, specifically mentioning positions in the Sandwich Islands (today's Hawaii) and Liverpool consulates, as well as the Patent Office, all of which were no longer available. Davis returned to Bloomington two weeks after the inauguration to find a disconcerted Swett, observing in a letter to Lamon, "Swett's pride is wounded deeply. He regrets deeply, I think, that he even applied for office." Davis, too, was overlooked in the appointment process and was keenly disappointed. Both Judge Davis and Swett reluctantly returned to legal practice in the Eighth Circuit courts, now reduced to McLean, Champaign, and Vermilion Counties.[2] After their deep involvement in presidential politics, and all the excitement that went with it, somehow, incredibly, Swett and Davis had been left behind.

Swett, who was a meticulous dresser, wrote to Lamon in early April, "I am quietly wearing out my old clothes, and try to pay the debts I have made this campaign." Lamon tried but failed to get a response from Lincoln on behalf of Swett. Apparently Lincoln was at a loss to know what to suggest. Swett's law partner, William Orme, visited Lincoln in May in pursuit of appointments for both Swett and Davis. Lincoln "spoke highly of you and Swett," Orme wrote to Davis. "He wanted to know if Swett would take a colonelcy in the regular army at a pay of $2500 to $3000 per annum. He said he had to make up some new regiments & would appoint him to one." According to Orme, Weed had mentioned Swett's name to Lincoln and submitted suggestions in connection with it, and Lincoln was glad Weed had recommended Swett. Orme advised Swett to go to Washington and make a case for himself in person.[3]

Two days later, however, Orme had another meeting with Lincoln that was not so positive in tone. Swett's partner wrote him the next day that the president's face showed displeasure when he raised the topic of Swett's appointment. Lincoln said that "Illinois already had over 50 per cent of her share of appointments, and he did not see how in the world he could give any more to her." Lincoln again suggested giving Swett a post in a new regiment, but Orme countered that this was not the place for Swett. Lincoln then said, in so many words, that if he lived and the government survived, he would try to find a place for Swett. Orme said the subject appeared to be "distasteful" to Lincoln. When Orme rose to leave, he indicated that he would convey what they had discussed to Swett, but Lincoln made no reply. Dismayed by this reaction, Orme did not even raise the issue of an appointment for Davis.[4] Why Lincoln passed over these two men for an appointment remains an interesting question with no easy answer.

Lincoln's focus on pulling together a team representing the various factions, parties, and geographic areas left little room for special attention or favor to those closest to him. His first two months as president were not easy, and he had little time to contemplate the appropriate niches for his many friends and applicants. Nor would the remainder of his 1,503 days in office provide much reflective respite.

Meanwhile, war preparations moved ahead in Washington. The heightened state of agitation in the nation was exacerbated by the death on June 3, 1861, of Illinois senator Stephen A. Douglas, the titular leader of Lincoln's Northern opposition, who succumbed to typhoid fever at only forty-eight years of age. The courthouse bell tolled in Bloomington when the news arrived, and that evening, Judge Davis chaired a meeting in Phoenix Hall at which he also spoke briefly. The next day, at a meeting of the McLean County bar in the courthouse to pass a series of resolutions, Swett "made an eloquent speech analyzing the character and deeds of the illustrious dead."[5] Douglas's death seems to have led to some personal reflection on the part of both Swett and Davis, and by their actions, it appears that they finally were able to put aside their postelection disappointments and rejoined the political process.

Governor Richard Yates, to whom Swett had given his convention votes slightly more than a year earlier, lost little time in appointing Douglas's replacement. Within a week, he named Orville H. Browning to fill the seat, passing over Swett and Davis, as well as several other likely candidates, who were "all good Republicans and all 'in a family way, too'—to select . . . another old-time Whig."[6]

Over the summer, Judge T. Lyle Dickey, an old-line Whig turned Democrat from Ottawa and the circuit just north of the Eighth, consulted with Swett and Davis as to how he could get authority to raise a cavalry regiment. Some of his family members and friends in his county wanted to serve, but he could not find sponsors. Swett knew that many men in his own county were in the same position, although he had decided that he would not go to war again. He had fought in one war as a private soldier, and now his sick wife and family were depending on him for support. He resolved, however, to take snatches of time away from work and home to find appropriate places for those who did wish to serve.[7]

In keeping with this intention, Swett returned to Washington for the first time since the beginning of the Lincoln administration to seek authority for the regiment and assist Dickey. The judge was on the outs with Lincoln, since he had supported Douglas in 1858, and Dickey thought he might need help gaining approval for the regiment. Swett also knew Simon Cameron, whom Lincoln had appointed as the secretary of war, so this visit to Washington offered him an opportunity to reengage with Lincoln.[8]

Swett and Dickey arrived on the evening of July 31, 1861. Swett attempted to see Cameron, Seward, and then the president, with frustrating results. He was eager to meet with them on his arrival, but it was the dinner hour and they were not available. By the time he got to the receiving room at the White House, Lincoln announced that he was tired and was going to bed. Once again, Swett gave Laura an inaccurate estimate of how long he would be away from home; in a letter he wrote her the next morning, he told her that he would return "tomorrow," but it turned out to be a two-week trip.[9]

Fortunately, Swett's reception in Washington improved. Swett met with Lincoln several times during his visit and must have broached the touchy subject of his letter and appointment requests, as he wrote to his wife after one meeting that Lincoln "was very kind & protested that there was no trouble."[10] Within a few days of their arrival, the secretary of war authorized Dickey to raise a regiment of cavalry from Ottawa, Illinois. Dickey also obtained orders for one thousand uniforms, guns, and swords to be sent directly from the manufacturers to Ottawa, as Swett and Dickey feared that if these items were shipped to Washington, they might be distributed to other regiments. Dickey returned to Illinois and quickly raised one thousand men, gathering them in camp at Ottawa.[11]

While in Washington, Swett spoke with Brigadier General Andrew Porter about the battle of Bull Run. He learned that the cabinet had opposed the advance, with the exception of Blair and Chase. General Winfield Scott had "wanted to wait a little longer" before making an aggressive move. The political pressure brought to bear for the Union assault and the subsequent disorganized retreat disappointed Swett. He understood the vulnerability of Washington after the battle, were it not that the Confederate army was just as inexperienced and confused as that of the Union. Bull Run was a serious defeat for both Lincoln and the Army of the Potomac. The Confederate officer in command, General Joseph E. Johnston, later admitted that with two green armies, the defending troops had the advantage over the aggressor.[12]

Swett also pressed Lincoln for a position for David Davis. Both Senator Browning and later Davis aspired to a vacancy on the U.S. Supreme Court that Lincoln wanted to fill from Illinois, although initially Davis was not sure he was up to being a "Supreme Judge."[13] Admiration for Browning as a new senator blossomed, and his supporters easily influenced Lincoln on his behalf. Davis's supporters, on the other hand, were Illinois circuit lawyers whose voices could not be heard in Washington. Before coming to Washington, Swett heard that Lincoln had said, "I do not know what I may do when the time comes, but there has never been a day when if I had to act I should not have appointed Browning." Swett, Davis, and Orme all thought this remark sounded too much like Lincoln to be mistaken, as "no man but he could have put the situation so quaintly."[14]

Now Swett took the opportunity to speak on Davis's behalf to counter the influence brought for Browning by his fellow senators. He started off by boldly reminding the president that it was the force of Davis and the lawyers of the Eighth Circuit that had brought Lincoln to prominence, and that without Davis, he would not now be president of the United States. Lincoln agreed. Then Swett launched into a courtroom-style argument asserting the common law of mankind that such a force as Davis must be recognized, making reference to Tsar Nicholas and Napoleon. When he concluded his summation for Davis, Swett felt that he had swayed Lincoln.[15]

Later that day, while replaying his interview with Lincoln in his mind, Swett seized on another idea. He quickly wrote a letter, went back to the

White House, read it to Lincoln, and left it with him. In the letter, Swett told Lincoln that if he appointed Davis to the Supreme Court, he could kill two birds with one stone: Swett would accept the appointment as being half for him and half for Davis. Should Lincoln receive any further requests for patronage for Swett, he could use the letter as an estoppel and Swett would honor this plea.[16] This letter, clearly stating that Swett would apply for nothing from any member of Lincoln's administration, was later found among Lincoln's papers. The letter and Swett's entreaties did not seem to have had much effect on Lincoln, however. A year passed while Lincoln was waiting for Congress to finish realigning the circuits for which Supreme Court justices were responsible, and he appointed two others to the Supreme Court before finally appointing Davis.

Swett went home to Bloomington after two weeks in Washington, having achieved limited success in what he had set out to do. Shortly after his return, his resolve to serve the needs of the regiments and soldiers was tested again when he received a letter from Lieutenant Colonel Harvey Hogg from Camp Butler near Springfield. A fellow attorney and prosecutor on the Eighth Circuit, Hogg now led the Second Illinois Cavalry. Knowing Swett had influence with the president, Hogg wrote to him on August 18, 1861, that they had no guns or other supplies. Without them, he could not train his soldiers and prepare them for their call to duty.[17]

Lincoln soon made Swett another offer of a military appointment. On September 2, the president named Eleazer A. Paine of the Ninth Illinois Volunteer Regiment a brigadier general of volunteers. Two and a half weeks later, on September 19, he endorsed Paine's request for staff officers, including Swett by name, and offered Swett an appointment as assistant adjutant general dated October 23.[18] Swett likely agreed to consider the appointment, but as with the earlier offer, he wound up declining it.

As late summer approached, Dickey's regiment was in a similar situation to Hogg's. The uniforms, sabers, and carbines they had ordered still had not arrived. The men were growing uneasy waiting in camp for supplies. While Swett was working on court matters in Danville, 135 miles from Dickey and his regiment in Ottawa, someone banging on the door of his hotel room awakened him at four o'clock one morning. To Swett's surprise, it was Dickey. His friend was there in hopes of enlisting Swett's help and started off with a graphic story: "I know it was mean, but in old Kentucky times, when we used to drive a six-horse team and were near miring down in a slough, we used to lick the best horse. It was awfully mean, but it was simply a necessity to get out of the mire, and that is what I have come clear from Ottawa tonight to do to you. I want you to get out of that bed and leave the court and go immediately to Washington and find out what has happened to our orders for clothing and arms. I cannot leave my regiment. They are all in camp in farmer's clothes, and you can not drill a farmer boy to become a soldier until you put a new uniform on him, and give him a new sword and bright carbine. You know all about this business at Washington, and can get it done." Swett agreed to help and set off for Washington.[19]

En route, Swett stopped at Harrisburg, Pennsylvania, on October 21 to see Secretary of War Cameron for input and influence. The same day, Colonel Edward D. Baker, a senator from Oregon who had been an Illinoisan and was Lincoln's close friend and political ally, was killed in the battle of Ball's Bluff, Virginia. The Lincolns had named their second son for him, and Baker had ridden with the Lincolns to the capital on Inauguration Day. Baker's body lay in state in the nation's capital, and Lincoln was in a state of shock. This was the scene that greeted Swett on his arrival in Washington.

When Swett met with Lincoln about the uniforms and arms for the regiments in Illinois, the arming of the North had been under way for about four months. The South had acquired many of the arms that had existed when the war broke out, and no surplus was available from Europe. The government had ordered that all arms be sent to Washington, which superseded the orders for the regiments in Illinois. Swett heard that men were not enlisted because industries needed to be changed and manufacturing increased, facts that had not been made public for fear of showing the nation's weakness. Lincoln told Swett in grave terms, "If your regiment were to wait and take an honest turn, the wool has not yet grown on the sheep's back to make their uniforms." Swett wrote, "Lincoln might have added with equal truth that the ore with which to make the swords and the carbines was still in its native mountains."[20]

A few days later, Lincoln asked Swett to deliver orders removing General John Fremont from the leadership of the Union armies in the West. Lincoln was concerned about the possible defection of the border states resulting from unauthorized actions by Fremont. These included a proclamation the general made on August 30 freeing Missouri slaves, which Lincoln had promptly countermanded. Swett went directly to St. Louis, where he met with General Samuel P. Curtis on October 29. A friend of Lincoln's,

Curtis was a three-term Republican congressman from Burlington, Iowa, who resigned to become a brigadier general in 1861. Fremont had kept his manifold command transgressions hidden from his generals, and thus Curtis now learned about them for the first time from Swett.

The *New York Times* had publicized this mission, alerting Fremont to make efforts to avoid his receipt of the orders. Fearing that Fremont might attempt to evade the orders, Curtis suggested they have several messengers carry multiple copies to Fremont. To avoid arousing Fremont's suspicion, Swett and Curtis selected several reliable men who had legitimate business inside Fremont's lines. Captain T. I. McKenny from Iowa, who had experience delivering dispatches in Mexico, took the originals for the first delivery attempt. He rode for a day and several nights to arrive at headquarters. There, disguised as a simple country farmer, he told Fremont's aide that he had to see General Fremont and no one else. The aide demanded several times that he reveal his business, but McKenny finagled until he managed to get admitted. After Fremont read the order, he asked McKenny how he had gotten through his lines. McKenny departed, but an aide came after him and told him not to reveal the order in camp. The aide came back to ask whether General David Hunter, who would relieve Fremont, had been advised. McKenny said that a duplicate order had been sent by messenger to Hunter. McKenny was subsequently forbidden to leave the camp, but later that night, he overheard the password to get out. He dug out an old pass General Curtis had given him, used the password, and departed under cover of darkness. He located General Hunter and then returned to headquarters.[21]

Swett learned from a friend, Captain J. W. Shaffer of Freeport, Illinois, that when Fremont received the discharge orders, he ordered all his men to arms and Hunter's division to march to join the battle. Once they had assembled, Fremont gave a farewell address and left with a bodyguard, fifty Indians, and a paymaster carrying two hundred thousand to three hundred thousand dollars. The paymaster was soon arrested with some of the money. After taking command, General Hunter sent scouts in every direction, but they found no Confederates in the area. Swett advised Lincoln of these events in a letter dated November 9, mentioning his outrage over Fremont's misdeeds. He requested punishment for the officers who had stolen from the government, lest theft become rampant amid the war.[22]

Before Fremont was removed, Ulysses S. Grant had been promoted to brigadier general and assigned to Cairo, Illinois, at the junction of the

Mississippi and Ohio Rivers. In early November, Fremont had directed him to make demonstrations along both sides of the Mississippi, and Grant moved a large contingent of troops to Belmont, Missouri, opposite Columbus, Kentucky, which had been recently occupied by a Confederate contingent. Rebels already in Belmont left when Grant's skirmishers went into action on November 7, 1861. When Grant's green troops witnessed the sudden evacuation of the Confederate camp in Belmont, they went on a looting spree, not easily quelled by untrained officers and enlisted leaders. Confederate General Leonidas Polk sent a force across the Mississippi River to cut off Grant's return to his steamboats, but Grant and his men made it back in time. Losses on both sides turned out to be significant but fairly balanced. This was Grant's first major military action, and he suffered adverse publicity from it. But to his credit, his forces gained experience and confidence, and they had disrupted Confederate activity in the area, at least for a time.

Shortly after the battle at Belmont, Swett met Grant for the first time. They spent the evening together at a hotel in Cairo discussing the action of the battle. Swett asked Grant how the Rebels got behind his troops when he could see them coming upriver. With his usual deliberation, Grant explained, "You see my army was a green one. The boys were never in a fight before. . . . They met the rebels, ran at them and whipped them with an ease that astonished themselves. They were exultant." As a result, some of them got drunk. Then "they became rather demoralized, and, after the battle," Grant said, "I had just about as little command over them as a herder has over a wild drove of Texas steers." In retelling the story later, Swett remarked, "It takes a small man to lie out of a difficulty; a big man alone can tell the truth." "It is not for the newspapers, however," he joked, which guaranteed its publication.[23]

Lincoln appointed a Commission on War Claims at St. Louis in November 1861, under the chairmanship of David Davis, to look into the malfeasance in the military administration of the West. Other members were Joseph Holt, who had served in the Buchanan administration as postmaster general and briefly as secretary of war, and Hugh Campbell, a prominent leader in St. Louis.[24] This also provided a great opportunity for Swett, who prepared claims at Davis's behest for presentation to and review by the commission. While doing this work in St. Louis, Swett finally revealed the extent of his indebtedness to his wife in several letters written in January 1862. He had attempted to obscure these details from her for some time, not wanting to worry her. Now, with the claims work, he hoped to make significant inroads toward eliminating his debts. A list he made in one letter to Laura suggests that he owed money for mortgages, houses, and farmland, as well as to banks, family members and other individuals, and a few hotels or boardinghouses. Despite the shock this information must have caused Laura, the tone of his letters suggests they had a remarkably warm and loving relationship. Swett's use of alcohol apparently had become another issue in his marriage, as he also took the time in two of these letters to assure his wife he was not drinking.[25]

While pursuing claim work related to Fremont's excesses and discharge, Swett also resumed his efforts to obtain a significant appointment for Judge Davis, taking up the cause with renewed vigor. "I write . . . because I am so impressed with the injustice of now overlooking Judge Davis," Swett wrote to Lincoln on January 25, 1862. In keeping with the direct and forceful approach that Swett alone brought to bear on Lincoln, he championed Davis's strengths once again, finding one mark of the judge's worth to be his lack of self-aggrandizement. Invoking the golden rule, Swett asked the president to consider whether Davis would have hesitated or swerved from his conviction in favor of Lincoln, describing him as "true as steel."[26]

Others joined him in the cause. Swett forwarded a letter to Lincoln from John Todd Stuart strongly recommending Davis for the Supreme Court. Three days later, Swett sent another letter with a petition from thirty-one members of the Illinois Constitutional Convention, then meeting in Springfield, urging Lincoln to appoint Davis to the Supreme Court. As the seventy-five-member convention included only twenty-one Republicans, Davis obviously had support from some Democrats. At least nineteen individuals wrote to Lincoln in early 1862 on the judge's behalf, as did several county bar associations and two Missouri groups. Despite this show of support, Lincoln still did not choose Davis, instead appointing Ohio lawyer Noah H. Swayne to the Supreme Court to ensure a quorum for the bench.[27]

While Swett was working in St. Louis, Laura and Bertie, now three years old, joined him for a time, and together they socialized with the group of leaders the war activities brought together in the hotels. These included General Curtis, with whom Swett had worked to deliver removal orders to Fremont, and Lieutenant James Shirk and his wife, who took a great interest in Bertie. Commodore Andrew H. Foote, who commanded the western navy, oversaw the building of a riverboat flotilla to assist in opening the

Mississippi, Ohio, Tennessee, Cumberland, and other rivers. It was reported that "while Foote was at St. Louis superintending the preparation of his fleet, one evening at the Planters' House one of the ladies, Mrs. Leonard Swett of Bloomington, congratulated him on the glory he was sure to win with his fleet, to which he replied with the Biblical quotation, 'Let not him that girdeth on his harness boast himself as he that putteth it off.'" Swett also met Brigadier General John M. Schofield, later a major general under Sherman in several battles, who spent some time in St. Louis as well.[28]

Also during this period, Swett visited some of the battle sites shortly after the fighting there ended. In February 1862, Grant took Forts Henry and Donelson and captured fifteen thousand Confederates. These twin victories opened the Tennessee and Cumberland Rivers to Union penetration deep into the South and constituted the first major military successes for the Union, producing a positive political effect in the free states. Swett joined General Halleck in his command boat to the Fort Donelson battlefield, arriving as hostilities ended. Soldiers from central and southern Illinois had fought in these battles, and Swett spoke with many of them.

Swett provided a geographic description of the landscape for these battles in a letter to his mother. The Confederates had built Fort Henry on the Tennessee River, intending it to protect from incursions farther south. They had also constructed Fort Donelson, twelve miles east on a sharp bend in the Cumberland River, and fortified it to avoid easy occupation. "Two thousand Union troops left Cairo . . . by steamboat" for Fort Henry, Swett wrote, and with the help of gunboats, they attacked and easily took possession of the fort. The Rebels fled to the Cumberland, where they joined the forces at Fort Donelson. Confederate reinforcements came in by railroad from Memphis to Bowling Green, Kentucky, within easy reach of Fort Donelson. Outside the fort, embankments constructed on the hillside protected the defending riflemen, along with felled trees that served as an obstruction.[29]

The battle at Fort Donelson lasted nearly four days in freezing rain and snow. Grant extended a line of soldiers about seven miles long in back of the fort to the river on each end. The soldiers slowly gained ground, but many of the men suffered frozen hands and feet. On the morning of the last day, the Rebels chose the weakest point in the line and unsuccessfully tried to escape through it. Sensing defeat, they returned to the fort and surrendered. Swett observed, "Every small twig is scarred with bullets[,] and trees the size of a man's body have often from 10 to 20 bullets in them."

Three soldiers from McLean County were killed and about forty wounded. Other companies from Illinois fared even worse. One company that had started with fifty-five men ended up with eight. Another company of sixty-two was reduced to twelve. In all, about twenty-five hundred Union soldiers were killed or wounded, along with a similar number of Confederates. Shortly thereafter, Nashville fell to the North and Kentucky was liberated, a substantial victory.[30]

In the aftermath of the Civil War, it came to light that Grant had attacked Fort Donelson before all the soldiers arrived, in keeping with his "maxim . . . to fight first and get ready as soon as he could." Colonel Dickey and his cavalry regiment from Ottawa arrived at the Union line but dropped back to a ridge to forage their horses. When the Confederate forces broke through the Union line, they fled straight into Dickey's force. Swett described the reaction: "Dickey immediately caused all his bugles to be blown . . . and fired his howitzers sharply in the face of the enemy. They hesitated, stopped and went back into the fort. . . . Grant was enabled, finally, to report the capture of fourteen thousand men with the fortifications." Later, Rebel officers said they had retreated because they thought they had run into the rest of Grant's army and feared being trapped between it and Grant's main force.[31]

The investigation by the Commission on War Claims against Fremont took four months, producing a final report dated March 10, 1862. During this time, they received "6,400 claims aggregating $9,500,000." Swett's harsh judgment of Fremont's actions in his letter to Lincoln was vindicated in the commission's findings: "If a commanding general, without ever advising with his government . . . is permitted, at will, to replenish his military chest from the banks and private fortunes of the nation, there is an end . . . of all just responsibility in the military service." Fremont had said on many occasions, according to the commission, that "the people of the United States were in the field; that he was at their head; that he meant to carry out such measures as they . . . expected him to carry out, without regard to the red tape of the Washington people." The day after the commission report was published, however, Lincoln, pressed by abolitionists supporting Fremont, gave him a lesser command in the Appalachian Mountains. This unfortunately created the impression that his misdeeds were inconsequential. Fremont's military career came to an end not long after when, in June 1862, he refused to serve under the new command of General John Pope and his request to be relieved was granted.[32]

After his work with the commission was finished, Swett spent a short time with his family in Bloomington before hearing the news of fighting at Shiloh in April 1862. Shirk, with whom Swett and his wife had socialized in St. Louis, was captain of one of two gunboats that had engaged the Confederates at Shiloh. Grant later acknowledged Shirk for his assistance on the first afternoon at Shiloh in repelling the effort of Confederate forces to turn Grant's left flank. That night, knowing where the enemy forces camped, the gunboats lobbed shells into their encampment every fifteen minutes. Swett now hastened back to Cairo, accompanied by his partner, William Orme, where they obtained permission from General Halleck to board his steamboat to Pittsburg Landing, adjoining the battleground on the west side of the Tennessee River. Swett spent several days tramping over the battle site and visiting with friends and soldiers, including Colonel Dickey, Shirk, and the other gunboat captain. Once Swett learned of their war efforts, he recommended both captains for recognition and promotion to Lincoln, who acted on his counsel.[33]

In a memorial he later wrote for Dickey, Swett recounted the tragic story of Colonel Dickey's extended family in the battle of Shiloh, which emphasized the human costs of war. Colonel Dickey had gone into the army with seven of his brothers and sons and one son-in-law. His eldest daughter was married to General W. H. L. Wallace. Haunted by the danger to her husband as the battle approached, she left home in Illinois and traveled to Cairo, where she was told that no woman was allowed up the Tennessee River. Undaunted, Dickey's daughter took the place of someone carrying a new flag to one of the regiments and arrived at Shiloh, six hundred miles from home, on April 6, 1862. At the height of the battle, her husband was brought back to camp with a gunshot wound in the head. As Dickey told Swett later that week, "She arrived in time to recognize him and be recognized by him, and a few days afterward, saying 'We shall meet again in heaven,' he died in the arms of that devoted wife."[34] Three of the eight men serving from Dickey's family were killed in this and associated operations, with another severely wounded and a fifth incapacitated by disease.

Now, a year into the war, with no end in sight and with Shiloh's heavy losses, a crisis developed among the Union military leadership. Lincoln began to watch a general in the West, and Swett kept an eye on him as well. General Henry W. Halleck did not like Grant and had supported McClellan's efforts to cut down Grant's command well before Shiloh.

After Shiloh, Halleck took over command of the armies from Grant, who received extensive criticism on his being caught by surprise the first day and the human costs of the battle. Halleck slowly moved his forces to Corinth, where the Union army again incurred heavy losses. Another friend of both Lincoln and Swett, General Richard J. Oglesby, was shot below the armpit in this battle. The ball passed through his lung and lodged next to his heart, where it stayed for the rest of his life, although he eventually recovered sufficiently to serve as governor of Illinois and as a U.S. senator. Away from Grant's control, Halleck dispersed his forces. True independence for Grant came when orders arrived for him "to relieve General McClernand from command of the Expedition against Vicksburg, giving it to the next in rank, or taking it yourself."[35] Not surprisingly, Grant took the second alternative. Lincoln guided him from a distance as if he were maneuvering some pieces on a chessboard.[36]

Late in May 1862, Swett and Davis received an urgent request from General Yates's office that Bloomington supply two hundred new recruits to replace troops guarding Confederate prisoners at Camp Butler near Springfield. Apparently Secretary of War Stanton was calling for more troops to meet a threatened attack on Washington while McClellan's forces fought in the Peninsula Campaign. Why the call was specifically for men from Bloomington is not clear, but the governor knew that Swett and Davis were close to Lincoln and would act quickly. Davis was away, however, but Swett managed on his own to accomplish the task, raising two companies. He arranged to have the courthouse bell ring at midnight, and 203 recruits responded to the call. Lieutenant Colonel William McCullough, who was home on sick leave, organized the men, and Swett accompanied them to Springfield within the next few days.[37]

In late July and August 1862, Swett finally heard the first hints of Davis's long-awaited appointment. In Washington again on behalf of the McLean County regiment, Swett called on Lincoln's wife, Mary, who informed him that she too was pressing for Davis. Judge Davis's "matter was all right," she told him confidentially. Lincoln did not express his intentions to Davis for another month, and it was not until October 19, 1862, that he announced the appointment of David Davis to the U.S. Supreme Court.[38] Once again, Swett proved to be the engineer behind the scenes. As he had served earlier as eyes and ears to Lincoln, now he was a determined voice to the president, even if his own personal ambitions in the political world had borne no fruit.

Leonard Swett, about age fifty, photographed in Chicago. Eckley Collection.

Leonard Swett, about age sixty. Courtesy of the McLean County Museum of History.

Original homestead where Leonard Swett grew up, three miles west of Turner, Maine. On a clear day, you can see Mount Washington in New Hampshire. This photograph was taken in 2005, and the house still stands as of this writing. Courtesy of George Ricker, Windham, Maine.

John Swett Jr. (1789–1859), Leonard's father. After serving in the War of 1812, John farmed near Turner, Maine. Charcoal rendering dated 1869. Courtesy of Wilma Irish, Livermore, Maine.

Remember Berry (1794–1883), Leonard's mother. She taught young Leonard to play the flute as part of the family orchestra she started. Courtesy of Wilma Irish, Livermore, Maine.

Josiah Drummond, Swett's roommate at Waterville (now Colby) College in 1845 and later a delegate to the 1864 Republican National Convention. Collections of the Maine Historical Society.

Abraham Lincoln, age thirty-seven, several years before meeting Swett for the first time at Mount Pulaski. Photograph by Nicholas Shepherd. Courtesy of the Library of Congress.

(*From left*) William T. Sherman, Ulysses S. Grant, Abraham Lincoln, and David D. Porter in *The Peacemakers* (1868), by the Chicago painter George P. A. Healy. Robert Lincoln wrote on two occasions in correspondence that Swett consulted with the painter and modeled for the role of Lincoln in the painting. Swett knew Lincoln well enough to emulate the Lincoln pose with the hand under the chin. The painting has hung in the White House since 1942. Courtesy of the White House Historical Association.

The Mount Pulaski Court House, in the town where Swett first met Lincoln on October 8, 1849. The original courthouse still stands on a prominent square in the small town in central Illinois. Courtesy of Robert George.

David Davis, age thirty-two. When Swett met him in 1848, he thought Davis's "immense tread was the tread of Hercules." Courtesy of the Library of Congress.

Brigadier General William Ward Orme, Swett's Bloomington law partner from 1855 to 1866. Courtesy of the McLean County Museum of History.

McLean County Courthouse, Bloomington, Illinois, the site of many Lincoln-Swett cases between 1852 and 1859. Courtesy of the McLean County Museum of History.

Ward Hill Lamon, Lincoln's and Swett's friend, Eighth Circuit prosecutor, and District of Columbia marshal. Photograph by Mathew Brady, circa 1855–65. Courtesy of the Library of Congress.

Sketch of the interior of the Wigwam from the May 19, 1860, issue of *Harper's Weekly* that depicts the Republicans in the nominating convention in May 1860. The Library of Congress catalog notes that the crowd is mostly women. Courtesy of the Library of Congress.

Thurlow Weed, New York newspaper editor, political leader, and supporter of Seward, whom Swett and Davis met the night of Lincoln's nomination. Swett attended both Lincoln-Weed meetings before Lincoln's inauguration. Weed was sometimes called "the dictator." Courtesy of the Library of Congress, Brady-Handy Collection.

William H. Seward, New York governor, U.S. senator, and Lincoln's (and later, Andrew Johnson's) secretary of state from 1861 to 1869. Seward was Swett's best friend in Lincoln's cabinet. Courtesy of the Library of Congress.

Simon Cameron, Pennsylvania senator and political leader. Swett had an instrumental role in Cameron's appointment as secretary of war, from which position he was removed after nine months. Courtesy of the Library of Congress.

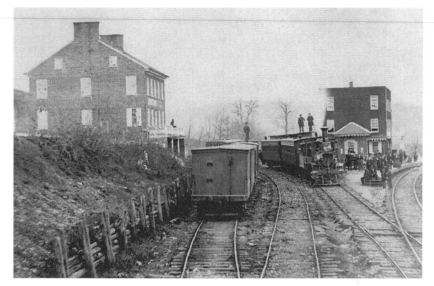

Presidential train stop at Hanover, Pennsylvania, east of Gettysburg, on November 18, 1863. Leonard Swett and his family were on board at Lincoln's invitation. They attended the dedication and Lincoln's famous address. Photograph by Mathew Brady, who ran down the tracks and set his camera atop another train car to photograph the group assembled at the depot.
Courtesy of the Library of Congress.

Close-up of mystery man standing alongside the station at the train stop. Is this Abraham Lincoln or Leonard Swett? Swett was occasionally mistaken on the street for Lincoln. Photograph by Mathew Brady. Courtesy of the Library of Congress.

Peter S. Grosscup, about 1892. Grosscup was Swett's third major law partner, from 1883 to 1889, after practicing in Ohio and losing two races there for Congress. He was made a U.S. district judge in 1892 and raised to the U.S. Circuit Court in 1897. Courtesy of the Library of Congress.

"Standing Lincoln" bronze statue in Lincoln Park, Chicago, by Augustus Saint-Gaudens. Leonard Swett gave the dedication speech for the statue in 1887. Photograph courtesy of Andrew Horne; from Wikimedia Commons and licensed under Creative Commons Attribution–Share Alike.

Lincoln . . . lifted our whole country to
a higher plane of civilization . . .

—Swett on the emancipation at the dedication of
Saint-Gaudens's "Standing Lincoln," 1887

7. Witness to the Emancipation

In July 1862, Leonard Swett made a fourth trip to Washington, motivated by his desire to serve the needs of the regiments and soldiers. This time he sought to gain authorization for his law partner and good friend, William Orme, to raise a regiment primarily from McLean County. The Illinois governor, Richard Yates, had refused to authorize the regiment because Orme had not supported some provisions of his proposed new state constitution. En route, Swett stopped in Harrisburg, probably to see Cameron or Casey, and in Baltimore, where he paid his respects to H. Winter Davis. On July 30, Swett spoke with Lincoln, who sent him to General Halleck with the following message: "Please see the bearer, Mr. Swett, who will tell you truth only about William W. Orme, whom I also know, to be one of the most active, competent, and best men in the world." As a result, the Ninety-Fourth Illinois Infantry Regiment mustered in on August 20, 1862. Swett also attempted to have William McCullough of Colonel Dickey's cavalry regiment promoted to the rank of colonel, but he found Lincoln less responsive on this matter. "I don't think I can succeed about McCullough," he wrote to Laura. He also made some observations about Lincoln: "He is in great trouble & care weighs heavily upon him," he wrote. "But the nation is in good hands. I have heard his views upon all the great questions and there is a deliberateness, a maturity of thought & a caution, which is in my opinion indispensable."[1]

During his trips to Washington, Swett also renewed former acquaintances and spent time with old friends. One was Ward Hill Lamon, who had served with him on the Eighth Circuit and was now U.S. marshal for the District of Columbia. The weather was oppressively hot and muggy, and while Lamon sought refuge at the beach, he left his carriage at Swett's beck and call. Swett also crossed paths with George F. Shepley, with whom he read law in Maine, who was now serving as the military governor of Louisiana under General Ben Butler. Shepley wanted more men for his force at New Orleans, fearing that the South would reinforce its numbers there and take the city. Swett took Shepley to see the president. Although Lincoln, too, wanted more troops there, he told Shepley that he had none to give.[2]

Swett had planned to visit his elderly mother in Maine while on the East Coast, but he delayed his departure when Lincoln invited him to speak at a "great war meeting" to explain the call for six hundred thousand additional troops and raise funds to support the war effort. On August 6, 1862, Swett joined Lincoln and almost a dozen other speakers on the platform on the east front of the nation's Capitol before a crowd of ten thousand. President Lincoln spoke for about five minutes, defending both McClellan and Stanton, despite the lack of military success and his growing frustration. Leonard Swett took his turn among a number of current and former elected representatives, government officials, and military leaders with whom he shared the stage.[3]

Introducing himself as a stranger from Illinois coming to the capital for the joint support of the nation, Swett went on to describe Washington, D.C., as "the pride of this country, founded as the city of constitutional liberty, bearing the name of the founder of this republic . . . but also the place of origin of the great rebellion." He spoke of the divergence of opinion in the nation: "The one cherished the memories of the past and found cause for pride in the illustrious deeds of our fathers . . . the other despised the government, despised constitutional liberty, and counted as noble only what contributed to the rebellion." He labeled the Confederates as "imaginary patriots [who] sought to take their people up through the beautiful paths of secession to a higher prosperity and a greater wealth." He congratulated the president and his cabinet for displaying a positive and strong sense of purpose in contrast to their prior indecision on the direction of the war and the draft for additional men.

Swett then answered for the states of Illinois and New York, saying that they would respond to the call. He reminded those in the crowd of words from the scriptures—"where the treasure is, there the hearts will be also"—and entreated them, "Weed out the traitors in your midst . . . and our soil will be clean and free from what had spread over it like a poisonous weed." He appealed for the assembled masses to respond to Lincoln's action, saying, "Do this not grudgingly, but cheerfully, and the six hundred thousand men will plant the flag in every hamlet from here to the gulf." He reminded them that the Union had already stripped the Rebels of two-thirds of their territory and power. Now the president was asking for additional men to "strip the balance." Swett closed by addressing the ambiguity of war: "A little boat that is launched upon the waves of the ocean, trusting to the drifts of its tide, never comes back and lands just where it was launched; neither does the great nation that embarks upon the seas of rebellion and revolution land where it started." No one could predict exactly when and how things would end, but if they had courage, faith, and energy, "then will He guide us safely through to the end." Swett mailed a copy of this elegant speech to the *Pantagraph*, which printed it for circulation. The *New York Times* also reported on the meeting, saying of Swett, "The speaker was frequently interrupted by applause."[4]

Swett left for Maine several days later, stopping in New York along the way to see Thurlow Weed. The refreshing breeze in New York City was a relief after the stifling heat of Washington. Like many others, Weed expressed despair about the war, which he felt had only made the South more resolute in its endurance. Swett wrote to Laura from New York about the pessimism in the North over the war and the failure of the Peninsula Campaign. He also talked of Lincoln's disappointment over McClellan's disposition of troops and gave her a long description of the president's positions relative to the campaign. Surprisingly, at this time Swett thought that Lincoln would not issue an emancipation proclamation. He also felt that Lincoln would not accept African American men as soldiers, as Lincoln believed that arming them would cause as much of a reaction as would a full-fledged proclamation.[5] When talking with Swett on the subject of a proclamation, Lincoln apparently was disguising his intent with a dissembling caution, as he did with others close to him. Horace Greeley, editor of the *New York Tribune*, demanded immediate action in an August 20, 1862, editorial titled "The Prayer of Twenty Millions." Two days later, Lincoln responded, "My paramount object in this struggle *is* to save the Union, and *not* either to save or destroy slavery."[6]

Swett stopped again in New York on his way back from Maine and returned to Washington on August 24 to see General Montgomery C. Meigs, the quartermaster general. In all probability, their discussion centered on patronage appointments David Davis had requested.[7] Swett then visited Lincoln again at about eight o'clock on the morning of August 26, arriving at the White House before breakfast.[8] He made his way down the corridor on the second floor, where he found Lincoln waiting for him.

"Come in here, Swett," the president said. "I want to talk to you and to hear your notions about some matters." Lincoln led him into the cabinet room, where they pulled their chairs close to a little cabinet with drawers. Swett sat in silence, wondering what Lincoln might want to tell him.[9]

Opening a drawer, Lincoln took out a letter from William Lloyd Garrison, a leading abolitionist and the founder of an antislavery newsletter called the *Liberator*. Lincoln read aloud Garrison's eloquent and passionate appeal for immediate emancipation of the slaves. Garrison described the devotion and loyalty of the North to the Union but advised that the president needed to take some step to cut out the roots of slavery to avoid disappointing the North's expectations. He believed the institution of slavery to be "the moral wrong that lay at the bottom of the war, and insisted that the war could not, in the nature of things, be ended until the wrong was at an end."[10]

Without any comment, Lincoln laid down this letter and brought out another, this one from Kentucky senator Garret Davis, a Constitutional Union Party supporter of slavery. Davis addressed the issue of emancipation from the point of view of a border state, underscoring the balance that existed in these states between the North and the South. The people in the border states had grown used to slavery, he said, and their prosperity depended on it. Therefore, emancipation, especially without some compensation, would affect their financial welfare and be regarded as a change in the North's original basis for the war. Davis called emancipation an "irretrievable mistake" and implored Lincoln not to allow abolitionist sentiment to influence him.[11]

Next, Lincoln brought out several letters from the prickly managing editor of the *New York Tribune*, Charles Dana. These letters, in essence, accused the president and his administration of "doing nothing and letting the country go to the dogs." "Now, that represents one class of sentiment," Lincoln commented.[12]

Lincoln then proceeded to read aloud a lengthy and well-written piece by former Indiana congressman Robert Dale Owen, who had written letters on emancipation to Lincoln and two other cabinet members. When he had finished reading, he said to Swett, "That is a very able paper indeed. He makes a very strong argument. I have written something on this subject myself. But it is not so able an argument as this."[13]

The final letter Lincoln shared with Swett came from the Swiss diplomat Agénor Étienne de Gasparin, who sympathized with the North but warned Lincoln that England and France favored the Confederacy and possibly were searching for a pretext on which to intervene in the war in the United States. Gasparin advised Lincoln that in his opinion, emancipation could lead to such intervention. As Europeans regarded interference with the South's ownership of slaves as an improper means to an end, Gasparin cautioned, an emancipation proclamation would be viewed as inciting insurrection by the slaves, a pretext for forcible foreign intervention.[14]

After reading from these letters and papers, Lincoln made no inquiry of Swett but instead began debating with himself the pros and cons of emancipation. For over an hour, he held forth on all matters related to emancipation, including the various issues and arguments the letters raised, taking first one side and then the other. "It was an instance of stating conclusions aloud," said Swett, "not that they might convince another, or to be combated by him, but that the speaker might see for himself how they looked when taken out of the region of mere reflection and embodied in words." Swett felt that he was "a witness of the President's mental operations. . . . The president was simply framing his thoughts in words, under the eye of his friend, that he might clear his own mind." Lincoln was weighing and evaluating the various points of view for his own enlightenment in a colleague's presence, using Swett as a sounding board. It was a soliloquy in front of an audience of one on a subject of monumental importance. The one-sided conversation in the cabinet room continued until it was time for the cabinet meeting. "I had intended to have shown you something else," Lincoln said; "but it has got so late I haven't time now." Swett departed as the members of the cabinet came in for the meeting.

That evening, Swett thought over Lincoln's words and reflected on one comment in particular: "I have written something on this subject myself. But it is not so able an argument as" Robert Dale Owen's. It occurred to him that Lincoln was implying that he had already written a draft of an emancipation proclamation. The next morning, before leaving Washington for home, Swett saw Lincoln again at the White House and alluded to his conjecture.

"Am I doing anything wrong?" Lincoln asked, adding a significant smile. "No, I can't say that you are," Swett replied.[15]

This occasion gives a glimpse into Lincoln's decision-making process—how he gathered information and thoughts, considered opposing views, balanced them against one another, and then tested his own version aloud as an argument in the company of a trusted friend. He asked for no opinion from Swett other than the nod of approval the next morning. Swett wrote later about Lincoln's self-reliance: "From the commencement of his life to its close, I have sometimes doubted whether he ever asked anybody's advice about anything . . . he rarely, if ever, asked for opinions. I never knew him in a case to ask the advice of any lawyer he was associated with. As a politician and as President, he arrived at all his conclusions from his own reflections, and when his opinion was once formed, he never doubted but what it was right."[16]

This meeting with Swett was another indication that Lincoln had been debating the proclamation and committed it to paper by late August 1862. The Preliminary Proclamation came less than a month later, and the final version was signed on January 1, 1863. As a friend, Swett had to accept that Lincoln would reveal only enough "of his plans and purposes to induce the belief that he had communicated all, yet he reserved enough to have communicated nothing."[17] This accounts for Swett's having written to Laura before he returned to Washington from New York that Lincoln did not intend to emancipate the slaves or use African American troops. During this interval, a committee of clergymen from Chicago also visited Lincoln, urging him to issue an emancipation proclamation. In response, Lincoln took an adversarial position, arguing, "If you call a sheep's tail a leg, how many legs will it have?" The natural answer was five. "No," said he. "Because calling the tail a leg will not make it a leg."[18] However, at the very time the Chicago clergymen and Swett visited Lincoln, he had a rough draft of the proclamation in his table drawer, which he had read to the cabinet more than a month before.

But Lincoln was waiting for a more opportune time to announce his decision to issue the proclamation, and the first clear Union victory in the east at Antietam afforded that opportunity. He issued the Preliminary Emancipation Proclamation on September 22, 1862. Emancipation dominated the political arena for the rest of the war, and it took a century longer just to remove the legal obstacles to fully effect it.

Shortly after Swett returned to Bloomington in early September 1862, he learned that Lieutenant Colonel Harvey Hogg, a friend and Lincoln supporter, had recently died in a battle at Bolivar near his native home in western Tennessee. Felled by eight balls in a saber charge against a superior Confederate force on August 30, Hogg was buried in Bloomington on his twenty-ninth birthday. In a letter two weeks after the funeral, Swett warned Colonel Orme, who was leading the Ninety-Fourth Illinois Infantry Regiment in Missouri, "Take care of yourself. Don't be reckless as I fear poor Hogg was."[19]

The day after Hogg was killed, John Todd Stuart, Lincoln's first law partner and Mary Todd Lincoln's first cousin, announced his candidacy for Congress in a new seven-county district. Stuart, an old-line Whig turned War Democrat, tried not to take a public position on the Emancipation Proclamation, but he actually opposed it as unconstitutional. Shelby Cullom, the Speaker of the Illinois House of Representatives in 1860, had laid out the district in anticipation that he himself would run. However, Cullom yielded the nomination to Swett, because Swett was his senior by four years and had done more in support of the Republican Party.

The district suited Cullom better than Swett, however. Both Cullom and Stuart were from Springfield, the seat of Sangamon County, and Sangamon had a larger population than McLean County, which included Bloomington. Earlier in the year, William Orme, serving as a member of the state constitutional commission, had arranged for a new district of eight counties in Illinois, primarily those east of McLean County. His proposed district happened to be more solidly Republican than the one arranged by Cullom. Unfortunately for Swett, the Orme-designed district went down to defeat with the proposed 1862 constitution.[20]

At the Republican Convention in Springfield on September 24, 1862, Swett became the unanimous nominee for the Eighth District congressional candidate. He had aspired to political office for more than a decade, and now many significant figures encouraged him to run. This time he had the support of many leaders in the Republican Party, including Lincoln and Davis. By now Lincoln had announced his Preliminary Emancipation Proclamation and a presidential proclamation suspending the writ of habeas corpus, subjecting those resisting the draft and aiding the rebellion to martial law. These measures, in addition to the disappointing military campaign, changed the nature of the political arguments. Voters feared the movement of contraband African Americans into central Illinois, and by late in the canvass, this issue seriously threatened the prospects for Swett, who had lost little time in declaring his full support for emancipation. The affable and politically experienced Stuart, on the other hand, avoided issues and controversy and effectively gained the Democratic endorsement. Swett lost the support of Republican adherents in heavily Democratic areas, especially in Sangamon, Tazewell, and DeWitt Counties.

Swett challenged Stuart to a series of debates early in the canvass, as publicized in the *Illinois State Journal* and the *Pantagraph*. Stuart dodged the challenge, however, and claimed that because Lincoln had "declared martial law in force," Swett's public arguments might be construed to make him "guilty of 'disloyal practice, or as offering aid and comfort to the rebels.'" Stuart goaded Swett: "You are young as compared with myself [Swett was thirty-seven, Stuart fifty-five], and excitable in debate . . . and some unguarded word or sentence . . . might expose you to be court-martialed in a 'fort or prison' without benefit of the writ of *habeas corpus*." In an effort to make his preposterous argument sound more reasonable, he added, "I feel, therefore, inclined for the present to postpone the further consideration of your proposition."[21] Clearly, Stuart had in mind Swett's elegant speaking ability and Lincoln's success in speeches during the Lincoln-Douglas debates from four years earlier and sought to avoid squaring off against him.

Once his adversary chose not to engage in open debate or discussion, Swett had little recourse. He published their exchange of correspondence, closing his rebuttal with this statement: "If I were not thoroughly and entirely for the Government, and thoroughly and entirely against the rebellion, I would do as he does. As it is I leave him to the safety of silence. . . . The door is still open for discussion." The Republican *Illinois State Journal* printed a long editorial on the subject on October 2, ending with two questions: "Who has had any doubts about the position of Leonard Swett? Who has been able to define Mr. Stuart's position?"[22]

Swett visited each of the seven counties two to six times between late September and Election Day, November 4. Whereas Swett wholeheartedly endorsed the Emancipation Proclamation and the war, Stuart stayed close to "the Constitution as it is and the Union as it was," believing that once the rebellion ended, the South should rejoin with slavery intact. He broke his refusal to debate on one occasion in Logan County, but he committed only to being "for the Union, Constitution, and enforcement of the laws."

According to the *Chicago Tribune*, when Swett pressed him, he "refused to endorse the democratic platform, and also the President's recent acts for vigorous measures." This posture worked for Stuart, however, especially when the movement of African Americans into central Illinois raised local residents' fears of worker competition. Secretary of War Stanton ordered this movement stopped on October 14, but it was too late to quell the alarm among voters. In response to questions about "bringing Contrabands to this State," Swett answered that he opposed their introduction into the local workforce because he viewed the restoration of the government as the purpose of the war.[23] Swett's response reflected the widely held view of many Northerners, particularly those in the West, who were concerned about the consequences of large numbers of freed slaves migrating into their areas following the success of the armies. Like Swett, many supporters of emancipation held inconsistent views with regard to what might follow.

Stuart avoided public appearances, despite his ability as a speaker, and instead did much pamphleteering. Stuart's strategy of inactivity seemed to be working, and some of Swett's friends quietly expressed the possibility of his defeat during the campaign. Orme wrote to Davis on October 19, "I very much fear that Swett will be beaten. . . . If defeated now it would be a severe blow to him—one from which he could scarcely recover." Davis responded to Orme the following day, "I would not have Swett beaten for a good farm. He is the most unselfish politician living and he has been so unlucky."[24]

With the Democratic threat showing its intensity, Swett redoubled his efforts, and in the closing days, he and his friends published and distributed information to counter his opponent. According to Davis, they spent an estimated fifteen hundred dollars on the effort, of which Swett's New York friend Thurlow Weed paid two-thirds. Thirteen days before the election, Weed offered more support, stating, "If there is any doubt about your District please draw on me for one thousand dollars at Astor House." Swett replied five days later: "Hard pressed. . . . I cannot tell you how indispensable it is to me. I shall succeed."[25] The election cost Swett hundreds of dollars in forgone practice fees and travel expenses.

The flavor of the campaign stayed the same from beginning to end. Stuart did not vary from his basic posture established in his opening public announcement letter: "When . . . the people of the South make the effort, by force to free themselves from the obligations which they owe under the constitution to the Union, they become rebels and traitors, seeking by revolution to destroy the Union, and it is the right, and becomes the duty of the general government, to put down that rebellion and slay that revolution by the use for that purpose, of all its constitutional powers. Were it to resort to any other powers, or to means *outside* of the constitution, the government would itself inaugurate a revolution. The southern revolution threatens us with anarchy; such a revolution, by the government, would lead to a military despotism."[26]

This position might have been plausible enough were it not for the pragmatic realities of holding a nation together. On the weekend before the election, the *Pantagraph* republished a response from the *Clinton Public*: "While such Democrats as McClernand and Logan have gone into the army, and Ingersoll and others have by their eloquence done good service in battling the enemies of our glorious Republic, Mr. Stuart has been sitting mutely at home, watching the chances for office, but offering no assistance to the government, making no effort to suppress the rebellion, proffering no counsel, giving no advice, venturing no remonstrance against southern sympathizers, and hurling no censures against the open traitors."[27]

On Halloween night, several men made speeches in Bloomington to bolster Republican support, but these came too late in the campaign to have much effect. William Gannaway "Parson" Brownlow, a newspaper publisher from Knoxville, Tennessee, a Methodist minister, and a Union supporter, spoke first "to an immense concourse of people assembled in the Court House yard." William "Deacon" Bross, a leading Presbyterian and editor and part owner of the *Chicago Tribune*, joined him on the stage that evening at Phoenix Hall, four days before the election. Both speakers were well received, but they did not sway many voters. Writing to Lincoln on October 30 to accept his Supreme Court appointment, Davis included this postscript: "I fear the result of the election in this state—Contest in this district: very doubtful—Swett is working as hard as mortal man ever did work to accomplish his object. My greatest fear is of Sangamon County."[28]

In the closing days before the election, Swett and his supporters maintained a rising optimism. They agreed that it would be close but that Swett would win, with David Davis predicting he would have only about a hundred-vote lead. Although Laura Swett had been suffering from an illness during a significant part of the campaign, she had assumed the responsibility for writing to Orme and sending him newspaper clippings while her husband remained absorbed in the race. Now she added her own burst of confidence in a letter to Orme penned at ten o'clock the night before the election. "I have just returned from the last political meeting of the canvass," she wrote. "I am all enthusiasm—I think Mr. Swett made a glorious speech, if I do say it. I have been so long debarred, by various circumstances, from going out and mingling with people, & listening to things of this kind, that it may affect me unduly, but I feel that I have enjoyed a rich treat, & that nobody in the world would be more gratified to know of Mr. Swett's success than yourself. . . . I am exceedingly gratified tonight. Tomorrow will tell the story."[29]

The margins for the Democratic counties wound up being more than twice what Swett's supporters had anticipated, however. Only McLean County produced the expected margin for Swett. Livingston and Logan Counties also went for Swett, but Sangamon, Woodford, Tazewell, and DeWitt Counties leaned toward Stuart. In the end, Swett lost to Stuart by 1,365 votes, a 5.6 percent margin, decisive but not overwhelming.

For Swett, several factors affected the outcome of the election. First, the war had not been going well for the Union forces, despite the strategic victory at Antietam, and it exacted a political price on the Republican Party as the chief architect of the war.[30] Second, many people felt more than minor discomfort about the Emancipation Proclamation. In addition to the massive social changes it portended, they questioned the legality of the president's authority to take such action. Third, the great number of men away at war and therefore absent from the polls likely contributed to Swett's loss in the Eighth Congressional District, as a large proportion of troops sympathized with the Republican position, although no reasonably accurate estimate is available of its impact on the voting.[31] Finally, cultural backgrounds and attitudes affected voting patterns in much broader areas of the old Northwest and Illinois and influenced voters adapting to extensive national changes. The district reflected these cultural characteristics in ways peculiar to central Illinois and its people.

Republican-backed candidates faced similar losses in all districts south of the northern third of Illinois in 1862. The "at-large" candidate, Ebon C. Ingersoll, also lost.[32] Owen Lovejoy narrowly won in the district including Peoria County, the southernmost Republican success that year. In all, nine of the state's fourteen congressional seats went to Democrats. Culturally and politically in transition, central Illinois received many migrants from both Northern and Southern states, while the northern and southern thirds distinctly represented one or the other. This was why Lincoln had focused his 1858 senate campaign against Douglas in central Illinois, where legislative votes could be gained or lost.

Swett was stunned and felt crushed, but Laura wrote that he accepted the verdict "more philosophically than I feared." Within three days, however, she reported that he was "now feeling—suffering from, the effects of his severe canvass. Defeat of course adds to the severity, since the heart of hope goes far in giving strength and vigor physically. It is terrible to be thus crushed down—thrust back."[33] He had pinned his hopes and ambitions on a political career for more than a decade, beginning with his first canvass as a Winfield Scott presidential elector in 1852. After striving for so long, his defeat now felt especially distressing and depressing. His party had thwarted his nomination attempts twice, for Congress in 1856 and governor in 1860, either of which likely would have resulted in victory in the polls. This time, however, the voters delivered the defeat. As Lincoln's political stature rose, Swett reveled in the participation and worked hard to help ensure his friend's success. But all of his efforts on his own behalf had failed. Now, after this bitter defeat, the thirty-seven-year-old Swett apparently made fundamental changes in his goals and aspirations. He never ran for public office again.

In the wake of this loss, Swett also began to feel overwhelmed by the enormity of his debts and obligations. His friends and acquaintances were keenly aware of his financial woes, but they did not criticize or blame him for his accumulated debts. Davis looked for work for Swett in Washington, feeling that Swett probably wanted to escape the reminders of his failure on his home turf. He later wrote to Laura about Swett's unselfishness, explaining that if her husband had worked for himself rather than others, he would be free of debts.[34]

Colonel Orme, who received news of the outcome via telegraph, wrote to his partner from his post in Missouri several days later with advice to "keep cool." He encouraged Swett: "There is something in the future for you, but what it is I can't now foretell. . . . Engage in your profession & let politics go to the devil or elsewhere, and you will be a much wiser, wealthier and happier man." A week and a half later, Orme wrote a long letter to Laura mentioning his own promotion to brigade responsibility and providing more counsel for her husband: "Now tell him to quit chasing these political *ignis fatuuses* [*sic*]. If he will only settle down & quietly practice law he can make a fortune and a reputation which will do him more good than a temporary seat in congress. He must quit politics. Have him tend to business. He can make both yourself & himself thrice as happy and comfortable by doing so. I wouldn't take a seat in Congress if it were offered me as a gratuity."[35] Although Orme offered advice and support, he could not alleviate Swett's deep disappointment in the people of his district for their failure to elect him.

A few days after the election, Judge Davis left Bloomington for New York and Washington. Letters he wrote to Swett in late November and December extensively explored Swett's alternatives. On November 26, now at his wife's family home in Massachusetts, he wrote his friend a letter full of political information, including Lincoln's reaction to the Swett-Stuart contest: "He spoke of you affectionately and in high terms and spoke of your defeat in a way that satisfied me that he regretted it more than the defeat of any other person in the State. He said that Stuart, he was afraid, w[oul]d get more votes than any other person in Sangamon & Tazewell." He added, "Governor Seward actually spoke of you in high terms & regretted exceedingly your defeat & wished that some thing was open for you, worthy of your acceptance."[36]

Two more letters from Davis followed in the first half of December with other ideas for Swett. Davis had met with Treasury Secretary Chase about giving Swett some cotton-trading privileges, but this possibility went no further. Lamon had suggested that Swett could make money in Washington as a claims agent, Davis said, but "it is not a very high toned employment." However, "if money is the object with you alone, it is worthy of consideration." He added, "I cannot see what Mr. Lincoln could give you that would be worth your acceptance."[37]

During this same period, Davis also wrote to Orme about Swett's possibilities: "Hill Lamon thinks that Swett had better come here, & practice law, & attend to the investigation of claims, & give up politics—He thinks he could make a fortune—There may be money in it—but he lowers his crest by doing so—What do you advise—Swett wants money terribly, & I doubt, hereafter, about his ever being able to enjoy himself in Bloomington—There is literally no chance for him in politics in Illinois, & besides he is too poor to be spending his life that way—There is no place that he can get, that is worth his acceptance—The plan of Hill's strikes me favorably, if money is the object *alone*."[38]

David Davis also exchanged correspondences with Laura Swett about her husband's situation. On December 10, Laura wrote to Davis, "Pardon me if my note seems presuming. I wish to add a word of my own heart-felt gratitude for your interest in my husband. Ever be a true friend to him. I have not been a wise wife to him, a loving one my soul testifies. When he is alone, be true to him. You know his nobleness of heart, but not as I do." Davis replied, "And now, my Dear matron a word about y[ou]r dear husband—I have loved him for years. I have ever found him to be noble disinterested, unselfish of high purposes great intellectual capacity & with qualities to attach friends to him such as few men ever had. . . . If he had devoted himself to his own interests as he has to the interests of others, he would have been this day independent of the world. . . . Be assured that I shall never desert him, & that my advice & counsel will be as *true* as if given to a brother. . . . My own impulses are warm, & my friendships strong."[39]

Just before Christmas, Davis wrote to Swett about the disaster at Fredericksburg on December 13 and the subsequent cabinet crisis, including the news that Secretary of the Interior Caleb Smith was leaving the cabinet. Davis believed that Smith's assistant, John P. Usher, would succeed him. "These Indianians seem to have the inside track of everybody," he wrote.[40] Swett's friends made efforts to persuade Lincoln to appoint him to the position. J. W. Parish and W. F. Schaffer sent a telegram to Lincoln from New York on December 27 stating, "At a meeting of the citizens of Illinois in New York this morning at the Metropolitan Hotel . . . It was unanimously resolved that this meeting earnestly urge you to appoint Hon Leonard Swett of Ill's Secy of the Interior."[41]

But again nothing happened for Swett. In January, Davis wrote to him, "Your name is mentioned here for assistant Secy of Interior—I *scorned* the thing I w[oul]d rather practice law in Ill. at 1500 a year. If the administration cannot offer anything better, so be it."[42] Usher had been named to the position of secretary two weeks earlier.

In addition to trying to find a place for Swett, his circle of friends experienced a number of traumatic events in the months surrounding Swett's November election loss. These tragedies did not reduce the impact of the loss for Swett, but they diverted his attention for a time. In late November, Swett traveled to Louisville, Kentucky, on a business matter involving a railroad contractor, taking with him an attorney friend, Lawrence Weldon from Clinton. Along the way, they stopped in Decatur to see another of Swett's friends, General Richard Oglesby. The general had been seriously wounded at the battle of Corinth, Mississippi, on October 3. Illinois newspapers stated in their October 8 and 9 editions that he "died of his wounds." Two or three days later, however, they reported that he was "not dead." Oglesby suffered a protracted and complicated recovery. On January 9, 1863, he gave a rousing speech in the State Capitol in Springfield encouraging trust for the people, who "may be misled and discouraged for a time, but they will always come out right," obviously referring to the October and November election results. Shortly afterward, Oglesby received confirmation of his promotion to major general and acknowledged Swett, Davis, and Lamon for their support.[43]

The Orme family endured several tragic losses during this period. The Swett and Orme families had become intertwined through the two men's affiliation as law partners and friends. All three of William Orme's brothers, Charles, Frank, and Joseph, lived in or visited Bloomington for a time. The youngest, Joseph, became affiliated with the law firm before he joined the Ninety-Fourth Infantry, the "McLean County Regiment," commanded by his brother. No records exist of Frank's military service, but he lived in Washington, D.C., and may have visited the Bull Run battlefield soon after the second battle on August 29–30, 1862. In late September, Swett informed his partner that the Confederates had captured Frank at Bull Run, took him to a prison in Richmond, and then released him.[44]

William Orme was married to Nannie McCullough, the eldest daughter of William McCullough, the McLean County circuit court clerk. Elected and reelected to the post four times, her father knew Swett, Lincoln, Davis, and Lamon well. In 1861, McCullough had joined Colonel T. Lyle Dickey's Fourth Cavalry Regiment with ninety-two other men from his county, receiving the rank of lieutenant colonel at age forty-nine. He had limited vision in one eye and had lost an arm in a threshing accident as a child. Although he could ride with one arm, fighting from atop his horse was another matter, but he was undeterred in his courage.[45]

On December 5, 1862, the fearless McCullough went on a night scouting mission near Oxford, Mississippi. Discovered by enemy forces, he waved his saber, upraised with his only arm, while he held the reins to his horse in his teeth. The Confederates shot him when he refused to surrender. Swett received notification of McCullough's death by telegram from Colonel Dickey three days later. He and Laura immediately spoke with Nannie, and the three together broke the news to McCullough's wife and younger daughter, Fanny. Fanny grew so agitated and inconsolable that Swett sent for a doctor. Shortly after seeing the doctor, she locked herself in her room and would not emerge for hours, until a friend finally persuaded her to open the door. Fanny was considered as a beloved member of both the Swett and Orme families, and over the next few days, Leonard and Laura Swett called on her regularly.[46]

Judge Davis told Swett that he would write to Fanny and also that Lincoln "had a warm attachment to McCullough & feels his loss keenly." On December 10, Laura wrote to Davis describing Fanny's state and imploring him to write words of encouragement to her. When he received Laura's letter, Davis was deeply touched and replied at some length, showing his affection and concern for Fanny. He also said that he would urge Lincoln to write to her.[47]

At the White House, Lincoln met the most serious challenge to his presidential leadership to date when he refused to accept the resignations of his secretaries of state and the treasury over a contentious disagreement that spilled into the Congress. Two days later, on December 22, he sent his congratulations and condolences to bolster and assuage the confidence of the Army of the Potomac, which had endured heavy casualties and defeat at the battle of Fredericksburg. The next day, Lincoln wrote a letter of consolation to Fanny, empathizing with her feelings of anguish and misery, and offering sage advice on the process of grief. "In this sad world of ours," he wrote, "sorrow comes to all. . . . You can not now realize that you will ever feel better. . . . And yet it is a mistake. You are sure to be happy again. To know this, which is certainly true, will make you some less miserable now."[48]

Unfortunately, Fanny soon faced another tragic loss less than a month after her father's death. She and Captain Joseph Orme had become close, and on December 31, the accidental discharge of a soldier's rifle killed Joseph as his company trudged back toward their base in southern Missouri from Prairie Grove, Arkansas.[49]

Two days after McCullough was killed, on December 7, 1862, Colonel William Orme led his brigade in an engagement at Prairie Grove. After a long march for three and a half days, they arrived just in time to prevent a Union defeat. This Orme brother had his own close brush with death when a cannonball nearly hit him, but it only blew him off his horse. Later that month, General Francis J. Herron wrote to Swett of William Orme's heroism and survival, prompting Swett and Davis to press Lincoln for Orme's promotion to brigadier general.[50]

As the events played out on the blood-sodden battlefields, more American families than ever before faced the reality of having loved ones involved in war. The extent of suffering and death grew ever more shocking as the deadliest war on American soil exacted a grim toll. Freedom versus slavery, fairness versus patronage, effort versus reward, benevolence versus greed, winning versus losing, life versus death—all of these struggles pressed upon Swett as he sought to reconcile his unrequited quest for recognition in the midst of the war.

I have entire confidence in [Swett's] Sagacity and prudence, and would leave the affair to him under the instructions.

—*Usher to Lincoln, 1863*

8. Quicksilver and New Almaden

At the beginning of 1863, William Orme went to Bloomington on leave to fulfill his increased family responsibilities after the death of his father-in-law, William McCullough. By the end of January, however, he decided to return to the military. Intent on getting Orme promoted to brigadier general, Swett made a fifth trip to Washington, arriving on February 17, 1863. As with his previous trips, he traveled at his own expense, sacrificing earnings and time at home. He and Davis approached President Lincoln about Orme more than once. After Lincoln agreed to the promotion, Davis took pains to make sure Orme's name was on the appropriate list for approval by the House of Representatives. But the House postponed action on this matter, so Swett remained in Washington to make sure that the promotion went through.[1]

Swett described his reactions to Washington on this visit in his letters home. He found the hotel to be crowded: "Often a seat to sit in cannot be had. It is a vast sea of strangers." One of those in the crowd that he met and visited with was William M. Evarts, who was "stately, scholarly, formal, a model."[2] Swett obtained a picture of Lincoln's son Tad from the president's valet and sent it to Bertie, commenting that Tad "is nine years old but he cannot talk plain." While he waited in Washington, Swett argued a patent claim, perhaps testing the waters of claims work in the capital as Lamon had suggested in December.[3]

During this visit to Washington, Lincoln confided in Swett about the recent court-martial trial of General Fitz John Porter, related to a military leadership controversy involving Generals Porter, John Pope, and George McClellan following the second battle of Bull Run on August 29–30, 1862. The court-martial addressed whether Porter had failed to follow orders to assist Pope, causing the Union army an embarrassing defeat. Lincoln received the record from the forty-five-day trial.

Swett recalled "standing in [Lincoln's] room in the White House, near the foot of the long table behind which he sat . . . when he called my attention to a large record lying near us on the table.

"'That,' said he, 'is the record in the Fitz John Porter case.' The trial had then just closed, and the record of the evidence taken in it was, as I understood, before him for action.

"'You know,' said he, 'If I know anything it is what evidence tends to prove and when a thing is proven. I have read every word in that record, and *I tell you Fitz John Porter is guilty and ought to be shot.*'

"He then added something the words of which I cannot remember, but the substance was: 'He was willing the poor soldiers should die while he from sheer jealousy stood within hearing of the guns waiting for Pope to be whipped.'"

The court-martial trial reached the same conclusion, but although the rules of war obligated Lincoln to uphold the death penalty for Porter, instead he ordered the general's cashiering and dismissal from the army and "forever disqualified" him from U.S. government service. This action demonstrated either Lincoln's application of his objection to capital punishment or his concern about the impact of such an order on other Union officers in the Army of the Potomac, as it might benefit the Confederacy in this time of crisis if other Union officers were to retaliate with reprisals.[4]

Over the winter, Davis had been trying yet again to get his friend an appointment. He wrote to Orme, "I mentioned to the President twice this winter that he ought to give Mr. Swett the first foreign appointment that was vacant but no word in reply." The suggestion may have had more effect than Judge Davis realized at the time. Sometime after Swett's arrival, Lincoln approached him about taking the position of special envoy or commissioner for the settlement of claims against Peru and Chile. These claims dated back to 1821 for the seizure of a cargo of silver from a privately owned U.S. brig, a vessel with two square-rigged masts. Lincoln sent a draft of Swett's appointment to the Senate in early March 1863, and the *Pantagraph* announced on March 9 that Lincoln had appointed Swett to be a commissioner to Peru.[5]

Within ten days, however, Swett declined the Peru commission for the stronger smell of money. After a U.S. Supreme Court decision that set the wheels in motion, Lincoln appointed Swett the emissary for the U.S. government to take possession of the New Almaden quicksilver mine in northern California. Swett considered this appointment the opportunity he had been hoping for, providing travel to a healthy climate and the prospect of financial fortune.

The New Almaden mine was in the Santa Cruz Mountains twelve miles west of San Jose, in Santa Clara County. It was the oldest mine in California, and since 1845, miners had been extracting from it large amounts of red sulfide mercury ore, called cinnabar, which was used in reducing gold from the California gold rush of 1849 and silver in Nevada after 1859. At the time of Swett's involvement, mercury, or quicksilver, was growing in demand as an essential ingredient for making percussion caps for use in battle.[6]

Litigation involving this mine and its competing ownership interests started in 1852 and continued for the next twelve years, until U.S. Supreme Court decisions in 1863 and 1864 finally brought the matter to a conclusion. Competing claims for title to the mine, based on both mining rights and landownership, were a problem from the earliest days of mining there in 1845, even before Mexico ceded the territories of Alta (Upper) California and New Mexico to the United States as part of the treaty ending the Mexican-American War in 1848.[7] Thanks to gold rush fever, by 1858, $7 million worth of mercury had been extracted and sold. That same year, U.S. attorney general Jeremiah Black sent the lawyer Edwin Stanton to California to clarify the mine and land titles. The U.S. District Court in San Francisco enjoined the New Almaden Company, owned by a British firm, Barron, Forbes and Company of Tepic, Mexico, from mining for more than two years while it decided on the validity of the company's mining title, called the Castillero claim. The District Court reached a decision that upheld the New Almaden Company's Mexican mining claim, derived from Spanish and Mexican law enabling miners to stake out a claim to a mineral deposit on land owned by another and used for agricultural purposes, so long as the miner reimbursed the landowner for fair value of the agricultural land.[8]

The District Court decision related only to the validity of the mining claim under Mexican law and left two other claims for title based on ownership of the land subject to review. In addition to holding the Castillero mining claim, the New Almaden Company also held another land claim called the Berreyesa claim, and significantly, it was in possession of the mine under dispute. The Quicksilver Mining Company of Philadelphia and New York had acquired yet another land claim for the same mine, called the Fossat claim, setting up a three-way contest over ownership of the land among the two competing companies and the U.S. government, which also became embroiled in the dispute.

The U.S. Supreme Court, including David Davis, heard arguments on the Castillero mining claim in December 1862. The court issued its decision on March 10, 1863, reversing the District Court decision and rejecting the New Almaden Company's Castillero mining claim. This decision left the competing land claims pending before the Supreme Court to determine who owned the mine. At this point, two cabinet members, Attorney General Edward Bates and Secretary of the Interior John Usher, misinterpreted the Supreme Court's decision and assumed that because the mining claim was faulty, the mine therefore was on property belonging to the U.S. government. They thus set out to reclaim the mine for the United States. Bates drafted a writ based on an obscure law from 1807 involving possible military seizure, of questionable application for this purpose. This was the point on which the entire matter turned, yet no one involved reviewed its validity.

Although the Supreme Court arguments in the Castillero case dealt extensively with the allegations of fraud in the mineral claim and title, the final decision in 1863 did not address the fraud issues, because the court considered only the preliminary issue of the technical validity of the mining claim. The court would determine mine ownership based on the competing land claims. Some of the ensuing confusion may be attributed to the justice writing the opinion, Nathan Clifford. He disagreed with the majority of the court, believing that fraud had occurred, and his sentiment may have spilled over into the language he used in writing the opinion for the majority. But his incidental remarks expressed only his opinion and were not binding—an obiter dictum, in legal jargon. The court's majority opinion did not go that far, yet apparently four able attorneys—Bates, Usher, Lincoln, and Swett (if the last two read the opinion)—misinterpreted it as being a ruling of fraud.[9]

Bates sent his writ, signed by Lincoln on May 8, 1863, to the U.S. marshal for the Northern District of California, C. W. Rand, directing that the New Almaden quicksilver mine be delivered to the possession of Leonard Swett as the agent for the U.S. government. The writ mistakenly used the words "is or are fraudulent and void" to describe the Castillero mining claim.[10] These inflammatory terms did not accurately reflect the Supreme Court's decision, which was based only on the validity of the mining claim and made no finding of fraud. Bates also said that the assistance of military force was available as needed. The threat of military force in the takeover of the mine added a provocative element to the planned action. Other free miners questioned whether the U.S. government also purported to end their lucrative activities and require acknowledgment of government ownership of their mines.

Several days before Lincoln signed the writ, Secretary Usher sent S. W. Butterworth, the president of the Quicksilver Mining Company, an unofficial proposal for the company to lease and operate the New Almaden mine from the United States after its seizure. Usher referenced Quicksilver's pending land claim before the Supreme Court, the delicate nature of Swett's trust, and the fact that the Castillero decision did not establish "any precedent inimical to the mining interests of California." Quicksilver responded that it would accept the proposed contract. On May 18, Usher sent the writ signed by Lincoln to Swett, enclosing his May 6 letter to Butterworth and the proposed contract. To his credit, Usher interjected words of caution in his letters to Butterworth and Swett about the exercise of the writ, specifically advising Swett to avoid the inference of possible government interference and forcible dispossession with other mining interests.[11]

However, the seventy-year-old Edward Bates, with his experience, personality, and seniority, was the driving force in the effort to reclaim the mine.[12] John P. Usher, a forty-nine-year-old attorney from Indiana, had served in the cabinet as secretary of the interior for only four months after several months as assistant secretary. At the time, Lincoln's attention was focused on the drubbing of the Army of the Potomac at Fredericksburg and Chancellorsville, so he was relying on Bates and Usher to handle and report back to him on the mine claim issue. Although Lincoln devoted most of his time to the war, he consulted with them as needed.

Swett, now age thirty-seven, showed no hesitation in accepting the appointment to carry the writ to California for execution. Always hasty and impulsive when opportunity and travel beckoned, he was especially so with the added inducement of reward. His political goals were diminished, even extinguished, by this time, and now he faced the prospect of fortune. The day after the Supreme Court decision, he wrote to Laura about his speculation with others in the purchase of Quicksilver stock. He also made arrangements to serve as a lawyer for Quicksilver, which agreed to pay him ten thousand dollars "in any event," half up front, plus a "large conditional fee" if he were successful on the company's behalf. The conditions for the extra fee were not specified, however. Thus Swett headed west not only as an envoy of the government but also as a counsel to and investor in Quicksilver, New Almaden's competitor and legal opponent. Clearly, he had high expectations for this assignment.[13]

On May 23, the date of his departure from New York, Swett wrote to Orme and told him he had purchased life insurance policies in the amount of $15,500 to cover his debts and provide for his family in the event of his death. The insurance gives a sense of the scale of his debts, as Swett specified that it would provide his wife and son "a competence," possibly half the amount of the coverage. The remainder would cover his personal debts from his travels and living large on the road while engaged in politics.

Although he may have approached the venture with a foolhardy spirit, this time Swett chose to take along his family—Laura and the now four-and-a-half-year-old Bertie, as well as a nurse for the child. Laura was glad to accompany him, as it was a long way from home and she suffered during his frequent absences. Now she felt healthy enough to travel, and Swett's expectations soared. "I begin to believe my wife will get well," he wrote in a letter to Orme. When rough seas made many passengers ill, she did not succumb, instead assisting the sick and caring for another baby in order for the ailing mother to have some rest.[14]

The quickest and most efficient way to get to California at that time was by way of the isthmus of Panama. The Pacific Mail Steamship Company carried passengers and mail to and from Panama on the Atlantic-Caribbean and Pacific sides, and the Panama Railroad Company crossed the forty-seven-mile isthmus "ocean to ocean" in about three hours.[15] The Swett family started off their trip by train to New York City, from where they departed on May 23 on a steamship for San Francisco. On June 2, they arrived at Colón on the Caribbean coast, then called Aspinwall for the New York merchant founder of the steamship line. They departed the same day from Panama City. As they crept along the coast of Central America in their coal burner, the *Orizaba*, they admired the conical volcanoes rising to fourteen thousand feet in Guatemala. The heat grew oppressive near Acapulco, where they stopped for half a day. While the ship took on coal, some of the passengers including the Swetts disembarked to attend mass at the cathedral and lunch at the El Dorado Hotel in the town of three thousand. The longer Pacific part of the journey ended on schedule, with the passengers arriving in California on June 19, nearly a month after their departure. Swett and his family stayed for the next two and a half months at the Lick House in San Francisco, at the corner of Montgomery and Sutter Streets.[16]

Four days after Swett arrived in San Francisco, Bates, the prime mover in the New Almaden mine action, went home to Missouri for a visit, leaving the tentative and less confident Usher at the switch in Washington to make decisions on the mine issue. Whereas Bates was eager to claim the mine and additional mineral properties for the government by whatever means necessary, Usher remained cautious about the use of force. Swett appeared on the spot ready to act with force if necessary to seize the mine. Believing that he was acting under government mandate based on the Supreme Court decision, he felt that the use of force was appropriate.

If any of the three—Bates, Usher, or Swett—questioned the basis of the seizure, they did not express it. The idea that the people of California might react to a challenge to their new economic livelihood based on private mineral claims eluded all of Lincoln's lieutenants. A state gubernatorial contest loomed in which secession-minded Democrats planned to broaden the challenge to all mineral claims. The political fireworks started in the San Francisco Bay Area a few days after the Fourth of July. The wise legal minds of the East remained unaware, however, that an intense negative reaction awaited them in the West.

Soon after Swett arrived, he began discussions with Rand and the army. He arranged through the Pacific Army commander, General George Wright, to have a cavalry detachment moved from its quarters at Benicia, between Suisun and San Pablo Bays north of San Francisco, sixty miles south to San Jose, where they would camp. This began on July 8 by order of Wright's assistant adjutant general. On the same day, Frederick Low, collector of the port of San Francisco and Republican candidate for governor in the September 2 election, telegraphed his superior, Treasury Secretary Salmon Chase, warning him of the political dangers of military seizure. The next day, Chase forwarded the telegram to Lincoln.

Lincoln immediately consulted with Usher, who presented the president with copies of his earlier letters to Butterworth and Swett, adding, "You will observe that in the event of the possession of the mine being obtained by

Mr. Swett, he is authorized to lease the premises to the Quick Silver Mining Company. The present occupants have no color or right to the mine, known to me, and I presume that if any is shown to Mr. Swett that he will not undertake to have the writ executed. I have entire confidence in his Sagacity and prudence, and would leave the affair to him under the instructions."[17]

That same day, Lincoln telegraphed Swett and Low, "Consult together, and do not have a riot or great difficulty about delivering possession." Also that day, Swett and Rand delivered the writ to the mine operators and sought possession. The mine superintendent asked for time to consult with his superiors in San Francisco. The following day, he responded that the New Almaden Company found the warrant invalid, and that the company's officers and employees would resist any illegal trespass with force. Swett determined that at least a hundred soldiers would be needed to quell the resistance. While Swett considered his next move, Major General Halleck received two telegraph messages from California: one from General Wright, recommending deferral of any present action, and the other from the commander of the California Militia, emphasizing the severity of the potential reaction.[18]

The next day, July 10, Lincoln received another message from Low, again stressing the political reaction and asking for suspension of execution, with concurrence from General Wright and Judge Stephen J. Field, the California chief justice, whom Lincoln had already named to the U.S. Supreme Court. After receiving Lincoln's initial telegram, Swett and Low sent the cavalry back to the north.[19] Apparently Secretary of War Stanton and General Halleck, not knowing of the president's writ, ordered Wright to suspend operations to claim the mine by force of arms.

General Halleck added fuel to the fire in a reply to Wright on July 11, stating, "I am directed by the Secretary of War to say that he has no information of any military order to take possession of New Almaden Mine. If there be any such order, it has been *surreptitiously obtained*. You will obey no order of this kind that does not come through the proper military channels. If you have done anything in the matter, you will withdraw and restore everything to the condition in which you found them." Halleck further compounded the situation two days later by repeating the incorrect and, indeed, offensive wording to the counsel for the New Almaden Company, Frederick Billings.[20] This action made the confusion public in a controversial and provocative way.

Over the next few days, the telegraph lines between San Francisco and Washington buzzed with messages of inquiry, political warnings, exculpatory statements, factual explanations, and various appeals from the owner. When Swett obtained confirmation from General Wright that the writ had been countermanded, he quickly sent a wire to Usher on July 11. This message informed Lincoln for the first time that the military action had been aborted. Swett wrote, "Go and see the Pres[iden]t. There was no danger of riot in the execution of his writ without his dispatch I should within three hours have been in peaceable possession of the Property."[21]

Swett spent several days at the mine and returned to San Francisco on July 14. Not ready to acquiesce, he sent three telegraph messages the same day to Lincoln. In the first, he advised that he had learned from the owner and attorney at the mine that they would not have resisted the seizure, and that he could still take possession if given discretion by Lincoln. He recommended instead that the attorney general provide authority for him to obtain an injunction and receiver for the government and reported that the company had refused the same lease terms as proposed to Quicksilver. In the second message, he reiterated that the New Almaden Company would have yielded without force, but emboldened by the government's inaction, it now took the position that the mine was on government land by order of the court and that the United States should do nothing. Swett warned that this intentional attempt to undermine the rights of the government should not be tolerated and requested again that an injunction be authorized, followed by a lease contract for the U.S. government to capture some of the $1 million in annual profits from the mine. In his third telegram, Swett told Lincoln of Halleck's telegraph message to the counsel for the New Almaden Company the day before. The next day, Swett also wrote to Usher about Halleck's telegram and reported that it had "been published that the President's order had been surreptitiously obtained."[22]

That same day, July 15, Lincoln replied to Swett, "Many persons are telegraphing me from California begging me, for the peace of the State, to suspend the military enforcement of the writ of possession in the Almaden case, while you are the single one who urges the contrary. You know I would like to oblige you, but it seems to me my duty in this case is the other way."[23] As the fever pitch of concerns subsided with the cessation of troop movement, Lincoln undoubtedly received requests for a summary statement relative to the entire mining question in California. On

August 17, a little over two weeks before the gubernatorial election slated for September 2, Lincoln obliged, using his inimitable ability to structure a reply so that all sides could save face. At the same time, he supported the Republican candidate for governor, to whom his message was addressed. Lincoln explained that the order referred only to the New Almaden mine, with no applicability to any other mine or miners. He still harbored the belief that "the claim of the occupants was decided to be *utterly fraudulent*" and stressed that "the Attorney General carefully made out the writ and I signed it. It was not obtained surreptitiously, although I suppose General Halleck thought it had been."[24]

After Lincoln's reversal, Swett and Usher attempted to salvage through legal means some resolution of the mine ownership and operation. Between July 13 and the end of the month, Swett sent four telegrams to Usher and one to Lincoln regarding the protection of the government's position by obtaining a U.S. District Court injunction. In three replies, Usher supported this recommendation.[25] In the heat of the controversy, Usher urged Swett to make a public explanation. Swett wrote a thousand-word letter to the *San Francisco Evening Bulletin* on July 22. The editors immediately contacted the owners of the contested New Almaden Company claim, and their response, titled "Foiled Attempt to Steal a Mine," ran the next day in both the *San Francisco Daily Alta California* and the *Evening Bulletin.* The opposing efforts did not influence the situation significantly but illustrate the intensity of the polemics.[26]

Before the government officials had reached any conclusion, however, New Almaden and Quicksilver started to discuss an out-of-court resolution. As the two contending claimants were negotiating a settlement, a new policy thrust emerged in early August that gave the Land Commission and the courts time to decide the legal rights of the companies. Swett telegraphed Usher on August 5 to inform him that negotiations had started and ask for authority to treat all parties alike by compelling the party in possession to execute the lease contract for the government. He also reminded the attorney general and the Supreme Court to send the March 10, 1863, decision to the San Francisco District Court.[27] The Lincoln White House accommodated this change in direction.

While these negotiations were taking place, an interesting exchange occurred in a cabinet meeting on August 11. Bates wrote in his diary that he had just returned from a five-week absence and read the president a newspaper article about Halleck's offensive telegram, which Bates strongly denounced. He also wrote to Halleck about it that evening and received an evasive letter in reply. Welles, too, recorded the incident in his diary, describing Bates's and Usher's criticisms of Halleck's integrity and Lincoln's response that "Halleck had been hasty and indiscreet but he hoped nothing worse."[28]

Although the competing claimants on both sides deserved the lion's share of the credit for seeking to settle, Swett's request for government fairness to both parties demonstrated his respect for evenhandedness in a matter involving his own self-interest as well as the interests of Quicksilver as his client. Lincoln telegraphed Swett his approval on August 29, stating, "If the Government's rights are reserved the Government will be satisfied; at all events, it will consider."[29]

Initially, the government offered to allow the New Almaden Company to lease and operate the mine under the same terms Quicksilver had agreed to earlier. New Almaden refused. Quicksilver offered to pay the New Almaden Company $1.75 million for the properties while it also continued to pursue its own legal rights to the land. Once the parties had agreed on the terms of the settlement, Quicksilver leased the mine from the government. Why Quicksilver would agree to a payment of this size is not clear. One investigator reported that an 1861 California geological survey had placed the value of the entire claim at $1 million to $2 million, an amount that the New Almaden Company concurred with at the time.[30]

On September 2, 1863, Frederick F. Low won election as the Republican governor of California. His victory was commanding, as he received almost twenty thousand more votes (45 percent more) than his opponent. The Swett family departed California the next day and arrived in New York about a month later, at the beginning of October. Instead of going directly home to Bloomington, however, the entire family traveled to Washington, as Swett wished to clarify and explain his side of what had happened in California.

Swett later returned to Washington when arguments resurfaced on California mining properties in the Supreme Court on February 25, 1864. Attorney General Bates represented the United States, and three former attorneys general represented Quicksilver: Jeremiah Black, who had been the lead attorney for the U.S. government in the mining case before the Supreme Court in 1863, assisted by Caleb Cushing, who also had represented the government a year earlier, and Reverdy Johnson. The sole issue for determination was who owned the land on which the mine was located. Studies by the land commission showed that the land was owned by Quicksilver, and thus the government was not the owner. The case terminated abruptly on April 4. Justice Samuel Nelson wrote the majority opinion, which now included Justice Stephen Field from California. This time Justice Nathan Clifford, who had written for the majority in 1863, wrote a dissent. Bates was disconsolate, as reflected in his diary.[31]

The decision could only have been bittersweet for Quicksilver. It had taken on debt to pay $1.75 million to purchase a mine it had already bought some years earlier, but now the court ruled it had owned the land the whole time. Not only that, but Quicksilver had made lease payments for seven months to the federal government, and the lease terms precluded any claim for restitution from the government.

As the cabinet secretaries who had sponsored and drafted the writ, Bates and Usher bore chief responsibility for its design and execution. The mine situation contributed to Bates's resignation from the cabinet, which he submitted to Lincoln in the third week of October 1864, six months after losing the government's case in the Supreme Court. In a retrospective and illogical statement, Bates blamed Swett for failing to actually seize the mine. Usher's relationship with Lincoln was "broken up" by "the New Almaden affair."[32] Bates and Usher both made a scapegoat of Swett and did not admit that their own misinterpretation of the 1863 Supreme Court decision led them to send him on an impossible mission. But Swett had been unaware that the attorney general and secretary of the interior had misinterpreted the law underlying the order they used for his assignment. No one emerged from the episode in good shape except for the British owners of the New Almaden Company, which prospered from the sale of a mine it had not even legally owned.[33]

Swett's actions in the New Almaden affair revealed an element of ethical or moral deficiency in his character, as he sought to use an official mission as an opportunity to reap his own financial reward. Certainly, a brash and foolhardy side of him emerged. Quicksilver paid him ten thousand dollars for his efforts, but he never received the conditional fee. Although his professional conflict of interests was questionable, with Swett representing both the government and one of the mining companies, as well as investing in Quicksilver stock, it was not illegal at the time.[34]

Although brilliant in the courtroom and in his support of his friend Lincoln, Swett displayed little aptitude for business, throwing himself wholeheartedly into what turned out to be an embarrassing event, and even ending up being blamed for the incident. He did not expose the flawed interpretations of the Supreme Court decision, nor did he display cunning in failing to save Lincoln from possible embarrassment and what could have been a costly mistake. Lincoln himself averted a potential disaster with his own quick thinking. By a stroke of fate, Swett played the unfortunate role of Mercury, the messenger in Roman mythology and god of commerce, to a mercury mine in the distant American West, an irony that perhaps crossed his mind, given his background in classical studies.

Swett is unquestionably all right.
—Lincoln to Burton Cook via John Nicolay, June 6,
1864, at the Republican National Convention

9. This Terrible War

The New Almaden misadventure appears not to have affected Swett's relationship with Lincoln, despite the allegations by various critics. Soon after Swett and his family arrived in Washington, Lincoln invited them to join the presidential party on a special four-car train to Gettysburg for a ceremony dedicating the military cemetery there. The president's invitation list was not long—the cabinet, a few members of the diplomatic corps, the Marine Band, and fifteen to twenty others, including Lincoln's old law partner, Judge Stephen T. Logan of Springfield, who had helped him sharpen his writing and legal skills in the past. Also accompanying the group was the usual crowd of generals, admirals, politicians, and journalists who normally attended such occasions.[1]

Only three members of the cabinet chose to attend. Judge Logan's daughter accompanied her husband, Ward Hill Lamon, who was chairman of the event and would introduce the president as speaker. Lincoln and his friends and guests boarded the train on November 18, 1863, and arrived in Gettysburg later that day after an eighty-mile journey. The Swetts found their hotel, and Lincoln had the night to prepare for the ceremony.[2]

The next morning, while Swett was taking a walk, a man mistook him for President Lincoln. Swett smiled to himself as he shook the man's hand and greeted him, then sent him on his way without acknowledging the mistake, allowing the man to think he had just met the president. This incident illustrates how similar in appearance the two men were. Such mistakes more readily occurred in the days when political figures were depicted only in black-and-white print media such as newspapers and handbills.[3]

Lincoln used the battlefield dedication ceremony to share his hopes for the nation. He delivered a short speech laden with stylistic innovations he had been formulating and writing since 1838. Lincoln appeared as the secondary speaker to Edward Everett, a well-known Massachusetts politician and the major orator of the generation.[4] Everett's lengthy speech of more than thirteen thousand words endured for several hours, causing many in the audience of fifteen thousand to nearly miss the brief Lincoln speech that followed. In fact, initially Lamon and others thought it was a failure. It would take time to measure the value of Lincoln's succinct speech, 272 words that Americans eventually came to know as the Gettysburg Address.[5]

On December 15, Lincoln invited Swett to accompany him, along with his private secretaries, John G. Nicolay and John Hay, to see James Henry Hackett's performance of Falstaff in Shakespeare's *King Henry IV* at Ford's Theatre. Lincoln had seen the show the night before with his family and, much taken with Hackett's rendition of his character, wanted to see it again. He also graciously sent a letter to Hackett regarding his acting and interpretation. Always a target for favors, Lincoln was mildly embarrassed when his letter was published and Hackett asked for an appointment as consul to London.[6]

Earlier that fall, Swett had spoken with Lincoln about political maneuvering prior to the next election, advising him that his opponents considered him to be too conservative and might outstrip him by catering to the radical element. Swett "tried to induce him to recommend in his annual message a constitutional amendment abolishing slavery." Lincoln demurred: "Is not the question of emancipation doing well enough now?" Swett confirmed that it was. Lincoln added, "I have never done an official act with a view to promote my own personal aggrandizement, and I don't like to begin now. I can see that emancipation is coming; whoever can wait for it will see it; whoever stands in its way will be run over by it."[7]

Although unable to persuade Lincoln, Swett considered running for office once again and using this platform for himself. Before the end of 1863, Swett exchanged correspondences twice with Jesse Fell back in Bloomington regarding his interest in making another congressional run in 1864. Fell encouraged Swett to pursue the congressional seat again. Swett considered it, waxing and waning in enthusiasm over a period of about five months.

On February 18, 1864, he wrote to William Orme, "I have determined that if nominated I will make the race for Congress in our district. My platform will be the changing of the constitution in a legal manner—the insertion of a clause forever prohibiting slavery." Three weeks later, however, his mood apparently had changed, as he wrote to Orme on March 7, "I am entirely indifferent about Congress. Don't care anything about it. If nomination comes I will take it, if not shall be glad." Then on March 26, he wrote, "I consider myself thoroughly cured of any *desire* to go to *Congress*. . . . I don't want anybody to put themselves to any trouble and I don't intend to put myself to any trouble. . . . I have become pretty eager to accumulate a competency [modest wealth]. This seems much more desirable to me than debts and Congress."[8]

During the first half of 1864, Swett engaged in legal work related to the war. He visited the War Department several times regarding supply contracts for J. W. Parish & Co. of St. Louis and another firm. On at least one visit, Swett and Browning had a long but inconclusive visit with Assistant Secretary Charles A. Dana.[9] General Richard Oglesby and Swett conferred with Lincoln on the evening of March 29 concerning "the Claim of Ill[inoi]s. to the Two Per Cent Fund," pertaining to the revenues from the sale of federal land allocated to the states.[10] Swett thus sought to benefit from some of the work created by the war, as so many others had done since its inception.

It seems that Swett was consuming alcohol excessively at this time, perhaps at least in part to calm his anxieties over all the uncertainties in his life. On March 31, 1864, he and Lamon signed an agreement titled a "Pledge on Drinking." This curious document, handwritten by Judge Davis on Executive Mansion stationery, states, "We the undersigned pledge to each other our Honor that we will not drink for the period of one year any spirituous, vinous or malt liquors—with this proviso, that either of us at dinner has the privilege of drinking wine. Dinner is not to be understood as coming before noon. If anything is used at dinner, but wine, the pledge is violated. To the time observance of this pledge, we deposit it in the hands of Judge Davis of Illinois, & each of us places in the hands of said Davis, a bond of the United States for $500. If either violates this pledge, the said Davis is to give to the other the two bonds for $500 each. The said Davis is to determine all questions arising under this pledge." Another clause, likely added by Davis, tightened it with a moral obligation: "Each gentleman pledges his honor to the other that if he violates this pledge, he will inform Judge Davis of it."[11]

The existence of this signed document indicates that Swett and Lamon had a serious desire to curb their excessive drinking. It also shows the lawyers' sense of humor over the wager. That the pledge did not require total abstinence suggests that they agreed the problem did not require such radical intervention. It also did not impose limits on the amount of wine they could consume at dinner. The clause stating that dinner could not be construed as starting before noon might be considered humorous if not for the correlation between alcoholism and drinking in the morning and the serious tone of the remainder of the pledge. At the time of the pledge, Swett was thirty-eight. There is no record of either man having broken this pledge or of alcohol abuse on Swett's part later in his life, after Lincoln's assassination and the end of the war. Whatever the reasons for the pledge, five hundred dollars was a sizable sum at the time and can be taken as a measure of the seriousness of the issue in the lives of the two men.

Swett apparently had finally decided not to run when he wrote to Orme on May 18, "I don't wish to be considered a candidate for Congress." He began a second letter to Orme the same day with an even firmer statement: "Your note in relation Congress just came. Let the matter drop. I am determined to make no contest in the matter and have very little desire upon the subject. I consider the elections next fall to hang upon the campaign and while there is much to hope there are many things to fear in reference to it. I have been with the President just now." Swett revealed his personal situation to Orme as well: "The panic tore me terribly & I am trying to get over its effects. As soon as I can do this I want to come and eschew politics and settle down. I regard the life of a lawyer as much more respectable & happy than any other I can lead."[12]

Both May 18 letters also dealt extensively with the battlefield action in Virginia. Swett predicted that the war would be over by the end of the year and assessed that the success or failure of Republican candidates in the fall elections would mirror the military fortunes of the Union. Almost from the beginning of the spring 1864 encounters in the Wilderness, Lee's forces did not appear easy to conquer. Not until the late-summer successes of Farragut at Mobile on August 5, Sherman at Atlanta on September 1, and Sheridan in the Shenandoah Valley at Winchester on September 19 and Cedar Creek on October 19 did the tide appear to turn.

Another factor in Swett's decision not to run for Congress was his anticipation that gains from his speculation in Quicksilver stock were his way to financial "competency." The case for ownership of the land title to the New Almaden mine was still under consideration by the U.S. Supreme Court at this time, and Swett spoke with Jeremiah Black, counsel for Quicksilver, and considered himself an authority on Quicksilver. Swett's speculation in Quicksilver stock in 1863 had been modest and his losses manageable. By early 1864, however, he plunged more aggressively into investing. After losing fifty-five hundred dollars on short trading of Rock Island railroad stock, he turned to Thurlow Weed for help. Apparently undeterred by his losses, he jumped into the ring again in early February with Colonel Thomas A. Scott, assistant secretary of war; Walter E. Lawton, treasurer of Quicksilver; and Anthony Arnoux of New York to sell ten thousand (later reduced to five thousand) shares of Quicksilver stock short. He provided for Orme's participation in some fashion and also that of Charles H. Ray, who had sold his substantial interest in the *Chicago Tribune* the prior November.[13]

Ten days later, Swett reported to Orme, "The short sale of Quick was a failure." They hoped they would at least get out even, and Swett assured Orme that he would shield his partner from any loss. After closing the shorts, the group took a long position of more than eight thousand shares. Swett elaborated more fully in response to Orme's concerns in early March and revealed that the group had held its short position too long, contrary to his advice, before shifting to a long position as the Quicksilver case was argued before the U.S. Supreme Court. The sole question for the Supreme Court's determination was who owned the land on which the mine was located. The result must have appeared favorable, as the stock price rose. Swett confided to Orme, "I am sick of partners in stocks," and conceded that he could have lost twelve thousand to fifteen thousand dollars had he not shifted his position promptly.[14]

As he waited for the court's decision to be released on April 4, Swett had regained his confidence in the prospects for Quicksilver, its heavy indebtedness of $3 million notwithstanding. He stated that he was "acting in concert . . . not in partnership with" the company people. He wrote several letters to Thurlow Weed that same month, relaying what he knew about the case and Quicksilver's prospects so that Weed might avail himself of the opportunity if he wished. An entry in John Hay's diary at the end of April revealed that Swett also lamented these problems at the White House:

"Tonight came in Swett and Lamon anxious about their line of stocks."[15] Despite the outcome of the case in Quicksilver's favor, the results of Swett's speculation were not favorable, but no records exist as to whether he lost any of his meager resources or simply failed to capture anticipated gains.

In May 1864, Grant crossed the Rapidan River in northeastern Virginia with an army of 118,000 men to press Lee's force of 61,000 Confederates toward Richmond. Within little more than two weeks, in the battles of the Wilderness and Spotsylvania Courthouse, the Union forces suffered casualties approaching thirty thousand. Although Lee's forces were diminished and seriously impaired, the entrenchments at Spotsylvania protected them. But he could less afford to lose men than Grant, because he could not replace them. Severe losses in leadership also occurred, including the Army of the Potomac's John Sedgwick at Spotsylvania and Lee's Jeb Stuart at Yellow Tavern near Richmond. The fighting continued, and by early June, with Grant at Cold Harbor near Richmond, both sides dug in and paused for a breather.

The wounded started arriving heavily in Washington by mid-May. Swett and Laura spent the summer attending to the wounded at the hospitals in the capital, going from man to man, trying to bring cheer, helping them write letters home, and listening to their tales of woe and sorrow. The men reported the fighting to be the worst in the war. Swett wrote to Orme about what they witnessed: "There is a world of wounded men here. The city is environed with sores."[16] Although the hospitals provided good care and the Sanitary Commission dealt appropriately with the dead, the agony and misery that surrounded him rendered Swett sick to his stomach.

After weeks of this work, Swett grew overwrought with the experience and felt that the nation could no longer stand the incredible sacrifice. "In mercy, both to the North & South," he wrote, "every man capable of bearing arms must be hurried forward to Grant to end this fearful slaughter at the earliest possible moment." He went to see Lincoln at the White House to share his thoughts and observations. Lincoln sat near an open window while Swett described the ordeals he had witnessed. During a pause in the conversation, the strains from a bird singing on a nearby branch came through the window, and both men heard the distinct sweetness.[17]

Lincoln imitated the bird: "Tweet, tweet, tweet; isn't he singing sweetly?"

Swett felt as if the wind had been knocked out of his sails. He stood up and reached for his hat, saying, "I see the country is safer than I thought."

As he walked toward the door, Lincoln called out to him in his familiar manner: "Here, Swett, come back & sit down. It is impossible for a man in my position not to have thought of all those things. Weeks ago every man capable of bearing arms was ordered to the front, and everything you have suggested has been done."[18]

The interaction between Lincoln and Swett regarding the singing bird demonstrates the essential differences in their natures as well as their ability to speak frankly to each other without fear of collateral damage to their relationship. Swett reacted viscerally and emotionally to the losses from the war. Inflamed and agitated by what he saw and heard, the younger man did not hesitate to spill his heart and sympathies to the president, jumping to the conclusion that the older, more experienced man had failed to recognize the enormity of the suffering. He did not stop to consider what Lincoln might think of his impassioned plea or whether he might offend him by insinuating that the president had failed to take the necessary actions to end the war. Lincoln did not take offense. He listened to Swett, stopped him from leaving, and gave him an explanation in order to avoid a misunderstanding. Lincoln valued Swett's impressions and suggestions, and Swett had sufficient self-confidence in their relationship to risk making such bold statements without fearing Lincoln's judgment.

Swett characterized Lincoln as having a "mental equipoise which is disturbed by nothing, and diverted from the pathway it has marked out by nothing. . . . The war, like all others, was prosecuted by alternate success and defeat. The first two years, it was generally defeat, and yet Mr. Lincoln in moments of disaster was not disheartened, but was cool, collected and determined. . . . In moments of victory, when everybody was carried away by the joyousness of the occasion, Mr. Lincoln had the same mental equipoise and was self-restrained and determined as before. In short, he was the strong man of the contest."[19]

As the nomination of Lincoln for a second term approached, Swett recalled that Lincoln actually "desired the second nomination, because that involved an approval by the common people, whom he had always loved and confided in, of the course which he had taken." Swett thought he wanted the second nomination more than the first, but again Lincoln discouraged the efforts of his friends and supporters on his behalf. Although he was aware that his opponents worked hard to promote themselves, Lincoln would not take direct action against them or for himself and would not allow others to do so. Swett described the strategy: "He managed his campaigns by ignoring men and ignoring all small causes, but by closely calculating the tendencies of events and the great forces which were producing logical results."[20]

Unlike any other politicians Swett had known, Lincoln kept an "account book of how things were progressing." It included "estimates . . . on the great scale of action, such as the resolutions of the legislatures, the instructions of delegates" and many other, similar items. These accounts served as the basis for Lincoln's unwavering belief in his second nomination. Whenever Swett worried that Lincoln might lose, the president would pull out his ledger to demonstrate that his predictions in various areas were on target. Once, when Swett was anxious about support in the Senate, Lincoln said he would make a list of his supporters, if Swett "would not show it." Swett challenged him on five or six of the men, certain that Lincoln was incorrect. "You may think so," Lincoln responded, "but you keep that until the convention and tell me whether I was right." Swett later saw that he was right, to the man.[21]

As he had the first time, Swett again encouraged Lincoln to take action on his own behalf and against his rivals. Swett wanted to use James Gordon Bennett of the *New York Herald* in support of Lincoln. All Bennett required was to be noticed by Lincoln, but Lincoln refused, saying, "I understand it; Bennett has made a great deal of money, some say not very properly, now he wants me to make him respectable. I have never invited Mr. Bryant [of the *New York Post*] or Mr. Greeley [*New York Tribune*] here; I shall not, therefore, especially invite Mr. Bennett." Lincoln assiduously avoided the risk of buying influence in the press by taking no position and giving no favors.[22]

Because Lincoln's second nomination was virtually assured, the selection of a vice presidential candidate became the main focus at the Republican National Convention in Baltimore in mid-1864. Swett's role in the process was confusing from the outset. Just before the Baltimore meeting, he apparently telegraphed the Illinois delegation to the Republican National Convention to recommend Joseph Holt of Kentucky for vice president. For the two previous years, Holt had served as judge advocate general for Lincoln, and he was a friend of Judge Davis's, having worked with him on the Commission on War Claims investigating General Fremont's activities. John Nicolay was in Baltimore looking after Lincoln's interests and met with Burton C. Cook, head of the Illinois delegation. Nicolay wrote to John Hay on June 5, 1864, that Cook was "suspicious that Swett may be untrue to Lincoln," as Swett had recommended Holt to the Illinois delegation. "Cook wants to know confidentially whether Swett is all right—whether in urging Holt for V.P. he reflects the President's wishes . . . or whether he wishes not even to interfere by a confidential indication."[23]

Hay visited with Swett in Washington in early June. That same day, Nicolay wrote in his diary, "Talking with Swett tonight, found he was talking Holt for Vice Pres[iden]t. I suggested to him that two Kentuckians from adjoining States were rather crowding his ticket." Lincoln's endorsement on the Nicolay letter read, "Swett is unquestionably all right." Hay answered Nicolay the following day by telegram and letter, adding that Swett "has never even mentioned Col. Holt's name to the Prest. For the place designated. The President wishes not to interfere in the nomination even by a confidential suggestion. . . . Do not infer from what I have said above that the President objects to Swett presenting Col. Holt's name. He is, and intends to be absolutely impartial in the matter."[24] Further, Lincoln apparently was not troubled by the Illinois-Kentucky contiguity, as six months later he appointed James Speed of Kentucky to replace Edward Bates as attorney general after first offering the position to Holt.

Both Swett and his former college roommate, Josiah Drummond, were delegates to the Baltimore convention and spent a significant amount of time there together—nineteen years after having gone their separate ways from Waterville, Maine. As Swett was a friend of Lincoln's and was originally from Maine, it was presumed he would support Vice President Hannibal Hamlin, who had a Waterville College affiliation. Swett's iconoclastic attempt to introduce Joseph Holt to the Illinois delegation invited question.

Drummond later wrote in support of his old friend, "I was in constant consultation with Swett, and I had not then and never have had since the slightest reason to believe that he had any knowledge of any views or wishes on Lincoln's part that any other man than Hamlin should be nominated. It is true that Swett told me at the time that Lincoln's position was that he could take no part whatever in the nomination for Vice President, or, indeed, in *any* matter that was to come before the convention." Further, Drummond directly addressed Swett's allegiance, writing, "The idea that Swett hesitated about the re-nomination of Lincoln is an absurd one. He was and always had been the *devoted personal friend* of Lincoln, and I knew from his correspondence and personal interviews, that *he never wavered in his devotion* to Lincoln during the latter's life. Swett was selected by the

Illinois delegation to thank the convention for Lincoln's nomination, and proceeded to do so in a very eloquent manner."[25]

Prior to the Baltimore convention, delegates from Massachusetts had invited some of the Maine delegates to a meeting in Boston. Many radical Massachusetts Republicans wanted to prevent Seward from continuing in the cabinet because of his conservative views and influence on Lincoln. Drummond and Charles J. Talbot attended and emphatically supported renominating Lincoln and Hamlin. A motion was made in favor of their renomination, but this "was voted down by quite a decisive majority" and accepted as "merely an expression of views." The remainder of the group sought to nominate a vice president from New York, as the secretary of state could not be from the same state, thereby ruling out Seward. The group proposed U.S. senator Daniel Dickinson for this purpose.[26]

At the Baltimore convention, Drummond watched a meeting of the New York delegation from an open door. The delegates from New York were divided into two camps: those determined not to choose a vice presidential candidate from New York, who supported Seward in his role as secretary of state and mostly favored Hamlin for vice president, and those who advocated Dickinson. Henry J. Raymond, editor of the *New York Times* and chairman of the Republican National Committee, called for Andrew Johnson. The resulting vote gave Dickinson more votes than Hamlin but not a majority. The delegates debated further and eventually shifted from Hamlin to Johnson. A plurality resulted for Johnson, whom they took to the convention.[27] In the meantime, New England delegates had split into those from Massachusetts opposing Hamlin and those from Maine in his favor. Lyman Tremaine of New York supported Dickinson, and "Parson" William G. Brownlow and Horace Maynard of Tennessee nominated Johnson. On the first roll call for vice president, Johnson had a clear lead but not enough to win: 300 votes, followed by Hamlin with 150 and Dickinson with 108, with 61 votes scattered over seven others. Vote switching followed, with Simon Cameron of Pennsylvania giving Johnson enough to be chosen. Maine shifted, then Illinois, and finally New York, with Tremaine calling for a unanimous vote for Johnson.[28]

The Maine delegates chose Drummond to formally advise Lincoln of his nomination. He spoke with Lincoln at the conclusion of the ceremony and took the occasion to mention his friendship with Swett. According to Drummond, Lincoln immediately said, "'Get Swett and come in after these people get away, and we'll have a good time'; and he did not release my hand until I had promised him I would do so."[29]

Swett never explained why he had proposed Joseph Holt to the Illinois delegation a few days before the convention. Perhaps he knew of the likelihood of strong support developing for Andrew Johnson, then in his abolitionist phase, and offered Holt as more compatible to Southerners. Or it is possible he made this suggestion in deference to Davis, who liked Holt but could not attend the convention and thus had asked Swett to act on his behalf.

On June 10, 1864, soon after the Baltimore convention, Governor Richard Yates of Illinois wrote to Lincoln asking for a district commander to be appointed for the state of Illinois. Some Peace Democrats, or "Copperheads," had made a raid on the *Illinois State Register* in Springfield. This followed on the heels of a riot in Charleston, Illinois, between local Copperheads and Union troops on leave, in which six soldiers and three civilians died and twelve more were wounded. After the New York draft riots in 1863, the Illinois riot was the most serious incident in the North involving civilians during the war. Lincoln asked Swett to carry the Yates letter to Stanton ten days later, writing on it, "I have asked Mr. Swett to have a full talk with the Sec. of War in this case."[30] Sixteen Copperheads awaited military adjudication in the hands of the army.

David Davis was presiding over the federal circuit court in Illinois as a Supreme Court justice at the time. Lincoln telegraphed him, asking for a summary of the facts and his reaction. Davis advised Lincoln, "The Govt. ought not to have taken these men out of the hands of the law." Lincoln later released them to civilian authority, and although some remained subject to prosecution for nearly a decade, all were ultimately released.[31]

There is no record of Swett's discussion with Stanton, but it is likely that Swett explained why the army should postpone any decision regarding a district commander, as well as any action by the staff of the judge advocate general, until Lincoln could review the case. The unrest reached close to home for the president, as his stepmother and several relatives lived in the Charleston area and were acquainted with some of those detained.[32]

After this assignment, Swett visited his family in Maine for an extended time in the summer of 1864. During this period, the Union army sustained many casualties, and hopes for military success of the Union greatly dimmed as the American public grew more impatient for military accomplishments.

Democratic opponents quickly capitalized on the situation, finding willing opportunists of varied persuasions ready to respond. Many felt that it was time to settle the Union's differences with the South and end the horrible bloodshed. Confederate leaders swiftly recognized the propaganda possibilities for weakening Northern support for the war, especially with the election approaching in November and the possibility of a presidential turnover. Lincoln saw the political danger associated with this unabashed wish for peace.

Lincoln faced a tough challenge in finding a solution to the political and peace crisis. He made two overtures toward the South during this period, but both were rebuffed. In early June, he authorized a journalist and a clergyman to visit Confederate president Jefferson Davis in Richmond as private citizens seeking peace. They presented Lincoln's principles of amnesty, pardon, emancipation, and union, but Davis immediately and soundly rejected them. Next, Lincoln allowed Horace Greeley and John Nicolay to meet with Confederate men in Niagara Falls, Canada, but they soon learned that these Southerners had no authority to negotiate and wanted only to disturb War Democrats and interfere with military efforts of the North.

Swett's involvement with the Republican concerns and reactions started when he stopped in New York in mid-August while en route to Washington from Maine. There he became alarmed at the extent of the disaffection by both radical and conservative Republicans, particularly the latter who had been steadfast and loyal in supporting Lincoln. Thurlow Weed strayed toward the Democratic position, conferring with the New York State Democratic chairman and other party leaders about a Democratic nomination not based on peace and disunion. Two weeks before the Democratic National Convention, he published a statement "flaying the abolitionist influence at Washington and declaring that, if the Democrats would nominate a man who would agree to prosecute the war on the basis of reunion rather than the subjugation of the South and interference with established state institutions, he would give his 'voice and vote for such a candidate.'"[33]

On August 15, Swett wrote to Laura from New York, "The fearful things in relation to the country have induced me to stay a week here. I go to Washington to-night, and can't see how I can get away from there before the last of the week." He summarized the activities ongoing against Lincoln, including the call for a convention at Buffalo to supplant him; Democratic efforts to resist the draft, manifested by a seizure of arms to be distributed; the possible nomination of a loyal War Democrat; and the alliance of the Peace Democrats with the Confederacy. He concluded the letter with his deepest fear: "Unless material changes can be wrought, Lincoln's election is beyond any possible hope. It is probably clean gone now."[34]

Swett met with Lincoln in Washington on August 18. Henry J. Raymond, chairman of the Republican National Committee, wrote to Lincoln four days later, arguing that even his "staunchest friends" thought the tide was turning against them, referring to U.S. congressman Elihu B. Washburne from Illinois, Simon Cameron from Pennsylvania, and Governor Oliver Morton of Indiana. He attributed this to "two special causes . . . the want of military success, and the impression in some minds, the fear and suspicion in others, that we are not to have peace *in any event* under this administration until Slavery is abandoned." Raymond proposed that Lincoln appoint a commissioner *"to make distinct proffers of peace to [Jefferson] Davis . . . on the sole condition of acknowledging the* supremacy *of the constitution."* Later he wrote, "I have canvassed this subject very fully with Mr. Swett of Illinois who first suggested it to me & who will seek an opportunity to converse with you upon it."[35]

It is questionable whether Swett went so far with Raymond, who may have simply used Swett's name in an effort to strengthen his own argument. Given Swett's esteem for Lincoln and statements in his next letter to his wife that he had met with Lincoln to fully explain the danger and see if Lincoln would assist in resisting, it seems likely that Swett informed Lincoln of where the various parties stood relative to Raymond's proposal.[36] In the interval between Swett's visit and receipt of the Raymond letter, Lincoln drafted a memorandum on whether or not he could be reelected, which he sealed and had the cabinet members sign. The day after receiving the Raymond letter, he drafted a reply authorizing Raymond to lead the negotiation, which he did not send; this was actually an exercise in considering various courses of action, as Lincoln occasionally did. A letter from Swett's friend John W. Shaffer to General Ben Butler, written to further the nomination of Butler for president to replace Lincoln on the Republican ticket, mentioned Swett as a party in the discussions and was further evidence of the chaos in the Republican ranks.[37]

Lincoln did meet with the "stronger half of the Cabinet" on August 25. According to Nicolay, "Seward, Stanton, and Fessenden, held a consultation" with Raymond "and showed him that they had thoroughly considered and discussed the proposition . . . giving him their reasons[.] [H]e very readily concurred with them in the opinion that to follow his plan of sending a commission to Richmond would be worse than losing the Presidential contest."[38] The Republican National Committee met the same day.

Swett next wrote to Laura on September 8, 1864. Since his last letter, two defining events in the war had occurred: Rear Admiral David G. Farragut led his Federal fleet to victory on Mobile Bay, and Union forces under Major General William Tecumseh Sherman took Atlanta. Another military success was pending by General Philip Sheridan in the Shenandoah Valley. Swett's reaction to these victories reflected the national sense of relief: "There has never been an instance in which Providence has kindly interposed in our behalf in our national struggles in so marked and essential manner as in the recent Union victories."[39] Notwithstanding these victories, neither Lincoln nor Swett felt confident of the election outcome.

When he had arrived in New York back in August, Swett found an alarming situation. Greeley, Beecher, Raymond, Weed, and many other politicians had given up and would do nothing on behalf of Lincoln's election. "There was not a man doing anything except mischief," Swett wrote to Laura in his September 8 letter. Swett felt it his duty to "see if some action could not be inaugurated."[40] One such action was to push Raymond to call a committee and meet with Lincoln. Swett made sure Lincoln fully understood the danger of the situation, with this faction of politicians simply sitting on its hands. Both victories on the battlefield and these negotiations with Swett to protect himself saved Lincoln.

In the same letter, Swett also told Laura about his activities to persuade Raymond to convene the Republican National Committee in Washington and the subsequent disorganization and lack of funding of the group. He worked fervently with Washburne to raise money, acquiring one hundred thousand dollars needed for the canvass. Swett again described the seriousness of the crisis to Laura: "We are in the midst of conspiracies equal to the French Revolution. I have felt it my solemn duty under these circumstances to stay here. I have been actuated by no other motive than that of trying to save our country from further dismemberment and war. People from the West, and our best people, say if we fail now the West will surely break off and go with the South. Of course that would be resisted, and the resistance would bring war."[41]

Although Swett seemed overwrought in his two letters to Laura during this period, statements by Weed to Seward at this same time put his anxiety in context: "When, ten or eleven days since, I told Mr. Lincoln that his re-election was an impossibility, I also told him that the information would soon come to him through other channels. . . . Mr. Swett is well informed in relation to the public sentiment. He has seen and heard much. Mr. Raymond thinks commissioners should be immediately sent, to Richmond, offering to treat for Peace on the basis of Union. That *something* should be done and promptly done, to give the Administration a chance for its life, is certain."[42] Swett's role during the peace crisis may have been more important than anything else he had accomplished for his country and his president since the 1860 nominating convention in Chicago.

Laura Swett's frustration with her husband's restlessness and absence finally spilled over in a letter to Swett's law partner and close friend William Orme on October 25, 1864. She and Bertie, now almost six, had spent several months at her parents' home in Westford, Massachusetts, while Swett stayed in Washington. Orme was home in Bloomington awaiting his departure for Memphis, where he had been posted by Lincoln to be a supervising special treasury agent for cotton trading. In response to a request from Orme that she visit his lonely wife, Laura replied that she could not, as she was suffering too much from the absence of her own husband. She wrote, "I think Leonard will be at Washington the greater part of the winter, whether he now proposes so doing or not. *I* am beginning to be anxious about a home—a settled place of rest. . . . I feel as though it would be better for our boy that we should have a permanent home and be alone in it, than have him longer subjected to the changeful life of the last two years. The times are such that I cannot & do not expect to keep Mr. Swett in one place; the idea & hope of *home* in *that* respect, has at last—after infinite struggle—been abandoned."[43]

Swett's letters to Laura demonstrate that he estimated time very poorly. Frequently he wrote that he expected to depart for home shortly, but then did not return until weeks later. He did not take the time commitments made to her seriously. Words in her letter to Orme suggest that Laura had adapted to her husband's time estimates as only simple propositions, but with every recurrence, she could not help but feel a promise broken. His raising her expectations but then failing to follow through exacerbated their marital strife, leading her to feel resentment, distrust, and a sense of being alone. Swett's inability to settle down and provide for Laura had taken its toll, especially with his willingness to leave her alone at home on short notice in order to support the causes of others. By the fall of 1864, when she penned the letter to Orme, her seemingly infinite patience was showing that it had limits.

"Will you write me one of your kind, *sound sense* letters, giving me your views?" she asked Orme. "I rely upon you as a brother, knowing your unfailing friendship, & that so my husband regards you. Tenderly attached to home, as he really is, yet in his frequent & prolonged absences I am often made to feel & realize that I stand alone, and I doubly prise the strong arm of a friend. If I am asking unreasonable things, or anything you would, for an instant, object to, do not hesitate so to tell me. I can appreciate, I believe, any course you may see best to pursue."[44] After this appeal, Orme likely suggested she join her husband in Memphis. Swett sent a note on December 14, 1864, to Orme from Philadelphia indicating that he was planning to "come to Memphis within a week with good papers." He added, "If I come I shall try to induce Mrs. S. to come with me. If she will come I shall telegraph you for some place to live."[45]

In November 1864, Swett decided to visit Grant at City Point on the James River, not far from Petersburg, Virginia. There he stayed with Brigadier General Rufus Ingalls, Grant's former roommate at West Point, now quartermaster general for the Army of the Potomac. Ingalls resided in the army headquarters house on a bluff overlooking the junction of the James and Appomattox Rivers, while Grant quartered in a tent in the yard.

Grant left early each morning before Swett had breakfast, but he joined Ingalls and Swett in the evening, "after smoking out his cigar," for one hot glass of punch and three hours of stories. One evening, Grant talked about several other leaders, including Sheridan, with his recent success in the Shenandoah Valley, and Sherman, in whom he had complete confidence. Grant described the overly cautious General Don Carlos Buell as a brilliant tactician who only fought battles he was "dead sure" he could win, "by which time the other fellow had found it out and could not be found."[46]

During and after his activities related to Lincoln's second nomination and election, Swett continued to seek work. In late June 1864, he had asked Lincoln to appoint him as a commissioner for the Pacific Railroad under a bill awaiting passage. He had also recommended another man for the job, but ultimately, neither was appointed.[47] Concurrently, Swett attempted to get involved in cotton trading, seeking permission under an act of Congress from July 1861 making controlled trade in Southern cotton lawful by the Union under Treasury Department supervision.[48]

After receiving cotton-trading privileges, in December 1864 Swett teamed up with Thurlow Weed as a venture partner. By now Weed's political influence had declined, and he stood accused of corruption in the form of financial manipulation and false testimony. After a monthlong trial, he was vindicated, but his standing further suffered from the acrimony.[49] As a friend, however, Swett clearly had no qualms about Weed's reputation, even though Weed had often faced accusations of corruption because of his long-standing political influence and many business activities. Essentially, the two men created a joint venture for the purposes of conducting the trading, and their collaboration in the cotton trade continued through the end of the war. By now, Orme had been in Memphis for several months in his position as supervising special agent of the treasury, and Swett went to join him there.[50]

Yet again, Swett went into this venture with hopes of making a quick fortune. After sizing up the situation in Memphis, he first made a trip up the Ouachita River in Arkansas and later visited a more promising area up the Yazoo River in Mississippi. His source in the latter region was Samuel Tate (1817–92), president of the Memphis and Charleston Railroad, on the Confederate side. For a time, things looked good. Swett wrote to Weed on February 6, 1865, that with several contingencies satisfied, "I will make a great deal of money here." However, as the war got closer to its end, the price of cotton softened, and Rebel authorities made desperate efforts to stop the trade. Swett explained to Weed on March 30, "If their officers did not despair of their cause, and in individual cases, permit the traffic, in order that they might have something when they come to grief, not another bale would be brought out except surreptitiously." As with political success, financial wealth remained elusive for Swett. He mentioned one hundred thousand dollars in cash held by the business, but it is doubtful that he ever realized much of this amount.[51]

On top of this financial disappointment, several major events occurred over the next few weeks that caused Swett's world to drastically change. On April 9, 1865, Robert E. Lee surrendered, and General Joseph E. Johnston signed an armistice on April 18. The Civil War was over. In between those two key dates, an unimaginable tragedy occurred when, on April 14,

John Wilkes Booth assassinated Lincoln at Ford's Theatre. That same night, an associate of Booth's, Lewis Powell, attacked Secretary of State William Seward at home and slashed him badly about the head and neck. This assassination attempt failed only because other family members were present. Less than two weeks later, on the night of April 27, the steamboat *Sultana*, carrying Union soldiers newly released from Confederate prisons, exploded as it made its way up the Mississippi River from New Orleans toward St. Louis. The overcrowded boat caught fire and sank a few miles north of Memphis, resulting in nearly two thousand casualties. This horrible maritime catastrophe on top of the loss of Lincoln and his failed cotton venture likely sent Swett reeling. Other than a brief note from Orme in a letter to his wife on May 21, mentioning only that "Swett has been in poor health for two weeks," no record exists of Swett's reaction to the assassination or the attack on Seward. Neither did he write about his attendance at Lincoln's funeral on May 4 in Springfield or the *Sultana* disaster. In all probability, he was in a state of shock and depression. Not only had Swett's anticipated fortune evaporated, but his good friend, former colleague, and mentor, Abraham Lincoln, whom he had aided in becoming and serving as president of the United States, was gone as well.[52] Indeed, Lincoln's assassination overshadowed the entire nation as a devastating chapter of war came to a close.

Herndon and Swett were [Lincoln's]
intimate personal and political friends.
                    —*David Davis to J. S. Holland, July 3, 1865*

10. A Strategic Decision

Lincoln's assassination, the end of the war, and the termination of cotton trading by federal agents initiated a career change for Leonard Swett. About to turn forty years of age, Swett moved to Chicago in the summer of 1865 and established a new legal partnership with Laura's brother, Colonel David Quigg, who had studied law at the Swett & Orme firm in Bloomington, and Van H. Higgins, a superior court judge in Chicago who was just a few years older than Swett.[1] He announced his new venture to posterity in a letter he wrote to an attorney friend in Bloomington, William H. Hanna, from the new office of Higgins, Swett, & Quigg at 88 Washington Street in downtown Chicago.[2] Swett had met Higgins during his term in the Illinois state legislature in 1859. Higgins also knew Lincoln and had recruited him to participate in the Chicago *Sandbar* case in the spring of 1860.[3]

Within five weeks of Lincoln's death, journalist Josiah Holland wrote to David Davis, inquiring whom he should contact for biographical information on the martyred president. In reply, Davis named Leonard Swett, as well as William H. Herndon, Joshua Speed, John Todd Stuart, and Stephen T. Logan, adding, "Messrs. Herndon and Swett were his intimate personal and political friends and can perhaps give you more detailed information concerning the past fifteen years of his life than perhaps any other parties."[4] Holland subsequently visited Herndon for a couple of days in Springfield, but there is no indication that he ever communicated with Swett.[5] As early as the decade after Lincoln's assassination, interest in Swett waned, most likely because he had not achieved a political post or held a position in the

Lincoln administration. It took only a few decades for him to fade away as a forgotten friend.

By late 1865, Herndon began collecting information on Lincoln and contacted Swett. In response to Herndon's inquiry, Swett wrote three letters to him in early 1866. The second letter contained a thirty-one-hundred-word essay that remains one of the most expressive and eloquent statements ever written about Lincoln. It is perhaps the most significant biographical legacy of Lincoln, describing his characteristics and attitudes on more than a dozen topics.[6]

Swett began by explaining Lincoln's political strategy, which was based on his belief that "the agitation of slavery would produce its own overthrow." He aimed "to get himself in the right place and remain there still, until events would find him in that place." "In his conduct of the war," Lincoln believed that "but one thing was necessary, and that was a united North." Swett felt that "it was here that he located his own greatness as a President." He recalled that Lincoln once told him, "'I may not have made as great a President as some other men, but I believe I have kept these discordant elements together as well as anyone could.'"[7]

Swett also described Lincoln's sense of humor, love of the ludicrous, wit, and storytelling ability. He expanded on Lincoln's need not to waste anything and his practice of giving "more to his enemies than he would to his friends" because he could count on his friends' affection, whereas he needed to "appease his enemies." Swett said that "there was always some truth in the charge that he failed to reciprocate their devotion with his favors. The reason was, that he had only just so much to give away—'He always had more horses than oats.'" Although Lincoln was always very kind and understanding of sensitivities, his generous nature never went beyond his own judgment. Swett spoke of Lincoln's compassion and his refusal to judge men based on his own like or dislike of them. "He was certainly a very poor hater," said Swett. If someone "was the fittest man for the place, he would give him that place just as soon as he would give it to a friend. I do not think he ever removed a man because he was his enemy or because he disliked him." Swett raised a question that was in his own mind: "I have sometimes doubted whether he ever asked anybody's advice about anything. He would listen to everybody; he would hear everybody; but he rarely, if ever, asked for opinions." Others, including David Davis, also emphasized this trait of Lincoln's.[8]

Swett's other letters to Herndon raised specific questions about aspects of Lincoln's life and habits. The second pertained to letters from John D. Johnston, Lincoln's stepbrother, asking for financial assistance from Lincoln in 1848 and 1851. Lincoln had declined to provide support because Johnston refused to work. Swett sent Herndon copies of Johnston's letters, which he had obtained from a banker friend in Richmond. "I never knew Mr. Lincoln had a brother," Swett wrote, indicating how closemouthed Lincoln had been about his family. General Grant had read to Swett something similar to Johnston's complaint when Swett visited Grant's camp at City Point in 1864. At that time, Swett had assured Grant that Lincoln had no brother.[9]

In the third letter to Herndon, Swett cautioned him about writing history, stating, "No man is great to his 'Valet de chamber.'" He provided an example from the Bible about Uriah, the husband of Bathsheba, whom David had arranged to have killed in battle: "If the history of King David had been written by an ordinary historian, the affair of Uriah would at most have been a quashed indictment with a denial of all the substantial facts." Then he generalized, "There's a skeleton in Every house." By the end of the letter, Swett turned the inquiry back to Herndon: "I would like to have you write me what the skeleton was with Lincoln. What gave him that peculiar melancholy? . . . I always thought there was something but never knew what."[10]

Herndon pursued his collection of biographical information on Lincoln vigorously through most of 1866. He ultimately contacted more than 250 people by interview or letter, including Davis, who was administrator of Lincoln's estate and temporarily controlled access to his papers.[11] During this collection phase, Herndon gave four lectures on Lincoln in Springfield between December 1865 and November 1866. The first three lectures were never published except as reported in the press, and initially they were well received.[12]

Herndon's fourth lecture focused on Lincoln's relationship with Ann Rutledge and his deep depression following her death. He speculated that Lincoln's difficulties in his marriage to Mary arose from his earlier romance with Ann. This time Herndon went a step further and provided the full text of his words for distribution at the time of his lecture. The reaction was immediate and negative. Although the Springfield papers abstained, others voiced disapproval. Lincoln's son Robert wrote to Davis three days after the lecture, "Herndon is making an ass of himself." A more tempered reaction came from an older friend, Judge T. Lyle Dickey, who wrote to Herndon after reading a copy of the lecture, "Romance is not your forte. . . . I don't like the garnishments."[13]

As a result of this reaction and other personal matters, Herndon set aside his project after 1867 and did not return to it for more than a decade. Ward Hill Lamon practiced law with Jeremiah Black, who had served as attorney general and secretary of state under President James Buchanan, for a while after the war and became acquainted with his son, Chauncey F. Black. Lamon and the younger Black decided to collaborate on a Lincoln biography. Learning of Herndon's collection of materials, Lamon purchased them from Herndon and sold Black a half interest. Together they made a contract providing that Black would ghostwrite the book, to be published under Lamon's name. However, the Blacks, both father and son, had not been particularly friendly with Lincoln.[14]

Meanwhile, Swett was busy building friendships in Chicago and trying to get his new legal partnership established. In July 1866, he made a trip to Washington to present a claim, for which he received five thousand dollars.[15] Shortly thereafter, Swett lost another close friend—William Orme, his former law partner. Orme had contracted tuberculosis while serving with his brigade in the Mississippi delta, and his health had been deteriorating steadily ever since, despite his efforts to seek refuge in the waters and the cooler climate of Minnesota. He finally succumbed to the disease on September 13.[16]

In Washington again in October, Swett wrote to Laura that he attended the funeral of Fanny Seward, the beloved twenty-one-year-old daughter of William Seward, also a victim of tuberculosis. Swett felt closer to Seward than to any other cabinet member, as they had become acquainted early on and got along well, and he had spent a lot of time visiting with Seward while in Washington. However, he had not seen the secretary of state since the assassination attempt against him the same night Lincoln was killed, and now he told Laura that he was shocked by the man's appearance. Seward bore the scars from the serious lacerations his intended assassin had inflicted on his head and neck. Life had not been easy for Seward, who had lived through an assassination attempt that maimed him, the loss of his president, the loss of his wife, and finally the loss of the daughter who had provided him with her cheerful support.[17]

During this same trip, Swett advised Thurlow Weed that "Stanton will go out of Cabinet." He sensed President Johnson's sentiments correctly, but Stanton held on to his position for another year and a half, until after Johnson's acquittal by the Senate on impeachment charges in May 1868. Swett attended the opera in Washington with a former Treasury colleague who had assisted him with the cotton-trading claims. Before returning home in late 1866, Swett visited Westford, Massachusetts, where Laura had been staying with relatives and friends during his absence. From there, he went on to Maine to spend a few days with his mother and other family members in Turner.[18]

Swett returned to Chicago before Christmas, but Laura and Bertie, now eight years old, remained in Massachusetts. Laura may have been undergoing treatment in the East for her malady, or she may have been releasing some of her resentment and frustration by turning the tables on her husband. She stayed there for at least three months, extending into 1867, during which she and Leonard remained in close contact with one another. Laura's tactic apparently worked, as Swett wrote fifteen letters to her in January alone. Unfortunately, no letters from Laura to Leonard survive from this period, but his affirmed not only the strife that was evident in their relationship but also their enduring affection.[19]

Swett told Laura about a dinner party in their home for fourteen guests in early January and gave another detailed description of a party for Wirt Dexter, a newly married contemporary and friend who was establishing himself in the Chicago bar. Swett gave the particulars of those who attended and described the dress of the women, and then moved on to "the subject of social life" and its relationship to his professional career in Chicago. "I must first of all, attend to my business," he explained, "but it is aided by a social acquaintance . . . so that I may have a standing, not through Judge Higgins but independent of him."[20]

While Laura was absent, her family members were very much present. Laura's father stayed with Swett in Chicago part of the time, as well as with her brother, David Quigg. Her mother also visited two of Laura's sisters in Clinton, 150 miles southwest of Chicago. Before the end of January, Laura's mother traveled to Chicago, and Swett took her and Quigg to a performance by the Italian actress Adelaide Ristori during the second of her four acclaimed tours of the United States. Swett also attended the opera twice in December and twice again in early January, taking his father-in-law along on at least one occasion. The opera *Medea* made such an impression on Swett that he described its plot by Euripides in a twelve-page letter to

Laura.[21] The bloody tragedy depicted feminine rebellion and reverberated in his mind, resulting in uncomfortable reflections on his own life and marriage. He may have intended his descriptions of his social life while Laura was gone to show her that he was carrying on quite well, but he responded intensely to statements she apparently made in her letters to him. "You tell me you feel so happy that I am free, as you term it, and are rejoiced to see me enjoy it," he wrote. "Those expressions . . . simply show how little you understand my real feelings."

He told Laura that he had attended a wonderful party and stayed out until past one A.M. The party was in honor of the Dexter couple, who had recently married and returned from their honeymoon. Swett described the fashions the women wore, down to the details of French lace. The party livened up with the arrival of the theater crowd. One woman looked like the queen of the Fiji Islands to him. He also made it clear that he did not wish to socialize too much: "I do not want to frisk and flirt and have the community get a frivolous opinion of me." He felt like a stranger in Chicago, he said, but was intent on working hard and building his professional standing. "I am determined . . . to make the practice of my profession here a success," he wrote.

In this same letter, he chided Laura for not being aware that he had stopped drinking. "I drink no liquor of any kind," he wrote, referring to an earlier topic of contention in their relationship. Whether he had maintained his abstinence after the time of his yearlong "Pledge on Drinking" with Lamon in 1864 is unknown, but there is no evidence that he had a drinking problem. The quantity and quality of his work in Chicago, the increasing demand for his legal services, and his constant availability to assist friends and clients seem inconsistent with alcohol abuse.

Swett ended this letter by restating an enigmatic remark that Laura had recently sent him, with his interpretation: "Don't talk to me of innocence. Tell me of greenhorns. If to be half witted is to be worldly wise[,] not to be is to be fooled—by a woman." He asked her to be explicit and he would explain, and then ended the letter abruptly with the words, "I am not half done but good bye now."[22] Another two months elapsed before she returned to Chicago. In the meantime, he continued to write, professed his love for her, and sent her a piece of jewelry.

In February 1867, while Laura was still in Massachusetts, Swett spent several weeks in Springfield working on a three-hundred-thousand-dollar case for his firm in which he estimated that his office would earn forty-five hundred to five thousand dollars. The amount of this fee indicates that he was well on his way to establishing himself as a successful attorney with his firm. Swett's reputation as a trial lawyer throughout central Illinois was well known, and he was also retained during this period as counsel for the plaintiff in a contest over the estate of Isaac Funk, a large case he brought into the firm that occupied him on and off over the next several years.

While in Springfield, Swett stayed with Lawrence Weldon, an old friend from the Eighth Circuit in Clinton. Weldon had recently resigned from his 1861 appointment by Lincoln as U.S. district attorney for southern Illinois. Swett also renewed and maintained other friendships on this trip. He saw Governor Richard J. Oglesby every day and made two visits to Bloomington, one to call on Orme's wife and the other to assist Jesse Fell in attempting to attract the new state university to that location. He felt that the proposed college could be an addition to the teachers university that Fell, Swett, Lincoln, and others had helped establish a decade earlier. As Swett predicted in correspondence to Laura, however, the institution instead went to Urbana-Champaign, to Fell's disappointment.[23]

In one of his letters to Laura, Swett wrote about his thoughts on a book he was reading, Daniel Schenkel's *Portrait of Jesus*, first published in 1864. The book followed on the heels of Ernest Renan's *Life of Jesus*, published in France the year before. Schenkel's book related to the rationalist interpretation of Christ's life and teachings. Swett's reactions to the text interested Laura, who was a dedicated Presbyterian. His interest in the book may have been stimulated by a leading Chicago minister, Reverend David Swing, who headed the church they attended. The pastor's liberal thinking sometimes brought him into conflict with some of the prominent Presbyterians of the day.[24]

The biggest matter on his plate during this period was the Isaac Funk estate contest. The case involved a famously wealthy landowner who had died without a will two years before, leaving twenty-five thousand acres of land near Bloomington. Along with an impressive group of attorneys, including John Todd Stuart of Springfield and Robert E. Williams and Lawrence Weldon of Bloomington, Swett represented James Funk, the illegitimate son of Isaac. The nine other Funk children were represented by William H. Hanna of Bloomington, Littler & Greene of Springfield, and Richard Harrison from Ohio. Isaac had migrated to central Illinois from Ohio, leaving James, then seven years old, with his mother, who died a short time later. Isaac married another woman in Illinois and raised a family but returned to Ohio to bring James home as a child. When James reached maturity, Isaac offered him land to farm adjacent to the family land, but James chose to live with his wife's family, so he was given a sum of cash instead. Over the next two decades, Isaac Funk grew immensely wealthy. Following Isaac's death in 1865, the lack of a will or distribution plan provided the opportunity for a claim by James Funk. The other nine children felt, however, that James had no valid claim against the estate.[25]

In early 1868, while Swett was working on the Funk case, Secretary of State Seward urged President Johnson to retain Swett as one of his defense attorneys in his impending impeachment trial by the Senate. Johnson's relationship with Congress had deteriorated steadily almost from the inception of his presidency, and he was facing a second attempt to remove him from office. Seward recommended Swett "because he was a special friend of Mr. Lincoln, and to retain him would gratify Mr. L's friends."[26]

When Seward encouraged Johnson to use Swett as a defense attorney, Secretary of the Navy Welles took the opposite course. Seward was the cabinet member who knew Swett best, and he also was close to the president. Treasury Secretary Hugh McCulloch knew Swett only slightly and said in the exchange that Montgomery Blair had told him "Swett was a tool of Stanton's," which Seward promptly denied. Although Secretary of the Interior Orville Browning was a former Illinois senator, he did not help on Swett's behalf. Had Swett been privy to the discussion, he would have taken satisfaction in knowing that the gossipy Welles strongly opposed the appointment of William Evarts, a New York attorney whom Welles called "cold, calculating, selfish," but who in the end provided winning leadership in the defense of Johnson.[27] A friend of Swett's, federal judge Lawrence Weldon, said that Swett had "declined an employment in the Presidential impeachment because of the obligations of a previous engagement."[28]

Swett did not record his opinion of Johnson, but it probably reflected some of the thoughts he heard from his friends Oglesby and Davis. Oglesby's support for Johnson began to falter as early as the summer of 1865, and he broke with the president the following April when Johnson opposed and ultimately vetoed the Civil Rights Act.[29] Oglesby's public break with Johnson occurred less than three weeks after his introduction of Frederick Douglass on April 3, 1866, as a speaker at a lecture in Springfield, praising the abolitionist leader as well as the loyalty of African Americans.[30]

By 1868, Davis had been in Washington as a member of the Supreme Court for six years. As such, he attempted to avoid partisan politics and expressed a more moderate and nuanced position, yet his Liberal Republican leanings were already ingrained. During Johnson's impeachment trial, Davis said to his brother-in-law, "I believe the President to be an honest man and a true patriot, but with qualities totally unfitting him to be the ruler of a people in the fix we are in . . . obstinate, self-willed, combative, slow to act . . . no executive ability." On the day the articles of impeachment were presented to the Senate, he wrote to his wife, Sarah, "I am opposed to impeachment. The trial must become one of the most celebrated in history."[31] Swett's prior and subsequent positions imply that his reactions would be similar to Davis's, but reaching in Oglesby's direction.

In retrospect, the Radical Republicans overplayed their authority, especially in the charges that applied largely to Johnson's removal of Stanton as secretary of war, claiming that he had violated the Tenure of Office Act. The defection of seven Republican senators provided a one-vote margin for defeating the removal of Johnson. The action revealed many unsettling issues, particularly that if Johnson had been impeached, Senator Benjamin F. Wade, who was president pro tempore of the Senate, was next in line for the presidency and would have served as such for ten months. Wade was not well regarded and lacked the confidence of many influential people.

Meanwhile, Swett had been preparing for the Isaac Funk estate case. Finally, in July 1869, after several years of preparation and a change of venue from McLean to Macon County, Swett made the opening statement at trial for James in Decatur. From existing records, it appears that the case was settled outside court, bringing in another large fee for the firm.[32]

The press made occasional references to Swett as he now moved more visibly into leadership positions in Chicago. In September 1870, he and his friend Wirt Dexter spoke along with three others at a mass meeting in Farwell Hall celebrating the new French Third Republic. The wisdom these two neophyte foreign commentators might have offered on the subject was not recorded, but their efforts were both commendable and precarious, considering the unfolding situation in France following the defeat of the Second French Empire in the Franco-Prussian War. The celebration was heady in a city with a population consisting of more than one-quarter ethnic Germans.[33]

While St. Louis clung to its reliance on the flow of commerce moving north-south along its extensive river system, Chicago had opened up to east-west railroads, and by 1870, it was the second-largest city in America, teeming with entrepreneurs and immigrants. Chicago was a growing metropolis with all the attendant grit and noise.[34] Fires broke out often, and in 1871, a devastating fire overtook the city at large, becoming one of the greatest disasters of the century.

Swett left only paltry bits of information relating to his experiences in the Great Chicago Fire, which burned him out of home and office in early October 1871. Apparently he suffered an injury during the incident, as he later wrote to his son, "The night of the Great Fire, I lamed my knee running upstairs." Like much of the rest of the population, he was forced to rebuild his life, and these efforts left him with little time for writing. Eleven days after the fire, Higgins, Swett, and Quigg advertised the firm's new location on Wabash Avenue, possibly in one of the five thousand temporary structures said to have been built in the first week. Swett's family moved temporarily to Hyde Park, where some of his wife's relatives lived.[35]

During this same period, Swett came to play a leading role in the Liberal Republican movement and the attempt to nominate David Davis as the party's presidential candidate for the 1872 election. Years of secession and war, Lincoln's assassination, an aborted attempt at reconstruction, and the failed presidential impeachment did not provide a viable background for new political directions, especially in the combination of divisive elements pulled together in the form of the Liberal Republican movement.[36]

Davis's prominence in Lincoln's Republican triumph in 1860 and his distaste for military reconstruction in the South had earned him increasing attention from political critics. He had also made a landmark Supreme Court decision in the December 1866 *Ex parte Milligan* case, ruling that military tribunals should not try civilians given the existence of civil courts. In early 1871, Swett and Jesse Fell, Bloomington's foremost promoter and a Lincoln enthusiast, emerged as comanagers of a "Davis for president" effort.[37]

Despite Grant's popularity as the incumbent president and his dedication to Lincoln's goal of emancipation, he lacked adequate political skills and experience to deal satisfactorily with problems of a reuniting nation. His opponents represented the fractured elements seeking a cohesion that could not be found in the inconsonant multiplicity of the new movement. Swett and Davis, as protagonists in this unfolding drama, might have known better, given their exposure to Lincoln's skillful fashioning of his miraculous coalition. But hope—in politics, as in everything else—often exceeds reality.

Correspondence flowed between Swett and Fell as they discussed their plans. One tactic of the campaign owed its ancestry to Lincoln's first nomination: capitalization on the railroad proximity of central Illinois, Davis's home and the base of his support, to Cincinnati, the location for the convention. This afforded the opportunity to transport about five hundred people to the convention.

One long letter Swett wrote to Fell espoused the Liberal Republican movement without mentioning Davis's candidacy. In March 1872, Fell, known in publishing circles because of his prior newspaper ownership, forwarded Swett's letter to the *Chicago Tribune* and the *Chicago Times*, the leading Republican and Democratic papers. Bloomington's *Pantagraph* carried it a few days later. The success of the movement depended on its ability to draw voters from the two major parties.

In his letter, Swett quickly identified the Liberal Republican view: "At the close of the war, the government enfranchised the negroes, and by attaching disabilities to men prominent in the rebellion, practically disenfranchised the property-holding and intelligent classes of the South. The next step was to empower the army quartered there to override civil authority." Swett then reduced the argument from the sectional level of the country to a personal one: "The same reason which made me sympathize with the negro, makes me the friend of the white man now that war and time have changed their mutual relations." This was definitely not the Lincolnian view, however. Perhaps Swett had forgotten the ratification of the Fourteenth Amendment less than four years earlier, providing that "no state shall . . . deprive any person of life, liberty, or property, without due process of law; nor deny to any person within its jurisdiction the equal protection of the laws." Further, he held, now that seven years had gone by, "we find the white man loaded with political disabilities, the control he used to exercise given to his former slaves, and his country a Botany Bay for every scalawag who wishes to plunder him." The intensity of the rhetoric increased still further: "Can we pin this country together permanently with bayonets?" Finally, his good humor returned at the conclusion: "The Cincinnati Convention will produce a new national organization, founded upon the principles of amnesty, liberty and reform, and through its agency the bitterness of the past may be forgotten, national friendships revived, and the blessing of free government dispensed to all people in the land." The *Pantagraph* editor, although courteous in his response to the letter, thought it one of Swett's "less able production(s)" and did not "yet see the need of destroying the Republican Party to reform . . . the carpet bag governments."[38]

The mix of participants at the Liberal Republicans' 1872 Cincinnati convention demonstrated the heterogeneity of the movement. Senator Carl Schurz, a Republican and German American, led the reformers in Missouri. He made the initial invitation, chaired the convention, and supported Missouri governor B. Gratz Brown for president. Senator Charles Sumner, the long-serving legislator from Massachusetts, came to the convention filled with righteous indignation toward Grant over his effort to annex Santo Domingo. For his opposition, Sumner had lost his position as the chairman of the Committee on Foreign Relations. He did not support any candidate in particular at the convention but contributed to the diverse interests of the group.

Although Illinois had a large contingent of Liberal Republicans, they divided their loyalties among four candidates: David Davis; Charles Francis Adams, wartime minister to Great Britain who carried strong support from those in the East; Senator Lyman Trumbull; and Illinois governor John M. Palmer. Besides Swett and Fell, Davis backers at the convention included John Wentworth, Lawrence Weldon, and Adlai Stevenson. Wentworth had served two terms as the mayor of Chicago and six terms as a congressman from Illinois, and he had been the managing editor and owner of the *Chicago Democrat*. Weldon and Stevenson were Bloomington Democrats, the former having served as U.S. attorney for southern Illinois. Davis gained much of his support from Democrats as a result of his stances against the civil rights legislation and military occupation of the South.

At the time of the convention, Davis seemed to be in a position to win the nomination. However, the editors of four newspapers met the afternoon before the start of the convention to attempt to take Davis out of the running. *Chicago Tribune* editor-in-chief and co-owner Horace White supported Trumbull. The editors of the *Springfield (MA) Republican* favored Adams. Both the *Louisville Courier-Journal* and the *Cincinnati Commercial* derided Davis in the next day's editions. One of the managers of Horace Greeley's *New York Tribune*, Whitelaw Reid, then joined the group. When the convention met, the *Cincinnati Commercial* printed and provided participants with flyers containing the disparaging editorials. White was able to control the Illinois vote to achieve a split among the three principal candidates. Without the overwhelming support of Illinois, and thanks to the opposition stirred up by the editors, Davis failed to make the requisite showing on the early ballots to command the lead.

In his opening remarks, the convention chairman, Carl Schurz, seemed to favor Trumbull or Adams, but he was committed to Governor Brown. However, Brown surprised everyone by throwing his support to Horace Greeley, sparking the editor's candidacy. Greeley ended up winning the nomination on the sixth ballot. This sudden change of favor deprived the delegates of the opportunity to carefully consider Greeley's drawbacks, including his denunciations of the Democratic Party, which burdened him heavily in the campaign.[39]

Swett acquiesced in Greeley's nomination. Three of the four editors leading the revolt against Davis had expected Adams or Trumbull to win and expressed some reservation and disappointment about the result. Brown ended up as the vice presidential nominee. Schurz wavered for an extended period, suggesting that Greeley withdraw, but finally he threw in his support for Greeley. In the end, the German Americans proved to be the most disaffected elements of the Liberal Republicans, including Schurz of Missouri, Gustav Koerner of Illinois, and the free traders of the Northeast.

Before the Democratic National Convention convened in Baltimore in July, twenty-six of the thirty state parties instructed their delegates to form some kind of coalition with the Liberal Republicans, and they quickly endorsed the Liberal Republican platform and candidates. Greeley had openly denounced the Democrats in the past, but now they tried to swallow their humiliation and appealed for adherence and unity with the Liberal Republicans in opposition to Grant and his running mate, Massachusetts senator Henry Wilson.[40] This posture provided the best opportunity for Southern Democrats to avoid four more years of Radical Reconstruction under Grant.

By the end of June, Swett outlined his agenda for the support of Greeley in the fall election canvass. He made speaking appearances in Chicago, Rockford, and Aurora, Illinois. During a speech at a Cook County meeting to name delegates to the statewide meeting in Springfield, he rationalized the move away from the Republican Party for the first time and explained its deterioration: "Like all parties, it has grown old, and with its twelve years of power has grown corrupt. . . . The only way on earth to reform them is . . . through disaster and defeat."[41] While some, like Davis, accepted this explanation, it did not go over well with the rank-and-file Republicans.

Swett and other Liberal Republicans made an effort, joined by the Democrats, but the results at the polls showed a poor response. In Chicago alone, the 10 percent gain in presidential ballots from 1868 to 1872 went almost entirely to Grant. Greeley obtained only 2 percent more votes than Horatio Seymour, the Democratic candidate for president, had in 1868 and carried only six states. Gustav Koerner, the Liberal Republican candidate for Illinois governor, fared somewhat better than Seymour had, yet Oglesby beat him by four thousand votes. After his defeat, Greeley died before the end of the month. The Liberal Republicans lingered a while longer in some areas, but the death knell had sounded for the party as well.

After the Liberal Republican defeat in the 1872 election, Davis became an independent, but Swett did not follow him. Instead, he resolved to stay out of national politics and had only limited involvement for about the next decade and a half. Though he had once been a kingmaker, he had been unsuccessful as a politician in his own behalf. Now he devoted his attention and energy to the law, which was where his true talents resided. An able speaker who once had the ear of important people behind the scenes, Swett now did most of his speaking in the courtroom and occasional public addresses.

One of the most persuasive who ever
addressed a jury at the American bar.
    —*Wirt Dexter, president of the Chicago Bar Association,*
speaking of Leonard Swett, June 9, 1889

11. Legal Advocate and Civic Leader

Swett's senior partner, Van Higgins, retired from the firm at the beginning of 1873, leaving Swett with his brother-in-law, David Quigg.[1] The
firm replaced Higgins with attorney Cyrus Bentley, who partnered with
Quigg while Swett practiced alone for much of the rest of the decade. Swett
was now clearly established among Chicago's leading lawyers. He had made
the transition from his days on the Eighth Circuit with Lincoln, handling
cases of trespass, land and property disputes, crop damage, and debt collection, to the more complicated and far-reaching issues of a major city, as
well as a society in the process of industrialization. Swett "was connected
with some of the most important cases of the day," his former partner John
Herrick noted after Swett's death, "and in both civil and criminal causes
his almost unbroken record of success gave him great prestige."[2] Although
his criminal cases garnered more attention from the press, his civil cases
constituted the majority of his Chicago legal work and the bulk of his
income. These cases were often connected with large private interests and
sophisticated clients, bringing Swett complicated legal problems involving
real estate, inheritances, and contracts.

In one prominent case, Swett defended Chicago treasurer David A. Gage
from 1870 to 1873. Gage was accused of failing to pay his successor $360,000
in public funds that were unavailable following the fire, economic recession,
and political upset in the city. The venue of the case shifted to Waukegan
in Lake County, and Swett won the jury trial on behalf of Gage. "The
telegraph flashed the result to the city and immediately, so great was the

interest in the case, the news was in the possession of everybody. It was an unexpected result. The most sanguine friends of the man on trial did not dare hope for such a triumph, and the general public were simply astounded." Appeals followed and eventually culminated in a loss and then a win for Gage in 1879.[3]

One of the largest and most important civil cases Swett became involved with during this period was that of the Northwestern Fertilizer Company (NWF). In early 1867, the Illinois state legislature granted the company a fifty-year charter to operate in Cook County for the purpose of converting dead animals and animal products into agricultural fertilizer and other chemical products. This legislation assisted Chicago's slaughterhouse industry by locating the fertilizer operation outside the city in a less densely populated area within Cook County. Relying on this charter, NWF invested about $250,000 to build its facilities in the village of Hyde Park, a swampy and sparsely inhabited area thought to have "little promise of future improvement."[4] Much of the Chicago area along the lake was originally a prairie bog, but as the city's population increased, Hyde Park expanded, resulting in more people living in close proximity to the odoriferous transporting and manufacturing business.

In 1869, two years after the first state legislation, the Illinois legislature upgraded the authorization powers of Hyde Park to allow police power "to define or abate nuisances . . . injurious to the public health" but expressly provided that those powers could not be exercised against NWF for two years. In November 1872, after the two-year period had expired but with close to forty-five years left on the company's charter, village authorities adopted an ordinance to stop NWF's operation by preventing the shipment of dead animals and debris into Hyde Park. On January 8, 1873, the police stopped a train for violating the ordinance, arrested the engineer and other railroad employees, and fined them each fifty dollars.[5]

At the outset, it appeared that the dispute could generate litigation proceeding from the local courts to the U.S. Supreme Court. On one hand, U.S. constitutional law forbade the states to interfere with the contracts of its citizens, the "Contract Clause" within Article I (section 10, clause 1). On the other hand, the states retained "police powers" to regulate conduct including "public nuisances" and hazards. These fairly novel, yet important, questions of federal constitutional law and state police or regulatory powers began to emerge in a society with more industrial activity and accompanying

government regulation. Accordingly, the combatants selected highly quali-
fied legal counsel. NWF chose Swett, who brought an injunction to stop the
fines and interference with the chartered operations. Swett's legal opponent
was the formidable attorney Charles Hitchcock, who had served as president
of the Illinois Constitutional Convention in 1870.[6]

The Cook County court ruled swiftly on Swett's injunction before mid-
March 1873, favoring NWF's position based on its charter. The village of
Hyde Park attempted to remove the case to federal court, but Swett argued
successfully that federal statutes did not authorize such a removal and the
case was returned to the Illinois Supreme Court.[7] About a year and a half
later, on September 24, 1874, the Illinois Supreme Court rejected the view
of the Cook County court finding that "this factory was an unendurable
nuisance . . . for many miles around its location. . . . And the transportation
of this putrid animal matter through the streets of the village was offensive
in a high degree both to sight and smell." The court implied a reservation
in the state's "police regulation" power to punish public nuisances. By this
time, the newspapers referred to the litigation as "the stink case," and the
two lead attorneys employed a number of impressive names to assist in
presenting their arguments.[8]

Swett's arguments for NWF were squarely on the cusp of those required
in America's adaptation to a new industrial form of society. The case stood
near the beginning of continuing controversies alleging public health as a
reason for regulating business, with the resulting issues of state versus federal
power and the Contract Clause versus the broadening of police powers.

The case then went on to the U.S. Supreme Court. Justice Noah H.
Swayne, Lincoln's first appointee to the court, wrote the majority opinion
in 1878. In a seven-to-one decision against NWF, Swayne characterized
the charter as a revocable license instead of a fifty-year contract in order
to allow the exercise of police power for a serious nuisance.[9] A foresighted
dissent by Justice William Strong recognized a palpable violation of the
constitutional provision against the impairment of contracts, as well as
the inappropriate application of calling a contract a license. Such a twist
or sidestep, he stated, took away contract rights "without compensation,"
falling directly in the path of one of Swett's arguments.[10]

The conclusions of the editor of *Chicago Legal News*, Myra Bradwell,
on this case at the time were especially telling: "The question involved in
this case, was not only of vital importance to the people of Hyde Park,

but to the people of every town and village in the United States as well as the company itself. . . . The present case has been warmly contested, it has extended through a number of years. The best of counsel were engaged on both sides, Charles Hitchcock, the president of the Convention that framed our present Constitution, represented Hyde Park, and Leonard Swett, the Fertilizing Company. The names of these gentlemen is [sic] sufficient guarantee that the case was well conducted."[11]

During this same time frame, Swett defended a prominent murder case in Yankton, Dakota Territory. The case against banker Peter Wintermute arose from a political argument in a saloon over the financing of the Dakota Southern Railway. The argument erupted into fisticuffs between Wintermute and former general Edwin S. McCook, then secretary and acting governor of the Dakota Territory.[12] McCook beat his opponent badly, upon which Wintermute threatened to shoot him. After McCook left to give a speech nearby, Wintermute showed up at the meeting with a pistol. A shot rang out, and McCook rushed the banker, who shot him fatally at close range. Wintermute claimed that he had acted in self-defense. This homicide in 1873 resulted in two protracted trials and an appeal, altogether lasting two years.[13]

Jason H. Brown, secretary of the Wyoming Territory, and two Yankton attorneys argued for the prosecution. Swett defended Wintermute with the assistance of three local attorneys. The trial court found Wintermute guilty of the lesser charge of manslaughter and sentenced him to ten years in the penitentiary. The defense appealed the case to the Territorial Supreme Court, claiming that a member of the grand jury had been challenged for partiality but the challenge was denied. The court ordered a new indictment for Wintermute requiring adjudication. Swett again defended Wintermute in the next trial, and this time Wintermute was acquitted. Public sentiment in the Dakota Territory ran strongly against Wintermute, and as the defense attorney, Swett was described as having cleared this case "against 'light and knowledge,' as well as law and evidence." A later review of the trials concluded, however, that "close examination . . . reveals the deliberate thoroughness with which the trials were carried out, as well as factual support in the record for the jury's determination that reasonable doubt existed."[14]

In early 1874, Swett was one of forty-two founders of the Chicago Bar Association, along with his former senior partner, Van Higgins, and his brother-in-law, David Quigg. Other notables included William Goudy, former senator Lyman Trumbull, Thomas Hoyne, Melville Fuller, Benjamin

F. Ayer, Grant Goodrich, Charles Hitchcock, Wirt Dexter, William Black, and Thomas Dent.[15] Swett served on the admissions committee to select individuals for membership from among Chicago's five hundred practicing attorneys at the time. He was well respected by his peers in the legal community, and he practiced in the top rank of attorneys not only in Chicago but also in the state of Illinois and throughout the nation. Ayer later said of Swett, "Few lawyers ever deserved or enjoyed in a greater degree the respect and confidence of the bench or the esteemed good will of his professional associates."[16]

Of the multiplicity of skills required for success as a trial lawyer, perhaps persuasion is of the greatest importance. Wirt Dexter, a president of the Chicago Bar Association, called Swett "one of the most persuasive who ever addressed a jury at the American bar." Swett's approach was to find the fundamental truth at the base of the action and develop his case around it. As James L. High, another bar association president, later described it, Swett "sought in every litigation a central and underlying principle upon which the conflict turned, and upon this principle he fought the fight to the end."[17]

During his twenty-four years in Chicago, Swett made many friends. Among these was David Swing, who came to Chicago a year after Swett to serve as the minister of Westminster Presbyterian Church, which Laura and Leonard Swett initially attended. Westminster merged with another church in 1871 to become Fourth Presbyterian, the leading church of its denomination in Chicago. Swing proved to be a popular minister, adapting his sermons and writings to the liberal Protestant theology of the day after the publication of Charles Darwin's *Origin of Species* in 1859 and *The Descent of Man* in 1871. In early 1874, a diligent keeper of the church's Calvinist doctrines, Professor Francis L. Patton of the Theological Seminary of the Northwest, filed heresy charges against Swing. A trial took place in April 1874 in the district of Chicago presbytery, and Swett testified in Swing's defense. Always strong in his role as advocate, Swett prepared by schooling himself thoroughly in Presbyterian doctrine, and David Swing was acquitted. Unwilling to yield, however, Patton appealed the case to the church synod, and Swing resigned rather than drag his parishioners through a bitter doctrinal feud. The strict Calvinists prevailed at the synod level, a hollow victory after Swing's resignation and a discouraging defeat for the area ministry, looking to adopt new and emerging ideas.[18]

Another notable Swett had befriended was General George Custer. Leonard and Laura Swett had become acquainted with the general and his wife, Elizabeth, earlier in Washington, and while Swett was in the Dakota Territory working on the Wintermute case, he visited the Custers at Fort Lincoln (near today's Mandan, North Dakota). But it was the Swetts' son, now called Bert, who developed a lasting relationship with the famous general and his family. In 1875, when he was sixteen, Bert attended a preparatory school in Woodstock, Illinois, sixty miles northwest of Chicago. After four months, he wrote home, "Everything is dull here," so Swett and Laura sent him to Phillips Exeter Academy in New Hampshire the next year.[19] However, things did not go well at Exeter either. Bert had difficulty in class and visited a doctor, who found the boy overly nervous and anxious and recommended that he take a vacation. At the urging of his parents, during the winter break he made a trip to Washington and New York City, meeting the general and his wife. The Custers took a liking to Bert and spent a considerable amount of time with him. They invited him to visit them at Fort Lincoln in the Dakota Territory the following summer.[20]

Not long after meeting Bert, the Custers stopped in Chicago while returning to Fort Lincoln and visited Leonard and Laura Swett at their home. Swett wrote to Bert about the general's upcoming assignment to protect immigrants and miners in the area of the Black Hills. The general described the planned military policy to move against the Lakota Sioux and again invited Bert to visit Fort Lincoln the coming summer.[21] If Bert had actually visited the Custers that summer, he would have found more excitement and tragedy than he bargained for. At the battle of Little Bighorn on June 25–26, 1876, Custer and his men were killed. The Native Americans wiped out Custer and 220 soldiers of the Seventh Cavalry in the battle that has since become a legend.[22]

In the spring of 1876, friends at Exeter invited Bert for a proposed yacht trip, but his father quashed the idea because of the cost and possibly other concerns. Laura also visited Exeter that spring.[23] Bert did not return to school the following fall, possibly because of a lack of funds. Swett was changing law partners, and money was tight.

During the mid to late 1870s, Swett also provided legal assistance to the Lincoln family. Erratic behavior on the part of Mary Lincoln led her son Robert to seek the services of his father's old friend Leonard Swett. Mary had experienced many tragedies during her life. She lost her mother at age seven, two of her sons died at a young age, and her husband was assassinated. Over her first decade of widowhood, indignities compounded for Mary Lincoln. Income from her late husband's estate was irregular. She lost a third son, Tad, who died of a respiratory disease in July 1871 at age eighteen. Just a few months later, while she was living with Robert, the Great Chicago Fire broke out and she had to evacuate. William Herndon's ongoing biographical lectures went from bad to worse for her, as they raised unpleasant questions about her husband's past, including Lincoln's religious infidelity and his love for Ann Rutledge. In their biographical collaboration, Ward Hill Lamon and Chauncey Black raised doubts about Lincoln's parentage, with Lamon claiming he could find no record of Lincoln's parents' marriage, adding further insult to Mary's Victorian sensibilities. Mary and Robert Lincoln attempted to restrain the Lincoln biography projects, and Swett was aware of their motives. Robert induced Swett to convey his objections on the Lamon book to its author, with the intent of eliminating certain passages. Apparently such aspersions concerning his old friend upset Swett as well, as Orville Browning described a dinner conversation at which Swett was highly critical of Lamon's book.[24]

In March 1875, as the tenth anniversary of her husband's martyrdom approached, Mary conceived the strange idea that her one surviving son was dying. Robert took a room next to hers at the Grand Pacific Hotel in Chicago to observe her odd behavior. Two weeks later, he tried to stop her at the elevator as she bounded for the lobby only partially clad. She objected, saying, "You are going to murder me." Following this incident, Robert initiated insanity proceedings as required by Illinois law.[25]

Leonard Swett had developed a comfortable relationship with both mother and son over two decades, based on his long friendship with Lincoln. Now Robert brought Swett into the case to take advantage of his expertise in insanity as well as his diplomatic skill. Swett assembled a team of current-day experts on mental illness, including one of the founders of the American Medical Association and the first president of the American Neurological Association. These experts "pronounced her insane by all the physicians and her confinement [was] recommended." Robert decided to move forward to trial for commitment and appointment of a conservator. Swett wrote a comprehensive twenty-three-page letter to Davis describing the trial and attending difficulties with Mary.[26]

Swett volunteered to try to talk Mary into accompanying him peaceably to trial, rather than being handcuffed and dragged by law officers. He wrote to Davis that the conversation was civil, "but with bitterness and sarcasm such as wounded me; it seems to me worse than bullets would." At one point, she said, "Mr. Swett, allow me to suggest that you go home and take care of your wife. I have heard some stories on that subject about her," referring to Laura Swett's chronic disability. Obviously she was very familiar with the Swetts from their ongoing relationship. It took Swett more than an hour to persuade her, but Mary finally consented to accompany him.[27]

For Mary's defense, Swett obtained the services of Isaac Arnold, a former congressman from Chicago and a Lincoln supporter and biographer who was associated with the Swett law firm from 1872 to 1875.[28] On the day of the trial, however, Arnold had second thoughts about defending Mary, feeling there was a conflict of interests in that she might truly be insane. Swett managed to persuade him to proceed nonetheless. Benjamin Ayer questioned the witnesses, and Swett gave only a brief summation to the jury. Then followed Arnold's defense, in which he proved to be a sympathetic friend to her.[29]

The jury voted for commitment and financial guardianship. The following day, Mary moved to a private facility, Bellevue Place, in nearby Batavia, Illinois. She carried more than fifty thousand dollars in bearer bonds in her petticoats, and another verbal tussle with Swett ensued when he tried to get her to give them up, although he finally got them from her with Arnold's assistance. That evening, she eluded her guards and slipped out to obtain some laudanum, a drug she could use for suicide. The first two druggists did not immediately respond to her requests, so she went on to a third, who gave her burnt sugar and water, which she swallowed.[30] Swett and Robert spent the night with her. As Swett was leaving the next morning, she treated him civilly and asked him to visit her in Batavia.[31]

With some assistance from Myra Bradwell, the editor of the *Chicago Legal News*, Mary was released from Bellevue after four months to live with her sister and brother-in-law, Elizabeth and Ninian Edwards, in Springfield. Another trial was held in June 1876 with only Ninian Edwards, Robert Lincoln, Leonard Swett, and the court and jury in attendance. This time Mary was declared competent. Four days after her funds were restored, she wrote to Robert, "You have tried your game of robbery long enough," demanding the return of "*all* my paintings . . . silver set . . . and other articles your wife appropriated." Swett recognized behavior potentially damaging to both mother and son and took immediate action. He drafted a stinging rebuke to Ninian Edwards, with the approval of Robert Lincoln and David Davis, in which he reminded him "that the removal of civil disabilities from Mrs. Lincoln" was done "to err on the side of leniency towards her." If Mary tried to ruin Robert, Swett swore, "I shall, as a citizen, irrespective of Robert, or anyone . . . have her confined as an insane person, whatever may be the clamor or consequences." He concluded by instructing Edwards to communicate this to Mrs. Lincoln "kindly but firmly." Edwards replied within two days with Mrs. Lincoln's promise not to sue or attack Robert. It was a firm approach based on sound reasoning, and it proved to be successful. Robert Lincoln expressed his appreciation for Swett's assistance in a letter to John Hay: "In the catastrophe, the value of Mr. Swett's earnestness, tact and resources have placed me in debt to him to an extent I can never repay."[32]

In the midst of assisting Robert with his mother, on December 22, 1875, Swett attended the wedding of David Davis's twenty-three-year-old daughter, Sallie Worthing Davis, and the son of Supreme Court justice Noah H. Swayne from Toledo, Ohio. The wedding took place in the Davis home in Bloomington, a grand Victorian estate in a pleasant grove of shade trees. Many of the three hundred guests undoubtedly recalled that Lincoln had been a frequent visitor in the Davis home and that this year was the tenth anniversary of his assassination. Swett likely remembered his buggy ride from the Davis home with Lincoln to the courthouse, where Swett introduced his friend to a vast audience during Lincoln's senate campaign against Stephen A. Douglas in 1858. At the wedding, Swett joined a large gathering of old and new friends, from Judge T. Lyle Dickey, just elected to the Illinois Supreme Court, to Ward Hill Lamon's daughter Dollie, whose mother had died in Bloomington when she was an infant. Although Swett was a close friend of Lamon's, he had not seen Dollie until now because Lamon's sister had raised her.[33]

By this 1875 wedding celebration, Swett had known for more than a year that his *Fertilizing Co. v. Hyde Park* case was headed for the U.S. Supreme Court. He had no idea what kind of opinion Justice Swayne, who was also at the wedding, would write. Swett had met Swayne while he was in Washington during the Civil War. He was pleased to run into Judge John Dean Caton, who had written, in his curt, caustic style, several decisions favorable to Swett. Caton had just completed writing a book titled

A Summer in Norway and regaled Swett with his travel adventures. Former U.S. congressman "Long" John Wentworth also attended the wedding with his daughter Roxanna.[34]

The stellar lights of Bloomington enjoyed the wedding and reunion as well: Jesse Fell and his attorney brother, Kersey; Asahel Gridley, a crusty businessman and banker; Judge John M. Scott, who replaced Davis as judge of the Eighth Circuit before moving to the Illinois Supreme Court bench; Democratic congressman Adlai E. Stevenson; and former Republican congressman John McNulta, leader of the McLean County Ninety-Fourth Illinois Regiment. Swett took the train to Bloomington from Chicago with his good friend and attorney colleague Wirt Dexter, who hailed from Dexter, Michigan.[35] For Swett, the wedding was both a homecoming, where he became reacquainted with his many friends in politics and the courts, and an opportunity to reflect on his personal achievements since moving to Chicago a decade earlier.

Early the next year, on February 20, 1876, Swett gave a lecture on Lincoln at Grew's Opera House in Chicago. The sponsors of the event had chosen Swett to speak on the former president to inaugurate what was to be a series of lectures, hoping that both the speaker and the subject would attract attention, and they were not disappointed. The *Chicago Press & Tribune* wrote, "The matter was of such unusual interest that [Swett] held the unflagging attention of his audience until its close." Swett repeated the lecture in Bloomington in early July.[36]

Throughout 1876, Swett's legal career also continued to keep him busy. He soon became involved in defending some of those caught up in the Whiskey Ring scandal. In 1875 and 1876, President Grant's treasury secretary, Benjamin Helm Bristow, had been finding evidence of extensive conspiracies to divert tax revenues in Chicago, St. Louis, Milwaukee, and other locations. Many distillers had been bribing revenue officers to defraud the government of funds. In the legal prosecutions that followed, up to three hundred people may have been accused, resulting in 110 convictions and fines amounting to a possible accumulated total of $3 million. Swett subsequently represented thirteen of those indicted. According to Judge Richard S. Tuthill of the Cook County Circuit Court, he asked Swett if he would try these cases, to which Swett responded, "They are not the sort of cases to take into court." Instead, Swett went to Washington to discuss settlements for those he was representing, possibly meeting with Secretary

Bristow, a protégé of David Davis's, and Swett's "great powers as a diplomat were shown by the result." He was able to negotiate settlements for every one of his clients, none of whom wound up spending any time in jail.[37]

Another hotly contested case in 1876 involved Swett's representation of Rodolphus K. and Howard A. Turner, who were indicted for forgery in connection with the title to $480,000 worth of land situated in South Chicago. In two trials, Swett claimed that the prosecution was malicious in that the attorneys for the parties holding adverse title to the land were orchestrating the criminal proceedings. After two trials in which the jury could not agree on a verdict, the prosecution abandoned the case. The lead prosecutor became a Cook County circuit judge and later wrote that the case "bristled with almost all conceivable questions of real estate and criminal law, and particularly the law of evidence, was full of dramatic incidents, and to relate it all in its details would make a novel of many pages and unabating interest." A *Chicago Times* editor apparently found the case quite interesting as well, later describing it as the "most remarkable litigation ever before a court in Chicago."[38]

Despite the demands of his busy legal practice, Swett also found time to participate in important civic activities in Chicago. In this capacity, he played a prominent role in two election reform meetings in April 1876, which demonstrated his political potential. The first followed alleged ballot-box stuffing in an aldermanic contest in South Town in early April. He participated in a planning session at the Palmer House, and as a result of his efforts, a call was issued for Chicago voters to attend a meeting designed to alert citizens to the problem. The first meeting took place on a Saturday evening in Farwell Hall. Several thousand people, mostly from Chicago's South Side, squeezed into the hall, and the *Chicago Times* reported that an estimated five thousand more were turned away. As the kickoff speaker, Swett informed the crowd that "the recent election was carried by fraud and violence, and the candidates actually defeated by the votes of the people have been declared elected by ballot-stuffing and by the obstruction of ballots actually cast." The newspaper reported the next day that "the audience . . . quickly became transformed into a howling mass, as [Swett] delineated the condition of the city." When Swett asked rhetorically what should be done, the crowd screamed, "Hang them! Hang them!!" Swett responded, "Before we do anything let us reflect." He ended his talk with a resolution calling for the protection of the ballots at the coming city election.

The *Chicago Times* reported that all the speeches "were warmly received; that of Leonard Swett especially being taken most enthusiastically to heart."[39]

Three days later, at the Exposition Building, an even larger meeting of more than forty thousand people convened to deal with the coming mayoral election. After a reception of loud cheering, Swett spoke, addressing the audience once from each end of the hall. He made a proposal that was accepted by the people. Thereafter, the reform group nominated the Democrat Thomas Hoyne, a highly respected attorney, hoping to force Mayor Harvey Colvin of the People's Party to resign because of heightened corruption in city affairs. Hoyne was nominated as an independent and elected. Colvin refused to yield and was backed by the court, so a special election was allowed at the direction of the city council. In this race, the Republicans backed a candidate of their own, Monroe Heath, rather than Hoyne, and they succeeded in getting Heath elected.[40]

Later that year, Swett became involved in yet another murder case, this time in defense of Alexander Sullivan, secretary of the Chicago Board of Public Works and a protégé of the city's mayor, Harvey Doolittle Colvin. Sullivan stood accused of killing Francis Hanford, a high school principal in Chicago and former assistant superintendent of schools, who had made scurrilous and insulting remarks about Sullivan's wife. Hanford accused Sullivan's wife of having an intimate relationship with the mayor, and on August 7, 1876, Sullivan shot him from a range of six feet. Swett took on the defense of the twenty-nine-year-old Sullivan at a very busy time in his practice. His motive for doing so is unclear, other than that he was good at this sort of defense. Swett apparently had become something of a legal specialist in dealing with homicides committed at close range while witnesses looked on. In this case, obvious challenges in the evidence may have attracted him, or maybe it was his tendency toward charity, as Sullivan was a young immigrant of socially inferior status.[41]

In the Sullivan trial in October 1876, Swett explained the fine points of the law applicable to self-defense in a Lincolnesque approach to the jury: "The circumstances of the killing, as charged, and the act of killing are both admitted. The motive with which the act was done alone remains, few will be the disputed facts even upon collateral points, but a human heart must be analyzed and the issues of life and death depend upon the accuracy with which you do it." At the end of the trial, Swett told the jury, in his eloquent manner, "I am oppressed by the solemnity of the occasion, and as I realize that a word by me injudiciously uttered or a false position assumed may put all my client holds dear at hazard." He closed: "All that hearts hold dear are in the scales you balance, and as in the final trial, when all deeds shall be weighed, you will bow with fear but with hope—so humbly, but hopefully we bow before you and wait for deliverance."[42]

The *Chicago Times* described the crowds attending the closing scenes of the trial: "It would have been as easy to turn a somersault in an oyster shell, as to have hung a pumpkin seed edgewise in that concourse of men and women."[43] However, as James L. High later described Swett's advocacy, "no applause of listening multitudes could tempt him from the supreme issue to which he addressed himself. Self was forgotten, and thus it was that we who sat under the spell of his eloquence, judges and jurors, associates and opponents, saw before us something more than a mere hired advocate. We saw a man of splendid presence, of magnetic voice which could cover the whole range of pathos and persuasion . . . and behind all, inspiring all, was the constant sense of a supreme conviction of the righteousness of his cause."[44]

The trial ended with a hung jury voting eleven to one for acquittal. After this trial, the *Chicago Tribune* accused the judge, William K. McAllister, of bias in favor of the prisoner, and the Chicago Bar Association moved to investigate his conduct. Swett attended this bar association meeting but declined to advocate or oppose an investigation, though he defended Judge McAllister by saying that his conduct "had been greatly misrepresented . . . and very generally misunderstood." The second trial was postponed for five months, until March 1877. This time the jury acquitted Alexander Sullivan.[45]

Meanwhile, in late 1876, Robert Lincoln called on Swett for assistance once again, this time to review the bizarre attempt of several counterfeiters to steal his father's body so they could demand a ransom for the release of their engraver, who was in prison. A Secret Service informant infiltrated this plot and alerted the police. Swett consulted with Robert and the Secret Service as the plot unfolded, and he oversaw the propriety of the arrest and handling of the prisoners. Over the objection of the Secret Service agent, Swett insisted that the counterfeiters had a right to legal counsel. This enabled one of them to plant a bogus story in the *Chicago InterOcean*, but the truth finally emerged.[46] Such unwanted notoriety was the price Robert paid for being the son of a famous president.

By 1876, Swett had rejoined the Republican Party and gave muted support to Rutherford B. Hayes. After the disputed presidential election of 1876 failed to result in a clear decision from the Electoral College between Hayes and Democrat Samuel J. Tilden, the latter of whom had won the popular vote, Swett wrote a draft speech or statement, probably at the request of a committee of the Chicago Bar Association. In this seven-thousand-plus-word document, Swett traced most of the congressional changes with regard to the tallies of the Electoral College since the birth of the nation. He took up the Hayes-Tilden controversy and invited legal scholars to consider the separate roles of the House and the Senate in the election of the president and the vice president under the Twelfth Amendment to the Constitution, in the absence of an appropriate decision from the Electoral College. Swett concluded, "The people of the country, therefore, ought to demand of the politicians that their councils shall be guided by moderation and wisdom, and that some peaceful solution shall be found in reference to the difficulties and dangers which unnerve us."[47]

The Chicago Bar Association may have backed away from the controversy as it became more involved politically, seeking to avoid such arguments in its early years. Congress waded in as the dispute worsened, setting up committees in both houses in late December. The Electoral Commission Act evolved in January, and a bill passed in the Senate and the House before the end of the month. Members of the Electoral Commission voted along party lines and gave all contested electoral votes to Hayes, creating a majority of one for him. Fourteen years of reconstruction efforts in the South thus ended in 1877, as much from Republican exhaustion as from Democratic pressure for white supremacy.[48]

By this time, Swett had garnered a reputation in connection with his successful use of the insanity defense, and he continued to employ this defense and even helped define it. In May 1877, while successfully defending Alvin Lancaster in a case in federal court brought by a New York City woman suing for damages, Swett argued the issue of what constituted insanity. The case resulted in Judge Henry W. Blodgett rendering a decision in Lancaster's favor.[49]

In July 1877, the Chicago mayor drew on Swett's speaking ability to recruit volunteers as troops to bring order in the midst of rioting. Railroad strikes in the East in mid-1877 had severely affected Chicago, the nation's most crucial railroad center. Riots and bloodshed began in Baltimore and Pittsburgh and spread to Chicago. For three days, all freight traffic in the city was halted, and the factories and businesses of meat-packing, grain handling, and manufacturing shut down. On July 26, Swett spoke at a mass meeting at the Moody and Sankey Tabernacle. Mayor Monroe Heath called for the recruitment of five thousand citizens, including as many former soldiers as possible, to assist in maintaining order. Swett suggested, in the interest of organization and expediency, that the mayor request that the U.S. government provide an army regiment (a thousand men) and expressed the opinion that four companies (four hundred men) could do the job of restoring order. Following this meeting, four companies of veterans organized locally, one mounted, and the Regular Army marched two companies down Madison Street. The violence peaked the following day but then subsided, perhaps because neither side really wanted a confrontation.[50]

After years of living in a seemingly endless series of hotels, apartments, rental houses, and several temporary homes that Laura considered inadequate, in 1878 the Swetts finally bought a family home, the absence of which had long been a point of contention in their household. Their new house was at 122 Ashland Avenue on the west side of Chicago, easily accessible to downtown. This residence was in the Central Park area, later known as Garfield. The Swetts' home was just north of Ogden Avenue, and their church, Third Presbyterian, was close by on the other side of Ashland Avenue.[51]

Bert now spent an extended period in Illinois, caring for livestock on a farm near Mendota, about ninety miles southwest of Chicago, and attending medical school on and off at Rush and Chicago Medical Colleges between 1878 and 1882. He also made a series of extended tours to Utah, Texas, and California with the newly created U.S. Geological Survey and army personnel, which his father arranged through geologist and explorer John Wesley Powell, whom Swett knew from his Bloomington days. Leonard and Laura hoped that these trips would strengthen their son physically.[52] While studying at Chicago Medical College in 1878, Bert wrote home that he had asked a doctor about his father's kidney disease. This may have been an early indication that Swett was suffering from type 2 diabetes. During his years of practice in Chicago, Swett added about fifty pounds to his formerly lanky frame, a risk factor associated with development of the disease.[53]

Swett found another opportunity to speak publicly in November 1879, on the occasion of the meeting of the Union Army of the Tennessee in Chicago. This time he shared the dais with several luminaries: President Ulysses S. Grant, General William Tecumseh Sherman, and Mark Twain, the most acclaimed American storyteller of the nineteenth century. Sherman gave the first toast and Grant the second. Swett gave the seventh toast, providing a tribute to the Mexican-American War officers and soldiers. His toast was formal and patriotic, paying obeisance to famous Greek leaders and battles, recalling the names of heroes and battlefields in this war, and recognizing the vastness of the veterans' accomplishments. Mark Twain finally rose to speak in the wee hours of the morning and plied his talents to poke some fun at the leader of the Union army. Twain's humor brought down the house, even getting a good laugh out of the ordinarily shy and reticent Grant. Twain thought his speech that evening was "the high point of his career as a speechmaker."[54]

During the 1870s, Swett also represented several clients in important Illinois Supreme Court cases related to the legalization of futures trading and the operating authority of its regulatory body, the Chicago Board of Trade. In representing these clients, Swett participated in the evolution of the key functions of the world's largest grain market, enabling owners and investors to find more efficient ways to exchange their interests in various commodities. In the decade since his failed stock market speculations of 1863–64, Swett had come to understand the essential function of futures trading in agricultural markets. If participants fully understood the risks involved, they could trade advantageously. Defining gambling as unlawful and distinguishing it from lawful speculation was difficult, and policing subtle differences was even more so. In one case Swett was involved in, he succeeded in getting the Illinois Supreme Court to remand the case to the lower court for further consideration on the trading rules and their application after customary contractual obligations were ignored.[55]

As the next decade got under way, Swett became involved when the Chicago Bar Association grew concerned about jury bribing and other interference with jurors. He played a role in the prosecution of these activities by bringing two resolutions to the association in March and April 1880: one to authorize the preparation of measures to prosecute and punish improper jury interference, and the other to raise funds to carry out these measures. The bar association adopted both of his resolutions.[56]

Also in April 1880, Swett gave a talk on Lincoln and Grant before a Union veterans group, and several months later, in July, he traveled north to Lake Bluff, Illinois, to give a speech on Lincoln at the Methodist church. Swett found time that year as well to organize a Sons of Maine group in Chicago, and he served as its first vice president, with Judge Thomas Drummond of the U.S. Circuit Court as president. At the group's initial banquet the following summer, in June 1881, former vice president Hannibal Hamlin and former minister to France Elihu B. Washburne shared the podium.[57]

Another speech Swett gave in 1880 was on behalf of the Illinois governor welcoming the Masons and Knights Templar to Chicago. Some fifty thousand Knights attended, with twenty-five thousand marching in parade in their white-plumed and black uniforms, accompanied by 125 bands. Swett did not detain them long, giving a brief speech paying homage to their long history and then focusing on their current missions.[58]

The Swett household had one guest from each side of the family for this meeting. In a letter to the now twenty-one-year-old Bert, Swett wrote that a relative from Turner, Maine, on the Swett side of the family "was pure Yankee genus—talked about the expense of the food he ate, came to the table once in his shirt sleeves and because of his entertainment at my house, was almost the happiest man I ever saw." In contrast, the Quigg cousin of Laura, "who represents the other side of your house, or whatever of iron, you may have in your nature . . . has been a merchant at Ithaca all his life, his father before him, having established his store 80 years ago. He is a good specimen of a country merchant and the Quiggs—honest, thrifty, bashful and tenacious in whatever he thinks or believes."[59]

Perhaps because Swett had seen Grant again in 1879, he initially supported him for a third term in 1880, but his busy legal practice did not accommodate much activity on Grant's behalf. As things developed, after the Chicago convention made James A. Garfield the Republican nominee on the thirty-sixth ballot, Swett gave Garfield modest support. This time, however, he did not set aside his practice of law to get involved in politics surrounding the presidential race.[60]

During this period, Swett's largest civil clients were insurance companies, and he had personal connections with two of them. Van Higgins, his first law partner in Chicago, became a financial agent for the Charter Oak Life Insurance Company of Hartford, Connecticut, at about the same time that he and Swett terminated their partnership at the end of 1872. As a result, Swett later represented the principals of Charter Oak and their customers in litigation in Illinois and Hartford. Swett developed an even more significant connection with Union Mutual Life Insurance Company of Maine. His former college roommate, Josiah Hammond, became general counsel for the firm when it moved its headquarters to Portland, Maine, in 1881, and Swett became its Chicago counsel.[61]

One of Swett's most important cases for Union Mutual involved the foreclosure of a trust deed held by the company for three hundred thousand dollars on the property of the old University of Chicago. In 1858, Stephen A. Douglas had conveyed ten acres of land to the former university. A building named Douglas Hall was erected and classes began. In 1876, the university borrowed $150,000 from the Union Mutual Life Insurance Company and executed a mortgage on the property. Two years later, payments ceased, and debt started to mount with interest accumulating. The insurance company offered to accept one hundred thousand dollars in full discharge of the entire debt the following year and made concessions concerning the repayment of the unpaid balance. When the university and its Baptist supporters could not raise the funds, the company retained Swett to file a foreclosure suit in 1881. Heirs of Stephen Douglas filed a cross bill for jurisdiction on contractual grounds, so initially Swett faced two suits. He eventually proved that the university had the right to mortgage the property and won his case for foreclosure four years after the initial suit, in 1885.[62]

I thank God . . . that in the mysteries of providence
He placed the lines of my life between two such great
men as David Davis and Abraham Lincoln.
                    —*Leonard Swett, "In Memory of David Davis," March 1887*

12. The Better Angels of Our Nature

While working on the University of Chicago foreclosure suit, Swett complained of poor health in letters to his mother in 1881–82, but without specifying his ailments.[1] He relaxed for several days on Mackinac Island in Michigan in the summer of 1881 but found limited relief from his maladies. At times, he said, he was "unable to work." As a consequence, he took an eighty-two-day vacation from July to September 1882, traveling to England and France. He booked first-class passage on Great Eastern's *Leviathan.* Apparently Laura did not feel healthy enough to travel, so once again she stayed behind to fend for herself. Among the 162 passengers on the ship were a number of Chicagoans, including Swett's minister friend David Swing. On arriving in Liverpool, Swett mentioned his "back and kidney" problems in a letter to his wife and son. He then visited the typical tourist sites in London and Paris. One of the highlights was seeing Queen Victoria pass by in a carriage; he described her as "simply a little old woman in black, plain and simple," a fitting description for the queen who continued to dress in mourning clothes long after the 1861 death of her husband, Prince Albert. He also made a few excursions to Derby, Sheffield, and Chester, possibly for work on an estate claim for a client in Chicago, John Drake, who had asked Swett to investigate a claim on an English Drake estate. Although John was a possible heir, nothing came from Swett's investigation. As they made preparations to return home, Professor Swing, as Swett called him, told his fellow Chicagoans he wanted to get home and get warm.[2]

After his return home, Swett got back to work on his legal cases. On referral from a southern Illinois family, in 1883 he represented Charles Stickney, a Harvard graduate living in Colorado, in a double murder case. Incensed at the alleged mistreatment of his wife, Stickney had killed Montgomery Campau and an innocent bystander. The prosecutor in the case was former congressman Thomas McDonald Patterson. Swett, who had become a master of the insanity defense, employed it successfully once again, winning an acquittal for the defendant.[3]

This same year, Swett established what was to be his final partnership in the legal arena, with Peter S. Grosscup. Grosscup had practiced for an extended period in Ohio before moving to Chicago. Like Swett, he had made two unsuccessful forays into congressional politics before settling fully into the practice of law. He proved to be an able partner.[4]

Swett made a second trip to Europe in the summer of 1884. The Swetts had sent their son on an extended trip to Europe to round out his education, and while on his travels, Bert had become ill in Paris. Leonard Swett's second European trip appears to have been motivated by parental concern for Bert's health. By the time Swett arrived, however, Bert had already recovered and met his father in London. Here, Swett saw some of the same sights as on his earlier trip, and then the two went to Paris, where Swett interviewed a potential teacher to instruct Bert in French. Leaving his son in Paris, Swett visited Switzerland, Brussels, and the battlefield at Waterloo, finally returning home. Bert remained in Europe longer, also visiting Switzerland, as well as the Riviera and Italy.[5]

Despite Swett's poor health and travel, cases kept flowing into his firm, and frequently the work required his presence on the East Coast. In August 1885, he wrote Laura from Turner, Maine, that he had all sorts of maladies and was thinking of going to Philadelphia to be treated by the nationally renowned doctor S. Weir Mitchell. Apparently he did not see Mitchell at that time, however. After returning to Chicago and spending the fall in poor health, Swett finally made the trip to Philadelphia at the end of the year. He took Bert along, hoping that his son could care for him while he sought treatment from Dr. Mitchell for what may have been prostate problems. While there, Bert contracted typhoid fever, and the two recovered slowly under the care of different physicians. Swett's nephew and junior law partner, Edward Swett, traveled to Philadelphia to assist them.[6]

By early March 1886, both Swett and Bert had recovered enough to head south for further recuperation. They left New York by the coastal steamship *Delaware*, bound for Charleston, South Carolina. While they were at sea, Laura, who had remained back home in Chicago, suffered a stroke and died on March 5 at age fifty-eight. When Swett and his son learned the news, they immediately headed for Chicago. En route, however, Swett realized they would not arrive in time for Laura's funeral, so they stopped to rest at Aiken, South Carolina. He wired their minister some thoughts for her service, describing her constant illness for nearly the last thirty years. As an invalid, he said, she had suffered great pain with heroic fortitude and was sustained by her religious faith, "living a life of Christian virtue and discharg[ing] every duty to the best of her ability. The help she gave her husband was of a high and gentle order."[7] Attending her funeral were relatives who lived nearby, including Laura's father; her brother, David; several sisters and their families from Hyde Park, Bloomington, and Clinton; and Leonard's brother and two nephews in Chicago. Her pallbearers included Robert Lincoln, Van Higgins, and Peter Grosscup.[8]

Although Leonard Swett had been absent for much of his relationship with Laura, and his habitual inclination for travel had added to her distress, he had the same great difficulty in adjusting to her loss as he did after Lincoln's shocking assassination and Orme's lingering departure. Swett stayed in Aiken about four weeks before returning to Chicago. His doctor advised him not to work until September, but in his usual fashion, by May 1886 he was already making preparations for another trip, this time heading for Mexico City to revisit his military mission from thirty-eight years earlier.[9] Before leaving, he went to Bloomington to visit David Davis and spent the day with him on May 10. Davis suffered from diabetes and had been ill for many months, and Swett said good-bye knowing he might never again see the man he had known longer and better than any other friend. By the time he returned to Chicago from Mexico at the end of June, he received word of David Davis's death on June 26, 1886. Swett had lost the last of his closest friends and allies. Those he had traveled to see often and returned home to for solace and support, the beacons of his life—Abraham Lincoln, William Orme, Laura Swett, and David Davis—all were gone.

Davis's funeral was the most remarkable he had ever witnessed, said Swett. "Twenty thousand people gathered there on that occasion, coming in mostly by wagons, and some coming twenty-five or thirty miles. This crowd, of course, could not get into the house, or even see the funeral, but they could line, in silence, the streets where it was known the cortege would pass, filling the sidewalks, the front yards, doors and windows every inch of the way from his house to the graveyard, a distance of more than two miles." Swett rode in the second carriage of 150 in the funeral procession, along with Chief Justice John M. Scott of the Illinois Supreme Court and attorney Hamilton Spenser. Swett and Scott served as pallbearers, along with Adlai Stevenson and Robert Lincoln. "Thus on a bright June day, at that gathering of the great and the small, of the proud and the humble, the rich and the poor, and all his friends, we consigned him to his final resting place, and all alike were real mourners."[10]

After Davis's funeral, Swett spent several months visiting with various members of his family and friends, from Montreal to Maine. He returned to Chicago refreshed and wrote to thank his sister Sarah Ricker, whose family lived on the Ricker-Swett home farm, for "one of the pleasantest vacations" he had ever had. He professed to need to do some work, but just enough to relieve him "of the tediousness of doing nothing."[11]

That same year, Rose Skillings, a relative by marriage from Swett's sister's husband's family, had joined the Swett household in Chicago, perhaps so she could attend school and work in the city. Rose enlivened the home and caught the attention of Bert, who enjoyed her presence. Swett soon was enjoying life again as well. He was a happy man by nature and not the sort to mourn forever. Although he did not forget his wife and friends, he was able to move on. In a letter to Sarah in October, Swett portrayed his current idyllic daily routine, beginning with a horseback ride around a nearby park at six A.M., breakfast with the family at seven, a trip to the office by nine, his return home between three-thirty and five P.M., and if still early enough, another ride before dinner at six. Then the family gathered for reading Homer's *Iliad* or a Homeric story until nine, at which point he retired.[12]

At this time, Swett's office was on the eighth floor of the Montauk Block, Chicago's first skyscraper, built in 1882. One of Chicago's most famous architectural companies of the time, Burnham and Root, had designed this ten-story building on Monroe Street between Dearborn and Clark. Although its architectural supremacy was brief, the building and its location captured the prominence of Swett's last seven years in Chicago. A *Chicago Herald* article titled "Great Illinois Lawyers" depicted the setting in late November 1886, describing Swett's office as having two windows and a gallery of fourteen photographs and engravings, which might have been called "the Eighth Circuit in Chicago." The "most conspicuous place" held William Edgar Marshall's 1866 sixteen-by-twenty-inch engraving of Lincoln. Two cabinet members were represented: William H. Seward in an engraving sent to Swett by his son, Frederick W. Seward, and Simon Cameron in a recent photograph. Cameron had disappointed Swett as Lincoln's first secretary of war, but he admired him as an astute Pennsylvania politician. Swett described Stephen T. Logan, Lincoln's second law partner, as "the greatest lawyer of them all," and his picture hung to one side of Lincoln's. Illinois lawyers filled the remaining spots in the gallery. One picture was missing at the time: Leonard Volk had borrowed Swett's picture of David Davis while working on his bust of Davis.[13]

It was in this office that Swett did most of his writing, preparing at least three articles for formal publication in 1885–87. Although Swett's writings on Lincoln were scattered throughout his life, he spent more time and energy on them in his late fifties and early sixties, reflecting his apparent intent to devote a portion of his later years to recording his reminiscences of his old friend. During this period, Swett authored more than half of his total writings on Lincoln. Swett described the first time they met for "Lincoln's Story of His Own Life," which appeared in Allen Thorndike Rice's collection titled *Reminiscences of Abraham Lincoln*, published in 1885. He made a further submission to Francis Fisher Browne's 1886 book, *The Every-day Life of Abraham Lincoln*, and wrote another article titled "The Conspiracies of the Rebellion" for Rice's *North American Review* in 1887.[14]

Intermittently during late 1886 and into 1887, Swett was also busy working on another important legal case, as he had become part of the defense counsel in the wake of the Haymarket massacre. In May 1886, a violent uprising had occurred at the McCormick Reaper Works, which ended with the police opening fire on a crowd of workers. Several were killed or wounded. The next day, a protest took place near Haymarket Square, eight blocks west of the center of Chicago. As the rally wound down in the evening, with only a fraction of the crowd remaining, the police ordered the protestors to end the meeting. Someone threw a bomb into the ranks of the police, causing serious injury. In the accompanying chaos, the police fired their weapons randomly, killing some and injuring others, including a number from their own ranks. In the end, seven police were killed and sixty civilians injured.

Eight anarchists were charged and tried for conspiring with the unidentified bomber, who had slipped away into the crowd. A forty-three-year-old Civil War hero, Captain William P. Black, became the chief defense counsel. At the end of the twenty-one-day trial, the jury condemned seven of the defendants to be hanged and sentenced the eighth to a fifteen-year prison term. Black sacrificed his future legal career with his spirited defense. He asked Robert Ingersoll to assist him in the appeal, but Ingersoll declined, recommending that he find someone accepted by the conservative establishment. The details of Swett's selection are not clear, although the Defense Committee, led by the respected labor leader George Schilling and physician Ernest Schmidt, recruited him, and he accepted the challenge.[15]

Swett and Black outlined twenty-eight procedural errors in their brief for the Illinois Supreme Court and requested a stay in early November 1886. Chief Justice John Scott, an old friend of Swett's from the McLean Circuit Court, immediately ordered a stay of the execution scheduled for December. Errors with regard to jury selection and cross-examination were alleged, possibly due to the inexperience of the trial counsel in criminal defense work. Swett and Black made oral arguments before the court in the Haymarket case in mid-March 1887, but the resulting decision by the seven-member body, rendered in September, was unanimously negative. The author of the opinion, Justice Benjamin D. Magruder, focused on the evidence of conspiracy and the intent to promote lethal violence as described in the workers' newspaper, *Arbeiter Zeitung*. The court rejected the defense appeal point by point.[16]

The action then moved to the U.S. Supreme Court, but Swett did not play an active role in presenting arguments. In the year following the trial, the tide of questions rose and public opposition mounted. Former senator Lyman Trumbull said simply, "These men did not have a fair trial."[17] Three eminent attorneys from the East argued the case, but in the end, Justice Morrison Waite wrote the unanimous opinion denying the writ of error. A single recourse remained—the executive clemency power residing in the hands of the governor of Illinois, Swett's old friend Richard Oglesby. The task of reading thousands of appeals asking for reconsideration fell on his shoulders. In what proved to be a classic failure of the courts to sort out what had happened, before justice could be served, four of the eight were hanged and another committed suicide. Oglesby commuted two of the sentences to life imprisonment. In 1893, the next governor, John Peter Altgeld, pardoned the three remaining prisoners.[18] The bomber was never found, and some of the police deaths were determined to be from friendly fire.

While Swett was in the midst of his efforts on the Haymarket case, the Illinois Bar Association asked him to present his memories of his old friend and colleague David Davis. Swett's speech, given on March 5, 1887, nearly a year after Davis's death, reflected his own values as well as those of Davis. Swett began with his first sight of David Davis in 1848 and concluded with a description of his last visit with Davis thirty-eight years later. He recounted their days on the Eighth Circuit, their nomination of Lincoln, Davis's appointment to the U.S. Supreme Court, his time in the U.S. Senate, and his final days. Along the way, Swett told stories and anecdotes to portray Davis as a judge and described the cases and decisions for which he would be remembered. He called Davis "one of the greatest judges this country has ever produced" and said that "he knew just enough law to be a great judge, and not enough to spoil him," meaning that he used the law as a guide to justice, not as an end in itself. Davis was a "natural judge" who "took to justice by instinct" and "the best character I have ever met in life." Swett concluded by expressing his gratitude: "As I recall the circumstances of my own early life in this State, I thank God and thank Him again that in the mysteries of providence He placed the lines of my life between two such great men as David Davis and Abraham Lincoln, permitted me, in the hours of my own weakness, to 'Lean on their own great arms for support.'"[19]

Just two months later, on May 9, 1887, Swett gave another memorial speech for an old friend, this time T. Lyle Dickey, whom he had known since his days on the Eighth Circuit, when Dickey had been judge of the adjoining circuit in Ottawa, Illinois. Dickey had asked Swett to give his memorial speech at the time of his death, as he believed Swett to be the person best able to commemorate his character and appreciate what was worthy of remembrance from his life. The Dickey memorial encompassed much more than Dickey's life and the war's high price for his family. Swett reached out from one life to another, revealing his own character as well as Dickey's, and touched on one of Lincoln's bitter disappointments, when Dickey defected from being an old-line Whig to a Democrat in 1858–60. In this speech, one of his best examples of Victorian prose, Swett displayed his mastery of the art of storytelling.

Sixteen months after Laura's death, Leonard Swett surprised his friends and family by marrying his legal assistant, Maria A. H. Decker, on July 14, 1887. Maria was twenty-nine years younger than Swett and had been a legal assistant in his firm since 1880. The eldest of seven children born to a Roman Catholic family in Cologne, Germany, she had attended Catholic convent schools in Cologne and Brussels and became exceedingly proficient in French and English in addition to her native tongue. She also studied music extensively. In 1869, her family migrated to Chicago, where her father started a business. After his business was destroyed in the 1871 fire, Maria quickly learned stenographic skills to assist in supporting the family.[20]

Swett's law firm had initially hired Maria as a stenographer, but she quickly developed the skills to become the firm's bookkeeper, cashier, and general office manager. Swett noted her business and organizational acumen and employed her skills with his clients. In 1885, she had traveled with him to Hartford, Connecticut, to assist with the liquidation of the Charter Oak Life Insurance Company. As a result of Swett's defense, the principals had been exonerated from charges of fraud, and he needed Maria's administrative abilities. When Laura questioned the propriety of his decision to take Maria with him, in an effort to alert him to potential criticism, Swett defended the necessity of her assistance.[21] Maria's abilities continued to develop, and after several years, she gained a partnership interest in the firm. Her growth at the firm reflected not only her abilities but also Swett's openness to the advancement of women professionally, and perhaps as well his appreciation of Maria as a young, attractive, and highly intelligent woman whose company he enjoyed.

The marriage of Maria and Leonard Swett was accompanied by much fanfare in the newspapers, one of which described the bride as a "tall, handsome brunette." The ceremony took place at the residence of Archbishop Patrick A. Feehan, who served as the officiant. Maria's family attended, but only Rose Skillings, whom the papers erroneously referred to as a niece, was present from Swett's side. It is unknown why Bert did not attend, as he did not mention it in his writings. He liked Maria and was happy for his father. For their honeymoon, Leonard and Maria traveled to Niagara Falls and Saratoga Springs, New York.[22]

On their return to Chicago, the newly married couple entertained Archbishop Patrick Feehan and two Protestant ministers in their home for dinner. Leonard and Maria shared many interests, including a love of music and riding on horseback together in the parks. Swett acquired a black riding horse for Maria and upgraded his own mount to an Arabian, purchased in Lexington, Kentucky.[23]

Three months after his wedding, the dedication of a splendid tribute to Lincoln in October 1887 became the occasion for Swett's final written words on his old friend. A gift from a Chicago businessman had enabled the American sculptor Augustus Saint-Gaudens to create one of the great memorial monuments of the former president: the sculpture called *Abraham Lincoln: The Man*, commonly known as "Standing Lincoln," at the south end of Chicago's Lincoln Park, not far from Lake Michigan.

Saint-Gaudens had seen Lincoln twice: once in life, when Lincoln passed through New York on his way to Washington in 1860, and a second time after his death, as Lincoln's body lay in state at City Hall when the funeral procession stopped in New York in 1865. There, Saint-Gaudens went through the long line twice to view the great man's face. Now, before undertaking his sculpture, he made a careful study of Lincoln, including photographs by Mathew Brady and Alexander Gardner, and Leonard Volk's life mask of Lincoln and casts of his hands. He devoted great consideration to the pose, including the thoughtful tilt of the head forward, as well as the overall composition, placing a chair behind the upright figure. In this landmark depiction of the president, Lincoln stands in his long coat, with his head bowed in great thought as he would have appeared in the moments before delivering a speech. For the design of a base, Saint-Gaudens collaborated with the well-known architect Stanford White.[24]

Leonard Swett was the obvious choice as the principal speaker for the dedication of this magnificent statue in memory of Lincoln. No person in Chicago—or, in fact, the nation—had known Lincoln better or appreciated him more in his life in American law and politics, and Swett was well known for his superb speaking ability. His thirty-minute tribute did not disappoint. Those attending on the cold, rainy afternoon of October 22, 1887, were treated to masterful visual and verbal portrayals of the late president.

After the opening ceremonies and a formal presentation of the statue, Robert Lincoln assisted his fourteen-year-old son, Abraham Lincoln II, in the unveiling as a thirty-eight-gun salute fired and a band played patriotic numbers. Swett studied the image of his friend in bronze and looked out across the sea of admiring faces amid the mist of chilly fall rain. As the assembled crowd gazed at Lincoln's likeness, Swett brought it to life with his vivid words on the kind of man Lincoln was and what his leadership had meant to the Union. He drew a brief sketch of Lincoln's life and the essentials of his political career, including his "house divided" concept and emancipation, his self-reliance, and the equanimity of his leadership. He spoke of Lincoln's doubt during the first two years that "this terrible war" could be won and moved on to its two final years, when no one should have doubted its outcome. He explained Lincoln's religious views as "simply a reflex of his own character. He believed in God, as the . . . controller of the great events and destinies of mankind. He believed himself to be an instrument and leader of the forces of freedom." Swett told his listeners that Lincoln believed in the Declaration of Independence and its well-known words "that all men are created equal" as the "perfect standard of political truth," not a generality to be taken lightly. By his proclamation emancipating the slaves, he "lifted our whole country to a higher plane of civilization, and finally, at the hand of malice, fell a martyr because of this character and this act."[25]

The next year, 1888, was an election year, and Swett responded once again to an invitation to engage significantly in the presidential nominating process. This time, Judge Walter Q. Gresham, who had been a friend of David Davis's, was running. Davis and Gresham had become well acquainted during their eight-year association in federal appeals court work in Indiana, part of Davis's annual circuit court responsibility. Like Davis, Gresham was a political conservative and favored a legalistic approach to judicial questions. Swett had known him well for three years and perhaps casually for much longer. It was in Gresham's courtroom that Swett had given his memorial to Dickey the previous year.[26]

Four years earlier, in 1884, Gresham had been an unannounced candidate for the Republican presidential nomination. Senator Benjamin Harrison, also from Indiana, contended unsuccessfully for the nomination that year, and animosity between these two Republicans had gradually intensified. Now both became open candidates for president. Gresham's backers asked Swett to make the nominating speech at the convention in the new Auditorium Theater in Chicago.[27]

On June 23, 1888, Swett introduced Gresham, who was a relatively unknown candidate outside Indiana and Illinois. Swett emphasized his Civil War record, his wounding at Leggett's Hill near Atlanta, his improvement in mail service as postmaster general, and his concern for the working classes. Gresham came in second on the first three ballots, but his support faded after Robert Ingersoll came out wholeheartedly in his favor and made himself obnoxious, offending the delegates with his partisanship. Harrison won on the eighth ballot and also succeeded in the fall election. Gresham's supporters and family were disappointed with Swett's speech, feeling that Swett could have created more excitement for their candidate, but they realized that their campaign managers had vetted it.[28]

In September 1888, as a member of the reception committee for the Chicago Bar Association, Swett attended a banquet in honor of the newly appointed chief justice of the U.S. Supreme Court, Melville Weston Fuller. Swett and Fuller shared a common background, although Swett's bar association colleague was a lifelong Democrat. From Augusta, Maine, and a graduate of Bowdoin College, Fuller had moved to Chicago to practice law in 1856.[29]

Early in 1889, Swett had the opportunity to honor his old friend David Davis once again. After Davis's death, Swett had assisted Leonard Volk, who had sculpted Lincoln's bust in 1860, in gaining permission from Davis's son to make a bronze bust of his father. Swett then sought out a dozen sponsors for the bust of Davis. After exploring various venues for its location, he finally presented it to the state of Illinois at a meeting with Governor Richard J. Oglesby on January 9, 1889. Accompanied by Robert Lincoln, Swett and Oglesby exchanged public comments in the State Capitol appropriate for the occasion. They noted that Davis had devoted a major portion of his life to a rare combination of public service: two years in the state legislature, the 1847 Illinois Constitutional Convention, fourteen years as Illinois Eighth Circuit judge, fifteen years as a U.S. Supreme Court justice, and six years in the U.S. Senate. The last year, as president pro tempore of the Senate, Davis had stepped in to fulfill the duties of vice president following Garfield's death. To the extent that he served in that role, he is the only American to have served in all three branches of the government. Assisted by his first wife, Sarah Walker Davis, he assembled sizable landholdings and died a millionaire.[30]

Five days after the Springfield dedication ceremony, Oglesby passed the leadership of the state to a fellow Republican, Governor Joseph W. Fifer of Bloomington, who as a seventeen-year-old had witnessed the Lincoln-Swett courtroom duel in the Isaac Wyant murder case. The Oglesby and Swett generation, though still active, was passing from the scene.

Swett's son, who as an adult went by Herbert, had continued his formal education at Cornell University in 1888, as he turned thirty. In late January 1889, he wrote his father and acknowledged his need to get on with the practicalities of life. He mused, "I think our sitting room at home, our talks, our books, the horses, Marie's [*sic*] piano, our little dinner parties—with you for President and Marie and . . . Myself as pupils constitute a better University than Cornell itself for acquiring a general education."[31]

In early April, Swett visited Bloomington with Maria to give a lecture on Abraham Lincoln at the opera house. The *Pantagraph* reported a few aspects of his remarks without covering them in detail. An old friend, Judge John M. Scott of the Illinois Supreme Court, introduced him.[32] They stayed a few days in Bloomington so that Swett could show Maria his old home, the town he had stumbled into nearly dead, and introduce her to his circle of friends there.

During the visit, Swett caught a cold that plagued him for some time and may have been evidence of his deteriorating health. Although he had been ill on and off during the past decade, he had made no comments that he felt his maladies were life-shortening. On the contrary, he had written to Lamon back in mid-1886, a few months after traveling to Philadelphia to see Dr. Mitchell, that he expected to recover completely.[33] He left no record of further illness after that time period. His weight remained around 220 pounds, filling out his six-foot, two-inch frame as it had for the last couple decades.

After returning home in the spring of 1889, Swett continued to keep busy with his legal work, and in late April or early May, he and Grosscup defended an appeal against the Union Life Mutual Insurance Company in the Illinois Supreme Court. The court reached a decision favoring Union Life on May 18. Meanwhile, Swett and Maria were enjoying their time together. They were eagerly planning a vacation to Maria's native Germany and were scheduled to set sail from New York on the SS *Werra*.[34]

But the trip was not to be. Just a few weeks after the Union Life case ended, on June 8, 1889, Leonard Swett died at age sixty-three. Swett's death did not occur suddenly, nor was it agonizingly prolonged. Herbert described the daily progression of events: "On the fifth day of June he enjoyed a horseback ride, [his] daily exercise; on the sixth, he was about the city in a carriage; on the seventh, he felt somewhat indisposed, but transacted business at his house. He retired early for the night . . . and sank gradually into a profound unconsciousness." Then, "on the eighth of June, at two o'clock in the afternoon, his heart simply ceased."[35] The newspapers of the day either overdiagnosed various maladies or emphasized his recent health. Swett's death certificate, however, showed his cause of death as diabetes mellitus.

Leonard Swett's funeral was held the following Tuesday, June 11, at the Third Presbyterian Church on Ashland Avenue near his home. Political and legal leaders attended from Chicago and elsewhere, including Chief Justice Melville Fuller of the U.S. Supreme Court, Illinois governor Joseph Fifer, U.S. senators Charles Farwell and Shelby Cullom, former senator Lyman Trumbull, U.S. circuit judge Walter Gresham, former circuit judge Thomas Drummond, U.S. district judge Henry Blodgett, and Chicago mayor DeWitt Cregier. Sixty-five members of the Chicago bar were also present, along with a contingent of sixteen Mexican War veterans. Surrounded by family members, numerous friends, and countless colleagues who had come to pay their respect, Swett was laid to rest in Rosehill Cemetery on the North Side of Chicago, along with Laura and a significant number of his contemporaries.[36]

Epilogue

On June 15, 1889, the Saturday following Swett's death, a number of friends and colleagues spoke about Swett at a memorial ceremony conducted by the Chicago bar in the U.S. district courtroom of Judge Henry W. Blodgett, and the words of several others appeared in succeeding issues of the *Chicago Legal News*. Memorial comments and eulogies have always tended to be excessively favorable, and this was especially so in the nineteenth century, but the descriptions of Swett reflect similar things his friends said about him in life, and they help provide color and detail for his portrait.[1]

Bar association president James L. High characterized Swett with these words: "As an advocate he won his most enduring fame, and as such he will be best remembered. . . . It is the simple truth, to say that as an advocate he was the peer of any lawyer of the northwest. . . . In a certain magnetic personality; in an earnest and impressive power of persuasion, and in the rare art of causing his hearers to see as he saw, to think as he thought, and to feel as he felt, he was unsurpassed by any lawyer of his time."

Benjamin Franklin Ayer, Illinois Central solicitor general and second president of the Chicago Bar Association, made the point in a somewhat different way: "In many respects, Mr. Swett was a remarkable man. Very few men in the legal profession have been endowed with stronger persuasive powers or greater dexterity and astuteness. He had a logical and well-disciplined mind, a keen and quick discernment, rare insight into human nature, and exquisite tact and judgment. . . . In the management of jury trials he had, I think, no superior and very few rivals in the courts of this State. His knowledge of the law was wide and various. In the discussion of legal questions he was always clear, vigorous and impressive. . . . Few lawyers ever deserved or enjoyed in a greater degree the respect and confidence of the bench or the esteem and good will of his professional associates."

Elijah B. Sherman, president of the Illinois Bar Association at the age of fifty and a fellow Alliance Club member, said of Swett, "He met, perhaps, with the most remarkable success in the trial of jury causes. His commanding presence, his earnest but dignified demeanor, his superb powers of analysis, his consummate skill in marshalling, grouping, and interpreting the evidence, his suave manner and persuasive speech, his uniform generosity and regal courtesy, his winning smile and air of perfect candor combined to render him a most formidable and dangerous antagonist. . . . From his great heart the amenities of the life flowed out impartially to all. The bootblack from the alley received from his lips an encouraging word, and an extra douceur for a perfect shine."

Several speakers dealt with his interest in civic or public concerns as well as the law, and many commented on his modesty and the breadth of his practice and competence. Edwin Walker, general counsel for the Chicago, Milwaukee, and St. Paul Railroad, noted that "he could successfully defend a man accused of murder one day, and the very next take part in the trial of a case involving the most intricate and important questions in corporation law." The Memorial and Resolutions Committee also emphasized, "He was a favorite with both the bench and the bar."

As these remarks were made in the U.S. District Court, a marble bust of Swett sat directly in front of the judge's desk, made for posterity the year before by Leonard Volk. The bust of Swett was similar to the one he had arranged three years earlier for Volk to make of David Davis, which had been placed in the State Capitol in a ceremony five months before Swett died. With a certain synchronicity, the same sculptor who had made a life mask and bust of Lincoln in 1860, then the bust of Davis, had now completed the third and final member of the "great triumvirate" of the Eighth Circuit.

Swett's family lived on for two more generations. Herbert married Rose Skillings six months after his father's death, on December 25, 1889, in Auburn, Maine. He wrote a comprehensive essay in 1901 on his father's life, revealing the depth of his respect and admiration, along with wonderment about his father's qualities. Herbert and Rose had one child, a daughter born in Aurora, Illinois, on June 17, 1897. They named her Laura Rose for her grandmother and her mother. The family migrated to Fort Collins, Colorado, around 1905–6. Herbert farmed just west of the town until he retired in 1917. Sometime later, he was a dealer in investment securities. Rose died in 1914, and Herbert continued to live in Fort Collins until his death in 1934.

Laura Rose Swett attended a preparatory school connected with Colorado State University and married Henry Ashley Burnham, born in Jackson, Minnesota. They moved to El Centro in California's Imperial Valley. By 1941, they had moved to Santa Maria, California. They had no children, and thus Leonard Swett's direct lineage ended when Laura died in Santa Maria in 1963. Henry died in Los Angeles County in 1985 at age ninety-one.[2]

Leonard Swett had an abundance of nieces and nephews, several of whom also became lawyers. His nephew Edward Ricker Swett (1855–1906) practiced law in Leonard's firm in Chicago. A great-nephew, Frank Wentworth Swett, practiced law for fifty years in Chicago, and his son, Leonard Wentworth Swett, graduated from University of Michigan Law School and practiced law in Chicago, New York, Cleveland, and Maine.[3]

Swett's marriage to Maria had lasted only twenty-three months before he died, and they had no children. There are only a few glimpses of her after that time. In 1893, she sought Robert Lincoln's assistance in applying for work at the Newberry Library in Chicago and appears to have had an interview with its president, but no connection with that institution developed. In 1900, she sued the city of Burlington, Iowa, after she fell on some ice and broke her leg. In 1911, she sold six acres of land, a possible inheritance from Swett, to a real estate developer just north of Kenilworth, Illinois. A short newspaper article in the *Chicago Tribune* in 1931 in Hermia Clark's column, "When Chicago Was Young," makes reference to her. Maria apparently found the love of her life in Swett, as she remained a widow for fifty-two years after his death. She died in 1941 at age eighty-one and was buried with him and Laura in Rosehill Cemetery, amid a coterie of Chicago mayors, Illinois governors, Civil War generals, and Swett's friends.[4]

Having never achieved political success or received a position in the Lincoln administration, Leonard Swett soon became largely forgotten to history. Historians have picked over his prose for quotable material, but for almost a century and a half he has essentially remained the forgotten friend of Lincoln. Like Lincoln and Davis, however, Swett stood out among his Eighth Circuit colleagues in his professional achievements. His greatest contributions lay in his aid in Lincoln's two nominations, his acting as a sounding board to Lincoln, his willingness to take on the appeal of the Haymarket anarchists, and his performance as a superb legal advocate in hundreds of other cases. His colorful life during which he traveled in circles that included some of the most important figures in American history, his noted skill in public speaking and ability to express ideas in unique and interesting ways—and most of all, his close connection with Lincoln for more than a decade and a half—all call for a fuller appreciation of Leonard Swett as a trusted and faithful friend.

Acknowledgments
Appendix
Notes
Bibliography
Index

Acknowledgments

As I am now in my tenth decade, the completion of this manuscript has become dependent on the extensive assistance of my daughter, Jane Lennon, joined on occasion by my son Robert George, especially in the area of his expertise, photography. Together with help from other family members, what seemed impossible has emerged in its final form. Sylvia Frank Rodrigue, executive editor of Southern Illinois University Press, has invested heavily in encouraging and assisting in the improvement and finishing of the project. Without the efforts of these individuals, my many years of interest in Leonard Swett might have come to naught.

Five readers gave me their frank comments on the first draft of the manuscript, pointing in directions that were helpful and encouraging in the next steps. They were Robert Bray, Colwell professor of English at Illinois Wesleyan University; Lee B. McTurnan, who headed a legal practice specializing in business litigation in Indianapolis; Mark Plummer, professor emeritus of history at Illinois State University; Ronald D. Rietveld, then professor of history at California State University in Fullerton; and Thomas F. Schwartz, then Illinois historian. Each made significant contributions that helped in future work on the manuscript.

The largest source of Swett information is the Abraham Lincoln Presidential Library in Springfield, Illinois. Librarian Kathryn M. Harris and the heads of the various components in the library have been extremely cooperative in my endeavors.

Another prime source of assistance was the Chicago History Museum Library, which Debbie Vaughn headed at the time I conducted my research there. This source contains the full run of the *Chicago Legal News*, essential in finding extensive information on Swett's legal career in Chicago. Inadequate indexes necessitated scanning the pages of the eleven hundred weekly copies. The museum also has Willard King's copies of the Davis Papers, filed chronologically with many other relevant letters.

The Huntington Library has the post–Civil War letters of Swett and his family, as well as a large collection of Lamon Papers, containing significant Swett correspondence. My son-in-law, David Gartshore, an attorney, assisted me there on one visit, and we found working in that source to be a pleasant experience.

The University of Illinois Library, Urbana-Champaign, has an extensive collection of Orme Papers. John Hoffmann was helpful in assisting with this material, as well as providing access to Lavern M. Hamand's doctoral dissertation on Ward Hill Lamon and a copy of Swett's specially printed memorial to T. Lyle Dickey.

The McLean County Museum, under the direction of Greg Koos, and its librarian, William Kemp, provided many specialty letters and information relevant to the project. The Bloomington Library has an extensive set of the *Pantagraph*, distributed widely in a multicounty area during Swett's lifetime.

George Buss of Freeport, Illinois, provided a digital copy of an early picture of Swett and a copy of Herbert Swett's journal, both for my use. The latter mentions that Leonard Swett also kept a journal, but this has not yet turned up.

Marcia Young, site manager of the David Davis Mansion, located near my home for twenty-five years, has been very helpful in providing access to an earlier and longer draft of Willard King's manuscript on David Davis and useful commentary relative to collateral information.

An extensive number of Abraham Lincoln Association board members have helped me in a variety of ways, the first being Rodney O. Davis and Douglas L. Wilson of Knox College in 1992, who provided access to several Swett and Swett-related letters.

Not surprisingly, Maine sources have contributed importantly. Colby College special collections librarian Patricia Burdick provided information on their curriculum and students when Swett was in residence, as well as an alumni article by a former president on Swett. My wife's niece and her husband, Linda and Rodney Mann, looked up articles in the *Portland Evening Express* from 1891 and recognized the relevance of Josiah Drummond's article on the 1864 Lincoln vice presidential nomination. Several others interested in history have been willing to follow up on local inquiries, including Dennis Stires and Jay and Ben Dresser.

Others have been important in limited ways. E. Hugh Henning offered encouragement early in this undertaking. The Newberry Library searched for a number of items and found Maria Swett's application for a job at the time the institution was opening. Bradley University's Charles Frey furnished extensive information on a Peoria case, which did not make the final cut. Illinois Wesleyan provided early help from a student, Emily Beaugureau, who was extremely effective and is now an attorney. Three members of the Swett extended family—George A. Ricker, Margery Swett Walker, and Leonard W. Swett—have also given me information. Dorothy McDavid, my wife's friend who volunteered at the Fort Collins, Colorado, library, found and supplied information on Leonard Herbert Swett, including a copy of his death certificate.

A supportive environment is always encouraging, and my wife, Nell, has been both tolerant of and interested in a project that seemed to have no end.

Appendix: Selections of Swett's Biographical Writing

This appendix contains seven of Leonard Swett's speeches and essays that are cited in the book. They are presented here to illustrate Swett's eloquent writing style and because they expand on Swett's relationship with Lincoln and his friends. Two appear in their entirety below; two already had omissions in the sources where they were printed; and portions have been omitted from the other three to avoid repetition when this text has been quoted elsewhere in the book or to eliminate brief statements not essential to the presentation.

Introduction of Lincoln at Bloomington, Illinois, September 4, 1858
Letter to Josiah Drummond on Lincoln's 1860 Nomination, May 27, 1860
Speech at Great War Rally, U.S. Capitol, August 7, 1862
Essay on Lincoln, Letter to Herndon, January 17, 1866, as Amended in 1887
In Memory of David Davis, Illinois Bar Association, March 5, 1887
Memorial of T. Lyle Dickey, U.S. Circuit Court, Northern District of Illinois, May 9, 1887
Dedicatory Speech at the Unveiling of Saint-Gaudens's "Standing Lincoln" Statue at Lincoln Park, Chicago, October 22, 1887

Introduction of Lincoln at Bloomington, Illinois, September 4, 1858

From the *Pantagraph*, 9-6-58, "Republican Mass Meeting," reception speech by Swett.

Mr. Lincoln:—I have been deputed on behalf of the citizens of this county to welcome you on this occasion. As a friend and known admirer of your talents and your character, I enter cheerfully upon this duty, sharing prominently with the thousands who surround us, the zeal and affection which have suggested this reception. For many years, in the exercise of the profession you have honored, you have frequently visited this county. With a great majority of its people your personal acquaintance, associated with the pioneer history of the West, has, in the lapse of years, ripened into affectionate regard: here now number many of your most devoted friends—here are associations of endearment deeply rooted in the past; and our whole people, by the intimacy of their acquaintance with your character and affectionate sympathy and regard claim you at least as "an adopted son of their race."

I should therefore but partially perform my duty, and violate greatly my own feelings, if I should extend to you on this occasion merely a political welcome. We would all give utterance to feelings of profound personal regard, as well as express to you our most ardent sympathies in the great struggle in which you are engaged.

Our government which has bequeathed the blessing of civil liberty to the millions of our land, is itself the child of political tyranny—the uprising throes of a people goaded to madness by oppression.

The present form of slavery was, at the achievement of our independence, an existing institution. It had been forced upon our forefathers during their colonial dependence by the power and cupidity of the mother country. After our independence the people for the first time controlled this subject. As a nation we were then weak and chastened by affliction; but the fires of liberty were aglow in every heart, and those generous hands which had rescued our freedom from the "perilous ridges of the battle" sought to bestow its blessings upon all. The first work of our forefathers, therefore, was to proclaim the territories, not polluted by slavery, forever free, to restrict as soon as practicable the further importation of slaves, and place the institution "where the public mind would rest in the belief that it was in the course of ultimate extinction." Since then time has wrought prodigious changes. State after State has been added to our domain, city after city of almost magic growth has sprung suddenly into life to adorn the slopes of our mighty rivers. Our commerce now floats on every sea, and luxury folds the nation in its easy and seductive embrace. A change perhaps consequent upon this in the political sentiment of the people is scarcely less striking. Our forefathers' policy of prohibiting the introduction of slavery into free territory is now claimed to be a violation of the very constitution they made and gave us. The sentiments of the great declaration for which they periled "their lives, their fortunes and their sacred honor," are now scoffed at and pronounced rhetorical flourishes. The whole policy to make this country the great heritage of free men is subverted, and in its stead prevail other maxims which, in their tendency, nationalize and perpetuate the crowning evil of our land.

Our State has the doubtful honor of furnishing the author and standard-bearer of these new and startling heresies. After deserting—in that final struggle his work had engendered and made essential to success—those companions with whom he started in a career which has shaken the institutions of our country to their centre, he has returned to his people to be honored or censured for the course he has pursued. You have been selected to enter the lists against him. You are the representative of those who repudiate his heresies, and content themselves with the wisdom and policy of Washington and Jefferson. Your great struggle with your adversary in this contest has not inappropriately been styled the "battle of the giants." The eyes of the nation are upon you. You are expected to deal heavy blows—to parry unscrupulous and artful thrusts, to unmask every sophistry, and drag to light the naked deformity of the dangerous policy you are combating. In this struggle I offer you to-day not only the affectionate welcome of this people, but their entire approval of your noble bearing on every field you have met your wary adversary. We have admired in your great debates with him your coolness and circumspection, and smiled at the raging of the fretted lion you have "bearded in his den." We approve the sentiments which in those contests you have uttered, and honor the ability and skill with which you have maintained them. "The past" with you "is at least secure." Go on as you have nobly begun; be cheered by the approval, the sympathy and unshaken confidence of the thousands assembled here to greet you. We will meet you again, when you shall have borne our standard to victory. We will then applaud your success, and commit the destinies of our beautiful Prairie State confidently into your hands.

Mr. Swett then introduced to the meeting the Hon. ABRAHAM LINCOLN; who came forward amidst loud applause.

Letter to Josiah Drummond on Lincoln's 1860 Nomination, May 27, 1860

Swett to Drummond, *Portland (ME) Evening Express*, 7-22-91, 1–2, copied by other papers; also published in Oldroyd, *Lincoln's Campaign*, available through Google Books.

My dear friend,—I have been intending for a long time, to write you, but my private business added to the interest I have of late, taken in politics, has prevented me.

The Chicago Convention is with us the great event and the nomination of Lincoln is to his friends a matter of great satisfaction. His nomination, under the circumstances, is very remarkable. I don't know whether you are pleased or not, but I am gratified enough to satisfy any two men and if you are displeased I will transfer some of my great joy to you.

I made the acquaintance of Mr. Lincoln early in the year 1849. Since then we have, twice a year, traveled over five counties, spending together most of the time from September until January, and from March until June, inclusive. Originally most of the lawyers did this, but lately one by one they have abandoned the circuit, and for perhaps five years Lincoln and myself have been the only ones who have habitually passed over the whole circuit. It seems to me, I have tried 10,000 [an abundant overstatement] lawsuits with or against him. I know him as intimately as I have ever known any man in my life, perhaps more intimately, if possible than I knew you when I left Waterville.

I was with him the week before the convention. In speaking of the propriety of his going to it he said "he was almost too much of a candidate to go, and not quite enough to stay at home." Our delegation was instructed for him, but of the 22 votes in it, by incautiously selecting the men, there were eight who would gladly have gone for Seward. The reason for this is in this fact: The northern counties of this State are more overwhelmingly Republican than any other portion of the continent. I could pick 25 contiguous counties giving larger Republican majorities than any other adjacent counties in any State. The result is many people there are for Seward, and such men had crept upon the delegation. They intended in good faith to go for Lincoln, but talked despondingly and really wanted and expected finally to vote as I indicated. We had also in the North and about Chicago, a class of men who always want to turn up on the winning side, and would do no work, although their feelings were really for us, for fear it would be the losing element, and would place them out of favor with the incoming power. These men were dead weights. The Centre and South, with many individual exceptions to the classes I have named, were warmly for Lincoln, whether he won or lost. The lawyers of our circuit went there determined to leave no stone unturned, and really they, aided by some of our State officers and a half dozen men from various portions of the State, were the only tireless, sleepless, unswerving and ever vigilant friends he had. The first thing after getting our headquarters was to have the delegation proper invite the cooperation of outsiders as though they were delegates. Thus we began. The first State approached was Indiana. She was about equally divided between Bates and McLean. Saturday, Sunday and Monday were spent upon her, when finally she came to us unitedly, with 26 votes, and from that time acted efficiently with us.

Seward came there with very nearly strength enough to nominate him, that is, men who intended to vote for him. Bates was the next strongest, but that element was an opposition to Seward, because he was not available in the doubtful States and would, as we well knew, come to the winning man in opposition to him. Pennsylvania wanted Cameron, and insisted Seward would not carry that State. New Jersey wanted Dayton, and insisted Seward would not carry that State. So the first point was gained, that is, the united assertion of the four doubtful States, Pennsylvania, New Jersey, Indiana and Illinois, that Seward would be defeated. We ran in this manner for several days, Indiana and Illinois for Lincoln and against Seward, Pennsylvania for Cameron and against Seward; New Jersey for her own man but against Seward, calling upon the various delegations as they concluded Seward could not be elected, we succeeded in getting them for our man, with Pennsylvania, we did nothing but got them for us as a second choice.

We let Greel[e]y run his Bates machine, but got most of them for a second choice. Our programme was to give Lincoln 100 votes on the first ballot, with a certain increase afterwards, so that in the convention our fortunes might seem to be rising, and thus catch the doubtful. Vermont had agreed to give us her second vote, so had Delaware, New Hampshire, an increase. It all worked to a charm. After the first days we were aided by the arrival of at least 10,000 people from Central Illinois and Indiana.

It was part of the Seward plan to carry the Convention by outside pressure. Thursday all the preliminary work was done. The friends of all parties Friday morning gathered to the capacious Wigwam. About 12,000 people were then inside, and more out. A line of men were stationed on the roof, the nearest to the speaker's stand, catching from an open skylight the proceedings within and reporting to his next man, and so on to the man on the front of the building, who, with stentorian lungs, announced to the thousands in the street. Stores were closed, and seemingly, the whole city was there. First, opening the war, was the nomination of Seward. It was greeted with a deafening shout, which, I confess, appalled us a little. Afterwards, Bates, McLean, Cameron and Chase came with moderate applause. Then came Lincoln, and our people tested their lungs. We beat them a little. They manifested this by seconding the nomination of Seward, which gave them another chance. It was an improvement upon the first, and placed us in the background. Caleb B. Smith, of Indiana, then seconded the nomination of Lincoln, and the West came to the rescue. No mortal eye before saw such a scene. The idea of us Hoosiers and Suckers being outscreamed, would have been as bad to them as the loss of their man. Five thousand people at once leaped to their seats, women not wanting in the number, and the wild yell made soft vesper breathings of all that had preceded. No language can describe it. A thousand steam whistles, ten acres of hotel gongs, a tribe of Comanches, headed by a choice vanguard from pandemonium, might have mingled in the scene unnoticed.

This was not the most deliberate way of nominating a President, I will confess, but among other things, it had its weight and I hope convinced the New York gentlemen that when they came to the West some other tactics must be resorted to.

Our increase after the first ballot was a little more than we calculated. On the third the ground swell was irresistible and bore our man through, and the shout from the Wigwam and the shout from the street, as the man from the top shouted "Old Abe, hallelujah!" and the cannon with its mimic thunder, told the city and surroundings we had won.

It was a glorious nomination. Seward could not have carried Illinois or Indiana; nothing is more certain than this. Our people, when they opposed Seward, did it from no other motive than for the reason that it lost us our State, our Senator Trumbull his place, and placed us under the ban of Loco Focoism [radical element of the New York Democratic Party] for 20 years. We felt as though we could not endure this, and hence the earnest effort for Lincoln.

No men ever worked as our boys did. I did not, the whole week I was there, sleep two hours a night. The nomination saves us. We will sweep the whole Northwest. The nomination is from the people, and not the politicians. No pledges have been made, no mortgages executed, but Lincoln enters the field a free man. He will continue so until the day of the election. He is a pure-minded, honest man, whose ability is second to no one in the nation. In 20 years he has raised himself from the captaincy of a flatboat on the Mississippi, to the captaincy of a great party in this nation, and when he shall be elected he will restore the government to its pristine purity. . . .

Your old friend, Leonard Swett

Speech at Great War Rally, U.S. Capitol, August 7, 1862

> This was a meeting to raise army recruits and money. President Lincoln,
> Treasury officials, and nine others spoke. Swett's speech followed those of
> the Treasury officials. *Pantagraph*, 8-12-62, "Speech of Hon. Leonard Swett
> at Washington"; also in ALPL, Swett Papers.

Mr. President: Like the gentleman who preceded me, I am a stranger to every
man and woman whom I address, and, like him, I will in the introduction
announce my home. It is the state of Illinois. A state which I trust has made
itself felt, in the war in which we are engaged, and which is progressing to
a successful issue.

We meet here today under singular auspices. This is the capital of a great
nation. I can only speak of it as a stranger, learning its peculiarities from its
national reputation. This city has been the pride of this country, founded
as the city of constitutional liberty, bearing the name of the founder of this
republic. . . . Yet, strange as it may seem, within the sound of my voice the
gigantic rebellion has been born and nurtured from its very inception. In
this city two opinions began to germinate! The one cherished the memories
of the past and found cause for pride in the illustrious deeds of our fathers,
and desired the perpetuation of this government and the blessings it conferred upon us; the other despised the government, despised constitutional
liberty, and counted as noble only what contributed to the rebellion, and as
ignoble what contributed to the perpetuity of the government. These two
portions, from the first formation of opinion, have been progressing in this
city. One is an active party, supporting the government; the other is a latent
party, permeating with treachery. The treasonable party have their hearts
with the rebellion. They are in your midst, and the appeal of this nation is
that they shall adopt those stern and decisive acts which the exigencies of
the war demands—to make this city either for this government or against it.

These men and sympathizers with treason are only found in company
with the sympathizers of [Jefferson] Davis and [Confederate secretary of
state Robert] Toombs, who, with the immaculate [John B.] Floyd [corrupt
war secretary under Buchanan, later a Confederate general], are to them
ideals of excellence. . . . But these imaginary patriots sought to take their
people up through the beautiful paths of secession to a higher prosperity and
a greater wealth; and what has been the result? Blood to the horses bridle;
and the angel of death is sweeping over the land today, and trailing his
bloody garments along her valleys. . . . The time is not for reasons, but for

actions, and I congratulate you, as well as the people of this whole country, on the recent acts of the president and the cabinet, displaying a sternness of purpose that inspires the whole people with confidence of success. It may, perhaps, have been right in the early inception of this rebellion to deal leniently with its sympathizers; but the day has passed, never to return.

I regard this day, or rather the day on which it was rumored that the administration had determined upon a policy which was stern, positive and decided, as the most auspicious event since this war began. Now you and I and some of the people of this vast country have, some of us, complained of the want of decisions on the part of the government. The tables, however, are now turned upon us, and the question to be determined now is, whether there is any energy in the people. The government has said to you, we want three hundred thousand men, and three hundred thousand more. That call requires an answer, not of words, but of six hundred thousand men. Where are they? . . . I can speak for the citizens of New York state, and say they will be here. My own state, and I speak of her with unfeigned pride, while she has already furnished sixty-three regiments of infantry, eleven of cavalry, two of artillery, five thousand men for three months service, twenty thousand men in companies in states adjoining us, making from ninety-five to one hundred thousand men, is ready for the call of twice as many more. . . .

There is one thing you should do immediately, and that is to weed out the traitors in your midst. You remember the words of the scripture, "That where the heart is there will the treasure be also." Now I want this government to say to these traitors in Washington, not exactly that language, but what in its conception it should be, "That where the heart is there the body should be also." And whenever a man or a woman shall be found in this city whose heart is in Richmond, I want the government to furnish him a train of cars to be there. Do this, and our soil will be clean and free from what had spread over it like a poisonous weed. Draft! Ah, I love that word. It is walking square up to this thing. It is not dodging at all. It falls equally on all men. It appeals equally to each man's pocket. Do this not grudgingly, but cheerfully, and the six hundred thousand men will plant the flag in every hamlet from here to the gulf. It is said by some that this rebellion will not be put down. Whoever says this does not understand the times in which he lives. Why will it not be put down. Because we have not put it down in a moment. This is a fainthearted answer. It will be put down because truth and strong arms, buckshot and patience will prevail.

These northern people have got all the element necessary for that success. With these six hundred thousand men, which we will get, we will have a million in the field. What have six hundred thousand men already done? . . . They have opened the Mississippi river, cutting the western banks away from this rebellion, taking from them over 400,000 miles of free territory.

They have occupied with gallant hearts the states of Missouri, Tennessee, Kentucky, part of Virginia, part of North Carolina, the coast, and a portion of Louisiana, making in square miles, added together with the country we have got from them, nearly all of their original territory. Now, the proposition is, if 600,000 men can strip from these boastful rebels two-thirds of their territory and power, cannot 1,000,000 of men strip the balance? Every man who speaks is expected to say something of the politics of this war. I do not intend to do it. Because I say put down this rebellion, and, in the language of scripture, "All these things shall be added unto you." He that runs may read. When you fight these rebels, don't do it with gloves. Use all the powers and facilities which God and our own ingenuity has given you to crush out this unholy rebellion. Shrink from nothing. . . .

A little boat that is launched upon the waves of the ocean, trusting to the drifts of its tide, never comes back and lands just where it was launched; neither does the great nation that embarks upon the seas of rebellion and revolution land where it started. We will not land where we started. . . . So with this people in its terrible trial. I cannot look down the long vista of time and see the end. No man can!

I can only gather around my own heart the courage that my nature is capable of enlisting. You can only do the same, trusting to God, to your energies, and the right to carry you safely through. If we will gloriously and safely do the right, use all the means in your power, then will He guide us safely through to the end.

Essay on Lincoln, Letter to Herndon, January 17, 1866, as Amended in 1887

This essay was published in Herndon & Weik, *Life of Lincoln*, 425–33, available through Google Books.

Lincoln's whole life was a calculation of the law of forces and ultimate results. The whole world to him was a question of cause and effect. He believed the results to which certain causes tended; he did not believe that those results could be materially hastened or impeded. His whole political history, especially since the agitation of the slavery question, has been based upon this theory. He believed from the first, I think, that the agitation of slavery would produce its overthrow, and he acted upon the result as though it was present from the beginning. His tactics were to get himself in the right place and remain there still, until events would find him in that place. This course of action led him to say and do things which could not be understood when considered in reference to the immediate surroundings in which they were done or said. You will remember, in his campaign against Douglas in 1858, the first ten lines of the first speech he made defeated him. The sentiment of the "house divided against itself" seemed wholly inappropriate. It was a speech made at the commencement of a campaign, and apparently made for the campaign. Viewing it in this light alone, nothing could have been more unfortunate or inappropriate. It was saying just the wrong thing; yet he saw it was an abstract truth, and standing by the speech would ultimately find him in the right place. I was inclined at the time to believe these words were hastily and inconsiderately uttered, but subsequent facts have convinced me they were deliberate and had been matured. Judge T. L. Dickey says, that at Bloomington, at the first Republican Convention in 1856, he uttered the same sentences in a speech delivered there, and that after the meeting was over, he (Dickey) called his attention to these remarks. [Actually, Dickey remembered it as September or October, and the content is similar to a Lincoln speech recorded at Jacksonville on September 6.]

Lincoln justified himself in making them by stating they were true; but finally, at Dickey's urgent request, he promised that for his sake, or upon his advice, he would not repeat them. In the summer of 1859, when he was dining with a party of his intimate friends at Bloomington, the subject of his Springfield speech was discussed. We all insisted it was a great mistake, but he justified himself, and finally said, "Well, gentlemen, you may think that speech was a mistake, but I never have believed it was, and you will see the day when you will consider it was the wisest thing I ever said."

He never believed in political combinations, and consequently, whether an individual man or class of men supported or opposed him, never made any difference in his feelings, or his opinions of his own success. If he was elected, he seemed to believe that no person or class of persons could ever have defeated him, and if defeated, he believed nothing could ever have elected him. Hence, when he was a candidate, he never wanted anything done for him in the line of political combination or management. He seemed to want to let the whole subject alone, and for everybody else to do the same. I remember, after the Chicago Convention, when a great portion of the East were known to be dissatisfied at his nomination, when fierce conflicts were going on in New York and Pennsylvania, and when great exertions seemed requisite to harmonize and mould in concert the action of our friends, Lincoln seemed to oppose all efforts made in the direction of uniting the party. I arranged with Mr. Thurlow Weed after the Chicago Convention to meet him at Springfield. I was present at the interview, but Lincoln said nothing. It was proposed that Judge Davis should go to New York and Pennsylvania to survey the field and see what was necessary to be done. Lincoln consented, but it was always my opinion that he consented reluctantly.

He saw that the pressure of a campaign was the external force coercing the party into unity. If it failed to produce that result, he believed any individual effort would also fail. If the desired result followed, he considered it attributable to the great cause, and not aided by the lesser ones. He sat down in his chair in Springfield and made himself the Mecca to which all politicians made pilgrimages. He told them all a story, said nothing, and sent them away. All his efforts to procure a second nomination were in the same direction. I believe he earnestly desired that nomination. He was much more eager for it than he was for the first, and yet from the beginning he discouraged all efforts on the part of his friends to obtain it. From the middle of his first term all his adversaries were busily at work for themselves. Chase had three or four secret societies and an immense patronage extending all over the country. Fremont was constantly at work, yet Lincoln would never do anything either to hinder them or to help himself.

He was considered too conservative, and his adversaries were trying to outstrip him in satisfying the radical element. I had a conversation with him upon this subject in October, 1863, and tried to induce him to recommend in his annual message a constitutional amendment abolishing slavery. I told him I was not very radical, but I believed the result of the war would be the extermination of slavery; that Congress would pass the amendment making the slave free, and that it was proper at that time to be done. I told him also, if he took that stand, it was an outside position, and no one could maintain himself upon any measure more radical, and if he failed to take the position, his rivals would. Turning to me suddenly he said, "Is not the question of emancipation doing well enough now?" I replied it was. "Well," said he, "I have never done an official act with a view to promote my own personal aggrandizement, and I don't like to begin now. I can see that emancipation is coming; whoever can wait for it will see it; whoever stands in its way will be run over by it."

His rivals were using money profusely; journals and influences were being subsidized against him. I accidentally learned that a Washington newspaper, through a purchase of the establishment, was to be turned against him, and consulted him about taking steps to prevent it. The only thing I could get him to say was that he would regret to see the paper turned against him. Whatever was done had to be done without his knowledge. Mr. Bennett of the [*New York*] *Herald*, with his paper, you know is a power. The old gentleman wanted to be noticed by Lincoln, and he wanted to support him. A friend of his, who was certainly in his secrets, came to Washington and intimated if Lincoln would invite Bennett to come over and chat with him, his paper would be all right. Mr. Bennett wanted nothing, he simply wanted to be noticed. Lincoln in talking about it said, "I understand it; Bennett has made a great deal of money, some say not very properly, now he wants me to make him respectable. I have never invited Mr. Bryant [of the *New York Post*] or Mr. Greeley [of the *New York Tribune*] here; I shall not, therefore, especially invite Mr. Bennett." All Lincoln would say was, that he was receiving everybody, and he should receive Mr. Bennett if he came.

Notwithstanding his entire inaction, he never for a moment doubted his second nomination. One time in his room discussing with him who his real friends were, he told me, if I would not show it, he would make a list of how the Senate stood. When he got through, I pointed out some five or six, and I told him I knew he was mistaken about them. Said he, "You may think so, but you keep that until the convention and tell me whether I was right." He was right to a man. He kept a kind of account book of how things were progressing, for three or four months, and whenever I would get nervous and think things were going wrong, he would get out his estimates and show how everything on the great scale of action, such as the resolutions of legislatures, the instructions of delegates, and things of that character, were going exactly as he expected. These facts, with many others of a kindred nature, have convinced me that he managed his politics upon a plan entirely different from any other man the country has ever produced.

He managed his campaigns by ignoring men and by ignoring all small causes, but by closely calculating the tendencies of events and the great forces which were producing logical results.

In his conduct of the war he acted upon the theory that but one thing was necessary, and that was a united North. He had all shades of sentiments and opinions to deal with, and the consideration was always presented to his mind, how can I hold these discordant elements together?

It was here that he located his own greatness as a President. One time, about the middle of the war, I left his house about eleven o'clock at night, at the Soldier's Home. We had been discussing the discords in the country, and particularly the States of Missouri and Kentucky. As we separated at the door he said, "I may not have made as great a President as some other men, but I believe I have kept these discordant elements together as well as anyone could," Hence, in dealing with men he was a trimmer, and such a trimmer the world has never seen. Halifax [George Savile, a seventeenth-century English statesman known as "The Trimmer"], who was great in his day as a trimmer, would blush by the side of Lincoln; yet Lincoln never trimmed in principles, it was only in his conduct with men. He used the patronage of his office to feed the hunger of these various factions. Weed always declared that he kept a regular account-book of his appointments in New York, dividing his various favors so as to give each faction more than it could get from any other source, yet never enough to satisfy its appetite.

They all had access to him, they all received favors from him, and they all complained of ill treatment; but while unsatisfied, they all had "large expectations," and saw in him the chance of obtaining more than from anyone else whom they could be sure of getting in his place. He used every force to the best possible advantage. He never wasted anything, and would always give more to his enemies than he would to his friends; and the reason was, because he never had anything to spare and in the close calculation of attaching the factions to him, he counted upon the abstract affection of his friends as an element to be offset against some gift with which he must appease his enemies. Hence, there was always some truth in the charge of his friends that he failed to reciprocate their devotion with his favors. The reason was, that he had only just so much to give away—"He always had more horses than oats."

An adhesion of all forces was indispensable to his success and the success of the country; hence he husbanded his means with the greatest nicety of calculation. Adhesion was what he wanted; if he got it gratuitously he never wasted his substance paying for it.

His love of the ludicrous was not the least peculiar of his characteristics. His love of fun made him overlook everything else but the point of the joke sought after. If he told a good story that was refined and had a sharp point, he did not like it any the better because it was refined. If it was outrageously vulgar he never seemed to see that part of it, if it had the sharp ring of wit; nothing ever reached him but the wit. Almost any man that will tell a very vulgar story, has, in a degree, a vulgar mind; but it was not so with him; with all his purity of character and exalted morality and sensibility, which no man can doubt, when hunting for wit he had no ability to discriminate between the vulgar and the refined substances from which he extracted it. It was the wit he was after, the pure jewel, and he would pick it up out of the mud or dirt just as readily as he would from a parlor table.

He had great kindness of heart. His mind was full of tender sensibilities, and he was extremely humane, yet while these attributes were fully developed in his character, and, unless intercepted by his judgment, controlled him, they never did control him contrary to his judgment. He would strain a point to be kind, but he never strained it to breaking. Most men of much kindly feeling are controlled by this sentiment against their judgment, or rather that sentiment beclouds their judgment. It was never so with him; he would be just as kind and generous as his judgment would let him be—no more. If he ever deviated from this rule, it was to save life. He would sometimes, I think, do things he knew to be impolitic and wrong to save some poor fellow's neck. I remember one day being in his room when he was sitting at his table with a large pile of papers before him, and after a pleasant talk he turned quite abruptly and said, "Get out of the way, Swett; to-morrow is butcher-day, and I must go through these papers and see if I cannot find some excuse to let these poor fellows off." The pile of papers he had were the records of courts martial of men who on the following day were to be shot. He was not examining the records to see whether the evidence sustained the findings; he was purposely in search of occasions to evade the law, in favor of life.

Some of Lincoln's friends have insisted that he lacked the strong attributes of personal affection which he ought to have exhibited; but I think this is a mistake. Lincoln had too much justice to run a great government for a few favors; and the complaints against him in this regard, when properly digested, seem to amount to this and no more, that he would not abuse the privileges of his situation.

He was certainly a very poor hater. He never judged men by his like or dislike for them. If any given act was to be performed, he could understand that his enemy could do it as well as anyone. If a man had maligned him or been guilty of personal ill-treatment, and was the fittest man for the place, he would give him that place just as soon as he would give it to a friend. I do not think he ever removed a man because he was his enemy or because he disliked him.

The great secret of his power as an orator, in my judgment, lay in the clearness and perspicuity of his statement. When Mr. Lincoln had stated a case it was always more than half argued and the point more than half won. It is said that some of the crowned heads of Europe proposed to marry when he had a wife living. A gentleman, hearing of this proposition, replied, how could he? "Oh," replied his friend, "he could marry and then he could get Mr. Gladstone to make an explanation about it." This was said to illustrate the convincing power of Mr. Gladstone's statement.

Mr. Lincoln had this power greater than any man I have ever known. The first impression he generally conveyed was, that he had stated the case of his adversary better and more forcibly than his opponent could state it himself. He then answered that statement of facts fairly and fully, never passing by or skipping over a bad point.

When this was done he presented his own case. There was a feeling, when he argued a case, in the mind of any man who listened to it, that nothing had been passed over; yet if he could not answer the objections he argued, in his own mind, and himself arrive at the conclusion to which he was leading others, he had very little power of argumentation. The force of his logic was in conveying to the minds of others the same clear and thorough analysis he had in his own, and if his own mind failed to be satisfied, he had little power to satisfy anybody else. He never made a sophistical argument in his life, and never could make one. I think he was of less real aid in trying a thoroughly bad case than any man I was ever associated with. If he could not grasp the whole case and believe in it, he was never inclined to touch it.

From the commencement of his life to its close, I have sometimes doubted whether he ever asked anybody's advice about anything. He would listen to everybody; he would hear everybody; but he rarely, if ever, asked for opinions. I never knew him in trying a case to ask the advice of any lawyer he was associated with. As a politician and as President, he arrived at all his conclusions from his own reflections, and when his opinion was once formed, he never doubted but what it was right.

One great public mistake of his character, as generally received and acquiesced in, is that he is considered by the people of this country as a frank, guileless, and unsophisticated man. There never was a greater mistake. Beneath a smooth surface of candor and apparent declaration of all his thoughts and feelings, he exercised the most exalted tact and the wisest discrimination. He handled and moved men remotely as we do pieces upon a chess-board. He retained through life all the friends he ever had, and he made the wrath of his enemies to praise him. This was not by cunning or intrigue, in the low acceptance of the term, but by far-seeing reason and discernment. He always told enough only of his plans and purposes to induce the belief that he had communicated all, yet he reserved enough to have communicated nothing. He told all that was unimportant with a gushing frankness, yet no man ever kept his real purposes closer, or penetrated the future further with his deep designs.

You ask me whether he changed his religious opinions towards the close of his life. I think not. As he became involved in matters of the greatest importance, full of great responsibility and great doubt, a feeling of religious reverence, a belief in God and his justice and overruling power increased with him. He was always full of natural religion; he believed in God as much as the most approved Church member, yet he judged of Him by the same system of generalization as he judged everything else. He had very little faith in ceremonials or forms. In fact he cared nothing for the form of anything. But his heart was full of natural and cultivated religion. He believed in the great laws of truth, and the rigid discharge of duty, his accountability to God, the ultimate triumph of the right and the overthrow of wrong. If his religion were to be judged by the lines and rules of Church creeds he would fall far short of the standard; but if by the higher rule of purity of conduct, of honesty of motive, of unyielding fidelity to the right, and acknowledging God as the supreme ruler, then he filled all the requirements of true devotion, and his whole life was a life of love to God, and love of his neighbor as of himself.

In Memory of David Davis, Illinois Bar Association, March 5, 1887

From Swett, "In Memory of David Davis," CLN, vol. 19, 3-5-87, 206–17. Also published in *Illinois Bar Association, Annual Meeting 1887*, available through Google Books.

In the autumn of 1848 I was sitting in Bloomington, where Baker's store then was, at the corner of Main and Front streets. The office of David Davis, before he was Judge Davis, was then across the street to the east, and a half block beyond the opposite corner. [The Davis office is still extant.] That was my first sight of him. I thought then, and still think, that immense tread was the tread of Hercules. He was then midway in his journey of life, or 35 [actually, 33] years old, and when the sun of life seems to stop and stand awhile in his course.

About this time he was elected judge of the eighth judicial circuit, itself an empire in extent, and remained as the judge of that circuit until A.D. 1862, when he was appointed by Mr. Lincoln, then President, one of the justices of the Supreme Court of the United States. I had myself, a little before, returned from a small service in the Mexican war, and was very much impaired in health, so, knowing the outside of a horse was very good for the inside of a man, I commenced about a year after this time to ride on horseback over a large portion of this eighth circuit. I continued this mode of life until about the year 1862, or a period of thirteen years. . . .

[A description of the circuit follows, which is omitted here.]

In this condition of things, at the age of 24 years, I first met Mr. Lincoln at Mount Pulaski in 1849, driving his horse, "Old Tom," which afterward became a fixture upon the circuit, and he and Davis, with two horses and buggies, David Campbell, the State's attorney, sometimes on horseback and sometimes in a buggy, commenced the traveling of the circuit together. . . . [The omitted lines present further descriptive information on the Eighth Circuit.]

Judge Davis became the leader of the bar and the community of the eighth judicial circuit. He was emphatically a hospitable judge, and when his court was visited by any stranger, he was immediately noticed and provided for by the judge. . . .

He was especially kind to young men, always knew when one came and settled in a county seat, and always helped them out of their troubles, often to the confusion and dismay of the older members of the bar, who were, many of them, inclined to sit down on them. I remember well an incident between Linder and the judge on this subject. A young man [Henry Clay Whitney] had settled in Danville, and in his pleadings, at court, he had written a plea wrong. Linder demurred to it, and the judge in sustaining the demurrer intimated to the young man how to amend the plea. The young gentleman amended it and got it wrong again. Linder demurred again, and the judge again sustained the demurrer, making plainer his suggestion. The plea was again amended and was again wrong, when the judge said: "Give me that plea." He took it, read it over to himself, amended it to suit himself, and handed it back. Linder could demur no more, but was very angry. That night he called round to the judge's room and found him alone and writing. "Come in, Linder," said the judge, "come in," "Oh, no," said Linder, "I see you are writing pleas in some of your numerous cases. I will not disturb you."

He was a preoccupied, absent-minded man. On one occasion, at the Champaign court, an old man and his wife, emigrants, were passing through the country and were robbed by a young man whom they overtook and who begged a ride. The occurrence took place just before his court, and the young man was arrested, tried and convicted at that term. The judge in passing sentence, gave the young man a lecture upon the baseness of his conduct in accepting a ride with the old man, and then knocking him on the head and robbing him. After pointing out in glowing language his conduct the judge proceeded: "And it is the judgment of this court that you be confined in the Legislature of the State of Illinois for the period of seven years." It was not until Ward H. Lamon, the prosecuting attorney, had gone to the judge and whispered in his ear, that he discovered his mistake and substituted the penitentiary for the Legislature of the State. Judge Davis was by nature faithful to a trust. Besides this natural make-up, this duty had been burned into him while young by the conduct of his own guardians. The judge's father and mother died while he was young. Twelve thousand dollars was left in his guardians' hands to be paid over to him when he should become 21 years of age, but his guardians in some manner invested this so as to lose the whole, or spent it, and when he became 21 he had nothing. He litigated these guardians for many years and finally lost the case, by an equal division of the Supreme Court of Maryland.

At the time he was presiding, no land of a minor could be sold under the laws of the State except on petition to the judge of the Circuit Court. Judge Davis always declined to order such sales, but kept the land in kind for the ward, until he or she became of age, and then not only was the estate preserved, but the ward got the benefit of the rise in the value of his estate, which then was rapid and universal.

On one occasion, about 1852, at the Champaign court, Mr. Murphy, a lawyer from Danville, filed a petition for a stepfather who was the guardian of a young girl whose mother he had married, asking permission to sell an improved farm which she owned. Everybody looked to the judge to see him refuse the application, when, contrary to his habit, he ordered the land sold, and that, when the money was collected it should be paid to Thompson R. Webber, who is still remembered for his honesty and fidelity, and as being the clerk of that court. In the course of a year afterward, Webber reported that he had a good pile of money. The judge ordered him verbally to go to Cincinnati, invest all the money in land warrants, which could then be had for about $1 an acre, and to meet him at the Danville court, which was held next after that of Champaign, and where the land office for the entry of land was then open. Mr. Webber went to Cincinnati, bought the warrants, came to Danville, when the judge adjourned the court, went to the land office in person and entered unimproved but rich farm-lands in Champaign, all in the name of the girl, and when she became of age she was worth $50,000.

His conduct was parental and patriarchal to all. If any of the lawyers got wild, the judge often made him stop it and go to bed and sleep it off. These may be said to illustrate the outposts or exterior layers of the judge's character. Dig through these and you come to a mine of pure gold.

Judge Davis was one of the greatest judges this country has ever produced. He knew just enough law to be a great judge, and not enough to spoil him. The poorest lawyers I have ever known are men who know the most law. . . .

A great judge must know not only law but must know things also [*sic*]. Judge Davis knew well the principles and rules of law, but he also knew that these rules were simply guideboards to justice. He did not look at the guideboard and go mad after it. He went straight for justice, using it so far as it would guide him, and when it would not he threw it away. He was a natural judge. He took to justice by instinct, as the hound takes the scent. He was of the same order as Chief Justice Marshall, and an anecdote of this great jurist illustrates the character of both. It is said of Judge Marshall that one time as he sat in consultation with his brother judges of the Supreme

Court some knotty and new question was under discussion. Judge Marshall stopped the discussion. Said he: "The law is so and so. Brother Such a One," turning to one of the judges, "you please hunt up the authorities to sustain my position."

Judge Davis knew that all legal rules were the result of a wise experience, and that they were intended simply as guides to the right. If, in any present complication, he found these rules used to further the wrong he would go through them like cobwebs. An anecdote of him illustrates this: Judge Davis and the eminent Judge Treat, of the United States District Court [in southern Illinois], were old and fast friends. They were one time holding the United States Circuit Court together in this city [Springfield]. One of the keenest land sharks this State ever produced had got some kink on a large farmer's farm, and had brought ejectment to take it substantially for nothing. The judge at the trial heard him, looked at him and finally, crossing his legs, swung around in his rotary chair, so as to turn almost his back to him, looked over his shoulder at the lawyer who was trying his own case, and said: "You can talk to Treat. You can talk to Treat. Before this court you can not steal a man's farm in that way."

I will give another illustration of this element of his character. The judge, after his promotion to the United States Supreme Court, was holding a Circuit Court of the United States in a neighboring State with the United States district judge, when a conflict arose between two sets of heirs, each claiming for itself an entire estate. The evidence tended to show that a man had married a wife in Germany, abandoned her and his family, came to Indiana, married another woman, raised another family, accumulated an estate of a million of dollars, and died. After his death the German heirs came for the estate, and the Indiana heirs resisted. There were some informalities in the proof of the first marriage in Germany, enough to create a doubt where one wants to doubt. The two judges were in consultation upon this case, after the trial. Judge Davis said: "It is a pity about this case. There is property enough for both. The situation is not the fault of either party, but of the man who is dead. Let us make them divide it." The district judge [probably Judge Gresham] replied: "That is right. You are good at that. Suppose you engineer the matter," and so they went into court and sent for the lawyers on opposite sides. . . . The true way was for each party to yield something, and settle the case. After again brushing up his grave doubts, at least as much as they would bear, the attorneys were left to consult and negotiate, and finally came into court with a decree, entered by consent, declaring both families to be heirs and dividing the million equally between them all. Each side went away happy and with a half million.

The great decision of Mr. Justice Davis' judicial life is what is generally known as the Milligan decision. By that he put his mark upon the constitutional history of this country which will never be obliterated. The substance of this decision is that peace is the natural condition of this country, and prevails except when actually interrupted by war where the question arises. That the rights of peace, including the right of trial by jury, exist in all persons, whenever the courts are open and the channels of justice uninterrupted, notwithstanding actual war may prevail in other parts of the country. War and not peace is the natural condition of mankind. War has left its fossil remains in the history of the ages, back to the fire-rock next to the creation of man. The doctrine of "Peace on earth and good will to men," in its application to governments, is new. War and force to-day is the rule of the world. If one would blot out from the map of the world every nation founded on force, and governed by force, he would blot out the map of nearly all the world. The doctrines of the Milligan decision were born in the United States and to the honor of the memory of David Davis be it said, he is the father of them. Let us who give our lives to the law see to it that this decision is preserved, and that it shall always live, as a memento of the judicial greatness of our friend, and as one of the great constitutional landmarks of our country. . . .

[The next three paragraphs, describing the part Davis played in the nomination of Lincoln, have been omitted.]

Judge Davis had been continuously upon the bench in this State and upon the Supreme bench for thirty-two years when he was elected United States senator, and by that Senate, before his term expired, was elected president of the senate and ex-officio vice president of the United States. The time allotted will not permit me to discuss his life there. . . . I used, as a rule, to visit Judge Davis, spending about half a day with him, every time in passing to and from Washington, he came through Chicago. . . . Suffice it to say of Judge Davis and his political career, that he was the only man in the United States who has ever been able to make a personal party, consisting solely of himself, respectable. By great capacity, by sterling qualities and character, he was able to retain his personal convictions on all subjects and vote with either party best representing them, and at the same time to retain the personal respect and confidence of the Senate and of the Nation.

He governed the Senate when presiding officer in the same paternal and patriarchal way he governed the Circuit Court in an early day. Some senator once moved about 3 o'clock in the afternoon to adjourn. "O pshaw," said the judge, "it isn't time to adjourn yet," and actually went on with the business paying no attention to and never putting to vote the motion to adjourn. He was the only man in the whole country who could have done this, and he could not have done it if he had not been entirely unconscious of what he was doing. If I were asked to state what was the leading trait of Judge Davis' character, I should say latent, unconscious strength. Almost everything in nature contains latent heat. This is a force which the object possesses unconsciously to itself and to every other person. Judge Davis was full of latent unconscious strength. He simply walked up to and did anything, almost impossible to be done, as a matter of course. In this way he acquired control over the most uncontrollable men, and accomplished with the greatest ease what seemed to others impossible of accomplishment. The judge's forecast was just as good as other men's actual sight of things. Away back in an early day when he looked down the channels of time and he saw the State of Illinois, with its smiling farms, its cities, its railroads and manufactories, as we see them now, and he made a colossal fortune in the simplest way possible. He never got the advantage of any man in a trade. He never loaned money for interest and never foreclosed anybody. Nobody ever left Illinois to "go west and try it again," on his account. Although I lived with him the last half of his life on most intimate terms, I never saw his promissory note, or ever saw anyone else who ever saw or heard of it. He simply entered land for $1.25 an acre, had it put into fertile farms, and when he died he left this same land worth $100 an acre.

Judge Davis was one of the kindest and most tender-hearted and most generous of men. At the Chicago convention, when Lincoln's nomination became a fixed fact, when delegations were changing their votes and everything was in the confusion of coming to Lincoln, when everybody was shouting and in the hurrah of Bedlam, Judge Davis threw his great arms around a friend and cried like a child.

He fulfilled the scriptural mandate in his charities of not letting his right hand know what his left hand was doing. He gave wisely but not ostentatiously, and never talked about his giving. Many a church and school house in Central Illinois, sits today on a lot given by the judge. I have, at different periods, in my intercourse with him, occasionally stumbled upon his charities. In this way I happened to know instances where he loaned or gave away to poor lawyers sums which when added together amount to $3,500. He had an immense landed estate and an army of tenants. I have known years of drought in which, as a rule, he remitted to his tenants his entire claims for rent. When visiting him in his last sickness, as I was walking over his palatial grounds with his wife, I said to her, noticing an old gardener: "How many of these old people have you?" She replied, "About twenty." These were permanent fixtures of the place, and when he died, a great light went out to them all.

I visited him last on the 10th of May, and spent a day at his home. He was then suffering intensely but heroically, and I bade him adieu, then thinking I might never see him again. I never did. In June I was called to Bloomington to the most remarkable funeral I have ever witnessed. Twenty thousand people gathered there on that occasion, coming in mostly by wagons, and some coming twenty-five or thirty miles. This crowd, of course, could not get into the house, or even see the funeral, but they could line, in silence, the streets where it was known the cortege would pass, filling the sidewalks, the front yards, doors and windows every inch of the way from his house to the graveyard, a distance of more than two miles. In the cortege, after the corpse, and after the family in carriages, and on that occasion the equals of the family they served, were the poor, the servants of the family, the gardeners, and even those who lived upon the bounty of the good judge. Thus on a bright June day, at that gathering of the great and the small, of the proud and the humble, the rich and the poor, and all his friends, we consigned him to his final resting place, and all alike were real mourners.

Judge Davis presented the best character I have ever met in life. He was not a religious man, in the sense of being a member of any church, yet he believed in all religions and in the good work of all churches, and they all alike called upon him in their wants to lend a helping hand, and to one just as cheerfully as to another he helped them all. He was broad and catholic in his beliefs and in his conduct. Intimately as I have known him, I can not, as I write these lines, recall one wrong act in all his life. He is the only man of whom I can say, if I had the making of him for time and eternity, I should alter nothing. Tender, considerate and kind, strong, robust and vigorous, he walked on, a model in character and a model of success. Judge

Davis is the only man I have ever known of whom I could conscientiously and without mental reservation say this, standing among people who knew him well, and standing as it were, over his grave.

Shakespeare makes his Portia say, speaking of the virtues and temptations of life: "If to do were as easy as to know what were good to do, chapels had been churches and poor men's cottages princes' palaces. It were easier to tell twenty what were good to do than be one of the twenty to follow my own instructions." Judge Davis was no exception to this rule. He was a man of strong human passions. . . . Judge Davis was a character full of humanity and full of moral sense. . . .

As I recall the circumstances of my own early life in this State, I thank God and thank Him again that in the mysteries of providence He placed the lines of my life between two such great men as David Davis and Abraham Lincoln, and permitted me, in the hours of my own weakness, to "Lean on their own great arms for support."

Memorial of T. Lyle Dickey, U.S. Circuit Court, Northern District of Illinois, May 9, 1887

From Swett, *Remembrances of T. Lyle Dickey*; also CLN, 5-14-87, 288–92, CHM.

May it please the Court:
"Take heed that in thy verse,
Thou dost the tale rehearse,
Else dread a dead man's curse:
For this I sought thee."

Mr. Longfellow, our greatest poet, being at Newport, Rhode Island, and seeing there the old round tower—that work of unknown date, of unknown architecture, and of unknown nationality—and hearing also that a skeleton had been recently found at Fall River, nearby, spun out that beautiful romance, "The Skeleton in Armor," in which he makes the tower the architecture of Norwegians in the twelfth century and the skeleton that of an old Viking or corsair of the same period, who built the house for his home, after stealing his wife and crossing the ocean, and when she died buried her under the tower, and, overwhelmed with grief at her loss and crying out, "Never shall the sun rise on such another," fell

full-armed upon his spear and lay there covered with the sands of time
until his body thus encased in corroded armor was found about the time
Mr. Longfellow was there.

The lines of this *true* story with which I begin this talk are what the
skeleton said to the poet, enjoining upon him the duty of telling this
dead man's tale.

These lines have rung in my mind many an hundred times during the
last two years, and the following is the history of their haunting me:

Once and only once, since I have had my offices in the Montauk block
[64–70 West Monroe, Chicago], some five years, Judge Dickey came up
there to see me. He being fourteen years my senior, I used to visit him. He
came up the eighth story, having apparently walked up some of the flights
of stairs and was considerably out of breath when he came in. "Swett," said
he, "as I was walking along the sidewalk below, I was thinking of you,
and have come up to see you." I replied: "I am very glad to see you, judge,
as I always am." "But I came of a special errand, and to see if you would
promise to do something for me." I replied: "It will give me great pleasure
to promise or do anything you could ask of me." He replied: "Well, I have
come up to ask you when I die to say something in commemoration of my
character. I believe you can appreciate and call out, better than any other
person I know, any points of my character worthy to be remembered, and
I have come in all seriousness to make this request." I replied, "Judge, I will
make the promise to you if you will make the same to me if I die first." He
said, "I will." And rose and offered me his hand across the table, which I
accepted, and there, alone, we confirmed to each other these promises. . . .

I first met Judge Dickey about thirty-five years ago in the autumn of
1852. He was then judge of the circuit and was holding court at Princeton,
in Bureau county. . . . I never knew him, in more than thirty years of
intimate acquaintance, to be guilty of a trick, or to be sharp or deceitful, and
never heard him accused of these faults of character by any one. He was an
open-hearted, kind, manly, but skillful and wise, man. It was, however, as
a trial lawyer in the circuit court that Judge Dickey pre-eminently excelled
and appeared most conspicuously and to advantage. Here he was always
at his best. Memory recalls him now, standing in a court-room, half way
through a long and complicated trial, a pleasant smile upon his face, in the
best of humor, and fully equal to the situation. Here he was gentlemanly,
overflowing with good nature, quick, sharp, and incisive as a Damascus

blade. Playing him under such circumstances was like playing with broken glass. Such moments with him were moments of supreme coolness and supreme good nature. He was thoroughly master of his place, smiling, happy, quick as a cat. When Dickey stood in a court-room and smiled and twirled the fob of his watch-chain, look out! It is conceded that Judge [Stephen T.] Logan of Springfield, was, for quickness and strength, the best trial lawyer this state has ever produced. Judge Dickey was more like him than any man I ever knew. If I had a long, tangled controversy in court and could have two associates, I would rather have Judge Dickey in his prime for one than any man living.

Judge Dickey was a man of unusually clear intellectual sight. . . . An anecdote of thirty years ago illustrates this, and may be useful to young men in the profession, and to old men, too. I was then about thirty-two years old. Dickey was forty-six, or in the prime of his professional experience. It had been seven years since I could call myself a lawyer in name, and I was defending the notorious Isaac Wyant, who had had an arm shot off in a fight, and who six months afterward walked into the court house at Clinton and shot four bullets through the man who had shot him. It was my first case of this kind. The trial lasted a week of long days and evenings, and the defendant was prosecuted by Abraham Lincoln. I had had the case in hand about a year and a half, and the facts and law of it were thoroughly tanned into me. I had been to Boston to consult Dr. Luther V. Bell, the great expert in insanity. I had also consulted Dickey, and he had promised if he could he would assist me at the trial; but, when the trial day came, my principal witness stampeded and wanted to go home, and Dickey was accidentally at the McLean court; and I was about scared to death. I fell on Dickey with his old promise that he would help me, but he declined. I offered him all the fee I was to get, but still not only he would not and went home, but he would give me no reason why he would not, and so I had "to tread the wine-press alone."

Afterward meeting Dickey, I said: "Now please tell me why you wouldn't help me?" He replied: "Because I could see you needed to be thrown on your own resources, and if I had been there you would have leaned on me, would have lost your own efficiency, and I was not familiar enough with the case to do the work well. No, when a young man is well prepared he should not undertake to filter his knowledge to the jury through an older man who is not prepared."

"Well," I replied, "why didn't you give me that reason?"

"Because you were strained then, and in a very useful state of distress, and if I had given you that reason I was afraid you would have beaten me out of it, and so I thought I would wait and tell you afterward. . . ."

Judge Dickey moved from Kentucky to Illinois before the panic of 1837. He brought a sum of money which he had accumulated there and invested it in Illinois, lost it all, and became crippled with debt, which he carried for a life-time. . . .

When the bankrupt law of 1841 was passed, a question of right and wrong was presented to Judge Dickey in reference to his old indebtedness. If there was ever a case in which a man was justified in taking the benefit of a bankrupt law, Dickey was, because there was no question but that the debt arose from misfortune, and he had nothing. The law was made for just such a case, but such a course did not accord with Dickey's conscientious notions of integrity, and he carried along the debt, paying as he could, until 1867, when the last of it, with interest, was finally liquidated. Thus he held it to be conscientious in himself, and a duty to pay the "uttermost farthing," although it took him thirty years, the best of his life, to do it.

And not only did he do this, but temptation came to him in this matter double-edged. About 1842, when everybody else was taking the benefit of the bankrupt act, Dickey inherited some seven or eight slaves, left to him by a relative in Kentucky. It would have been very convenient to have sold these to relieve him from debt, but this too he conscientiously declined, and freed all his slaves. . . .

He entered the service in the war of the rebellion in the spring of 1861. His name had been before Governor Yates for a colonel's appointment, but there was some hitch about it, and he came to Bloomington where Judge Davis and I lived, from Ottawa, where he lived, to consult with us as to how he could get into the service of his country. Besides himself, he had sons and sons-in-law and friends in La Salle county, who also wanted to get in, but couldn't. We told him the region of Bloomington was also full of men who wanted to do the same thing, but couldn't. This was an unusual thing in the history of patriotism in any country, but is a fact of those times that the country was full of men who wanted to serve it, but they could not get the chance. It was finally determined that Dickey and I should both go to Washington. We both knew Mr. Lincoln, and I knew General Cameron,

Secretary of War, and he for past favors was indebted to Judge Davis and myself. The object of this mission was to get into the service these people in the various capacities they were best fitted to fill, in La Salle and McLean counties. I was the more ready for this mission, because I had made up my mind not to go into the service personally, because I had a sick wife and a sick son wholly dependent upon me for care, and if I left them nobody was to take care of them. Besides, I had in my life been to one war, and that, too, as a private soldier. So I made up my mind that I would not go, but that I would serve every regiment and every man who did go. I could be absent from home in snatches of time. I need not add, as this became known I had plenty of business.

At Washington we got authority for Dickey to raise a regiment, which was done mainly in LaSalle and McLean counties, and appoint all the officers of it. He appointed William McCullough, of Bloomington, as lieutenant-colonel. He was the most thoroughly courageous man I have ever known, and entered the service at the age of fifty, with one arm and one eye. Afterwards he fell in a hopeless charge, at the head of his regiment in Mississippi [near Coffeyville]. We also obtained an order for 1,000 cavalry uniforms and 1,000 sabers and accoutrements and 1,000 Sharp carbines, to be sent directly from the manufactories to Ottawa. We were afraid if they were sent to Washington they would be needed by other regiments and we would not get them, and so we got this order directly on the factories for the first made. The regiment was soon and easily raised, but it was in the summer and quite late, and the uniforms, sabers, carbines, etc, had not come. They had a thousand men in camp at Ottawa and had written letters without number, and telegraphed until they had nearly burned the wires off, but no uniforms, accoutrements or carbines came. The men had become uneasy waiting about camp in farmer's clothes, and something had to be done.

It was finally decided by the officers in council to send me to Washington to see why these things did not come. I had already been there two or three times for them, and Dickey and his officers knew I didn't want to go again. I was then at the Danville court and Dickey came down there, about 150 miles, coming in the night, and about 4 o'clock in the morning I heard him pounding at my door at the hotel. I give you the interview as illustrative of his appropriateness, in saying always just the right thing to move a man and to effect his own purpose. "I know it was mean," he began, as he entered my room, I lying in bed. "I know it was mean but in old Kentucky times, when we used to drive a six-horse team and were near miring down in a slough, we used to lick the best horse. It was awfully mean, but it was simply a necessity to get out of the mire, and that is what I have come clear from Ottawa to-night to do to you. I want you to get out of that bed and leave the court and go immediately to Washington and find out what has happened to our orders for clothing and arms. I can not leave my regiment. They are all in camp in farmer's clothes, and you can not drill a farmer boy to become a soldier until you put a new uniform on him, and give him a new sword and bright carbine. You know all about this business at Washington, and can get it done, and Col. McCullough and I have held a council of war and we have concluded you must go." What was left for me but to get up and start for Washington?

I will not, in a long time, forget my interview with Mr. Lincoln on this subject, and herein I want to correct a popular error in reference to the beginning of the war. Everybody says: "Pshaw! What made Lincoln call for 75,000 men? Why didn't he call for 500,000 at once?" I will tell you. The government did not call for 500,000 men, simply because it could not utilize them. The time of which I speak was the spring and summer of 1861.

The arming of the nation had been in progress for about four months. At the beginning the government had no arms. They had all been transported south. Europe had no surplus of good arms it could sell. All we could buy were mainly old Austrian muskets, the refuse of Austria, and they were good for nothing but to teach men to drill.

I learned when I arrived at Washington that the government in a pinch had ordered all the arms it could lay its hands on to Washington, to arm regiments there, and this order had been held to supersede our order. Mr. Lincoln, in not the best of humor, said: "Swett, if your regiment were to wait and take an honest turn, the wool has not yet grown on the sheep's back to make their uniforms." This is the key to the explanation why the government did not take men faster. It is also a reason which could not then be publicly told, for it would have shown to foreign nations our weakness. The industries of the nation had all to be changed. All the wool on the sheep's backs in the country, and all that could be bought, had to be diverted to uniforms, and the manufacturing capacity of the country had to be increased, and Mr. Lincoln might have added with equal truth that the ore with which to make the swords and the carbines was still in its native mountains. All the manufactories in the country had to be set in operation to make arms. New factories had to be built and new industries created, and even then whole regiments had to wait for their turn to be uniformed and armed. . . .

Judge Dickey and his sons and sons-in-law have rendered marked services to their country, and deserve a monument more enduring than brass. They deserve the WARM thanks of their countrymen, for whom they made these sacrifices. Let me recount the history of these two families, and let us pause and think whether their services and sacrifices do not equal the Fabii or the Gracchi or any other family of antiquity.

Theophilus Lyle Dickey left Ottawa for the Mexican war in 1846 as a captain of Company I, which became a part of Col. John J. Hardin's regiment. At San Antonio his regiment left him behind in camp to die of disease, but after hanging in the balance for a long time between life and death, he finally recovered.

Gen. William H. L. Wallace, Col. Dickey's son-in-law, had been a student in Dickey's law office, was the first lieutenant of Capt. Dickey's company, and afterward was made adjutant, and was at Col. Hardin's side when he fell at the battle of Buena Vista. He entered the service again in April, 1861, as colonel of the 11th infantry, was made a brigadier-general, and fell at Shiloh while endeavoring to stay the retreat of our army on Sunday, the first day of that terrible fight.

Cyrus C. Dickey, Col. Dickey's oldest son, entered the service at the same time Col. Wallace did, and as a private in his regiment. Col. Ransom, a very young man, was a lover of battle for its own sake. His bright face seems to pass before me now. He was the son of the old veteran Ransom, who fell at Chepultepec. He became colonel of the 11th after Col. Wallace's promotion, and Cyrus Dickey was made adjutant upon his staff, and finally fell in Banks' expedition up the Red river, at Mansfield, Louisiana [Sabine Cross Roads, April 8, 1864].

Charles H. Dickey, the youngest son of Judge Dickey, entered the service with his father as a private in the 4th cavalry in July, 1861. He was made first-lieutenant, and was severely wounded while commanding Gen. McPherson's body-guard in the State of Mississippi. He is now a merchant in the Sandwich [Hawaiian] Islands.

M. R. M. Wallace, the brother of Col. Wallace, entered the service in the summer of 1861 as a major in the 4th cavalry with Col. Dickey, and was promoted for gallant service to the positions of colonel and brigadier-general. He was formerly the Probate judge of this county [Cook], and is now a practicing lawyer in this city.

John F. Wallace, another brother of Gen. Wallace, entered the service as lieutenant in Company C, with Col. Dickey, in the 4th cavalry, served gallantly through the war, was consolidated with Gen. Custer's 12th in the last part of the war in Texas, practiced law in Texas after the war, and died. In a letter received from Mrs. Gen. Wallace, that lady, in speaking of him, says: "I always felt that he, too, was a victim of the war."

Matthew Wallace, another brother, a farmer, entered the fourth cavalry in the summer of 1861, and in February, 1862, while embarking on a steamer with the troops at Cairo in a sleet storm to move up the Ohio, the guard-rail of the boat, on which he was leaning, broke, and he was plunged into the water with his carbine in hand with his knapsack, haversack and saber strapped upon him, and a cavalry overcoat and boots on, and, although a splendid swimmer, sank beneath his load and was drowned.

C. H. Wallace, who married Belle Dickey, Col. Dickey's youngest daughter, another brother, also served in the quartermaster's department under Col. Fort. He was broken in health by his service and by the small-pox which he contracted, and has never since fully recovered. He is also now a merchant in the Sandwich Islands with Charles Dickey. Thus Col. Dickey, with all his sons but one, and Col. William H. L. Wallace, his son-in-law, with all his brothers, entered the service of their country in the war of the rebellion, and the seven were together at Shiloh.

Mrs. General W. H. L. Wallace, who was Judge Dickey's eldest daughter, as the battle of Shiloh approached, became impressed with the sense of impending danger to her husband, then with Grant's army. This impression haunted her until she could stand it no longer, and in one of the most severe storms of the season, at twelve o'clock at night, she started alone for the army where her family were. At Cairo she was told that no woman could be permitted to go up the Tennessee river. But affection has a persistency which will not be denied. Mrs. Wallace finding a party bearing a flag to the 11th infantry, from the ladies of Ottawa to be used instead of theirs, which had been riddled and was battle-worn, got herself substituted to carry that flag, and thus with one expedient and another she finally reached Shiloh, six hundred miles from home and three hundred through a hostile country and through the more hostile guards of our own forces.

She arrived on Sunday, the 6th of April, 1862, when the great storm center of that battle was at its height, and in time to receive her husband as he was borne from the battle-field terribly mangled by a shot in the head, which entered the eye and passed inside the skull and came out a little back of the ear, and which he had received while endeavoring to stay the retreat of our army as it was falling back to the bank of the river on that memorable Sunday, the first day of that bloody battle. She arrived in time to recognize him and be recognized by him, and a few days afterward, saying "We shall meet again in heaven," he died in the arms of that devoted wife surrounded by Judge Dickey and his sons and brothers of Gen. Wallace, and, as I am informed, in the very room then occupied by your honor [Circuit Judge Gresham] as commander of the post at Savannah.

The story of the tragic death of Gen. Wallace and the circumstances of his wife's coming was told me by Judge Dickey on the battle-field of Shiloh, about Thursday or Friday of the same week.

It was through one of the accidents which so often changes the fate of battle, and which made Frederick the Great say battles were fought beyond the stars, that we are indebted to Col. Dickey more than any other man for the fact that the rebels did not effectually break through our lines at Fort Donelson and escape. Fort Donelson was on an ox-bow or sharp bend of the Tennessee river. The object of placing the fortification there was to command the river, and this position gave a shot nearly lengthwise down the river. Grant's maxim was to fight first and get ready as soon as he could, and thus have the selection of where the fight should be. His attack upon Donelson was made before his whole force arrived, and his tactics were to extend his line back of the fort from river to river, and thus hold the enemy in a *cul de sac*. To do this he had to stretch his lines like a piece of rubber—too far and make them too thin. The object of the enemy when this line was extended and the fort could not be held was to break through and escape; so, finding the weakest point near the river, they bent back our lines as a wrestler bends back and dislocates the arm of his adversary, and began to pour through this opening, but finally voluntarily went back within the fortifications. These facts are well known, but the reason that induced the rebels to fight their way out and then voluntarily go back has not been known until since the war, and since the officers upon opposite sides have had an opportunity to compare notes.

Dickey had come to our lines at the fort, but his cavalry was unfit for such siege work, and there was no food for the horses there, so he was ordered back to a ridge and where he could get forage. This happened to be along the line of the road over which the remainder of Grant's army was expected by Grant and the rebels. As the soldiers pent up in the fort poured through our lines at the broken place and had proceeded a little way, they struck Dickey's force, which was about eighteen hundred men with some howitzers. Dickey immediately caused all his bugles to be blown and beat the long roll, and fired his howitzers sharply in the face of the enemy. They hesitated, stopped and went back into the fort, and thus Grant was enabled, finally, to report the capture of fourteen thousand men with the fortifications.

This attack was wholly unexpected, and it has since the war been learned from rebel officers who were there, that they did not expect to meet any force, and that they hesitated, stopped and turned back, their exit from the fort being in process of completion, because they supposed they had encountered the remainder of Grant's army and retreated, fearing they would be caught between this force coming and Grant's main force.

In all that adorns a man Judge Dickey was as bright as a new blade. . . . His professional and judicial character was pure and was never even sullied by suspicion or accusation. He occupied the public position of circuit judge in this state way back in the '50s, was a captain in the Mexican war, the colonel of 4th Illinois cavalry, brigadier general, and Gen. Grant's chief of the cavalry in the west. After the war he became assistant attorney-general of the United States, and finally was for many years one of the justices of our Supreme court of this state. In all these instances of holding official position he discharged the duties to the satisfaction of every one whose interests were affected, and the place he filled was honored by the fact that he filled it. . . .

One morning [in 1858], as I went to my office at Bloomington, I met Dickey at the door. He had come down from Ottawa on a night train which arrived about daylight, and was standing at my office door awaiting admission. Said he: "Where is Davis?" I told him, and he replied he wished I would send for him. When the judge came into my private office, Dickey said: "Gentlemen, we have been friends a great while; we have thought alike and acted alike; now I am going to leave you, and so I have come down to spend the day with you and bid you good-by. *I am going to join the democratic party.* I have not come to discuss whether I shall join it. In reference to that my mind is made up; but I thought, considering our past relations, it but fair, before leaving you, that I should come down and spend the day with you and bid you good-by. Then I shall go."

We had been old Henry Clay whigs together, and no men ever thought so exactly alike as Henry Clay whigs. The formation of the republican party was an element of disruption. Dickey had been raised in Kentucky, had a holy fear of abolition tendencies, although, as stated, he abolished his own slaves, and a tendency himself toward the democratic party, and by and by he determined to plunge in and join it.

We gave him a cordial welcome, went by ourselves, and gave up all business to the visit of the day. At noon we had a dinner together with a little Catawba, best the town afforded, and talked the day away. Politics, in fact, was the only subject absolutely avoided, for all the ground there had in many an interview been tramped over before. We talked over the olden times, told stories of circuit life, recalled those who had gone before, and when 4 o'clock in the afternoon, the time for Dickey to leave, came, we went with him to the train, shook him by the hand, bade him good-by. He did not stop until he ran into the very heart of the democratic party.

But old age let fall his mantle on the dear old judge, as it will let fall that mantle on us all. The pinched look and the feeble tread were finally his, and at the ripe old age of seventy-four, and ripe in character, ripe in the affection and esteem of all good men, and ripe in good works, he was gathered to his fathers.

Dedicatory Speech at the Unveiling of Saint-Gaudens's "Standing Lincoln" Statue at Lincoln Park, Chicago, October 22, 1887

From *Ceremonies at the Unveiling,* 10-22-87. Also published in Whitney, *Life on the Circuit,* 557–64, available through Google Books.

And here we are again illustrating either the follies or the hopes of mankind! All the nations of the world have tried in their turn to perpetuate in some manner the memory of the worthy dead. Nearly, and perhaps all, nations have believed in the resurrection and a life after death. Hence their efforts to perpetuate the human figure or an exact memory of the human body. . . .

Greece grew out of Egypt and succeeded her. Many of her gods, goddesses, and myths migrated from Egypt into Greece, about 600 miles away, and the fertile and imaginative Greek mind vivified and idealized them, and hence we find in Greece, not the revolting mummy, or the actual flesh and form preserved, but the memory of that form idealized in the beautiful marble or bronze which recalls the likeness such as we see to-day, of form, figure, and feature, in the most pleasing manner, and the memory of the very man who has lived and passed away.

This Grecian art, the art of Phidias and Polyclites in marble, and Myron in bronze, we have endeavored to imitate, and as a result we have unveiled and now look upon this beautiful pedestal and colossal statue of Abraham Lincoln, a gentleman born within our own age, who lived within our own state, who was known to many of us, and adorned our own times.

We have been and are now constructing one of the most attractive parks in the whole country, upon the margin of the beautiful Lake Michigan, and about three miles from the central part of our city, which now contains nearly 900,000 souls. In the highest and not in the modern sense of that term, the honorable Eli Bates, in life, by his will, gave $40,000 in trust to Thomas F. Withrow, Geo. Payson, and James T. Brooks, who, associating with them Joseph Stockton, of the Park Commission, have erected at the southern or city entrance of this park the noble statue of Abraham Lincoln, which we now behold. Here, we see his tall, lithe form, his earnest face, recalling to all who knew him the figure and the look of the real man.

And why is the form of Abraham Lincoln thus selected, and placed at this entrance, to be observed for all time, we hope, by our citizens, and the admiring throngs who will pass this point visiting this park? Why is he selected from the 50,000,000 of people with whom he lived? The answer is, because he was, in life, the most simple and direct in character, and at one time the humblest citizen in the land, at another the most exalted. His patriotism was the purest, and he was the most far-seeing and wise, and having many years ago first predicted that this country could not exist, half slave and half free, but the antagonism and contest would go on until we should become either all slave or all free, he himself took the patient leadership of that contest, and by his proclamation freed 4,000,000 slaves, lifted our whole country to a higher plane of civilization, and finally, at the hand of malice, fell a martyr because of this character and this act.

The character of Abraham Lincoln sprung upon American soil and was of American growth. It would not have been possible for any other soil on the globe, or any country other than America, or any other civilization than our own, to have produced him. He was emphatically the child of the Republic and the product of our institutions. He was of the people and for the people.

Born in Kentucky, of the most humble and unknown parentage, he walked in early life the pathway of the poor. At about six years old, his parents moved to Southern Indiana, where his mother died and he lived there until about 19 [actually he was 21], when his father again loaded all his earthly possessions upon an ox wagon, and young Lincoln, with goad in hand, in the main, drove the team, on a new migration to Coles County, Illinois. [Swett always got Coles and Macon Counties reversed.]

When he thus left Indiana he had been in school in a log school house but six weeks, and this period constituted his entire education received at school. Having arrived here in August, they erected a log cabin and ploughed some land for a crop the coming year. He remained with his father until the next fall, when about to become 21 years of age the next February, his father gave him his time, and his step-mother, a kind, good mother to him, tied all his earthly possessions in a pack, and Lincoln running a stick through where the knot was tied, started on foot from Coles County to Macon County.

Cast your eye back sixty years and look on that tall, lithe young man, partly concealed by the tall grasses of the prairie as he then walks alone, along the Indian trail, with a pack on his back and hope in his heart, on that wonderful journey of life, which first took him to Macon County, and the life of a rail-splitter, thence to Sangamon County and Sangamon River, and the life of a flat-boatman upon the Sangamon, Illinois and Mississippi Rivers; thence to a captaincy in the Black Hawk War; thence to a membership in the Illinois Legislature for four [actually, eight] years, in which and in the political campaigns of 1840 and 1844 he acquired a name as an orator; thence to a leadership at the bar; thence to one term in Congress, and finally to the Presidency of the country he then walked over so humbly, and to martyrdom for the principles he advocated and the noble life he lived.

Arrived in Macon County, he met some cousins, and with one of them took a contract for splitting rails at a stipulated price per hundred. He then went to Sangamon County, and worked for a farmer who lived near the Sangamon River. Products were easily raised, but there was no market for them, and so Lincoln conceived the idea of building a flat-boat and floating it loaded with the products of the farm down the Sangamon into the Illinois River, and thence down the Illinois to the Mississippi, and then down the Mississippi to New Orleans. This as yet had never been done. It being agreed upon, Lincoln with his own hands felled the timber, hewed the beams, made the boat, loaded it with produce, and then was elected to his first office, which was the captaincy of that flat-boat. . . . Having made successfully the voyage to New Orleans he worked his passage back by firing upon a steamer coming up the river. Upon one of these trips down the river an occurrence took place which very nearly prevented him from ever being President or from ever making the slave free. His boat on a downward trip was one night hauled up to the shore near Natchez, in Mississippi. Captain Lincoln and his crew were asleep below when the steps of some one was heard on deck. Lincoln came up to see who was there. As his head reached up through the hatchway of the boat, a negro who was pilfering, struck him a blow with a large stick, which at the same time struck Lincoln's head and the floor beyond it and stunned him, and left upon his head a large scar which he carried through life.

After this he was a clerk and partner in a small store near New Salem. After this again the Blackhawk war broke out, and Lincoln was elected captain of a company raised at New Salem. After that war he was elected four times to the Legislature, to which he walked from Sangamon County on foot a part of the time. There, for the first time, he came in contact with the prominent men of the State, and distinguished himself as a speaker. He then moved to Springfield, and commenced about the same time to study and practice of the law, and soon rose to distinction and eminence in that profession.

When he was nominated for the Presidency in 1860 some campaign book-maker called upon him to get the prominent features of his life, and well he replied, in the language of Gray's Elegy, that his life presented nothing but

"The short and simple annals of the poor."

The most marked characteristic of Mr. Lincoln was his personal isolation or peculiarity from all other men with whom he lived. No one who knew him ever knew another man like him. He stands out from the whole world of his time isolated and alone.

I rode the Eighth Judicial Circuit with him for eleven years, and in the allotment between him and the large Judge Davis, in the scanty provision of those times, as a rule, I slept with him. Beds were always too short, coffee in the morning burned or otherwise bad, food often indifferent, roads simply trails, streams without bridges, and often swollen and had to be swum, sloughs often muddy and almost impassible, and we had to help the horses when the wagon mired down, with fence rails for pries, and yet I never heard Mr. Lincoln complain of anything. His character was that of great directness and extreme simplicity. Clothing to him was made for covering and warmth to the body, and not for ornament. He never in his life once got the better of his fellow men in a trade, and never loaned money for interest. I never knew him but once to borrow money or give his note. He never tasted liquor, never chewed tobacco or smoked, but labored diligently in his profession, charging small fees, and was contented with small accumulations. He was, however, very generous in expenditures for his family. In this manner he accumulated less than $10,000 before his election to the Presidency, and, when he left Springfield, had to borrow, and then, so far as I know, gave his note for the first time, for enough to pay his expenses and tide him over until he could draw from the government for the first quarter of his salary. He, in his life, has lived in all circles, moved in every grade of society, and enjoyed it all equally well. To his present companions in every station he was equally entertaining and equally happy.

As a politician he was also peculiar. He employed tactics wholly different from any other politician we ever had. He believed in the results to which certain great causes tended, and did not believe those results could be hastened, changed, or impeded by personal interference. Hence he was no political manipulator. He believed from the first the agitation of slavery would produce its overthrow, and his personal tactics consisted simply in getting himself in the right place, and staying until events found him there. This belief caused him to say and do many things which could not be understood when considered in reference to immediate surroundings. In his campaign against Douglas in 1858 he defeated himself in the first ten lines of the speech he made. "The House divided against itself can not stand." "We must become either all slave or all free." And yet he always justified and defended the utterance of these sentences, whatever may have been their immediate consequences, on the ground that they contained elementary truth, necessary in the growth of the Republican party, and should be uttered and defended.

At a private dinner at Bloomington at which some friends, after he was beaten, were criticizing these utterances as fatal to his campaign, he replied:

"Well, gentlemen, you may think that a mistake, but I have never believed it was, and you will see the day in which you will consider that the wisest thing I ever said."

He would not in politics willingly have any one do anything for him, and did not believe in the favorable results of personal efforts in any campaign. He did believe in the "vox populi," and to him it was indeed "vox dei," but he wanted it to be the genuine "vox populi." He did not believe in any interference with or efforts to control it. When first nominated to the Presidency in 1860, his name, in connection with that exalted office was new to the people at large to the country, and his nomination was almost wholly unexpected. Signs of party lukewarmness and lethargy existed in the East, and friends proposed sending delegations there to induce union and partisan activity, but he opposed it. It was not until late in the summer that he consented that Judge Davis should go, purely on his own behalf, on a tour of inspection, and it is my candid opinion, from all I know, that he consented to this reluctantly, and would in his heart of hearts rather he would not have gone.

He believed the necessities of the party and the great coercive force of a campaign were the real causes of union, and if they failed nothing else could act as a substitute for them. No individual effort could aid or hasten them, and none could defeat them. And so he sat at his Mecca in Springfield, received everyone who came, heard what everyone said, told a story, and said nothing himself, but watched the operation of the great forces as they gradually but slowly brought order out of chaos and led him on to final triumph. After his election he consented, also, after persuasion, to have Thurlow Weed invited to Springfield, but this had to be urged upon him.

I believe he desired the second nomination, because that involved an approval by the common people, whom he always loved and confided in, of the course which he had taken, often in great doubt during the first administration, yet he would do nothing and allow no friend to do anything to get it.

His rival aspirants were actively at work, and were doing and saying more radical things than the responsibilities of the position he occupied would permit him to say or do, but he was resolved and unmoved. One time after his first emancipation proclamation, he was urged by some friends to follow it up, in his next message to the Congress of 1863, which preceded his second nomination by only about five months, by a recommendation of an amendment to the Constitution, abolishing slavery. It was urged upon him that this was an outside position of radicalism, and if he did not take it his rivals would. Turning to the gentlemen present he said: "Is not the question of emancipation doing well enough now?" "Yes," was the reply. "Well," said he, "I have never yet done an official act because of its bearing upon my renomination, and I don't like to begin now. I can see the emancipation coming; whoever can wait for it will also see it; whoever gets in the way of it will be run over by it."

He looked with indifference over machinations against him in his Cabinet, and with indifference over the Senate and members of Congress in the action of the common people, as expressed in their preliminary conventions, and resolutions of State Legislatures, as though an electrical chord [sic] of sympathy extended from him to the people. They did not disappoint him, and finally, when the second convention convened in Baltimore, in May [actually, June], the only contest there was as to who should have the honor of putting Mr. Lincoln in nomination.

He never recognized a duty in himself to appoint any man to office simply because he had been a political friend, and would remove no man simply because he had been his political enemy.

I was present once in an interview between the most prominent politician in New York and Mr. Lincoln, at the White House, in reference to the removal of an office-holder in New York. Every reason was urged in favor of the removal that could be thought of, and finally it was urged that this officeholder abused Mr. Lincoln personally, and was opposed to his second nomination. Mr. Lincoln at last got out of patience, and ended the interview as follows: "You can not think —— to be half as mean to me as I know him to be, but I can not run this thing upon the theory that every officeholder must think I am the greatest man in the Nation, and I will not." The man named, notwithstanding his meanness to Mr. Lincoln, remained in office as long as he was President.

The sublime and crowning characteristic of Mr. Lincoln, however, was his self-reliance. During the eleven years I was with him at the bar of this State, I never knew him to ask the advice of a friend about anything. During the four years of his administration I never knew and never heard of his doing this. I never knew him in the preparation of a trial, or the perplexity of it in court, to turn to his associate and ask his advice. The nearest I knew him to do this was at Bloomington, in 1858, and about ten days before his joint debate with Douglas, at Charleston. He sent for a half dozen lawyers to meet him at Judge Davis' house before he was to speak in Bloomington on the same day, and when they were assembled he said: "Gentlemen, I am going to put to Douglas the following questions, and the object of this meeting is to have each of you assume you are Douglas, and answer them from his standpoint."

And yet he was the best listener I have ever known. He would hear any one on any subject, and generally would say nothing in reply. He kept his own counsels or his bottom thoughts well. He weighed thoroughly his own positions, and positions of his adversary. He put himself in his adversary's position or on the opposite side of a question, and argued the question from that standpoint. For instance, you will remember when a committee of Chicago clergy went to Washington to urge upon him to issue an emancipation proclamation, when he said: "If you call a sheep's tail a leg, how many legs will it have?" The natural answer was, "Five." "No," said he, "Because calling the tail a leg will not make it a leg." He was taking, in that argument, the opposite side of the question.

I was in Washington the next week after these clergy men. I got an interview with him early in the morning, and arising to go, he said, "What have you got to do? How long have you been in the city?" and being told that I came there the day before, he said, "Sit down; I want to consult you. If you had been here a week I would not give a cent for your opinion," and then himself occupied all the morning until 12 o'clock, when the Cabinet came, talking about the emancipation proclamation, considering every objection to it, asking in the whole interview my opinion of nothing, going over the whole question, and simply making me a friendly audience; and yet, at the very time I was there, and at the time the Chicago clergy were there, the proclamation in its rough draft, as I have since learned, was then written out and was lying in his table drawer in the room where we were talking.

And this, indeed, was his general way of arriving at a conclusion, but with him, when a conclusion was reached, he was at rest. . . . [H]e became one of the best educated men I have ever known by considering all life a school.

He was the most inquisitive man I have ever known. Traveling the circuit, he would perhaps sit with the driver, and before we got to our journey's end, he would know all the driver knew. If we stopped at a cross-road blacksmith shop, he would sit by the blacksmith over his forge and learn how to make nails; walking along the sidewalk of a country town, he would see a new agricultural implement set out on the walk; he would stop, and before leaving, learn what it would do, how it would do it and what it was an improvement upon. He is the only man I have ever known who bridged back from middle age to youth and learned in middle life to spell well. Mr. Lincoln's manuscripts are as free from mistakes as any college graduate's. I have seen him upon the circuit with a geometry or astronomy and other elementary books, learning in middle life what men ordinarily learn in youth.

I remember a scene I once witnessed at Barnett's Tavern at Clinton, at a session of the Circuit Court. Lincoln had a geometry which he was carrying and studying in leisure moments. One time he was sitting on the sidewalk near the building and had just got the point of a nice demonstration of a proposition, and wanting some one to enjoy it, he seized upon an ostler [a person who takes care of horses] and explained to him, until the ostler said, probably in self defense, he understood it.

The first two years of the war were years of doubt with Mr. Lincoln. He did not see any way in which we could conquer a people so numerous, so brave, and who occupied more than half of the territorial extent of the whole country. I do not believe that during this time any man ever heard him say that he could see we were going to be successful in the war. After about the second year, after he had issued the emancipation proclamation and began to see that it worked according to his expectations, I do not believe any man ever heard him express a doubt of success.

And herein may I be permitted to mention another very remarkable and useful trait of his character. It was that mental equipoise which is disturbed by nothing, and diverted from the pathway it has marked out by nothing. Although prosecuting the war for two years simply from a sense of duty and not from a belief in its success, yet he kept right on and was neither depressed by disasters nor elated by success. He seemed to comprehend the magnitude of the contest in which he was engaged more thoroughly than any other man. The war, like all others, was prosecuted by alternate success and defeat. The first two years it was generally defeat, and yet Mr. Lincoln in moments of disaster was not disheartened, but was cool, collected and determined. He was a monument of strength, upon which even the great men of the Nation and members of his own Cabinet could lean. In moments of victory, when everybody else was carried away by the joyousness of the occasion, Mr. Lincoln had the same mental equipoise and was self-restrained and determined as before. In short, he was the strong man of the contest, and the great men at Washington learned to gain renewed strength from his calmness, to lean upon his own great arm for support.

The religious views of Mr. Lincoln were simply a reflex of his own character. He believed in God, as the Supreme Ruler of the world, the guider of men, and the controller of the great events and destinies of mankind. He believed himself to be an instrument and leader of the forces of freedom. He knew the toils of the slave and of the poor whites at the South, and their sufferings and privations were his personal experiences, and he felt their burdens to be his own. He believed that the Declaration of Independence, "That all men are created equal," was not, as said by Richard Choate, a glittering generality, but was a standard of political truth. Our Saviour in the closing sentences of His sermon on the Mount said, "Be ye perfect as your Father in heaven is perfect;" not that He expected perfection in the persons to whom He addressed these words; not that he expected perfection of us in our day and generation; but He laid down a religious standard which no one can surpass and to which all nations might aspire. Happiest is that man and happiest are those peoples who shall most nearly approach this standard of religious requirement. So with Mr. Lincoln and the Declaration of Independence. He found here his perfect standard of political truth, and happiest he pronounced the man and the people who approached most nearly to this standard.

And he has made the journey to the great unknown. Before him Washington, Franklin, Hamilton, and Knox had gone. Before him all the great and good men who laid securely and well the broad foundations of this Republic, had fallen before the only foe their valor and courage could not meet.

They all have gone! All we know of that great and final journey to the unknown is that our race goes, but none return.

Let us hope that after "life's fitful fever" he sleeps well. Let us hope that on the eventful night of the 14th of April, A.D. 1865, when his spirit first left the earth and crossed the great divide between the here and hereafter, the angel at the gate met him with a smile, and said, "Well done, thou good and faithful servant, enter thou into the joy of thy Lord."

We see him in this image of bronze above us, and recall his real presence. All we know is that in the hereafter, wherever the slave shall groan under the lash, or the poor shall sigh for something better than they have known, there his name will be honored and his example imitated.

Notes

Abbreviations

ALPL   Abraham Lincoln Presidential Library
CHM   Chicago History Museum
CLN   *Chicago Legal News*

Introduction

1. Wilson & Davis, *Herndon's Informants*, 629; David Davis to Josiah G. Holland, Bloomington, 7-3-65, ALPL and CHM, Davis Papers; McClure, *Abraham Lincoln*, 75; Goodwin, *Team of Rivals*, 8.
2. Rice, *Reminiscences*; Weik, *Real Lincoln*, 192–93; *Chicago Tribune*, 2-10-84, "Lincoln's Opinion of Porter"; Browne, *Every-day Life*, 666–67; Swett to Orme, Washington, 5-27-64, Illinois Historical Survey, Univ. of Illinois; Swett, "Conspiracies of the Rebellion"; Swett, "In Memory of David Davis," CLN, vol. 19, 3-5-87, 206–7; *Ceremonies at the Unveiling*, 10-22-87.
3. Herndon & Weik, *Life of Lincoln*, 405–8 & 425–33.
4. Herndon to Mrs. Swett, Springfield, 11-10-89 to 3-14-90, ALPL, Swett Papers. Douglas Wilson and Rodney Davis assembled an extensive and comprehensive collection of information from more than 260 sources in *Herndon's Informants: Letters, Interviews, and Statements about Abraham Lincoln*, published in 1998. This work includes five letters from Swett, as well as comments about him by others.
5. Letters from Swett to Lamon, Huntington Library, Lamon Collection. Lamon's shortcomings notwithstanding, historian Rodney Davis later concluded that by introducing Herndon's rescued materials, which Lamon and coauthor Chauncey Black had purchased, the result "was significant," requiring subsequent Lincoln biographers "to come to terms" with them. (Davis, "Lincoln's 'Particular Friend' and Lincoln Biography," 21–37.)
6. See, e.g., Wilson & Davis, *Herndon's Informants*, 629–30. Whitney quote is from *Life on the Circuit*.
7. McClure, *Abraham Lincoln*, 75 & 457–81.
8. Burlingame, *An Oral History*, 58–59; Nicolay, *Personal Traits*, 18.
9. Pease & Randall, *Browning Diary* (see also Donald, *"We Are Lincoln Men,"* 101–39, on Browning's close friendship with Lincoln); Arnold, *The History of Abraham Lincoln and the Overthrow of Slavery* and *The Life of Abraham Lincoln*.
10. Lincoln to Davis, Springfield, 7-7-56, & Lincoln to Whitney, Springfield, 7-9-56, in Basler, *Collected Works*, vol. 10, 27, & vol. 2, 347.
11. Lincoln to Colfax on 3-8-61 in answer to Colfax letter to Lincoln 3-6-61, in Basler, *Collected Works*, vol. 4, 278.
12. Weik, *Real Lincoln*, 300–302; Lincoln to Oglesby, Springfield, 9-8-54, in Basler, *Collected Works*, vol. 10, 24.

13. Swett to Herndon, Chicago, 8-29-87, in Wilson & Davis, *Herndon's Informants*, 709–11.
14. Browne, *Every-day Life*, 666–67.

1. A Wandering Youth

1. Stackpole, *Swett Genealogy*, 166, 194; Swett, "Leonard Swett," 332–65; and author correspondence with Swett family descendants.
2. The president, a clergyman, taught intellectual and moral philosophy, as well as two terms of French to sophomores, and offered private instruction in Hebrew, German, and Spanish. The other four professors taught mathematics and natural philosophy, chemistry and natural history, Latin and Greek languages and literature, and rhetoric and oratory. One of the professors also served as the librarian. Waterville College information taken from catalogs for two of the three years Swett was in residence and from Colby College, *General Catalogue, 1820–1920*.
3. Waterville College catalogs; Colby College, *General Catalogue, 1820–1920*; Maine Historical Society.
4. Maine Historical Society website, collection 117, George Foster Shepley, 1819–78. Later, in 1869, President Ulysses S. Grant appointed Shepley the first U.S. Circuit Court judge in Maine.
5. Leonard Swett to Rose Swett (sister), Gray, Maine, 1-9-47, Swett Papers, ALPL.
6. Swett to Rose Swett, Pottsville, PA, 12-17-47, ALPL.
7. Swett, "Leonard Swett," 332–65.
8. Swett to Rose Swett, ship *Robert Burton*, off St. Augustine, 1-12 to 1-20-48, ALPL.
9. Ibid.
10. Swett to Rose Swett, Bloomington, IL, 8-11-48, ALPL. Swett's moral generalization seems excessive, but Hirsch & Logsdon, *Creole*, state in their preface (p. xi) that "its bawdy sensual delights" were in "counterpoint to the rest of urban America."
11. Swett to Rose Swett, Bloomington, IL, 8-11-48, ALPL. According to Hirsch & Logsdon in *Creole* (p. 100), "In 1850 . . . some 650 free people of color owned land in New Orleans."
12. Swett to Rose Swett, Bloomington, IL, 8-11-48, ALPL.
13. Swett to Rose Swett, Clinton, IL, 10-31-50, ALPL; also in Pratt, "A Beginner," 245.
14. Swett to Rose Swett, Bloomington, 9-4-48, ALPL, Swett Papers.
15. Swett, "Leonard Swett," 335–37; Carpenter, "Abraham Lincoln and Leonard Swett," 19–22.
16. Swett, "Leonard Swett," 335–37; Carpenter, "Abraham Lincoln and Leonard Swett," 19–22. It appears that what was convened was not a formal court-martial but rather an inquiry that might have led to a court-martial. However, the proceeding was terminated before it reached that stage.
17. Swett, "Leonard Swett," 335–37; Carpenter, "Abraham Lincoln and Leonard Swett," 19–22.
18. Swett, "Leonard Swett," 335–37; Carpenter, "Abraham Lincoln and Leonard Swett," 19–22.
19. Swett, "Leonard Swett," 335–37; Carpenter, "Abraham Lincoln and Leonard Swett," 19–22.

20. Swett, "Leonard Swett," 335–37; Carpenter, "Abraham Lincoln and Leonard Swett," 19–22.
21. Swett, "Leonard Swett," 337.
22. Ibid.
23. Swett to Rose Swett, Bloomington, 9-4-48, ALPL.
24. Swett, "In Memory of David Davis," CLN, vol. 19, 3-5-87, 206–7; King, *Lincoln's Manager*, 307–12.
25. King, *Lincoln's Manager*, ch. 2 & 3.
26. Swett to Rose Swett, Bloomington, 1-12-49, ALPL.
27. Dirck, *Lincoln the Lawyer*, 21. Many McLean County court records were destroyed by fire in 1900, and no record survives to confirm this date or say who administered the exam.

2. The Road to Mount Pulaski

1. Sutton, *Prairie State*, 19.
2. Sutton, *Prairie State*.
3. Krause, *From Log Cabins*, 21.
4. Pratt, "A Beginner," 241–48.
5. Swett, "Leonard Swett," 338–39.
6. *Chicago Tribune*, 2-21-76, "The Rostrum: Abraham Lincoln"; Rice, *Reminiscences*, 67–80; and Swett, "In Memory of David Davis," CLN, vol. 19, 3-8-87, 206–7. A faux version is found in Weik, *Real Lincoln*, 192–93, repeated in Wilson and Davis, *Herndon's Informants*, 131–32, and elsewhere.
7. Miers, *Lincoln Day by Day*, 6-21 to 7-24-49 entries.
8. Swett, "Leonard Swett," 340–41.
9. Ibid.
10. Ibid., 342, 338–39.
11. Ibid., 341, 339.
12. Hamand, "Ward Hill Lamon," 80–81; Swett, "Leonard Swett," 340–41; U.S. Congress, Congressional Biographical Directory.
13. Basler, *Collected Works*, vol. 2, 210, 218 note, & 347; Lamon, *Recollections*, 15–19; Hamand, "Ward Hill Lamon"; the author also acknowledges assistance from Roberta Allen, Danville Public Library archivist.
14. *Chicago Tribune*, 2-21-76.
15. *Chicago Tribune*, 2-21-76, "The Rostrum"; *Ceremonies at the Unveiling*, 10-22-87; Guy Fraker, "Move to the Mount," *Pantagraph*, 2-22-2004.
16. Swett, "Leonard Swett," 338; *Chicago Times*, 6-9-89, "The Last Case Tried," Swett obituary; Lamon, *Recollections*, 16–17.
17. Benner & Davis, *Law Practice of Lincoln*, "Thorpe v. Thorpe," L00379; "Lincoln, Herndon, and Divorce," *Lincoln Legal Briefs*, no. 17, March 1991.
18. Benner & Davis, *Law Practice of Lincoln*, "People v. Bosley," L02011.
19. Swett to Josiah Drummond, Bloomington, 5-27-60, first published in the *Portland (ME) Evening Express*, 7-22-91; Pratt, "A Beginner."
20. *Illinois State Journal*, 11-1-52.
21. Swett to Rose Swett, Bloomington, 1-12-49, Clinton, 10-31-50, 5-15-52, & Bloomington, 4-22-54, ALPL, Swett Papers.

22. Records are not available regarding Laura's education, but her two younger sisters attended Westford Academy in Massachusetts, which was a feeder school for Harvard. Existing writings show that her intelligence and knowledge made an impression on not only Leonard Swett but also Henry Clay Whitney, as evidenced in the quote from Whitney that appears later in the text. Correspondence also indicates that she read good literature and that later in life, while she was suffering from her illness, she spent her time reading French literature in the original language.

23. Swett to Rose Swett, Bloomington, 4-22-54, ALPL, Swett Papers. The pass was issued by the St. Louis provost marshal, Missouri Nineteenth Regiment, 11-11-61, ALPL, Swett Papers.

24. Whitney, *Life on the Circuit*, 69.

25. Wilson & Davis, *Herndon's Informants*, 350–51, 9-20-66 interview with David Davis.

26. Partnership agreement, manuscript at McLean County Historical Society, Bloomington; Wight, "Lincoln's Most Influential Friends," including Orme; and several of Swett's letters.

27. Orme to Mrs. Orme, Bloomington, various dates in July & Aug. 1855; Swett to Rose Swett, Bloomington, 1-24-60; Swett to Lincoln, Bloomington, 3-4-61; Laura Swett to Orme, Bloomington, 10-15-62.

3. The Great Triumvirate of the Eighth Judicial Circuit

1. Wilson & Davis, *Herndon's Informants*, 631, 8-27-87, Whitney to Herndon, quoting Swett; Swett dedication in *Ceremonies at the Unveiling*, 10-22-87.

2. Whitney, *Life on the Circuit*, 85. When Lamon became the prosecuting attorney on the circuit in 1857, he traveled with the other three, but he was not considered part of the "great triumvirate."

3. Rice, *Reminiscences*, "Lincoln's Story of His Own Life," by Leonard Swett, 67–80.

4. Swett, "In Memory of Judge Davis," CLN, vol. 19, 3-5-87, 206–7, before the Illinois State Bar Association.

5. Ibid.

6. Ibid.

7. Ibid.

8. Wilson & Davis, *Herndon's Informants*, 631, 8-27-87, Whitney to Herndon, quoting Swett; Swett makes the same point in *Chicago Tribune*, 2-21-76, "The Rostrum: Leonard Swett."

9. *Chicago Tribune*, 2-21-76, "The Rostrum: Leonard Swett."

10. Elijah B. Sherman, Comments on Swett, CLN, 6-22-89.

11. *Chicago Tribune*, 2-21-76, "The Rostrum: Leonard Swett."

12. Herndon & Weik, *Life of Lincoln*, 432; *Chicago Tribune*, 2-21-76; CLN, vol. 21, 6-15, 6-22, and 6-29-89.

13. *Ceremonies at the Unveiling*, 10-22-87; "Lincoln's Story of His Own Life," by Leonard Swett, in Rice, *Reminiscences*, 67–80.

14. *Ceremonies at the Unveiling*, 10-22-87.

15. Hamand, "Ward Hill Lamon," 80–81; King, *Lincoln's Manager*, 309.

16. "Lincoln's Story of His Own Life," by Leonard Swett, in Rice, *Reminiscences*, 67–80. Other sources back up some of Swett's statements. According to Benjamin Thomas in his biography of Lincoln, "Local tradition maintained that disagreement over

the sale of liquor caused the dissolution of the Lincoln-Berry partnership soon after they obtained the liquor license." (Thomas, *Lincoln*, 37.) And Ida Tarbell and John McCan Davis wrote of Lincoln's store partnership that "Berry rapidly squandered the profits of the business in riotous living." (Tarbell & Davis, *Early Life*, 160.)

17. Benner & Davis, *Law Practice of Lincoln*, cases involving Swett; Stowell et al., *Papers of Abraham Lincoln*, vol. 3, ch. 35, "*Allen v. Illinois Central Railroad et al.* (1854–1859)," 1–23.

18. Herndon & Weik, *Life of Lincoln*, 73–75. Whitney may have picked up Lincoln's preference for Swett's assistance from Herndon, whose book was published three years earlier. If so, it affirms the contention. The earlier slander case that Swett won was *Richey v. Adams*, DeWitt County, May 1854 (Benner & Davis, *Law Practice of Lincoln*, L00590). The case, with the names reversed, is discussed in Steiner, "Lawyer as Peacemaker," 21–22; *Spink v. Chiniquy* is found on 15–16.

19. Benner & Davis, *Law Practice of Lincoln*, L01488, *Spink v. Chiniquy*, Champaign Circuit Court, Oct. 1856.

20. Chiniquy, *Fifty Years in the Church of Rome*, 481–510; George, "Lincoln Writings of Chiniquy"; Hanchett, *Lincoln Murder*, 233–41.

21. The case is described most completely by Pratt in "The Famous 'Chicken Bone' Case," and quotations and much of the narrative are from this source; see also Benner & Davis, *Law Practice of Lincoln*, L01566.

22. Benner & Davis, *Law Practice of Lincoln*, "*People v. Wyant*," L01676; *Pantagraph*, 4-15-57, 1–2; Swett, Notebook on Insanity, Swett Papers, ALPL, O-10, bound volume.

23. *Clinton (IL) Register*, 1-26-1912, "Ann (Gideon) Parker, Aged Woman Is Called to Rest," obituary available at http://dewitt.ilgenweb.net/obits-p.htm, listing for Mrs. Abraham Parker.

24. Swett, Notebook on Insanity, including notes on Isaac Ray's *Treatise on Medical Jurisprudence of Insanity*, probably the 3rd ed., 1853; Story, *Commentaries on Equity Jurisprudence*; Chitty, *Treatise on Pleading*. Swett also visited with the superintendents of the McLean Asylum for the Insane in Boston, the Jacksonville State Hospital for the Insane in Illinois, and the Albany Insane Hospital in New York and interviewed another doctor who had practiced in Illinois, California, and Russia.

25. Swett, "Leonard Swett," 343. However, the anatomy book written by Henry Gray, initially titled *Anatomy: Descriptive and Surgical*, was first published in England in 1858, the year after this trial took place, and not until 1859 in the United States. Thus Herbert had to have been mistaken about which anatomy book his father used and perhaps whether this incident even occurred at all. Herbert was not born until 1858 and therefore did not witness the trial firsthand but must have based his story on other accounts, from either his father or others who actually had attended the trial. It is possible that the cross-examination occurred as described but that the story was later embellished to add the name of the well-known anatomy book.

26. *Pantagraph*, 4-15-57; Swett, "Leonard Swett," 343.

27. Benner & Davis, *Law Practice of Lincoln*, "*People v. Wyant*," L01676; *Pantagraph*, 4-15-57, 1–2; Swett, Notebook on Insanity.

28. Herndon & Weik, *Life of Lincoln*, 278; Wilson & Davis, *Herndon's Informants*, Weik interview of McDonald, 1888, 667.

29. Swett, "Leonard Swett," 344.

30. Howard, *Illinois*, 291.
31. Swett, "Leonard Swett," 343–45; *Pantagraph*, 8-26-57.
32. Bloomington, 5-27-60, Swett to Josiah Drummond, first published in the *Portland (ME) Evening Express*, 7-22-1891; Whitney, *Life on the Circuit*, 85.

4. Politics Overtakes the Law

1. Swett to Lincoln, Bloomington, 12-12, 12 14, 12-19, & 12-22-54, CHM, David Davis Papers. In the end, Judd supported Lyman Trumbull.
2. Ibid.
3. King, *Lincoln's Manager*, 107–8; Donald, *Lincoln*, 185–86. Davis and Swett never were thrilled with Judd, either, likely reflecting their Whig roots.
4. *Pantagraph*, 6-11-56, "Candidate for Congress."
5. Swett to Mrs. David Davis, 1-22-87, UIUC, Orme Papers, vol. 6.
6. Swett to Rose Swett Briggs (sister), 8-24-60, Swett Papers, ALPL. One of Danville's two sons, John A. Swett, eventually established a successful farm near Saybrook, farther east in McLean County, and served for eleven years as superintendent of Haskell Institute, a school for Indians in Lawrence, Kansas. His other son, Edward, joined the Swett firm later in Chicago.
7. Lincoln to Davis, 7-7-56, Springfield, in Basler, *Collected Works*, vol. 10, 27; Lincoln to Whitney, 7-9-56, Ibid., vol. 2, 347.
8. King, *Lincoln's Manager*, 113–15.
9. *Pantagraph*, 5-31, 6-11, & 7-16-56, "Congressional Convention, 3rd District," 9-3-56, "Fremont Club," 9-24-56, "Local News," "The Leroy Delegation," & "Stephen A. Douglas on the Missouri Compromise," 10-1-56, "Republican Meetings," "Local News, Republican Club," & "Republican State Convention." Wood became the governor three and a half years later, after Governor William H. Bissell died in office of a mysterious illness at age forty-eight.
10. *Pantagraph*, 10-15-56, "Mass Meetings—to Be," & "Republican Meetings at Bloomington," 10-22-56, "The Clinton Meeting," & "The Fremont Club"; *Illinois State Journal*, 11-3-56, "The Meeting in Jacksonville."
11. *Pantagraph*, 5-13, 5-27, 7-1-57; Morehouse, *Life of Fell*, ch. 4; *Pantagraph*, 7-7-57, "The Fourth in Bloomington."
12. Basler, *Collected Works*, vol. 2, 398, 6-26-57.
13. Bray, *Reading with Lincoln*, 182, background from Parker begins 175.
14. Swett to Herndon, 1-17-66, Wilson & Davis, *Herndon's Informants*, 162–63.
15. Swett to Mrs. Swett, 8-15, 8-16-58, Chicago; 8-17, 8-18-58, Milwaukee; 8-19-58, Port Washington; 8-23-58, Manitou Island & Mackinac Island, CHM, Davis Papers. According to King, *Lincoln's Manager*, 345, n. 12, "Putnam was the leading Fillmore man . . . in New York in 1856."
16. *Pantagraph*, 9-6-58, "Republican Mass Meeting," reception speech by Swett.
17. Ibid.
18. Basler, *Collected Works*, vol. 3, 86.
19. Swett, *Remembrances of T. Lyle Dickey*; also found in CLN, 5-14-87, 288–92, CHM.
20. Basler, *Collected Works*, vol. 2, 476–81.

21. *Pantagraph*, 9-7-58, "Republican County Convention"; Davis to Lincoln, 8-3-58, Lincoln Papers, ALPL.

22. *Pantagraph*, 9-7-58, "Republican County Convention."

23. Ibid., 9-25-58, "Bloomington Republican Club"; 9-29, 3; 9-30, 2; 10-4, 2.

24. Ibid., 9-27-58, "Republican Club," 3; 10-15, 3.

25. Ibid., 11-3-58, "McLean County Election Returns," table, & 11-4, "The County Vote."

26. Swett Papers, ALPL.

27. Pratt, "A Beginner," 241–48.

28. Wilson & Davis, *Herndon's Informants*, 550–51, Davis interview, 9-20-66.

29. Swett to Lincoln, Bloomington, 3-4-61, ALPL, Lincoln Papers.

30. Lincoln's Chicago speech, 3-1-59, in Basler, *Collected Works*, vol. 3, 365–70.

31. The court in Bloomington adjourned for the afternoon of April 14 to allow attendance at the funeral of Angeline Lamon, wife of their close friend, Ward Hill Lamon, the prosecutor on the circuit. Her death left a very young daughter, Dorothy, who was raised by Lamon's sister and her husband.

32. Wilson & Davis, *Herndon's Informants*, Patterson case, Davis interviews, 347 & 529, Whitney statements, 632–33, 650, & 733.

33. Benner & Davis, *Law Practice of Lincoln*, "*People v. Patterson*," L01488.

34. Swett to Lincoln, Bloomington, 3-4-61, ALPL, Lincoln Papers.

35. Lincoln to Dole, Hubbard, & Brown, Springfield, 12-14-59, in Basler, *Collected Works*, vol. 3, 507–9.

36. Davis to Henry E. Dummer, 2-20-60, Bloomington, Davis Papers, ALPL; also in Pratt, *Concerning Mr. Lincoln*, 22–23.

37. Caton served on the court from 1842 to 1864 and was a stickler for detail. Dan Bannister, a pre–Civil War Illinois Supreme Court historian, also implied that Lincoln and Herndon, who were doing a significant portion of the state appellate work by that time, may have taken on more cases than they could adequately handle, considering their involvement in politics. Bannister, *Lincoln and the Common Law*, 225–26, "*Gill v. Hoblit* 23 Ill. 420"; Bannister, *Lincoln and the Illinois Supreme Court*, 167.

38. Baringer, *Lincoln's Rise*, 142–43; Herndon & Weik, *Life of Lincoln*, 366–67; Whitney, *Life on the Circuit*, 99.

39. Swett to Rose Swett Briggs (sister), 3-18-60, Swett Papers, ALPL.

40. Reprinted in *Pantagraph*, 4-19 & 4-21-60.

41. Judd to Hatch, 3-29-60, Chicago, Ozias Hatch Papers, ALPL.

42. Davis to Hatch, 4-2-60, Bloomington, ALPL; Hogg to Hatch, 4-23-60, Bloomington, ALPL.

43. James P. Root to Yates, 4-30-60, Richard Yates Papers, ALPL.

44. *Chicago Tribune*, 5-9-60, "Illinois Republican Convention," & 5-12, "The Informal Ballot for Governor at Decatur"; Whitney, *Life on the Circuit*, 86–87.

45. *Chicago Tribune*, 5-9-60.

46. Ibid., 5-10-60.

47. Lincoln to Judd, 2-9-60, in Basler, *Collected Works*, vol. 3, 517; see Fehrenbacher, *Prelude to Greatness*, 150–53, for a fuller account; Lincoln to Trumbull, 4-29-60, in Basler, *Collected Works*, vol. 4, 45–46.

48. Donald, *Lincoln*, 246.

5. From the Wigwam to Washington

1. Swett, "David Davis Memorial," CLN, vol. 19, 3-5-87, 206–7, CHM.
2. The Tremont House was destroyed in the Great Chicago Fire in 1871. The site is now on the north side of the elevated loop for commuter trains.
3. Swett, "David Davis Memorial."
4. Ibid.
5. Swett to *Chicago Tribune*, /-14-78, "Lincoln & Weed," 5.
6. Swett to Drummond, *Portland (ME) Evening Express*, 7-22-91, 1–2.
7. Ibid. Nine days after the national convention, Swett wrote a description of the nomination to his college roommate from Waterville, Maine, Josiah Drummond, from which these details are taken. His letter was published in 1891, two years after his death, first appearing in the *Portland Evening Express*. The *New York Sun* quickly reprinted it, and within a few years, it appeared in Ida Tarbell's *Life of Abraham Lincoln* and Osborn Oldroyd's *Lincoln's Campaign; or, The Political Revolution of 1860*.
8. Swett to *Chicago Tribune*, 7-14-78, "Lincoln & Weed," 5.
9. King, *Lincoln's Manager*, 135–36.
10. Swett to Drummond, *Portland Evening Express*, 7-22-91, 1–2.
11. King, *Lincoln's Manager*, 136.
12. Swett to *Chicago Tribune*, 7-14-78, "Lincoln & Weed," 5.
13. Swett to Drummond, *Portland Evening Express*, 7-22-91, 1–2.
14. Swett, "David Davis Memorial"; Swett to *Chicago Tribune*, 7-14-78, "Lincoln & Weed," 5.
15. Swett to Drummond, *Portland Evening Express*, 7-22-91, 1–2.
16. Ibid.
17. King, *Lincoln's Manager*, 141.
18. Swett to Drummond, *Portland Evening Express*, 7-22-91, 1–2.
19. Swett, "David Davis Memorial."
20. Swett to Drummond, *Portland Evening Express*, 7-22-91, 1–2.
21. Swett and Davis, along with Davis's biographer, Willard King, and variously by Joseph Casey, Thurlow Weed, and historian William Baringer (*Lincoln's Rise*, 214, 266–67, 277, & 334), have denied the many permutations of these charges. Historian Don Fehrenbacher took no position on these disputes but clearly attributed Lincoln's nomination to the delegates' "hardheaded decision that the leading candidate (Seward) could not win." He concluded that "never in the presidency did he [Lincoln] surpass the political skill with which he shaped the Republican party of Illinois [after] 1854, held it together, and made himself its leader." (Fehrenbacher, *Prelude to Greatness*, 154 & 161.)
22. Swett to Drummond, *Portland Evening Express*, 7-22-91, 1–2.
23. Swett to *Chicago Tribune*, 7-14-78, "Lincoln & Weed," 5.
24. Ibid.
25. *Pantagraph*, 5-22-60, "Ratification Meeting." George G. Fogg of New Hampshire, secretary of the Republican National Committee, and another convention delegate from New York preceded Swett on the platform. Fogg, a newspaper publisher from New Hampshire, met and corresponded with Lincoln over the next eight months. Lincoln rewarded him with an appointment as minister to Switzerland.
26. Swett to Lincoln, 5-20, 5-27, & 7-13-60, Abraham Lincoln Papers, ALPL.

27. Swett to Lincoln, 5-25 & 5-27-60, Abraham Lincoln Papers, ALPL; Basler, *Collected Works*, vol. 4, 55, 57, 83–84, 312n. Lincoln later corresponded several times with Putnam and appointed him as consul in La Havre, France.
28. *Ceremonies at the Unveiling*, 10-22-87.
29. Herndon, *Life of Lincoln*, 425–33.
30. *Ceremonies at the Unveiling*, 10-22-87; Herndon, *Life of Lincoln*, 425–33.
31. *Ceremonies at the Unveiling*, 10-22-87.
32. Lincoln to Swett, 7-16-60, ALPL, Swett Papers.
33. *Chicago Tribune*, 8-6 & 8-9-60; *Illinois State Journal*, 8-4 & 8-17-60; Swett to Lincoln, Bloomington, 8-17-60, ALPL.
34. Representative "worry" letters can be found in Basler, *Collected Works*: John P. Sanderson to Swett, 6-16-60; Lincoln to Medill, 8-30-60; and Lincoln to Alexander K. McClure, 9-6-60.
35. Basler, *Collected Works*, vol. 4, 54, 70, 82, & 84.
36. All three of these men went on to serve in Lincoln's administration. Voorhees served in the House of Representatives from 1861 to 1865 and later in the U.S. Senate. Usher became secretary of the interior in 1863. Lincoln appointed Nelson as minister to Chile in 1861.
37. Swett to Davis, 10-1-60; Davis to Lincoln, Bloomington, 10-4-60, Davis Papers, CHM.
38. Davis to Mrs. Davis, Springfield, 10-15-60, CHM.
39. *Pantagraph*, 11-6-60.
40. King, *Lincoln's Manager*, 160; Neely, *Lincoln Encyclopedia*, 99, table.
41. Senator Lyman Trumbull participated in a conference Lincoln had with vice president–elect Hamlin and also advocated for Norman Judd. Lincoln gave Hamlin the privilege of naming the secretary of the navy from New England because of its interest in foreign trade and maritime activities. Lincoln asked Orville Browning to carry his offer for attorney general to Bates as a tactical courtesy because Browning previously supported him. George Fogg, secretary of the Republican National Committee from New Hampshire, corresponded with Lincoln and met with him in Springfield on three occasions. Fogg supported Chase and Welles but not Seward or Cameron. Lincoln listened to him patiently, as he did many others. Lincoln explored Joshua Speed's interest and eventually picked his brother, James, as attorney general to replace Bates in 1864. Far beyond the well of the consenting Senate, Mary Lincoln exercised influence as she saw fit in the process, making it known that she opposed Judd for the cabinet. In all, various influential politicians sponsored three dozen candidates, in addition to the original seven chosen, and these were considered to varying degrees.
42. Casey to Swett, Harrisburg, 11-27-60, CHM, Davis Papers.
43. Swett to Lincoln, 11-30-60, Davis Papers, CHM; this closely follows King, *Lincoln's Manager*, 164, but the author's transcription differs slightly from King's and includes excerpts from two later paragraphs.
44. Drummond to Swett, Portland, ME, 12-7-60, Davis Papers, CHM.
45. Baringer, *House Dividing*, 95; Swett to *Chicago Tribune*, 7-14-78, "Lincoln & Weed," 5.
46. Weed, *Weed Autobiography*, 604.
47. Swett to *Chicago Tribune*, 7-14-78, "Lincoln & Weed," 5.
48. Ibid.

49. Weed, *Weed Autobiography*, 604.

50. Swett to *Chicago Tribune*, 7-14-78, "Lincoln & Weed," 5.

51. Basler, *Collected Works*, vol. 4, 141–62.

52. Ibid.

53. Basler, *Collected Works*, vol. 4, 211. Lincoln and the secession leaders applied different concepts to the meaning of "crisis," however.

54. Swett to Mrs. Swett, Harrisburg, PA, 12-28-60, Davis Papers, CHM; Basler, *Collected Works*, vol. 4, 168, 12-31-60.

55. The letter, marked "not sent" by an archivist, is not dated clearly and can be found in Swett Papers, ALPL. Swett probably misplaced it among his travel papers and did not discover he had not sent it for some time.

56. Swett, "Conspiracies," 181.

57. The letter "not sent."

58. Swett to Mrs. Swett, Washington, 12-29-60, Davis Papers, CHM.

59. DeGregorio, *Presidents*, Buchanan, 220; the letter "not sent."

60. Swett to Lincoln, Washington, 12-31-60, ALPL, Lincoln Papers; King, *Lincoln's Manager*, 174.

61. Swett to Lincoln, Washington, 12-31-60. Although Swett's report of Seward's choices for cabinet differs from what has traditionally been reported, Swett was seeing Seward daily in Washington, and he was describing Seward's thoughts and choices in letters to Lincoln as he heard them. Seward changed his choices as the threats increased.

62. Swett to Davis, Washington, 1-1-61; King, *Lincoln's Manager*, 171–72.

63. Swett to Mrs. Swett, Washington, 1-1-61, CHM, Davis Papers.

64. H. Winter Davis to David Davis, Baltimore, 1-4-61, CHM, Davis Papers. H. Winter Davis dealt systematically with the problem of naming a cabinet member from a slaveholding state and where he might possibly come from—North Carolina, Tennessee, or Kentucky. He placed North Carolina first in line after some lengthy explanation involving loyalty, geographic position, and military considerations. Then he suggested four possible candidates and narrowed the choice down to Gilmer or Badger. In the process, he characterized Bates as "impudent" and Seward as "milk and water." For good measure, he endorsed former congressman and senator William C. Rives of Virginia, then returned for a reprise of Gilmer and Badger.

65. Swett to Lincoln, Washington, 1-4-61.

66. Swett to Lincoln, Washington, 1-5-61; Basler, *Collected Works*, vol. 4, 169–70.

67. Swett to Lincoln, Washington, 1-5-61.

68. Swett to Lincoln, Washington, 1-5, 1-6-61; *New York Times*, 1-7-61.

69. Swett to Lincoln, Washington, 1-5, 1-6-61.

70. Swett to Lincoln, Washington, 1-8-61; Lincoln's telegram has not been found, but it is mentioned in Basler, *Collected Works*, vol. 4, 169–70 & 174–75.

71. Basler, *Collected Works*, vol. 4, 174.

72. Swett to Lincoln, Washington, 1-14-61; Neely, *Lincoln Encyclopedia*, 318; Swett to Lincoln, Washington, 1-15-61.

73. Baringer, *House Dividing*, 315; Swett to Mrs. Swett, Pittsburgh, 1-24-61, CHM, Davis Papers.

74. Washburne to Lincoln, Washington, 1-6, 1-20-61, CHM, Davis Papers.

75. Mississippi seceded on January 9; Florida, on January 10; Alabama, on January 11; Georgia, on January 19; Louisiana, on January 26; and Texas, on February 1. The other four states that joined the Confederacy did not secede until after the Confederate attack on Fort Sumter on April 12: Virginia, on April 17 (with a secession referendum on May 23); Arkansas, on May 6; North Carolina, on May 20; and Tennessee, on June 8.
76. Nevins, *Emergence of Lincoln*, vol. 2, ch. 13.
77. Swett to Mrs. Swett, Harrisburg, 1-18-61; Swett to Lincoln, 1-19-61, CHM, Davis Papers.
78. Swett to Lincoln, Pittsburgh, 1-24-61, CHM, Davis Papers. In this letter, Swett also mentioned Congressman Thomas Corwin of Ohio, who was a moderate Republican of the Lincoln stripe. Corwin had also formerly held offices as Ohio governor, U.S. senator, and treasury secretary under President Fillmore. Swett asked Corwin to write to Lincoln with his cabinet suggestions, which he did immediately, recommending Seward, Bates, and Smith, with the possibility of Robert C. Schenck from Ohio. Lincoln promptly named him minister to Mexico, a good choice at a critical time for both countries.
79. Leonard Herbert Swett Journal.
80. Swett to Ward Hill Lamon, Bloomington, 2-25-61, Lamon Papers, Huntington Library.

6. And the War Came

1. Swett to Lincoln, Bloomington, 3-4-61, ALPL, Swett Papers; Swett to Thurlow Weed, Bloomington, 3-6-61, CHM, Davis Papers.
2. Weed to Swett, Albany, 3-13-61; Davis to Lamon, Bloomington, 3-24-61, CHM, Davis Papers; King, *Lincoln's Manager*, 182. In a lighter note in the same letter, regarding Lamon's dalliance with the attractive daughter of the McLean county clerk, Davis added, "Fanny McCullough is as sweet as ever. I have told her that I thought if she wrote Mr. Lincoln she could settle the matter in your behalf, without much trouble."
3. Swett to Lamon, Bloomington, 4-4-61, CHM, Davis Papers; Orme to Davis, Washington, 5-11-61, CHM, Davis Papers.
4. Orme to Davis, 5-14-61, CHM. Scholars wishing to review the entire correspondence pertaining to Swett's initial appointment effort should refer to the following letters: Davis to Lamon, 3-24, 3-30, 4-14, 4-24, 5-15, & 5-17-61; Davis to Weed, 5-7-61; Orme to Davis, 5-11-61; Orme to Swett, 5-13 & 5-14-61; Swett to Lamon, 4-4 & 4-7-61; Weed to Davis, 4-17 & 5-13-61, Albany, CHM.
5. *Pantagraph*, 6-5-61.
6. Hamilton, *War Governors*, 205. Browning served in the Senate until the 1863 legislature replaced him with a Peace Democrat, William A. Richardson.
7. Swett, *Remembrances of T. Lyle Dickey*; also, CLN, 5-14-87, 288–92, CHM.
8. Thanks to Swett's assistance in smoothing things over when Cameron was offended over Lincoln's rescission letter, Lincoln's apology worked and Cameron subsequently behaved himself. Lincoln wound up taking Swett's advice and appointing Cameron to his cabinet after all, making him his secretary of war.
9. Swett to Mrs. Swett, 8-1-61, Washington, CHM, Davis Papers.
10. Swett to Mrs. Swett, 8-6-61, ALPL, Davis Papers.

11. Swett, *Remembrances of Dickey.*

12. Swett to Sister (Rose), 8-16-61, ALPL, Swett Papers; Joseph E. Johnston, "Responsibilities of the First Bull Run," in Johnson & Buel, *Battles and Leaders*, vol. 1, 252 (also in McPherson, *Battle Cry*, 345; Boatner, *Civil War Dictionary*, 101).

13. King, *Lincoln's Manager*, 194.

14. Herndon & Weik, *Life of Lincoln*, Swett on Davis appointment, 406–7.

15. Ibid.

16. Swett to Lincoln, Washington, 8-15-61, CHM, Davis Papers, & ALPL, Lincoln Papers.

17. Harvey Hogg to Swett, 8-18-61, Camp Butler, CHM, Davis Papers. A supporter of emancipation, Hogg had freed his last slave when he and his wife moved to Bloomington in 1855. He succeeded Swett as McLean County representative in the Illinois legislature in 1861, and his service there won him an appointment in the Second Illinois Cavalry in response to Lincoln's initial call for troops in July 1861.

18. Basler, *Collected Works*, vol. 4, Lincoln to Cameron, 9-2-61, 504–5, & 9-19-61, 529; Reyburn & Wilson, *Jottings from Dixie*, 84, n. 1.

19. Swett, *Remembrances of Dickey.*

20. Ibid.

21. Swett to Lincoln, St. Louis, 11-9-61, CHM, Davis Papers. Although Swett referred to McKenny as a captain in his letter to Lincoln, McKenny was a brigadier general by the end of the war. Vol. 2 of Tarbell's *Life of Abraham Lincoln* includes McKenny's own first-person account and describes him as a general.

22. Swett to Lincoln, St. Louis, 11-9-61, CHM, Davis Papers.

23. *Chicago Times*, 4-27-80, and *Chicago Tribune*, 4-27-80; Grant, *Memoirs*, vol. 1, 269–81. Some have claimed that Grant altered his battle reports; see, e.g., Conger, *Rise of U.S. Grant*, appendix A, which Mark A. Plummer called to my attention.

24. In 1862, Lincoln named Holt the judge advocate general of the Union army. Likely as a result of their friendship in St. Louis, Davis suggested him as a vice presidential candidate two years later, and Swett attempted to introduce his name as a candidate at the Baltimore convention. Also, the fact that Holt was a War Democrat from Kentucky made him a logical choice for Lincoln in 1864.

25. Swett to Mrs. Swett, St. Louis, 1-8, 1-12, & 1-18-62, CHM & ALPL, Davis & Swett Papers.

26. Swett to Lincoln, St. Louis, 1-25-62, CHM, Davis Papers.

27. King, *Lincoln's Manager*, 352–53, n. 15. King believed that letters from Stephen T. Logan, a federal judge and Lincoln's second law partner, and Judge John Caton of the Illinois Supreme Court particularly influenced Lincoln.

28. *Transactions of the McLean County (IL) Historical Society*, vol. 2, 401; Boatner, *Civil War Dictionary*, 287; Swett to Mrs. Swett, St. Louis, 1-18-62. The scripture quoted is from 1 Kings 20:11, KJV. Foote later led the gunboats at Fort Henry and Fort Donelson, where he was severely wounded. He received the Thanks of Congress for his leadership and became a rear admiral in mid-1862. He died in 1863 en route to Charleston to relieve Admiral Samuel DuPont of his fleet there.

29. Swett to mother, Bloomington, 3-2-62, Swett Papers, ALPL.

30. Ibid.

31. Swett, *Remembrances of Dickey.*

32. King, *Lincoln's Manager*, 186–88.

33. Grant, *Memoirs*, vol. 1, 347, 337–68; Lincoln to Gideon Welles, 7-30-62, in Basler, *Collected Works*, vol. 10, 144; James Shirk to Swett, off Helena, Arkansas, 8-29-62, ALPL, Davis Papers.

34. Swett, *Remembrances of Dickey.*

35. *War of the Rebellion [Official Records]*, vol. 17, pt. 2, 555.

36. Thirty years after Fort Donelson and Shiloh, Alexander K. McClure, a political figure during the Civil War and a publisher, stated that he "had repeated conferences with some of [Lincoln's] closest friends, including Swett and Lamon, all of whom agreed that Grant must be removed from his command." Both of these men no doubt heard the chorus of calls for Grant's removal, but it is questionable that Swett would have argued for his removal. Swett carefully observed Grant's first significant engagements and probably learned Halleck's thoughts about Grant while traveling on his riverboat to Fort Donelson and Pittsburg Landing. Beyond that, neither Swett nor Lamon claimed any expertise in military command, and Lincoln would not have paid much attention to them if they had tried to meddle in the matter. Historian Brooks Simpson reviewed McClure's chapter on Lincoln and Grant and doubted much of the writing but conceded that Lincoln may have said, "I can't spare this man; he fights," as McClure reported. McClure may simply have been burnishing his own significance in his discussion of meetings with Lincoln. (McClure, *Lincoln and Men of War-Times*, 195–96; Simpson, "McClure on Lincoln and Grant.")

37. Munson, *It Is Begun!*, 67–68; Swett to Orme, Bloomington, 5-27-62, UIUC, Orme Papers; Swett to Mrs. Swett, Springfield, 5-28-62, ALPL, Swett Papers.

38. Swett to Mrs. Swett, 7-31-62, Washington, & 8-10-62, New York; King, *Lincoln's Manager*, 196, 199.

7. Witness to the Emancipation

1. Lincoln to Halleck, Washington, in Basler, *Collected Works*, vol. 5, 353–54; Swett to Mrs. Swett, Pittsburgh, 7-25-62; Swett to Mrs. Swett, Baltimore, 7-27-62; Davis to Swett, Bloomington, 7-27-62, Davis Papers, ALPL; Swett to Mrs. Swett, Washington, 7-31-62, David Davis Papers, CHM.

2. Swett to Mrs. Swett, Washington, 7-31-62, David Davis Papers, CHM; Swett to Mrs. Swett, New York, 8-10-62, Davis Papers, CHM.

3. Basler, *Collected Works*, vol. 5, 358–59, copy from the *New York Times*, 8-7-62; *Pantagraph*, 8-12-62, and ALPL, Swett Papers. Prior to Lincoln's speech, Edward Jordan, solicitor of the treasury, read several resolutions, followed by a brief talk by Lucius E. Chittenden, register of the treasury. Lincoln was followed, in this order, by George S. Boutwell, commissioner of Internal Revenue; Leonard Swett; General George F. Shepley; General James Shields; Robert J. Walker, former secretary of the treasury under Polk; former Indiana congressman Richard W. Thompson; Senator James Harlan of Iowa; Edward Carrington, U.S. marshal of the District of Columbia; Missouri congressman James S. Rollins; and a Virginia state senator named Close. Aside from the three speakers from the Treasury Department, no others are listed in the *Collected Works*.

4. *New York Times*, 8-7-62; *Pantagraph*, 8-12-62, and ALPL, Swett Papers.
5. Swett to Mrs. Swett, New York, 8-10-62, Davis Papers, CHM.
6. Lincoln to Horace Greeley, Washington, 8-18-62, in Basler, *Collected Works*, vol. 5, 388–89.
7. Davis to Swett, Bloomington, 7-31-62, and Frank Orme to Mrs. Swett, ALPL, Davis Papers.
8. The newspaper journalist Noah Brooks presented a portrait of the Lincoln White House—its furnishings, schedule, and activities—based on his personal observations. In 1863, a year after Swett's visit, he wrote in dispatches that the corridors and waiting rooms upstairs stirred with people at all hours. Because of the press of business and visitors, the president had three secretaries, all men, to assist him. Lincoln liked to arise very early in the morning to use the freshest hours of the day for reading and writing before breakfast. Burlingame, *Lincoln Observed*, 79–88.
9. There are six sources on this Lincoln interview regarding emancipation with Leonard Swett: Swett to John Nicolay in 1878, Burlingame, *Oral History*, 58–59; *Boston Herald* interview with Swett copied in the *Chicago Tribune*, late 1878, Swett Papers, ALPL, black scrapbook, 16–17; articles on Swett's talk on "Lincoln and Grant" in both the *Chicago Tribune* and *Chicago Times*, 4-27-80; Swett dedication in *Ceremonies at the Unveiling*, 10-22-87; and an account by Swett's partner Peter Grosscup in Tarbell, *Life of Lincoln*, vol. 2, 113–15. The five writers Lincoln quotes in the following paragraphs are mentioned a total of ten times in these sources.
10. Tarbell, *Life of Lincoln*, vol. 2, 113–15.
11. Ibid.
12. Swett to John Nicolay in 1878, Burlingame, *Oral History*, 58–59.
13. Ibid.
14. Ibid.; *Boston Herald* interview with Swett copied in the *Chicago Tribune*, late 1878, Swett Papers, ALPL; Tarbell, *Life of Lincoln*, vol. 2, 113–15.
15. Swett to John Nicolay in 1878, Burlingame, *Oral History*, 58–59; *Boston Herald* interview with Swett copied in the *Chicago Tribune*, late 1878, Swett Papers, ALPL; Tarbell, *Life of Lincoln*, vol. 2, 113–15.
16. Swett in Herndon & Weik, *Life*, 431–32.
17. Ibid.
18. *Ceremonies at the Unveiling*, 10-22-87.
19. Munson, *It Is Begun!*, 80–82; *Transactions of the McLean County (IL) Historical Society*, vol. 2, 302–9; Swett to Orme, Bloomington, 9-27-62, UIUC, Orme Papers.
20. Cullom, *Fifty Years*, 78–80; Orme to Mrs. Swett, Springfield, MO, 11-17-62, ALPL, Swett Papers; Mattingly, "Lincoln's Confidant," 90–93; Neely, "'No Confidence' Vote," 1–3.
21. *Illinois State Journal*, 9-30-62, "Messrs. Swett and Stuart's Correspondence."
22. Ibid. & 10-9-62, "The Swett and Stuart Correspondence."
23. *Pantagraph*, 10-9-62, "Stuart Still Dodging," & 10-21-62, "Mr. Swett on Immigration."
24. Orme to Davis, Springfield, MO, 10-19-62, CHM, Davis Papers; Davis to Orme, Bloomington, 10-20-62, CHM, Davis Papers.
25. Weed to Swett, New York, 10-23-62, & Swett to Weed, Bloomington, 10-28-62, ALPL, Swett Papers.

26. *Pantagraph*, 10-14-62, "Position of Mr. Stuart," & "John T. Stuart's Letter," first published in Springfield, 8-31-62.

27. *Pantagraph*, 11-1-62, "Mr. Stuart and Mr. Swett Compared."

28. *Pantagraph*, 11-1-62; *Chicago Tribune*, 11-1-62; *Pantagraph*, 11-3-62; Orme to Davis, Springfield, MO, 10-19-62, CHM, Davis Papers; Davis to Orme, Bloomington, 10-20-62, CHM. Davis Papers. Brownlow proved to be a good enough politician and speaker to be elected governor of Tennessee and a U.S. senator after the war.

29. Mrs. Swett to Orme, Bloomington, 11-3-62, misdated 11-2, UIUC, Orme Papers.

30. Historians generally believe that if things had not changed dramatically two years later, Lincoln and the Republicans would have gone down in defeat despite the Gettysburg and Vicksburg victories in 1863.

31. Pratt, "Repudiation," and Neely, "'No Confidence' Vote," are the only published analyses of the contest.

32. Ebon was the younger brother of Robert Ingersoll, the noted orator, activist, and political leader.

33. Mrs. Swett to Orme, Bloomington, 11-3-62, misdated 11-2, UIUC, Orme Papers.

34. Davis to Mrs. Swett, Washington, 12-21-62, ALPL, Davis Papers.

35. Orme to Swett, Springfield, MO, 11-7-62; Orme to Mrs. Swett, Springfield, MO, 11-17-62, ALPL, Swett Papers.

36. Davis to Swett, Lenox, MA, 11-26-62, in Pratt, *Concerning Mr. Lincoln*, 94–99 (orig. in ALPL, Davis Papers).

37. Davis to Swett, Washington, 12-7 & 12-16-62, Davis Papers.

38. Davis to Orme, Washington, 12-9-62, UIUC, Orme Papers.

39. Mrs. Swett to David Davis, Bloomington, 12-10-62, & Davis to Mrs. Swett, Washington, 12-21-62, ALPL, Davis Papers.

40. Davis to Swett, Washington, 12-22-62, Davis Papers. Usher had practiced in Danville on the Eighth Circuit.

41. Parish and Schaffer to Lincoln, New York, 12-27-62, Library of Congress, Lincoln Papers.

42. Davis to Swett, Washington, 1-23-63, CHM, Davis Papers.

43. *Pantagraph*, 10-8-62, "Telegrams, from Corinth, Death of Gen'l Oglesby," 1; Plummer, *Lincoln's Rail-Splitter*, 85; Oglesby to Lamon, Decatur, 3-24-63, in Lamon, *Recollections*, 330.

44. Swett to Orme, Bloomington, 9-27-62, UIUC, Orme Papers; Frank Orme to Davis, Washington, 10-30-62, ALPL, Davis Papers.

45. Wight, "Lincoln's Most Influential Friends."

46. Swett to Orme, Bloomington, 12-9-62, UIUC, Orme Papers. Fanny McCullough attended Monticello College for young ladies in Godfrey, Illinois, a small town near Alton. On May 13, 1861, she presented a flag made by the ladies for the First Cavalry Company, the "Loomis Dragoons," led by Captain John McNulta. In her dedicatory speech to a large crowd in the courthouse square, her words captured the Union's bold and confident manner a month after Fort Sumter: "Take with you this banner, the Star-Spangled Banner, the pride and boast of your country's heritage, the emblem of your country's honor, a priceless gift which the mothers and daughters of McLean place in your keeping. . . . And though . . . death assume command of the battle field, oh, let there be a noble and loyal hand to uphold this standard amid all the desolation." (Munson, *It Is Begun!*, 18–19 & 85–86.)

47. Swett to Orme, Bloomington, 12-9-62, UIUC, Orme Papers; Wight, "Lincoln's Most Influential Friends"; Mrs. Swett to Davis, 12-10-62, ALPL; Davis to Swett, Washington, 12-16-62, CHM, Davis Papers; Davis to Mrs. Swett, Washington, 12-21-62, ALPL.

48. Lincoln to Fanny McCullough, Washington, 12-23-62, Basler, *Collected Works*, vol. 6, 16–17.

49. A year later, another Orme brother, Charles, suffered from hepatitis and was relieved from command. He had fought at Prairie Grove, Arkansas, the siege of Vicksburg, and Yazoo City, Mississippi. While trying to get home from the Ninety-Fourth Regiment stationed at Brownsville, Texas, he made it as far as Jonesboro in southern Illinois and telegraphed Nannie that he had stopped to rest. He died there that afternoon. As did many others, the Orme family paid an extraordinary price in the Civil War. Swett wrote condolences again to his partner in late January 1864, recalling his own trip upriver after the Mexican War: "I know the wasting & wearing of a journey to a sick man up the Miss River. . . . I suppose it wore him out." Orme to Davis, Chicago, 1-24-64, CHM, Davis Papers; Swett to Orme, Washington, 1-27-64, UIUC, Orme Papers.

50. Brig. General F. J. Herron to Swett, Prairie Grove, AR, 12-31-62, copy courtesy J. Orme Evans, Grace Wight, unpublished manuscript.

8. Quicksilver and New Almaden

1. Davis interview, 9-19-66, in Wilson & Davis, *Herndon's Informants*, 347; Swett to Mrs. Swett, Washington, 3-5-63, ALPL, Swett Papers; Davis to Orme, Washington, 2-16-63, UIUC, Orme Papers.

2. Swett to Mrs. Swett, Washington, 2-24-63, ALPL, Swett Papers. Years later, Evarts opposed Swett in a U.S. Supreme Court case and served as both U.S. attorney general and secretary of state.

3. Swett to Leonard Herbert Swett, Washington, 2-23-63, ALPL, Swett Papers; Swett to Mrs. Swett, Washington, 3-5-63, ALPL, Swett Papers.

4. *Chicago Tribune*, 2-10-84, "Lincoln's Opinion of Porter," 5. Porter spent the next twenty-four years attempting to vindicate his actions. In 1878, the Schofield Commission reviewed his case and found that the presence of General James Longstreet's Confederate forces in addition to those of General "Stonewall" Jackson would have compromised the effectiveness of General Pope's orders for Porter to attack. The commission recommended remission of his sentence. Years later, on February 9, 1884, learning of the reconsideration and possible restoration of Porter to his rank, Swett revealed his memory of his conversation with Lincoln in a letter to the editor of the *Chicago Tribune*. Military analysts continued to argue both sides of the case (and still do to this day). Finally, President Chester A. Arthur remitted Porter's sentence and Congress restored him to rank. Interestingly, Robert T. Lincoln served as President Arthur's secretary of war at that time. (Basler, *Collected Works*, vol. 6, 54 & 57; Boatner, *Civil War Dictionary*, Porter Case, 662–63.)

5. Davis to Orme, Washington, 2-16-63, UIUC, Orme Papers; ALPL, Swett Papers; *Pantagraph*, 3-9-63.

6. Shutes, *Lincoln and California*.

7. These territories included all of present-day California, Nevada, and Utah, and most of Arizona, New Mexico, and Colorado.

8. Wiel, *Lincoln's Crisis*; Ascher, "Lincoln's Administration"; Shutes, "Lincoln and the New Almaden Mine"; Shutes, *Lincoln and California*. Wiel was an attorney and the author of several books on water rights, Ascher was an economic historian, and Shutes was a historian. Jane Lennon, a California attorney, assisted in reviewing and interpreting sources for this chapter.

9. Wiel, *Lincoln's Crisis*, 36–41.

10. Ibid., 26–27.

11. Ibid., 44 & 46.

12. From St. Louis, Edward Bates had been a serious contender for the Republican presidential nomination in 1860, as a former Whig who was not a member of any party. Lincoln named him to the cabinet as a conservative border state representative. His reach for political prominence dated back to the River and Harbor Convention in 1847, where he had made a lasting impression as president and principal orator.

13. Swett to Mrs. Swett, Washington, 3-11-63, CHM, Davis Papers.

14. Swett to Orme, New York, 5-23-63, UIUC, Orme Papers.

15. McCullough, *Path between the Seas*, 33–40 & 466–92; Cobb, "Panama Ever at the Crossroads," 466–92. The steamship line opened before the California gold rush of 1849, and the railroad had started up, with great loss of life, eight years before. A competing route existed across Nicaragua, and if Swett investigated it, he may have found it more troublesome for his party. It required two additional transfers, one from a steamboat on the San Juan River to another steamboat on Lago de Nicaragua, and again for the short land crossing to the Pacific Ocean. Several writers refer to the Swetts' transit as having been across Panama *or* Nicaragua. However, Leonard Herbert Swett's journal manuscript and Usher's biographers indicate that they made the crossing in Panama. The path Swett traveled with his entourage was reconstructed when the Panama Canal was built, and part of it today lies submerged under Gatun Lake. (McCullough, *Path between the Seas*, 33–40 & 466–92; Cobb, "Panama Ever at the Crossroads," 466–92; Richardson & Farley, *Usher*, 43.)

16. Leonard Herbert Swett Journal.

17. Wiel, *Lincoln's Crisis*, 61.

18. Ibid.; Ascher, "Lincoln's Administration," 43 (Ascher compiled this information from newspaper sources).

19. Wiel, *Lincoln's Crisis*, 60–62.

20. Ibid., 63 & 64 (emphasis added).

21. Ibid., 65.

22. Ibid., 66–67.

23. Ibid.

24. Basler, *Collected Works*, vol. 6, 393–94; Wiel, *Lincoln's Crisis*, 65–69 (emphasis added). Wiel also said Swett "discusses free mining incoherently." Another view would hold that Swett was supporting what he thought was the policy of Bates, Usher, and Lincoln in this matter.

25. Swett's telegrams and Usher's replies appear in Wiel, *Lincoln's Crisis*, 67–68 & 82–83: Swett to Lincoln, San Francisco, 7-16-63; Swett to Usher, San Francisco, 7-13, 7-25 (2 telegrams), & 7-30-63; Usher to Swett, Washington, 7-23, 7-27-63 (2 telegrams).

26. Shutes, "Lincoln and the New Almaden Mine," 12–14; *San Francisco Evening Bulletin*, 7-25-63. The *New York World*, a Democratic paper, reprinted a few articles, but they did not attract much attention in the East.

27. Wiel, *Lincoln's Crisis*, 83–84, Swett to Usher, San Francisco, 8-5-63, National Archives, Interior Dept. Lands and Railroads Division.

28. Wiel, *Lincoln's Crisis*, 75–76, quoting from Bates, *Bates Diary*, 303–4; ibid., 78, quoting from Welles, *Welles Diary*, vol. 2, 93. A year later, when Welles and Bates spoke of the matter again, Bates's charges against Halleck had not softened.

29. Basler, *Collected Works*, vol. 6, 422; Shutes misdated the communication as from August 19 in *Lincoln and California*, 137.

30. Ascher, "Lincoln's Administration," 50; Shutes, *Lincoln and California*, 137; Wiel, *Lincoln's Crisis*, 85–86. Wiel refers to the valuation in Brewer, *Up and Down California*.

31. Wiel, *Lincoln's Crisis*, 88–93, Bates, *Bates Diary*, 4-5-64.

32. Cain, *Edward Bates*, 311; Wiel, *Lincoln's Crisis*, 93; Bates, *Bates Diary*, 338–42; Richardson and Farley, *John P. Usher*, 73.

33. Shutes, *Lincoln*, 138–39; Wiel, *Lincoln's Crisis*, 95–96. Similarly, the three Californians—economist, historian, and legal scholar—who analyzed the episode more than seventy years later blamed the messenger rather than the instigators. Two of the three backed off from their original criticism, Milton Shutes partially and Samuel Wiel more fully. Bates emerged as the principal perpetrator of the near catastrophe.

34. Swett's behavior and fee should be viewed in the context of the times and alongside the actions of others involved with the case. The Securities and Exchange Commission, with its prohibitions and restraints, did not come into existence until 1934. Conflicts of interest were viewed differently in the mid-nineteenth century, and Swett would have been well aware of them. There is no indication that his representation revealed secrets or privileged information between Quicksilver and the government. He speculated less in Quicksilver stock than implied by his critics, but his investments nevertheless did raise suspicion. Former attorney general Jeremiah Black received twenty thousand dollars to represent the U.S. government in the mining case before the Supreme Court in 1863, and a year later he switched sides and received an unknown amount to act as lead counsel for Quicksilver. (Shutes, "Lincoln and the New Almaden Mine," 17.) Assisting Black were Caleb Cushing and Reverdy Johnson, who also switched sides with him from the earlier case. In addition, General Halleck served as superintendent of the mine from 1850 to 1858 and headed a San Francisco law firm that represented Quicksilver in the District Court. Secretary of War Edwin Stanton also represented Quicksilver as counsel, although the government had sent him to review the mining and land claims in 1858. About a dozen other prominent individuals had similar conflicts, but their activities fit the perspective of their own century.

9. This Terrible War

1. Ascher, "Lincoln's Administration," 49–50; Shutes, *Lincoln and California*, 141; Leonard Herbert Swett Journal.

2. Garry Wills analyzed the formulation and background of the epic speech in his book *Lincoln at Gettysburg*. A common myth is that Lincoln composed the speech on the back of an envelope during the train ride, but that was not the case.

3. Leonard Herbert Swett Journal; ALPL, Swett Papers, black bound scrapbook, 56.
4. Wills, *Lincoln at Gettysburg*, 79–87, 154–56.
5. As a skilled orator and an attorney who had gotten the best of Lincoln in the courtroom, Swett also may have wondered about Lincoln's brevity, especially following Everett's expansive speech. Swett did not mention the speech in any correspondence until later writings on Lincoln, further evidence that the importance of the speech was not recognized in its own time.
6. Miers, *Lincoln Day by Day*, 12-15-63; Dennett, *Lincoln and the Civil War*, 139; Burlingame, *At Lincoln's Side*, 136, 262 n. 42.
7. Herndon & Weik, *Life of Lincoln*, Swett essay, 427.
8. Morehouse, *Life of Fell*; Swett to Orme, Washington, 2-18, 3-7, 3-26-64, UIUC, Orme Papers. Fell was considered the savant of central Illinois concerning Whig and Republican politics, city and town development, and higher education, and Republican supporters asked him to run for the Stuart seat in Congress. He declined, as he had earlier when asked to run for the state legislature. Fell, a Lincoln and Swett supporter, became a sponsor and close friend of Owen Lovejoy as well.
9. Four entries in the diary of former senator Orville Browning record these visits by Swett: Pease & Randall, *Browning Diary*, vol. 1, 1-21, 1-23, 2-10 & 6-1-64, 655–56, 660, & 671, ALPL. Dana, the former managing editor of the *New York Tribune*, appraised Grant favorably for Lincoln in March 1862.
10. Plummer, *Lincoln's Rail-Splitter*, 92.
11. Pledge by Lamon and Swett, Washington, 3-31-64, Huntington Library, Lamon Collection. The appendage to the agreement increasing the personal responsibility of the signatories is consistent with Judge Davis's approach in other mediations and therefore was likely his addition.
12. Swett to Orme, Washington, two letters from 5-18-64, UIUC, Orme Papers.
13. Swett to Orme, Washington, 1-28-64, UIUC, Orme Papers; Swett to Weed, Washington, 1-2-64, CHM, Davis Papers; Swett to Orme, Philadelphia, 2-8-64, UIUC, Orme Papers; Wendt, *Chicago Tribune*, 143, 191, 210.
14. Swett to Orme, Washington, 2-18 & 3-7-64, UIUC, Orme Papers.
15. Swett to Orme, Washington, 3-26-64, UIUC, Orme Papers; Swett to Weed, Washington, 3-3 & 3-24-64, CHM, Davis Papers; Dennett, *Lincoln and the Civil War*, 178.
16. Swett to Orme, Washington, 5-27-64, UIUC, Orme Papers.
17. Browne, *Every-day Life*, 666–67.
18. Ibid.
19. *Ceremonies at the Unveiling*, 10-22-87. Frances Fisher Browne later described Lincoln's affect under these circumstances: "Amidst his terrible trials, [he] often exhibited a forced and sorrowful serenity, which many mistook for apathy." (Browne, *Every-day Life*, 41.) Swett referred to this characteristic of Lincoln as a "very remarkable and useful trait."
20. *Ceremonies at the Unveiling*, 10-22-87; Herndon & Weik, *Life of Lincoln*, 428.
21. *Ceremonies at the Unveiling*, 10-22-87; Herndon & Weik, *Life of Lincoln*, 428.
22. Herndon & Weik, *Life of Lincoln*, 427–28.
23. Dennett, *Lincoln and the Civil War*, 185; Basler, *Collected Works*, vol. 7, 376; Dobyns, *Patent Office Pony*, 151. The telegram from Swett recommending Holt has not been found.

24. Basler, *Collected Works*, vol. 7, 376; Dennett, *Lincoln and the Civil War*, 186. Twenty-seven years later, two years after Swett's death, controversy arose between John Nicolay and Alexander K. McClure over whether Lincoln had supported Andrew Johnson and how he won the nomination for vice president. Following Hamlin's death on July 4, 1891, McClure published an exposé in the *Philadelphia Times* claiming that Lincoln had wanted a Southern vice president. McClure, who also had been a delegate to the Baltimore convention, said he had been privy to confidential information during a visit with Lincoln in Washington before the convention. His position was simple, but it became more animated during three exchanges with Nicolay, who stated that Lincoln had taken no position on the selection of vice president and that McClure's claim was "entirely erroneous." Eight others subsequently corroborated McClure's claim. (McClure, *Lincoln and Men of War-Times*, appendix, 457–81.) Drummond responded with observations about Swett and the Baltimore maneuvering in a letter to the editor in the July 17 *Portland Evening Express*. He also forwarded a copy of Swett's lengthy May 27, 1860, letter containing a summary of Lincoln's first nomination in Chicago. (Drummond to *Portland Evening Express*, 7-17-91, 3.) Drummond's letter supports Nicolay's argument that Lincoln did not take the initiative from the convention delegates to choose Andrew Johnson. As James A. Rawley has noted, for a hundred years, the majority of historians took McClure's side. But more recently, Brooks Simpson and Don Fehrenbacher have raised doubts about McClure's claims, causing Rawley to believe that "his case stands unproved." (McClure, *Lincoln and Men of War-Times*, 15–16, n. 4.)

25. Drummond to *Portland Evening Express*, 7-17-91, 3 (emphasis added). Actually, Hamlin really did not help the ticket. Lincoln did not need Radical Republicans so much as he needed War Democrats and border-state voters.

26. Ibid.

27. Ibid.

28. Ibid. Although Andrew Johnson had an extensive public record—Tennessee legislator; congressman for ten years, including the tenure of Lincoln's term; governor of Tennessee; U.S. senator; and military governor of the state—his performance had been less than stellar. As historian Eric Foner described Johnson's prior record, "Early in his career other less commendable qualities had also become apparent, among them stubbornness, intolerance of the view of others, and an inability to compromise. As governor, Johnson failed to work effectively with his legislature; as military governor he proved unable to elicit popular support for his administration." (Foner, *Reconstruction*, 177.) The New York leaders, a critical faction in Johnson's selection, included Thurlow Weed, William Seward, and Henry J. Raymond, *New York Times* editor and chairman of the Republican National Committee, any of whom could have examined Johnson's background. And as party leader, Lincoln cannot be excused in the vice presidential choice. He knew of his vulnerability to assassination, and he and many others were well aware of the two prior Whig policy miscarriages in vice presidential successions. In fact, Weed called John Tyler (president from 1841 to 1845) a "despised imbecile," and Seward said of Millard Fillmore (president from 1850 to 1853), "Providence has at last led the man of hesitations and double opinions where decision and singleness are indispensable." (DeGregorio, *Presidents*, 159 & 194.)

29. Drummond to *Portland Evening Express*, 7-17-91, 3; Raymond, *Life and Public Services*, 512.
30. Basler, *Collected Works*, vol. 11, 97; Barry, "Charleston Riot."
31. Davis to Lincoln, 7-4-64, Davis Papers, ALPL. Davis's response to Lincoln was a precursor to his most famous opinion, issued in 1866 for the U.S. Supreme Court case known as *Ex parte Milligan*, holding that civilians should not to be tried in military tribunals where civil courts existed for the purpose.
32. Basler, *Collected Works*, vol. 11, 97; Barry, "Charleston Riot."
33. Van Deusen, *Thurlow Weed*, 310.
34. Swett to Mrs. Swett, New York, [8-15-64], Tarbell, *Life of Lincoln*, vol. 3, 200–201.
35. Swett did not write about this meeting with Lincoln, so the substance of their discussions can only be inferred from contemporaneous letters. Basler, *Collected Works*, Lincoln's Memorandum, Washington, 8-23-64, vol. 7, 514–15; Lincoln to Raymond, 8-24-64, 517–18, Tarbell, *Life of Lincoln*, vol. 3, 200–201.
36. Swett to Mrs. Swett, Washington, 9-8-64, ALPL, Swett Papers.
37. Shaffer to General Butler, New York, 8-17-64, Marshall, *Correspondence of Butler*, vol. 5, 67–69.
38. Basler, *Collected Works*, vol. 7, 518.
39. Swett to Mrs. Swett, Washington, 9-8-64, ALPL, Swett Papers.
40. Ibid.
41. Ibid.
42. Ibid.
43. Mrs. Swett to Orme, Westford, MA, 10-25-64, UIUC, Orme Papers.
44. Ibid.
45. Swett to Orme, Washington, 12-14-64, UIUC, Orme Papers.
46. Swett talk titled "Lincoln and Grant," separate reports on Union veterans talk, Palmer House, published in both the *Chicago Tribune* and *Chicago Times*, 4-27-80; Perret, *Ulysses S. Grant*, 24, 100, 348.
47. Basler, *Collected Works*, vol. 7, 451, & vol. 8, 38–39.
48. During and after the Civil War, the propriety of cotton trading drew heated arguments. Lincoln sought pragmatically to supply the needs of the North and provide some flow to Europe, but Grant and Sherman opposed any potential benefit to the Confederacy. Jefferson Davis favored prohibition, but General Robert E. Lee understood the political needs and reality. Others felt that it was fraught with corruption like other wartime trade. (Roberts, "Federal Government," 262–75; McPherson, *Battle Cry*, 620–25.)
49. Van Deusen, *Thurlow Weed*, ch. 19, esp. 312–16.
50. This chronology of the cotton-trading venture was assembled from seven letters from Swett to Weed, Dec. 1864–March 1865, CHM, Davis Papers, originals at Rochester University; several from Swett to Orme before they joined, UIUC, Orme Papers; and eight letters from Swett to Lamon written in the same period, Huntington Library, Lamon Papers.
51. Swett to Weed, Memphis, 2-6, 3-30-65, CHM. Although Swett made several trips to Washington in 1866 to press his cotton-trading claims, visiting with Treasury Secretary Hugh McCulloch and President Andrew Johnson, he finally concluded that these efforts were futile. (Swett to Mrs. Swett, Washington, 6-27, 9-24, & 11-14-66, Huntington Library, Swett Papers.)

52. Potter, *Sultana Tragedy*; Orme to Mrs. Orme, 5-22-65, CHM, Davis Papers. One of the boilers of the paddle wheeler exploded, and the overcrowded boat caught fire and sank a few miles north of Memphis. An estimated eighteen hundred passengers died of burns or drowned in the rapid river currents. A large proportion of these were Union prisoners released from Confederate prisons at Cahaba in Alabama and Andersonville in Georgia. Bodies floated down the Mississippi to Memphis and beyond for days. It remains a little-known fact that more passengers perished on the *Sultana* than in any other American maritime disaster in history. While artifacts from the *Titanic* tour museums around the world, the *Sultana* lies buried in the shallow Arkansas silt, a forgotten epitaph to the terrible war. (Potter, *Sultana Tragedy*.)

10. A Strategic Decision

1. Quigg had been captured by Confederate forces during Stoneman's Raid in Georgia in the latter part of 1864. By the end of the year, he was suffering in a Columbia, South Carolina, prison. (Swett to Weed, Clinton, 1-16-65, CHM, Davis Papers.) Swett worked diligently to free Quigg, who was eventually released and sent home to recover. Higgins (1821–93) migrated from upstate New York to the Midwest in 1837 and gained admittance to the bar in Iroquois County, Illinois, in 1844. He located permanently in Chicago in 1852.
2. Swett to Hanna, Chicago, 8-20-65, CHM & ALPL, Davis Papers. Hanna had visited Washington in 1862 and joined Swett and Lamon in persuading Lincoln to accept a detachment of troops as guards on his trips to and from the Soldiers' Home. (Swett, "Conspiracies," 187–88.)
3. Stowell, *Papers of Lincoln*, vol. 3, 384–453, "*Johnson v. Jones & Marsh*."
4. Davis to J. S. Holland, Bloomington, 7-3-65, CHM & ALPL, Davis Papers.
5. Donald, *Lincoln's Herndon*, 169.
6. Herndon & Weik, *Life of Lincoln*, 425–33, and other editions; Wilson & Davis, *Herndon's Informants*, 162–68. These are the only sources containing the complete essay. This essay is the most quoted of Swett's writings on Lincoln, but unfortunately it usually is seen only in bits and pieces. William Herndon and Jesse Weik published the entire essay in their 1889 biography in slightly amended form, after it was reviewed by Swett in 1887. His amendments were not substantial except in the ultimate paragraph, where Swett sought to soften his description of Lincoln's religious views. He affirmed Lincoln's "belief in God," saved Lincoln's emphasis on "religious reverence" and "natural religion," but excised his failure to attend church regularly and the statement that he read Petroleum V. Nasby as much as the Bible. Douglas Wilson and Rodney Davis republished the letter in its original form, 134 years after it was written, in *Herndon's Informants*. The essay as amended in 1887 appears in the appendix to this book.
7. Herndon & Weik, *Life of Lincoln*, 425–33; Wilson & Davis, *Herndon's Informants*, 162–68.
8. Herndon & Weik, *Life of Lincoln*, 425–33; Wilson & Davis, *Herndon's Informants*, 162–68.
9. Wilson & Davis, *Herndon's Informants*, 159–60; Basler, *Collected Works*, vol. 2, 15–16 & 111–12.

10. Wilson & Davis, *Herndon's Informants*, 213. This query called attention to a characteristic also noted by others; see Shenk, *Lincoln's Melancholy*.

11. Wilson & Davis, *Herndon's Informants*, esp. xiii–xxiv.

12. Donald, *Lincoln's Herndon*, 197–241.

13. Ibid.

14. Ibid., 231; Dickey to Herndon, 12-8-66, Herndon-Weik Collection, Library of Congress; Donald, *Lincoln's Herndon*, 266–84.

15. Although correspondence between Davis and Orme mentioned Swett's July trip to Washington and reported in August 1866 that "Swett is keeping quiet and still," it is odd that there are no copies of letters from Swett written during this period. (Davis to Orme, Bloomington 7-6 & 8-6-66, CHM, Davis Papers, box 14, folder 88.)

16. Davis to his son, George Perrin Davis, Washington, 2-28-66, ALPL, Davis Papers, box A-45.

17. Swett to Mrs. Swett, Washington, 10-31 & 10-25-66, Huntington Library, Swett Papers.

18. Swett to Weed, Washington, 10-31-66, CHM Davis Papers; Thomas & Hyman, *Stanton*, ch. 24, esp. 501–7; Swett to Lamon, Boston, 12-5-66, & Swett to Mrs. Swett, Boston, 12-19-66, Huntington Library, Lamon and Swett Papers.

19. Huntington Library, Swett Papers.

20. Swett to Mrs. Swett, Chicago, 1-23-67, Huntington Library, Swett Papers.

21. This was likely Giovanni Pacini's 1843 melodious composition rather than the version composed by Luigi Cheribini in 1797 and repopularized by Maria Callas in her 1960s revival.

22. Swett to Mrs. Swett, Chicago, 1-23 & 1-24-67, Huntington Library, Swett Papers.

23. Swett to Mrs. Swett, Springfield, 2-5, 2-6, 2-9, 2-21, & 2-22-67, Huntington Library, Swett Papers. Initially known as Illinois Industrial University, this future land-grant institution later changed its name to the University of Illinois.

24. Swett to Mrs. Swett, Chicago, 3-25-67, Huntington Library, Swett Papers; Schweitzer, *Quest*, ch. 14; more broadly, Pelikan, *Jesus*, ch. 15 & 16, esp. 189–202.

25. The Funk case was described similarly by two sources: *Chicago Legal News*, 10-10-68, & *Decatur (IL) Magnet*, 7-8-69, copied by *Chicago Tribune*, 7-12-69. The shortened account given here closely follows these sources. Subsequent biographies of Isaac Funk (Kerrick, "Life and Character of Funk," 498–520; Cavanagh, *Seed, Soil, and Science*) largely corroborated this information, except that they made no mention of James Funk or the estate contest. The size of Funk's landholdings is taken from the later sources, as they likely are more accurate.

26. Welles, *Welles Diary*, 306. As Eric Foner explained the situation, "Why the President so quickly abandoned the idea of depriving the prewar elite of its political and economic hegemony has always been something of a mystery. . . . Most likely, he came to view cooperation with the planters as indispensable to two interrelated goals—white supremacy in the South and his own reelection [*sic*] as President." (Foner, *Reconstruction*, 191.)

27. Welles, *Welles Diary*, 3-9 & 3-10-68, 306–7.

28. Statement before the Chicago Bar Association, 12-1-89, ALPL, Swett Papers. Weldon made this statement two decades later, at the time of Swett's death. He had been co-counsel with Swett on the Funk case, and it is likely that his memory

was faulty after learning so many years later that Swett had been considered for Johnson's defense.

29. This was the second of the president's twenty-nine vetoes, and the first of fifteen that were overridden by Congress. Foner noted that "for Republican moderates, the Civil Rights veto ended all hope of cooperation with the President." (Foner, *Reconstruction*, 250.)

30. Plummer, *Lincoln's Rail-Splitter*, 129–33. Although Oglesby did not adopt all the Radical Republican positions, he moved steadily in their direction. In 1866, he assisted in getting eleven Republicans elected in races for fourteen Illinois congressional seats. The importance of these acts is relevant to the later findings in civil rights cases.

31. King, *Lincoln's Manager*, 260; Davis to Mrs. Davis, Washington, 3-4-68, 267.

32. *Chicago Legal News*, 10-10-68; *Decatur (IL) Magnet*, 7-8-69.

33. *Chicago Tribune*, 9-23-70; Miller, *City of the Century*, 468.

34. Erik Larson graphically portrayed the city in the late nineteenth century, especially the filth and disease, the billions of flies, the rats, and the horse urine running in the gutters of the streets. (Larson, *Devil in the White City*, 28–35.)

35. Swett to Herbert Swett, Chicago, 7-20-74, Huntington Library, Swett Papers; CLN, 10-21-71; Miller, *City of the Century*, 16.

36. The following discussion of the Liberal Republican movement and its defeat in 1872 is based primarily on King, *Lincoln's Manager*, ch. 12, "Candidate for President, 1868–72," 271–83; Ross, *Liberal Republican Movement*; & Foner, *Reconstruction*, 499–511.

37. King, *Lincoln's Manager*, 277.

38. *Pantagraph*, 3-26-72.

39. King, *Lincoln's Manager*, 280 & 281–83.

40. Ross, *Liberal Republican Movement*, 140 & 144.

41. *Chicago Tribune*, 6-24-72.

11. Legal Advocate and Civic Leader

1. Higgins became president of the Babcock Manufacturing Company and served as a financial agent for the Charter Oak Life Insurance Company. By 1876, however, he returned to the practice of law. He also ran for the Illinois Supreme Court that year but was defeated by Swett's old friend T. Lyle Dickey. Myra Bradwell was impressed by Higgins's ability and wrote in 1888 that he was the "greatest case lawyer that ever appeared at the Chicago Bar" (CLN, 4-7-88, editorial comment).

2. CLN, 6-22-89, John J. Herrick; editorial in the *Chicago Inter Ocean*, 6-9-89.

3. *Chicago Times*, 12-5-74; CLN, vol. 8, 11-6-75, 49, 8-12-76, 371; vol. 11, 5-31-79, 279; & vol. 12, 12-13-79, 113.

4. *Fertilizing Co. v. Hyde Park*, 97 U.S. 659, 664, 24 L.Ed. 1036, 1038 (1878).

5. CLN, vol. 5, 3-15-73, "Circuit Court of Cook County," 291–92.

6. Hitchcock (1827–81) was a graduate of Dartmouth College and a member of the Cook County board elected after the fire to share leadership in rebuilding Chicago.

7. CLN, vol. 5, 3-15-73, "Circuit Court of Cook County," 291–92; 3-29-73, "U.S. Circuit Court," 313–14; & 4-12-73, "U.S. Circuit Court," 337–38. Shortly after

the U.S. Circuit Court cases were completed, Chief Justice Salmon Chase of the U.S. Supreme Court died on May 7, 1873, and Swett led several members of the Chicago bar, including former senator Lyman Trumbull and former congressman Burton Cook, in presenting remembrances of him.

8. CLN, vol. 7, 10-3-74, "Supreme Court of Illinois," 10–12.

9. 97 U.S. 659, 670, 672, & 679; CLN, vol. 11, 11-30-78, 81–82. The justices in the Waite Court (1874–88) then included one appointed by Buchanan (Clifford), three by Lincoln (Swayne, Miller, and Field; the last did not take part), four by Grant (Waite, Strong, Bradley, and Hunt), and one by Hayes (Harlan). Waite was in his fifth year as chief justice, and his fourteen-year tenure was marked by the first wave of business regulation connected with agrarian complaints. Swayne was nearing the last two years of his nineteen on the court and wrote few opinions. The full case is available from several court sources, including the U.S. Supreme Court Center.

10. These issues are still undergoing accommodation, as more recent cases attest. Judges and attorneys have referenced the *Fertilizing Company* case for more than a century. The 1878 Supreme Court opinion has been cited in various state and federal court opinions several hundred times (at least thirty-five of these in U.S. Supreme Court opinions) and in legal articles or publications close to a hundred times. Two late-twentieth-century cases emphasize the enduring nature of the arguments. In *United States Trust Co. v. New Jersey* (1977), 431 U.S. 1, called the *Port Authority* case, Justice William J. Brennan wrote a dissent joined by two others, pressing for a broad reliance on the state's police power to protect a wide range of social interests and claiming that the U.S. Supreme Court's majority opinion rejected the *Fertilizing Company* decision. A 1987 decision in the U.S. Seventh Circuit Court of Appeals by Judges Richard Posner and Frank Easterbrook upheld a Chicago ordinance limiting and changing important terms in existing apartment leases, contracts between private parties. They observed that "the Supreme Court had defanged the Contract Clause" on the basis of nineteenth-century decisions in cases such as the *Fertilizing Company*, cited earlier in their opinion. These twentieth-century cases broadened the social interests affected by the Constitutional Contract Clause, and several recent law review articles addressed the expansion of "takings" of contract rights, in conjunction with environmental concerns, for example. (*Chicago Board of Realtors, Inc. v. City of Chicago*, 819 F.2d 732, 743–44; two *California Law Review* articles in 1989 and 1990 were subtitled "The Takings Clause: In Search of Underlying Principles.") Epstein explores the contract clause beginning with the framers of the Constitution and its history, including police power and just compensation. (Epstein, "Toward a Revitalization of the Contract Clause," 703.) One of Swett's five arguments before the U.S. Supreme Court raised the question of just compensation.

11. CLN, vol. 11, 11-30-78, editorial by Myra Bradwell, 85.

12. The former general was one of the "Fighting McCooks" from Ohio, who, along with two brothers and their fifteen sons, fought in the Civil War. Six McCooks became generals during the war, and four were killed in action. After division of the Dakota Territory into two states in 1889, McCook County in South Dakota was named for the general. (Boatner, *Civil War Dictionary*, 528.)

13. Whitney, *Life on the Circuit*, 87; Simmons, "Territorial Justice," 91–112.

14. Whitney, *Life on the Circuit*, 87; Simmons, "Territorial Justice," 91–112.

15. Among those founding members, Goudy served as the first president of the Chicago Bar Association, Ayer was its second president, and Fuller became chief justice of the U.S Supreme Court.

16. CLN, 7-13-89, Benjamin F. Ayer.

17. *Chicago Times*, 6-9-89, Dexter; CLN, 12-7-89.

18. Pierce, *History of Chicago*, vol. 3, 429–34; Presbyterian Church of the U.S.A. Presbyteries, *Swing Trial*. The trial brought publicity to both Swing and Patton. Patton later joined Princeton Theological Seminary and became president of Princeton University from 1888 to 1902. Swing became a Congregational minister and went on to found the Central Church of Chicago. Swett, Wirt Dexter, and Abraham M. Pence, a prominent attorney who had a hand in initially bringing Swing to Chicago, provided financial and other assistance, and they served as members of the church's first board of trustees. Central Church opened in 1875 in McVicker's Theatre and moved to the newly opened Central Music Hall in 1879. Swing attracted five thousand to seven thousand weekly worshipers until he died in 1894. Historian Bessie Louise Pierce wrote that "Swing courageously and at times eloquently answered the increased questioning of those longing to reconcile their religious faith and the new urban setting in which they now found themselves." Mary Lincoln attended Swing's church when she was in Chicago. She developed a friendship with his family, which for a time resided only a few doors away from her son Robert. (Pierce, *History of Chicago*, vol. 3, 431–32; Grossman et al., *Encyclopedia of Chicago*, "Protestants," Martin E. Marty, 1016.)

19. Herbert Swett to Mr. & Mrs. Swett, Woodstock, IL, 1-13-75, Huntington Library, Swett Papers.

20. Herbert Swett to Mr. & Mrs. Swett, Exeter, NH, 1-14-76, a twenty-six-page letter on the trip, Huntington Library.

21. Swett to Herbert Swett, Chicago 2-13-76, Huntington Library.

22. The general's widow, Elizabeth Bacon Custer, remained in touch with the Swett family for many years, making multiple visits that were recorded in correspondence. Swett encouraged her to write and publish the first of her three books on her life with Custer, *Boots and Saddles; or, Life in Dakota with General Custer*, which was published in 1885. (Leckie, *Elizabeth Bacon Custer*, 234–35.) Herbert Swett and Elizabeth were still in contact as late as 1929, following the fiftieth anniversary of the battle of the Little Bighorn, as evidenced by notes in his journal.

23. Swett to Mrs. Swett, Chicago, 4-2-76, Huntington Library.

24. Baker, *Mary Todd Lincoln*, 263–65, 267–79, & 311–12; King, *Lincoln's Manager*, ch. 19, 233–44; Pease & Randall, *Browning Diary*, vol. 2, 366.

25. Neely & McMurtry, *Insanity File*, 8; Emerson, *Madness of Mary Lincoln*, esp. ch. 4.

26. Neely & McMurtry, *Insanity File*, 6–8; Swett to Davis, Chicago, 5-24-75, CHM, Davis Papers, box 18, folder 112. Swett's letter to Davis is a useful and reliable source on this painful episode.

27. Swett to Davis, Chicago, 5-24-75, CHM, Davis Papers, box 18, folder 112; Neely & McMurtry, *Insanity File*, 14–17.

28. Arnold, *History of Lincoln*; Arnold, *Life of Lincoln*.

29. Neely & McMurtry, *Insanity File*, 26.

30. Ibid., 135–36; Baker, *Mary Todd Lincoln*, 326–27. Mary's biographer Jean Baker raises doubts that this incident actually happened, however.

31. Swett to Davis, 5-24-75, CHM, Davis Papers, box 18, folder 112. Any old animosities on Mary's part as a result of Swett's involvement in her insanity hearing apparently faded from her mind, as she wrote in a letter to Robert, after learning that he had been discussed as a potential presidential candidate prior to 1880, that she "fantasized about the formation of his cabinet," including Leonard Swett. (Mary Lincoln to Edward Lewis Baker, Pau, France, 6-22-79 in Turner & Turner, *Mary Lincoln*.)

32. Neely & McMurtry, *Insanity File*, 101–7; Robert Lincoln to John Hay, Chicago, 6-6-76, Brown University, Hay Collection.

33. *Pantagraph*, 12-23-75. Twenty years later, Dollie edited her father's *Recollections of Abraham Lincoln* and got it published, something her father had not been able to accomplish. (Lamon, *Recollections*, preface & preface to 2nd edition.)

34. Caton (1812–95) served twenty-two years on the Illinois Supreme Court, including five years as chief justice. He participated in establishing telegraph lines throughout Illinois and other midwestern states. Wentworth served six terms as a U.S. representative from Illinois, first as a Democrat and later as a Republican, as well as six years as mayor of Chicago. He edited Chicago's first and largest newspaper, the *Chicago Democrat*, which he sold to the *Tribune*.

35. *Pantagraph*, 12-23-75. Dexter's grandfather had served in both houses of Congress and as secretary of war and the treasury under President John Adams.

36. *Chicago Press & Tribune*, 2-21-76; *Pantagraph*, 7-3-76.

37. *Chicago Times*, 6-9-89; McDonald, *Secrets*; Perret, *Ulysses S. Grant*, 437–46; Gresham, *Life of Gresham*, vol. 2, 438ff.; *Chicago Times*, 6-9-89; King, *Lincoln's Manager*, 287.

38. Swett, "Leonard Swett," 350, quoting Judge William H. Barnum, who wrote a history of the case at Goodspeed's Industrial Chicago, vol. 6, 768; *Chicago Times*, 4-27-79, editorial.

39. *Chicago Tribune*, 4-7 & 4-11-76; *Chicago Times*, 4-8 & 4-9-76, 6 (triple sheet).

40. *Chicago Times*, 4-12-76; Pierce, *History of Chicago*, vol. 3, 345–46. Further information appears in these sources and those in the previous note, especially in Pierce's notes found on the pages cited.

41. Wood, "Sullivan Trial," 385–92. Thomas Dent, an attorney from central Illinois who practiced in Chicago, observed that Swett was "a friend of man of all the various spheres of life, whether in a conspicuous position or in lowly walks." (CLN, 6-22-89, Thomas P. Dent, later president, Chicago Bar Assoc., labeled T.D., Swett opponent in Chicago Board of Trade cases.) Or perhaps it was the Maine connection. Sullivan was born in Waterville, Maine, to Irish immigrant parents, but there are no records suggesting that Swett knew the family. At the time of Sullivan's birth, Swett was a student at Waterville College (now Colby).

42. Swett, "Leonard Swett," 351, quotation from *Andrews' History*, vol. 3, 253; *Chicago Times*, 10-27-76, 4.

43. *Chicago Times*, 10-27-76, 4.

44. CLN, 12-7-89, James L. High.

45. CLN, 11-11-76, Swett, 60 & 62; Swett, "Leonard Swett," 352. Judge McAllister continued to preside over the courts of Cook County for many years.

46. Neely, *Lincoln Encyclopedia*, 310; Craughwell, *Stealing Lincoln's Body*, esp. 114–18; *Chicago Tribune*, 11-8, 11-9, & 11-18-76. As an ironic footnote to this quirky story, Lincoln had created the Secret Service on the very last day of his life, April 14, 1865, with the initial purpose of investigating the crime of counterfeiting. The assassination of two more presidents, Garfield and McKinley, took place before the Secret Service added presidential protection to its activities.

47. ALPL, Swett Papers, which contain extensive references to Benton, *Thirty Years' View*.

48. King, *Lincoln's Manager*, 289–92; *Encyclopaedia Britannica* and others; Foner, *Reconstruction*, 575–87.

49. CLN, vol. 9, 12-5-74.

50. Pierce, *History of Chicago*, vol. 3, 244–51; *Chicago Tribune*, 7-26-77, "The Mass Meeting."

51. Chicago History Museum, Chicago City Directory, 1878–79. Central Park was laid out in 1869 as the middle of a three-park system, with Humboldt Park two miles to the north and Douglas Park two miles to the south. The avenue's name came from Henry Clay's home in Kentucky, and former Kentuckians gathered in the neighborhood, including Congressman Carter H. Harrison, who became the mayor of Chicago the following year. (Mayer & Wade, *Chicago*, 56, 62, & 64; Miller, *City of the Century*, 440.)

52. Herbert Swett to Swett and/or Mrs. Swett, Chicago, 11-4, 12-17, & 12-28-78, Salt Lake City, 7-12 & 7-14-79, Chicago, 10-4 & 10-6-79, Huntington Library.

53. Herbert Swett to Swett, Chicago, 10-28-78, Huntington Library. Also known as adult-onset or non-insulin-dependent diabetes, type 2 diabetes is the most common form of the disease and is attributed to a combination of genetic and lifestyle factors, including poor diet, obesity, and lack of physical activity. It can cause damage to various parts of the body, including the kidneys and blood vessels. At the time Bert wrote his letter, medical science still had a lot to learn about the complexities and gravity of the disease, and blood glucose regulation and the use of insulin were decades off. Today, despite these modern treatments, research is ongoing for better ways to prevent, treat, and even cure diabetes, and it continues to be a major cause of death. NIH, "Diabetes"; *New York Times*, 10-16-2007, Schaffer, "Diabetes," 1.

54. Perret, *Ulysses S. Grant*, 458–60; Fatout, *Mark Twain*, 131–33; Smith & Gibson, *Twain-Howells Letters*, vol. 2, 139; Kaplan, *Mr. Clemens*, 225.

55. CLN, vol. 8, 2-5-76, 153–54, Supreme Court of Illinois, *John B. Lyon et al. v. Charles M. Culbertson et al.*, & 7-15-76, 337–38, Supreme Court of Illinois, *The People v. Board of Trade of Chicago*; both cases are also cited in Lurie, *Chicago Board of Trade*. The practices from the grain pits evolved into subsequent growth in foreign exchange markets and derivatives or futures for interest rates and additional commodities and services a century later.

56. CLN, vol. 12, 3-27-80, 241, & 4-10-80, 259.

57. Article published in both the *Chicago Tribune* and the *Chicago Times*, 4-27-80; Swett to Herbert Swett, Chicago, 7-18-80, Huntington Library, Swett Papers; Andreas, *History of Chicago*, vol. 2, 409; U.S. Congress, Congressional Biographical Directory.

58. Swett to Herbert Swett, Chicago, 8-21-80, Huntington Library, Swett Papers.

59. Ibid.

60. Swett to Herbert Swett, Chicago, 10-4-79, Huntington Library, Swett Papers; *Chicago Tribune* clipping, scrapbook, Swett Papers, 1880, Swett speech, 4th Ward Republican Club talk, and editorial, ALPL.

61. *Chicago Tribune*, clipping, scrapbook, Swett Papers, ALPL; *Chicago Tribune*, 12-4-78 to 1-2-79; CLN 3-2-72, *Morton v. Noble.*

62. CLN, vol. 13, 1880–81, 4-2-81, 234–35, *Union Life Insurance Co. v. The University of Chicago et al.*; Goodspeed, *History of the University of Chicago*, ch. 1; Pierce, *History of Chicago*, vol. 3, 390. The old University of Chicago ceased to operate in 1886, but interest developed in its reorganization. The second University of Chicago rose like a phoenix within six years after it reincorporated and began operation on a new campus two miles farther south. (Miller, *City of the Century*, 395–96.)

12. The Better Angels of Our Nature

1. Swett to mother, Remember Berry Swett, Chicago, 9-13-81 & 12-22-82, ALPL, Swett Papers.

2. Swett to Mrs. Swett &/or Herbert Swett, London, 7-11, 7-17, 7-19, & 8-20-82, Huntington Library, Swett Papers; in all, there are nineteen letters, mostly from Liverpool, London, or Paris.

3. CLN, vol. 9, 12-5-74; Dr. Andrew McFarland, "Insanity as a Defense," *Chicago Tribune*, 6-20-89.

4. Solomon, *History of the Seventh Circuit*, 49–58. In 1892, President Benjamin Harrison appointed Grosscup as a U.S. district judge in Chicago. Because Grosscup helped William McKinley in his first congressional race, when McKinley became president in 1897, he moved the judge to the U.S. Circuit Court in Chicago. (Ibid.)

5. Swett to Herbert Swett, Chicago, 10-4-79, Huntington Library; Swett to Mrs. Swett, aboard SS *Gallia* off Scotland, London, Brussels, and Liverpool, 7-8, 7-10, 7-15, 7-16, 7-17, 7-20, 7-22, 7-26, & 8-15-84, Huntington Library; Herbert Swett to Mrs. Swett, Genoa, 2-5-85. Swett also met a client for unidentified legal work, which prevented him from making a planned visit to Scotland.

6. Swett to Mrs. Swett, Turner, ME, 8-26, 12-30, & 12-31-85 (2); Thomas Jefferson University, "S. Weir Mitchell"; Edward Swett to Mrs. Swett, Philadelphia, 1-28-86, Huntington Library.

7. *Chicago Tribune*, 3-6 & 3-10-86.

8. Ibid.

9. Swett to Ward Hill Lamon, Las Vegas Hot Springs, 5-18-86, Huntington Library, Lamon Papers. Montezuma Hot Springs is just north of Las Vegas, New Mexico, where the Montezuma Castle Resort was built in 1879, accessible by the Santa Fe Railroad.

10. Swett, "In Memory of David Davis," CLN, vol. 19, 3-5-87, 206–7; King, *Lincoln's Manager*, 307–12. Scott practiced in Bloomington and became the Eighth Circuit judge following Davis's appointment to the U.S. Supreme Court. Spenser was a Bloomington attorney and close friend of Davis's who managed the Chicago and Alton Railroad.

11. Swett to Mrs. Addie Davis, Montreal, 7-24-86, ALPL, Davis Papers; Swett to Sarah Ricker (sister), Chicago, 10-14-86, ALPL, Swett Papers.

12. Swett to Sarah Ricker (sister), Chicago, 10-14-86, ALPL, Swett Papers.

13. *Chicago Herald*, 11-21-86, 13, "Great Illinois Lawyers." The portrayed lawyers included Sidney Breese, U.S. senator and longtime member of the Illinois Supreme Court; Archibald Williams of Quincy, named by Lincoln to be a federal district judge in Kansas; John M. Scott of Bloomington, who served on the Illinois Supreme Court; Asahel Gridley, a "sharp" Bloomington attorney and businessman; Robert E. Williams, another Bloomington attorney in practice there for forty-three years; John Todd Stuart, Lincoln's first law partner, who had defeated Swett for Congress; Ward Hill Lamon, the Eighth Circuit state's attorney and marshal of the District of Columbia; W. E. Terry, Danville judge; Clifton H. Moore, Clinton attorney and David Davis's farmland investment partner; and Oliver L. Davis, Danville attorney and judge.

14. Swett, "Lincoln's Story of His Own Life," in Rice, *Reminiscences*, 67–80; Browne, *Every-day Life*, 276–77, 364–72, 666–67; Swett, "Conspiracies," 180–89. The outpourings of Lincoln memorabilia in the late nineteenth century were tremendous and excessive. In *Lincoln in American Memory*, Merrill D. Peterson wrote that "Swett contemplated a biography but produced nothing more weighty than reminiscence and oratory" (69–70). Peterson must have been familiar with Swett's long essay appearing in the summation of Herndon's biography. It is unclear, however, whether he read Swett's introduction of Lincoln in the 1858 Lincoln-Douglas senatorial campaign or his well-crafted essay on T. Lyle Dickey and his family, especially regarding Dickey's changing position in Lincoln's two senatorial campaigns and the family's later role in the Union army. Two close friends also mentioned shortly after Swett's death that he had been planning to write his reminiscences. "He has told me that he intended to do this," Cook County circuit judge Richard S. Tuthill said, "and I have repeatedly urged him to do so." (*Chicago Times*, Tuthill, 6-9-89, "His Last Case Tried.") And at a memorial for Swett, his last law partner, Peter Grosscup, said that "he was about entering preparation" of his reminiscences. (CLN, Grosscup, 6-22-89, 365.) Both Grosscup and Tuthill had listened to Swett's well-crafted stories on many occasions, but neither knew of the trove of written material Swett left behind in various nooks and crannies over his life. Nor have historians interested in Lincoln and his cadre of followers sought to gather and assemble these disparate works.

15. Green, *Death in the Haymarket*; Avrich, *Haymarket Tragedy*; for a brief summary, Pierce, *History of Chicago*, vol. 3, 275–88; Kogan, *First Century*, 71–72.

16. Avrich, *Haymarket Tragedy*, esp. ch. 19 & 21; Plummer, *Lincoln's Rail-Splitter*, 190–201.

17. Avrich, *Haymarket Tragedy*, 339.

18. Ibid., esp. ch. 19 & 21; Plummer, *Lincoln's Rail-Splitter*, 190–201.

19. Swett, "In Memory of David Davis," CLN, vol. 19, 3-5-87, 206–7; King, *Lincoln's Manager*, 307–12.

20. Newberry Library, Mrs. Leonard [Maria] Swett to [library president] E. W. Blatchford, Chicago, 11-22-93, & Genealogy and Local History Collection.

21. Swett to Mrs. Swett, Turner, ME, 8-26-85, Huntington Library, Swett Papers.

22. *Chicago Tribune, Times, Daily News, Herald,* & *Mail,* plus a number of eastern papers.

23. Ibid.

24. Percoco, *Summers with Lincoln*, ch. 4, 89–116. Art critics immediately expressed favorable reactions to the new monument. The grandeur of Saint-Gaudens's work and his naturalistic style vaulted him into the top ranks of sculptors in America. He earned subsequent commissions for works on Boston Common and in Central Park in New York, then returned to Chicago to create another Lincoln bronze for Grant Park, this time depicting him seated. A replica of "Standing Lincoln" was sent to London to overlook Parliament Square.
25. *Ceremonies at the Unveiling*, 10-22-1887. This speech has been reprinted in the appendix to this book.
26. Calhoun, *Gilded Age Cato*. From Indiana, Gresham had achieved the rank of major general in the Union army. Grant appointed him as U.S. district judge in Indiana in 1869. He served as postmaster general and briefly as secretary of the treasury under President Chester A. Arthur, who appointed Gresham to the U.S. Circuit Court bench in Chicago at the end of his presidency. At the battle of Shiloh, Gresham had accommodated the dying husband of the eldest Dickey daughter in his quarters. (Ibid.)
27. Ibid. The Gresham campaign had first thought about asking Robert G. Ingersoll, who had made the "Plumed Knight" speech for James G. Blaine in the 1876 convention, to make the nominating speech, but after considering his atheism, they turned to Swett. (Ibid.; Swett's Nominating Speech, CLN, vol. 20, 6-23-88.)
28. Swett's Nominating Speech, CLN, vol. 20, 6-23-88; Calhoun, *Gilded Age Cato*, 100. Gresham switched parties in 1892 and supported the election of President Grover Cleveland. His reward was an appointment as secretary of state, and he served in the second Cleveland administration until his death two years later.
29. CLN, vol. 20, 5-5-88, 291 & 9-1-88, 431; CLN, vol. 21, 9-22-88, 21 & 9-29-88, 25; King, *Melville Weston Fuller*. Fuller began his twenty-two-year tenure as chief justice in October 1888. He joined the eight-to-one majority in the *Plessy v. Ferguson* case in 1896, with Justice Harlan dissenting, establishing the "separate but equal" segregation of African Americans for the next sixty years. (King, *Melville Weston Fuller*.)
30. CLN, vol. 21, 1-12-89, 160. Donors are listed as follows, with identification added: Henry Walker Bishop, Chicago attorney and son of Davis's legal mentor in Lenox, Massachusetts; Thomas B. Bryan, Chicago business leader; George P. Davis, son of Davis; Wirt Dexter, Chicago attorney; William C. Goudy, Chicago attorney; William H. King, Chicago attorney; Robert Todd Lincoln; Clifton H. Moore, Clinton attorney and Davis's land acquisition partner; Frank Orme, brother of William Orme; Mrs. Henry S. Swayne (Sally Davis); Leonard Swett; Edwin Walker, Chicago attorney and counsel of Chicago, Milwaukee, and St. Paul Railroad; and Judge Lawrence Weldon, U.S. Court of Claims. (King, *Lincoln's Manager*, 309–10.)
31. Herbert Swett to Swett, Ithaca, NY, 1-27-89, Huntington Library, Swett Papers.
32. "The Lecture by Hon. Leonard Swett," *Pantagraph*, 4-6-89.
33. Swett to Lamon, Las Vegas Hot Springs, 5-18-86, Huntington Library, Lamon Papers.
34. CLN, vol. 21, 5-18-89, 324.
35. Swett, "Leonard Swett," 363.
36. *Chicago InterOcean*, 6-12-89.

Epilogue

1. CLN, vol. 21, 6-22-89, 363–65; 6-29-89, 366; 7-13-89, 387; vol. 21, 12-7-89, 112–13. The friends and colleagues who spoke on Swett or had their remarks published in the *Chicago Legal News* were James L. High, Benjamin Franklin Ayer, Elijah B. Sherman, Edwin Walker, Lawrence Weldon, Theodore Dent, Richard S. Tuthill, John J. Herrick, Peter S. Grosscup, H. S. Monroe, and the Reverend Dr. Thomas. It is not clear from existing sources which of these people spoke at the memorial as opposed to having their remarks appear only in print. *Chicago Legal News* editor Myra C. Bradwell covered Swett's life and funeral on the day of the Chicago Bar Association's memorial session.

2. Fort Collins (CO) Public Library, personal communication with Dorothy Mc-David; *Santa Maria (CA) Times*; Huntington Library, Swett Papers.

3. Correspondence from Swett and Ricker family descendants.

4. Newberry Library, Mrs. Leonard [Maria] Swett to [library president] E. W. Blatchford, Chicago, 11-22-93; *Chicago Tribune*, 5-2-1900, 5-12-1911, "Real Estate Transactions of Week," & 3-29-1931.

Bibliography

Books and Articles

Andreas, A. T. *History of Chicago*. 2 vols. Chicago: A. T. Andreas Co., Pub., 1885.

Angle, Paul M. *The Complete Lincoln-Douglas Debates of 1858*. Chicago: Univ. of Chicago Press, 1958 & 1991.

———. *Here I Have Lived: A History of Lincoln's Springfield, 1821–65*. Springfield, IL: Abraham Lincoln Association, 1933.

———. "The Recollections of William Pitt Kellogg." *Abraham Lincoln Quarterly*, September 1945, 326.

Arnold, Isaac N. *The History of Abraham Lincoln and the Overthrow of Slavery*. Chicago: Clark & Co., 1866.

———. *The Life of Abraham Lincoln*. Chicago: A. C. McClurg & Co., 1884.

Ascher, Leonard. "Lincoln's Administration and the New Almaden Scandal." *Pacific Historical Review* 5 (1936): 38–51.

Avrich, Paul. *The Haymarket Tragedy*. Princeton, NJ: Princeton Univ. Press, 1984.

Baker, Jean H. *Mary Todd Lincoln: A Biography*. New York: W. W. Norton & Co., 1987.

Bannister, Dan W. *Lincoln and the Common Law*. Springfield, IL: Human Services Press, 1992.

———. *Lincoln and the Illinois Supreme Court*. Springfield, IL: Dan W. Bannister, 1994.

Baringer, William. *A House Dividing: Lincoln as the President Elect*. Springfield, IL: Abraham Lincoln Association, 1945.

———. *Lincoln's Rise to Power*. Boston: Little Brown & Co., 1937.

Barry, Peter R. "The Charleston Riot and Its Aftermath: Civil, Military, and Presidential Responses." *Journal of Illinois History* (summer 2004): 82–106.

Basler, Roy P., ed. *The Collected Works of Abraham Lincoln*. 9 vols. New Brunswick, NJ: Rutgers Univ. Press, 1953; vol. 10, First Supp., 1974; vol. 11, Second Supp., 1990.

Bates, Edward. *The Diary of Edward Bates, 1859–1866*. Ed. Howard Kennedy Beale. Washington, DC: Government Printing Office, 1933. Reprint, New York: Da Capo Press, 1971.

Baxter, Maurice G. *Orville H. Browning: Lincoln's Friend and Critic*. Bloomington: Indiana Univ. Press, 1957.

Bench and Bar of Chicago, The: Biographical Sketches. Chicago: American Biographical Publishing Co., 1883.

Benner, Martha L., Cullom Davis, et al., eds. *The Law Practice of Abraham Lincoln: Complete Documentary Edition*. Urbana: Univ. of Illinois Press, 2000. 3 DVD-ROM discs. Specific cases listed under Legal Cases below.

Benton, Thomas Hart. *Thirty Years' View; or, A History of the Workings of the American Government for Thirty Years, from 1820 to 1850*. 2 vols. 1854–56. Reprint, New York: Greenwood Press, 1968.

Blassingame, John W. *The Slave Community: Plantation Life in the Ante-Bellum South*. New York: Oxford Univ. Press, 1972.

Boatner, Mark M., III. *The Civil War Dictionary*. Rev. ed. New York: David McKay Co., Inc., 1988.

Bradley, Erwin Stanley. *Simon Cameron: Lincoln's Secretary of War*. Philadelphia: Univ. of Pennsylvania Press, 1966.

Bray, Robert. *Reading with Lincoln*. Carbondale: Southern Illinois Univ. Press, 2010.

Brewer, William H. *Up and Down California in 1860–64*. New Haven: Yale Univ. Press, 1930.

Browne, Francis Fisher. *The Every-day Life of Abraham Lincoln*. Lincoln: Univ. of Nebraska Press, 1995. First published 1886.

Bruce, Robert V. *Lincoln and the Tools of War*. Indianapolis: Bobbs-Merrill, 1956.

Burlingame, Michael. *Abraham Lincoln: A Life*. Baltimore: Johns Hopkins Univ. Press, 2008.

———. *At Lincoln's Side: John Hay's Civil War Correspondence and Selected Writings*. Carbondale: Southern Illinois Univ. Press, 2000.

———. *Lincoln Observed: Civil War Dispatches of Noah Brooks*. Baltimore: Johns Hopkins Univ. Press, 1998.

———, ed. *An Oral History of Abraham Lincoln: John G. Nicolay's Interviews and Essays*. Carbondale: Southern Illinois Univ. Press, 1996.

Cain, Marvin R. *Lincoln's Attorney General: Edward Bates of Missouri*. Columbia: Univ. of Missouri Press, 1965.

Calhoun, Charles W. *Gilded Age Cato: The Life of Walter Q. Gresham*. Lexington: Univ. Press of Kentucky, 1988.

Carpenter, Kay. "Leonard Swett and the Fifth Indiana Regiment in the Mexican War." *Indiana Military History Journal* (Indiana Historical Society), October 1980, 19–22.

Cavanagh, Helen M. *Seed, Soil, and Science: The Story of Eugene D. Funk*. Chicago: Lakeside Press, 1959.

Ceremonies at the Unveiling of the Statue of Abraham Lincoln, at Lincoln Park, Chicago, Illinois, October 22, 1887. Chicago: Brown, Pettibone & Co., 1887, ALPL, Swett Papers.

Chase, Henry. *Representative Men of Maine: A Collection of Biographical Sketches*. Portland, ME: Lakeside Press, 1893.

Chiniquy, Charles. *Fifty Years in the Church of Rome*. Rev. ed. London: Robert Banks & Son, 1886.

Chitty, Joseph. *A Treatise on Pleading*. 3 vols. 8th American edition. Springfield, MA: G. and C. Merriam, 1840.

Clinton, Catherine. "Wife versus Widow: Clashing Perspectives on Mary Lincoln's Legacy." *Journal of the Abraham Lincoln Association* 28 (winter 2007): 1–19.

Cobb, Charles E., Jr. "Panama Ever at the Crossroads." *National Geographic* 169 (April 1986): 466–92.

Colby College. *General Catalogue of Officers, Graduates, and Former Students of Colby College, Centennial Edition, 1820–1920*. Waterville, ME: Colby College, 1920. Courtesy of Patricia Burdick, Special Collections, Miller Library, Colby College.

Conger, Arthur L. *The Rise of U. S. Grant*. New York: Century Co., 1931.

Craughwell, Thomas J. *Stealing Lincoln's Body*. Cambridge, MA: Belknap Press, 2007.

Cullom, Shelby M. *Fifty Years of Public Service: Personal Recollections of Shelby Cullom*. Chicago: A. C. McClurg & Co., 1911.

Davis, Rodney O. "Lincoln's 'Particular Friend,' and Lincoln Biography." *Journal of the Abraham Lincoln Association* 19 (winter 1998): 21–37.

DeGregorio, William A. *The Complete Book of U.S. Presidents*. 2nd ed. New York: Dembner Books, 1989.

Dennett, Tyler, ed. *Lincoln and the Civil War in the Diaries and Letters of John Hay.* New York: Da Capo Press, 1939.

Dirck, Brian. *Lincoln the Lawyer.* Urbana: Univ. of Illinois Press, 2007.

Dobyns, Kenneth W. *The Patent Office Pony: A History of the Early Patent Office.* Fredericksburg, VA: Sergeant Kirkland's Museum & Historical Society, 1994.

Donald, David Herbert. *Lincoln.* New York: Simon & Schuster, 1995.

———. *Lincoln's Herndon: A Biography.* New York: Alfred A. Knopf, 1948. Reprint, New York: Da Capo Press, 1989.

———. *"We Are Lincoln Men": Abraham Lincoln and His Friends.* New York: Simon & Schuster, 2003.

Emerson, Jason. *The Madness of Mary Lincoln.* Carbondale: Southern Illinois Univ. Press, 2007.

Epstein, Richard A. "Toward a Revitalization of the Contract Clause." *University of Chicago Law Review* 51 (summer 1984): 703–51.

Fatout, Paul, ed. *Mark Twain Speaking.* Iowa City: Univ. of Iowa Press, 1976.

Fehrenbacher, Don E. *Prelude to Greatness: Lincoln in the 1850s.* Stanford, CA: Stanford Univ. Press, 1962.

Foner, Eric. *The Fiery Trial: Abraham Lincoln and American Slavery.* New York: W. W. Norton & Co., 2010.

———. *Reconstruction: America's Unfinished Revolution, 1863–1877.* New York: Harper & Row, Publishers, 1988.

Fraker, Guy C. "The Lincoln Landscape: The Real Lincoln Highway: The Forgotten Lincoln Circuit Markers." *Journal of the Abraham Lincoln Association* 25, no. 1 (winter 2004): 76–97.

Friedman, Jane M. *America's First Woman Lawyer: The Biography of Myra Bradwell.* Amherst, NY: Prometheus Books, 1993.

Friedman, Lawrence M. *A History of American Law.* 2nd ed. New York: Simon & Schuster, 1985.

George, Joseph, Jr. "The Lincoln Writings of Charles P. T. Chiniquy." *Journal of the Illinois State Historical Society* 49 (February 1976): 17–25.

Goff, John S. *Robert Todd Lincoln: A Man in His Own Right.* Norman: Univ. of Oklahoma Press, 1969.

Goodspeed, Thomas W. *A History of the University of Chicago: The First Quarter Century.* Chicago: Univ. of Chicago Press, 1916. Reprint, 1972.

Goodwin, Doris Kearns. *Team of Rivals: The Political Genius of Abraham Lincoln.* New York: Simon & Schuster, 2005.

Grant, Ulysses S. *Personal Memoirs.* 2 vols. New York: Charles L. Webster & Co., 1885.

Green, James. *Death in the Haymarket.* New York: Pantheon Books, 2006.

Gresham, Matilda. *Life of Walter Quintin Gresham, 1832–1895.* 2 vols. Freeport, NY: 1919. Reprint, 1970.

Grossman, James R., Ann Durkin Keating, & Janice L. Reiff, eds. *The Encyclopedia of Chicago.* Chicago: Univ. of Chicago Press, 2004.

Hamilton, William B. *Lincoln and the War Governors.* New York: Alfred A. Knopf, 1955.

Hanchett, William. *The Lincoln Murder Conspiracies.* Urbana: Univ. of Illinois Press, 1986.

Henig, Gerald S. *Henry Winter Davis: Antebellum and Civil War Congressman from Maryland.* Boston: Twayne, 1973.

Herndon, William H., & Jesse W. Weik. *Life of Lincoln.* Cleveland: Fine Editions Press, 1949. First published 1889.

Hess, Stephen. *America's Political Dynasties: From Adams to Kennedy.* Garden City, NY: Doubleday & Co., Inc., 1966.

Hicken, Victor. *Illinois and the Civil War.* 2nd ed. Urbana: Univ. of Illinois Press, 1991.

Hirsch, Arnold R., & Joseph Logsdon, eds. *Creole New Orleans: Race and Americanization.* Baton Rouge: Louisiana State Univ. Press, 1992.

Howard, Robert P. *Illinois: A History of the Prairie State.* Grand Rapids, MI: William B. Eerdmans Publishing Co., 1972.

Illinois State Preservation Agency. *Lincoln Legal Briefs* 17 (January–March 1991).

Johannsen, Robert W. *Stephen A. Douglas.* New York: Oxford Univ. Press, 1973.

Johnson, Robert U., & Clarence C. Buel. *Battles and Leaders of the Civil War.* 4 vols. New York: Century Co., 1887.

Kaplan, Justin. *Mr. Clemens and Mark Twain: A Biography.* New York: Simon & Schuster, 1966.

Kerrick, Leonidas H. "Life and Character of Hon. Isaac Funk." *Transactions of the McLean County Historical Society* 2 (1903): 498–520.

King, Willard L. *Lincoln's Manager: David Davis.* Cambridge: Harvard Univ. Press, 1960.

———. *Melville Weston Fuller: Chief Justice of the United States, 1888–1910.* New York: MacMillan, 1950.

Kogan, Herman. *The First Century: The Chicago Bar Association, 1874–1974.* Chicago: Rand McNally & Co., 1974.

Krause, Susan. *From Log Cabins to Temples of Justice: Courthouses in Lincoln's Illinois.* Springfield: Illinois Historic Preservation Agency, 2000.

———. *Judging Lincoln: The Bench in Lincoln's Illinois.* Springfield: Illinois Historic Preservation Agency, 2002.

Lamon, Ward Hill. *The Life of Abraham Lincoln.* Boston: James R. Osgood, 1871.

———. *Recollections of Abraham Lincoln.* Ed. Dorothy Lamon Teillard. Lincoln: Univ. of Nebraska Press, 1994.

Larson, Erik. *The Devil in the White City: Murder, Magic, and Madness at the Fair That Changed America.* New York: Random House, 2003.

Leckie, Shirley A. *Elizabeth Bacon Custer and the Making of a Myth.* Norman: Univ. of Oklahoma Press, 1993.

Lurie, Jonathan. *The Chicago Board of Trade, 1859–1905: The Dynamics of Self-Regulation.* Urbana: Univ. of Illinois Press, 1979.

Marshall, Jessie A., ed. *Private and Official Correspondence of Gen. Benjamin F. Butler during the Period of the Civil War.* Vol. 5. Norwood, MA: Plimpton Press, 1917.

Mayer, Howard M., & Richard C. Wade. *Chicago: Growth of a Metropolis.* Chicago: Univ. of Chicago Press, 1969.

McClure, A. K. *Abraham Lincoln and Men of War-Times.* 4th ed. Lincoln: Univ. of Nebraska Press, 1996.

McCullough, David. *The Path between the Seas: The Creation of the Panama Canal, 1870–1914.* New York: Simon & Schuster, 1977.

McDonald, John. *Secrets of the Great Whiskey Ring.* Chicago: Belford, Clarke & Co., 1880. Reprint, New York: Burt Franklin, 1969.

McPherson, James M. *Abraham Lincoln and the Second American Revolution.* New York: Oxford Univ. Press, 1990.

———. *Battle Cry of Freedom: The Civil War Era.* New York: Oxford Univ, Press, 1988.

Mearns, David C. *The Lincoln Papers.* 2 vols. Garden City, NY: Doubleday & Co., 1948.

Miers, Earl Schenck, ed. *Lincoln Day by Day.* Dayton, OH: Morningside House, 1991.

Miller, Donald L. *City of the Century: The Epic of Chicago and the Making of America.* New York: Simon & Schuster, 1996.

Morehouse, Frances Milton. *The Life of Jesse W. Fell.* Urbana: Univ. of Illinois Press, 1916.

Morison, Samuel Eliot. *The Oxford History of the American People.* New York: Oxford Univ. Press, 1965.

Munson, Don, ed. *It Is Begun! The* Pantagraph *Reports the Civil War.* Bloomington, IL: McLean County Historical Society, 2001.

Neely, Mark E., Jr. *The Abraham Lincoln Encyclopedia.* New York: Da Capo Press, 1982.

———. "A 'No Confidence' Vote on the Lincoln Administration." *Lincoln Lore,* no. 1729 (March 1982).

Neely, Mark E., Jr., & R. Gerald McMurtry. *The Insanity File: The Case of Mary Todd Lincoln.* Carbondale: Southern Illinois Univ. Press, 1986.

Nevins, Allen. *The Emergence of Lincoln.* Vol. 2, Prologue to Civil War, 1859–61. New York: Charles Scribner's Sons, 1950.

Nicolay, Helen. *Personal Traits of Abraham Lincoln.* New York: Century Co., 1913.

NIH (National Institutes of Health). "Diabetes." Pamphlet. No date.

Oldroyd, Osborn H. *Lincoln's Campaign; or, the Political Revolution of 1860.* Chicago: Laird & Lee, 1896.

Paludan, Phillip Shaw. *The Presidency of Abraham Lincoln.* Lawrence: Univ. of Kansas Press, 1994.

Pease, Thomas C., & James G. Randall, eds. *The Diary of Orville Hickman Browning.* Springfield: Illinois State Historical Library, 1925.

Pelikan, Jaroslav. *Jesus through the Centuries: His Place in the History of Culture.* New Haven: Yale Univ. Press, 1995.

Percoco, James A. *Summers with Lincoln: Looking for the Man in the Monuments.* New York: Fordham Univ. Press, 2008.

Perret, Geoffrey. *Ulysses S. Grant: Soldier & President.* New York: Random House, 1997.

Peterson, Merrill D. *Lincoln in American Memory.* New York: Oxford Univ. Press, 1994.

Pierce, Bessie Louise. *A History of Chicago.* 3 vols. Chicago: Jansen, McClurg & Co., 1974.

Plummer, Mark. *Lincoln's Rail-Splitter: Governor Richard J. Oglesby.* Urbana: Univ. of Illinois Press, 2001.

Potter, Jerry O. *The Sultana Tragedy: America's Greatest Maritime Disaster.* Gretna, LA: Pelican Publishing Co., 1992.

Pratt, Harry. "A Beginner on the Old Eighth Judicial Circuit." *Journal of the Illinois State Historical Society* 44 (autumn 1951): 241–48.

———. *Concerning Mr. Lincoln.* Springfield, IL: Abraham Lincoln Association, 1944.

———. "The Famous 'Chicken Bone' Case." *Journal of the Illinois State Historical Society* 45 (summer 1952): 164–67.

———. *The Personal Finances of Abraham Lincoln*. Springfield, IL: Abraham Lincoln Association, 1943.

———. "The Repudiation of Lincoln's War Policy in 1862: Stuart-Swett Congressional Campaign." *Journal of the Illinois State Historical Society* 24 (April 1931): 129–40.

Presbyterian Church in the U.S.A. Presbyteries. *The Trial of the Rev. David Swing, before the Presbytery of Chicago*. Chicago: Jansen, McClurg & Co., 1874.

Raymond, Henry J. *The Life and Public Services of Abraham Lincoln*. New York: Derby & Miller, Publishers, 1865.

"Rev. George Washington Minier." *Transactions of the McLean County (IL) Historical Society* 1 (1899): 523.

Reyburn, Phillip J., & Terry L. Wilson, eds. *Jottings from Dixie: The Civil War Dispatches of Sergeant Major Stephen F. Fleharty, U.S.A.* Baton Rouge: Louisiana Univ. Press, 1994.

Rice, Allen Thorndike, coll. & ed. *Reminiscences of Abraham Lincoln by Distinguished Men of His Time*. New York: Harper & Brothers Pub., 1909. First published 1885.

Richardson, Elmo R., & Alan W. Farley. *John Palmer Usher: Lincoln's Secretary of the Interior*. Lawrence: Univ. of Kansas Press, 1960.

Ricker, Ann. "Mary Lincoln and the Swings." *For the People* (newsletter of the Abraham Lincoln Association) 2, no. 1 (spring 2000): 1–2, 6, 8.

Ricker, Jewitt E., Jr. "The Other Side of Mary Lincoln," part 1. *For the People* (newsletter of the Abraham Lincoln Association) 8, no. 4 (winter 2006): 1, 3–8.

———. "The Other Side of Mary Lincoln," part 2. *For the People* (newsletter of the Abraham Lincoln Association) 9, no. 1 (spring 2007): 1–2, 7–9.

Roberts, A. Sellew. "The Federal Government and Confederate Cotton." *American Historical Review* (January 1927): 262–75.

Ross, Earle Dudley. *The Liberal Republican Movement*. New York: Henry Holt & Co., 1919.

Schaffer, Amanda. "In Diabetes, Complex of Causes." *New York Times*, October 16, 2007, "Science Times," 1.

Schenkel, Daniel. *The Portrait of Jesus*. Wiesbaden, 1864.

Schnell, Christopher A. *Stovepipe Hat and Quill Pen: The Artifacts of Abraham Lincoln's Law Practice*. Springfield, IL: Illinois Historic Preservation Agency, 2002.

Schwartz, Thomas F. "A Death in the Family." *For the People* (newsletter of the Abraham Lincoln Association) 9, no. 3 (autumn 2007): 1, 4.

Schweitzer, Albert. *Quest for the Historical Jesus*. New York: MacMillan Co., 1961.

Shenk, Joshua Wolf. *Lincoln's Melancholy: How Depression Challenged a President and Fueled His Greatness*. Boston: Houghton Mifflin Co., 2005.

Shutes, Milton H. "Abraham Lincoln and the New Almaden Mine." *California Historical Society Quarterly* 15 (March 1936): 3–20.

———. *Lincoln and California*. Stanford, CA: Stanford Univ. Press, 1948.

Simmons, Thomas E. "Territorial Justice under Fire: The Trials of Peter Wintermute, 1873–1875." *South Dakota History* 31, no. 2 (summer 2001): 91–112.

Simpson, Brooks D. "Alexander McClure on Lincoln and Grant: A Questionable Account." *Lincoln Herald* 95 (fall 1993): 83–86.

Slap, Andrew L. *The Doom of Reconstruction: The Liberal Republican Movement in the Civil War Era*. New York: Fordham Univ. Press, 2006.

Smith, Edward Conrad, ed. *The Constitution of the United States: With Case Summaries.* 11th ed. New York: Barnes & Noble, 1936–79.

Smith, Henry Nash, & William N. Gibson, eds. *The Mark Twain–William Dean Howells Letters.* 2 vols. Cambridge: Harvard Univ. Press, 1967.

Solomon, Rayman L. *History of the Seventh Circuit, 1891–1941: A Bicentennial Project.* Washington, DC: Bicentennial Committee of the Judicial Conference of the United States, 1941.

Stackpole, Everett S. *Swett Genealogy: Descendants of John Swett of Newberry, Massachusetts.* Lewiston, ME: Journal Printshop, 1913(?).

Steiner, Mark E. "The Lawyer as Peacemaker: Law and Community in Abraham Lincoln's Slander Cases." *Journal of the Abraham Lincoln Association* 16 (summer 1995): 1–22.

Story, Joseph. Commentaries on Equity Jurisprudence, as Administered in England and America. 2 vols. Boston: Hilliard, Gray & Company, 1835–36.

Stowell, Daniel W., et al., eds. *The Papers of Abraham Lincoln: Legal Documents and Cases.* 4 vols. Charlottesville: Univ. of Virginia Press, 2008.

Sutton, Robert P., ed. *The Prairie State: A Documentary History of Illinois, Colonial Years to 1860.* Grand Rapids, MI: Wm. B. Eerdmans Publishing Co., 1976.

Swett, Leonard. "The Conspiracies of the Rebellion." *North American Review* (February 1887): 180–89.

———. *Remembrances of T. Lyle Dickey.* Chicago: Barnard & Gunthorp, Printers, 1885, privately printed. Courtesy of John Hoffmann, Univ. of Illinois, Illinois Historical Survey.

Swett, Leonard Herbert. "Leonard Swett." *Transactions of the McLean County Historical Society* 2 (1903): 332–65.

Tarbell, Ida M. *The Life of Abraham Lincoln.* 4 vols. New York: Macmillan Co., 1917.

Tarbell, Ida M., & John McCan Davis. *The Early Life of Abraham Lincoln.* New York: S. S. McClure, 1896.

Taylor, John M. *William Henry Seward: Lincoln's Right Hand.* New York: HarperCollins, 1991.

Thomas, Benjamin P. *Abraham Lincoln: A Biography.* Carbondale: Southern Illinois Univ. Press, 2008.

Thomas, Benjamin P., & Harold M. Hyman. *Stanton: The Life and Times of Lincoln's Secretary of War.* New York: Alfred A. Knopf, 1962.

Thomas Jefferson University. "S. Weir Mitchell." In *10 Notable Jefferson Alumni of the Past.* Philadelphia: Thomas Jefferson Univ., 2001.

Turner, Justin, & Linda Turner. *Mary Lincoln: Her Life and Letters.* New York: Alfred A. Knopf, 1972.

U.S. Congress. Congressional Biographical Directory. http://bioguide.congress.gov.

Van Deusen, Glyndon G. "Thurlow Weed's Analysis of William H. Seward's Defeat in the Republican Convention of 1860." *Mississippi Valley Historical Review* 34, no. 1 (1947): 101–4.

———. *Thurlow Weed: Wizard of the Lobby.* Boston: Little, Brown & Co., 1947.

War of the Rebellion, The: A Compilation of the Official Records of the Union and Confederate Armies. Washington, DC: Government Printing Office, 1880–1901.

Weed, Harriet, ed. *Autobiography of Thurlow Weed*. Boston: Houghton, Mifflin & Co., 1883.

Weick, Carl F. *Lincoln's Quest for Equality: The Road to Gettysburg*. DeKalb: Northern Illinois Univ. Press, 2002. Theodore Parker, *Additional Speeches, etc.*, 91–123.

Weik, Jesse W. *The Real Lincoln: A Portrait*. Boston: Houghton Mifflin Co., 1923.

Welles, Gideon. *The Diary of Gideon Welles*. 3 vols. Ed. Howard K. Beale. Boston, 1911.

Wendt, Lloyd. *Chicago Tribune: The Rise of a Great American Newspaper*. Chicago: Rand McNally & Co., 1979,

Whitney, Henry Clay. *Life on the Circuit with Lincoln*. Introd. Paul M. Angle. Caldwell, ID: Caxton Printers, 1940. First published 1892.

Wiel, Samuel C. *Lincoln's Crisis in the Far West*. San Francisco: Privately printed, 1949.

Wills, Garry. *Lincoln at Gettysburg: The Words That Remade America*. New York: Simon & Schuster, 1992.

Wilson, Douglas L., & Rodney O. Davis, eds. *Herndon's Informants: Letters, Interviews, and Statements about Abraham Lincoln*. Urbana: Univ. of Illinois Press, 1998.

Wood, Charles H. "The Sullivan Trial." *American Law Register (1852–1891)* 25, no. 7 (July 1877): 385–92. Courtesy Debbie Vaughn, Chicago History Museum.

Manuscripts, Letters, Collections, and Library Resources

Abraham Lincoln Presidential Library (ALPL). David Davis Papers and Leonard Swett Papers.

Bajuyo, F. Karmann. "John Milton Scott: Bloomington's Benefactor." Unpublished manuscript. Illinois Wesleyan Univ., 1994.

Carpenter, Kay. "Abraham Lincoln and Leonard Swett on the 8th Judicial Circuit." MA thesis. Eastern Illinois Univ., 1980.

Chicago History Museum (CHM). Chicago City Directory, 1878–79, and David Davis Papers.

Colby College, Waterville, ME. Special Collections.

Dunn, Mark. "Chicago's Political Samurais: Joseph C. Mackin & Michael C. McDonald, Fraud, Perjury, Prison & Pardon." Unpublished manuscript. Bloomington, IL.

Fort Collins (CO) Public Library. Personal communication with Dorothy McDavid.

Hamand, Lavern M. "Ward Hill Lamon: Lincoln's Particular Friend." PhD diss., Univ. of Illinois, Urbana, 1949.

Huntington Library, San Marino, CA. Ward Hill Lamon and Leonard Swett Papers.

Letter from Herbert Swett to Mrs. Swett, Genoa, dated February 5, 1885. Courtesy of Doug Macrae, of Washington, who found this letter in a used book he purchased.

Library of Congress. Abraham Lincoln Papers.

Maine Historical Society. *Portland Evening Express*. George Foster Shepley Collection.

Mattingly, Michael A. "Lincoln's Confidant Leonard Swett of Bloomington, Illinois," MA thesis, Illinois State Univ., 1984.

McLean County Historical Society, Bloomington, IL.

National Archives. Old Military and Civil Records.

Newberry Library, Chicago. Genealogy and Local History Collection, and letter of application for a job from Mrs. Leonard [Maria] Swett to [library president] E. W. Blatchford, Chicago, 11-22-93.

Swett, Leonard Herbert. Journal, manuscript copy from George Buss, Freeport, IL.

University of Illinois at Urbana-Champaign (UIUC). William Orme Papers.

Wheeler, Samuel P. "Leonard Swett." MA thesis, Univ. of Illinois, Springfield, 2002.

Wight, Grace Cheney. "Lincoln's Most Influential Friends in Bloomington." Unpublished manuscript. Bloomington Public Library. Copy courtesy of Florence Fifer Bloomer. (Includes Fell, Davis, Swett, Lamon, Weldon, and Orme.)

Newspapers and Periodicals

Bloomington (IL) Pantagraph
Chicago Daily News
Chicago Herald
Chicago InterOcean
Chicago Legal News (CLN)
Chicago Mail
Chicago Press & Tribune
Chicago Times
Chicago Tribune
Clinton (IL) Public
Clinton (IL) Register
Decatur (IL) Magnet
Illinois State Journal, Springfield, Illinois State University Microfilms
Journal of Illinois History
Journal of the Illinois State Historical Society
Lincoln Herald
Lincoln Legal Briefs, Quarterly Newsletter of the Lincoln Legal Papers, Illinois Historic Preservation Agency, Springfield
Lincoln Lore
Peoria Daily Transcript, Peoria Public Library, Bradley University Library
Portland (ME) Evening Express
Santa Maria (CA) Times
Transactions of the McLean County (IL) Historical Society

Legal Cases

Chicago Board of Realtors, Inc. v. City of Chicago, 819 F.2d 732, 743–44.
Fertilizing Co. v. Hyde Park, 97 U.S. 659, 664, 24 L.Ed. 1036, 1038 (1878).
Lyon and Co. v. Culbertson, Blair and Co., 83 Ill. 33 (1876).
People v. Sloo, Weekly Pantagraph, 8-26-1857, Shawneetown, Gallatin County, IL.
Spies v. People ("The Anarchists' case"), 12 N.E. 865 (Ill. 1887); also *Spies v. Illinois*, 123 U.S. 131 (1887).

The Law Practice of Abraham Lincoln

Fleming v. Rogers & Crothers I.D.: L01566
People v. Bosley I.D.: L02011

People v. Patterson I.D.: L01488
People v. Wyant I.D.: L01676
Richey v. Adams I.D.: L00590
Spink v. Chiniquy I.D.: L01448
Thorpe v. Thorpe I.D.: L00379
See also Stowell et al., eds., *The Papers of Abraham Lincoln: Legal Documents and Cases.*

Index

Lincoln, 1–2, 9–10, 142–43, 145–46, 47, 169; at Gettysburg Address, 8, 137; as Greeley supporter (1872), 167–68; as gubernatorial candidate (1860), 5, 64–67; Haymarket anarchists' defense, 192–93, 203; health of, 57, 183, 187, 188, 198, 282n53; health of family, 61, 62–63, 93–94, 129; on Holt for vice-president (1864), 144, 147; home life of, 61–63; Illinois Supreme Court cases, 184; and insanity defense, 43, 46–48–49, 175, 182, 188, 259n24, 259n25; and insurance clients, 185–86; as law apprentice, 13; law partnership with McWilliams, 29–30, 31; law partnership with Orme, 30, 44; law partnership with Quigg and Higgins, 155; law practice in Chicago, 9, 155, 169–99; law practice in Clinton, 20, 22; as lawyer, 5, 9, 24–25, 28, 139, 161; and legal assistance to Lincoln family, 174–77, 181; and Liberal Republican movement, 165–66; on Lincoln, 32, 35, 36, 39–41, 72–73, 75–76, 97, 107, 112, 144, 156–57, 276n6; as Lincoln biographical source, 155, 156; in Lincoln-Douglas debates (1858), 57–58; as Lincoln political supporter, 13, 51–52, 65, 69–92, 151, 262n7; on Lincoln's "House Divided" position, 57, 75–76; Lincoln's lack of political support for, 54, 64; on Logan, 25–26; loyalty to Lincoln, 6; Maine ties of, 11; malaria contraction of, 17–18; on McWilliams as law partner, 30; meeting Grant, 101; meeting Lincoln, 23–24; as mine claim emissary for U.S., 8; in New Orleans (1848), 15–16; on nomination of Davis to U.S. Supreme Court, 3, 98, 102; and omission of appointment by Lincoln, 5, 6, 94, 120, 265n4; on omission of appointment by Lincoln, 7–8; and "peace crisis" (1864), 148–51; petitioning Lincoln for Union supplies, 99; and "Pledge on Drinking", 139–40, 273n11; political aspirations of, 5; and political contacts, 57, 66; purchase of

Chicago home, 183; and Quicksilver stock holdings, 129, 141–42, 272n34; representing Quicksilver Mining Company, 129, 272n34; requesting position in Lincoln's administration, 94, 152; resemblance to Lincoln, 24, 90, 137–38; sea voyage of, 14; on secession, 88; on slavery, 57–58, 138–39; as a speaker, 12, 40, 203; speeches of, 55, 57–58, 61, 63, 74, 77–78, 108–9, 167, 179–80, 183–84, 197; speeches on Davis, 193; speeches on Lincoln, 178, 184–85, 195–96, 198, 275n46; as state legislative candidate (1858), 59–61; as state legislator, 5, 8, 60, 63; as teacher, 14; in "triumvirate" of the Eighth Circuit, 32, 50, 201; on Trumbull, 53; types of cases of, 25, 27, 28, 169, 184, 259n18; on Union victories, 150; unsent letter to Lincoln, 85, 264n55; as U.S. Congressional candidate (1856), 5, 53–54; as U.S. Congressional candidate (1862), 6, 118; on Washington, D.C., 91; as Whig, 58–59; as Whig leader, 32; as Whig presidential elector, 28; and Whiskey Ring scandal defense, 178–79; writings on Lincoln, 2–3, 191, 258n16, 273n5, 284n14
Swett, Leonard Herbert "Bertie", 8, 61–62, 63, 102–3, 124, 129, 159, 174, 185, 188, 194, 198; and biography of Swett, 47, 201–2; in Europe, 188; marriage of, 201; medical school education in Chicago, 183; and U.S. Geological Survey, 183
Swett, Maria A. H. Decker, 3, 198, 202; L. Swett's marriage to, 193–94
Swett, Remember Berry, 11, 12
Swett, Mary Ellen. See Briggs, Mary Ellen Swett
Swett, Rose. See Briggs, Rose Swett
Swett, Stephen, 11
Swing, David, 173, 187, 280n18

Talbot, Charles J., 146
Taney, Roger B., 56
Tate, Samuel, 153

Robert S. Eckley (1921–2012) was the president of Illinois Wesleyan University from 1968 to 1986, and served as president emeritus thereafter. He was the president of the Abraham Lincoln Association from 2002 to 2004 after serving in the same capacity for the David Davis Mansion Foundation. In 2007 the Abraham Lincoln Association awarded him the prestigious Logan Hay Medal in recognition of his noteworthy contributions to promoting and preserving the memory of Abraham Lincoln. Eckley authored several articles on Swett and Lincoln, including two published in the *Journal of the Illinois State Historical Society* in 1999.